WORKING PROCESS (video 9:32)

EXPERIENCES FROM OUR EVERYDAY LIFE SHOW
THE PRIMARY DIFFERENCE BETWEEN SPACE AND TIME.
WE CAN MOVE BACK AND FORTH BETWEEN POINTS
IN SPACE, BUT WE CANNOT REVERSE TIME.

ILL

YET WE CAN DESCRIBE THE PAST.
I BUY OLD FILMS,

TRANSLUCENT

MOTION PICTURES

I PUT IN A CLASSIFIED AD
AND BOUGHT ABOUT 700 KILOS OF FILMS,

ROUGHLY FOUR HUNDRED 16 MM FILMS,
WHOSE FORMER OWNER BOUGHT THEM
FROM A DEFUNCT CINEMA IN ŽATEC
PICTURES OF THE PAST FROM 1957 - 1988

LEGIBLE

INSTRUCTIONAL AND EDUCATIONAL FILMS
TIRING AND DEPRESSING TO WATCH,
DEPICTING COMMUNIST CZECHOSLOVAKIA

TRACES OF TIMES THAT ARE HARD TO IDENTIFY WITH
WITHIN THE CADRE OF A "NORMAL SOCIETY"

ONE OF THE POSSIBLE WORLDS

A SIMPLE DESCRIPTION

THE PICTURES OF THE PAST USED HERE
HAVE BEEN TAKEN FROM AN ARCHIVE,
FROM WHICH I COULD HAVE
ASSEMBLED A DIFFERENT PROGRAMME EACH TIME

LAYERS

INSTRUCTIONAL AND EDUCATIONAL FILMS
FILMS WITH A CLEAR PURPOSE
VOID OF ANY ARTISTIC AMBITION
AN INCONGRUOUS PICTURE OF THE PAST

THERE IS NO CONTINUITY BETWEEN A SPECIFIC
PRESENT AND A SPECIFIC PAST.
A STRUCTURE OF EVENTS IS NOT
TREE-LIKE IN ESSENCE
A SPECIFIC BRANCH IN THE PRESENT DOES NOT SHARE
A TIGHTER BOND WITH
A SPECIFIC BRANCH IN THE PAST THAN
WITH A SPECIFIC BRANCH IN THE FUTURE

LEGIBLE

ILLEGIBLE

THE PAST AND FUTURE CAN EXIST NEXT TO EACH OTHER
AND SPLINTER AT ANY MOMENT INTO AN ENDLESS NUMBER
OF OTHER VERSIONS OF REALITY
I'VE MADE 15 DIFFERENT VERSIONS

EACH VERSION WAS AUTHENTIC

THE YEAR BEFORE HIS DEATH

THE PICTURES ALWAYS BROKE DOWN INTO SMALL
UNRELATED STORIES

BUT THAT'S NOT WHAT I WANTED TO SHOW

RELATEDNESS IS DEVELOPED IN TIME:

THE AVANT-GARDE COMPOSER ERWIN SCHULHOFF
WROTE A CANTATA IN 1932:
A COMMUNIST MANIFESTO
IN 1941 HE SENT A SCORE TO MOSCOW
AND IT WAS LOST THERE

THE MUSIC YOU HEAR
WAS COMPOSED BY FRANZ SCHUBERT
HE WROTE IT IN VIENNA IN 1827
THE YEAR BEFORE HIS DEATH

THE NAME OF BOTH COMPOSERS ARE LISTED
ON THE SAME PAGE IN THE DICTIONARY

MUSIC OF THE RADICAL ARTIST AS A MOTIF

A COLLECTION OF FILMS OF THE SUCCESSES
OF CZECHOSLOVAK SOCIALISM AS THE BACKDROP

CZECHOSLOVAK SOCIALISM

THE SEPARATE DESCRIPTIONS INTERTWINE

SCHUBERT AND HIS FINAL SUCCESS IN LIFE

SCHULHOFF AND HIS FAITH IN A BETTER FUTURE

CZECHOSLOVAK SOCIALISM

A SIMPLE DESCRIPTION

A SIMPLE CAUSATION

BUT IT CAN ALSO BE SAID,
THAT THERE IS NO STREAM OF TIME
AND NO SEPARATE PRESENT MOMENT,
EXCEPT FOR ITS SUBJECTIVE FEELING

Zbyněk Baladrán

Content

Zbyněk Baladrán
001–004

Azorro
007–010

Foreword
Vít Havránek, Sabine Schaschl-Cooper, Bettina Steinbrügge
011–012

Klub Zwei
013–016

The Need to Document
Sabine Schaschl-Cooper, Bettina Steinbrügge
017–030

Jiří Skála, Mark Ther
031–034

The Documentary — An Ontology of Forms in Transforming Countries
Vít Havránek
035–047

Big Hope
049–052

Politics of Truth — Documentarism in the Art Field
Hito Steyerl
053–064

Kaucyila Brooke
065–068

The Documentary Method
Christoph Behnke
069–072

Edgar Arceneaux
073–076

The Expanded Working Field of Documentary Production
Jan Verwoert
077–083

Olivier Zabat
085–088

The Document as Present Becoming
Gerald Raunig
089–098

Ella Ziegler
099–102

A Question of Display
Georg Schöllhammer
103–104

Johanna Kandl
105–108

Worktop Video
Søren Grammel in collaboration with Gerhard Zarbock
109–132

Duncan Campbell
133–136

The Slaves Freely Choose their Masters — A Few Strategies of Representation Through the Use of the Documentary Form
Dóra Hegyi
137–142

Dorit Margreiter
143–146

What are Documentary Films Doing in Museums!?
Claudia Spinelli
147–149

Kirsten Pieroth
151–154

Future Amnesia (The Need for Documents)
Pascale Cassagnau
155–173

Boris Ondreička
175–178

Ruins, Archaeology, and the Gap Between Images
Zbyněk Baladrán
179–186

Mircea Cantor
187–190

The Photographic Documentary Effect vs. Hyper-Real Mutations
Marina Gržinić
191–215

Joachim Koester
217–220

CAC TV — Every Program is a Pilot, Every Program is the Final Episode
Raimundas Malasauskas
221–222

Jens Haaning
223–226

Issuing Publications
Attila Tordai-S.
227–231

Hinrich Sachs
233–236

Make Film Political
Dorit Margreiter
237–239

Oliver Ressler, Dario Azzellini
241–244

Bibliography
245–251

Laura Horelli
253–256

Biographies
257–262

Ursula Biemann, Angela Sanders
263–266

List of Illustrations
267–270

Colophon
273–275

Done before.

We could do a sculpture too...

So, what can we do then?

VIÄRTÄ:	- Ja äbä. Miär müänd nisch äswas Nüüsch uusdeichä.
ZWEITÄ:	- Äswas. Asä äswas, waas no nid gää hed.
VIÄRTÄ:	- Ja.
ZWEITÄ:	- Preziis.
	(Schwiigä)
DRITTÄ:	- Vilicht chönntämär äs Viäregg malä, vor mä Hindärgrund.
VIÄRTÄ:	- Nei, das heds schon gään.
ZWEITÄ:	- Ehmm...(nadänkläch) miär chönntänd äs Viäregg und ä Chreis malä...
DRITTÄ:	- Nei, was deichscht au?
VIÄRTÄ:	- Nei, ä Chreis imä Viäregg... und um z Viäregg zringum noch äswas?
ZWEITÄ:	- Zringum?
VIÄRTÄ:	- Chönnti um z Viäregg zringum äswas sin?
DRITTÄ:	- I hans! Um z Viäregg zringum äs Driiegg. Und än Chreis.
VIÄRTÄ:	- Äs Driiegg um z Viäregg.
ERSCHTÄ:	- Vilicht chönntämär driidimensionali Figurä infüägä?
ZWEITÄ:	- Än Chegäl...
VIÄRTÄ:	- Nei, das heds schon ämal gään.
ZWEITÄ:	- Än Chegäl.
VIÄRTÄ:	- Mä chönnti...(värsuächt in där Uufregig zoWort zcho)
	mä chönnti au än Skulptur machä.
DRITTÄ:	- Oh, eini us Lätt odär eini us Bronze?
VIÄRTÄ:	- Än Chuglä chönntämä machä.
DRITTÄ:	- Än Chuglä...
ZWEITÄ:	- Uf ärä Grundlag?
VIÄRTÄ:	- Uf ärä Grundlag.
DRITTÄ:	- Ufmä Sockäl?
VIÄRTÄ:	- Anhand vu Berächnigä chönntämä schä...
DRITTÄ:	- Berächnä anhand var Grundlag. Odär än Grundlag ohni Berächnig?
VIÄRTÄ:	- Hmm...Wiä geid d Formlä var Grundlag vurä Chuglä?
ZWEITÄ:	- I deichä, di Grundlag sötti... di Proportionä iinhaltä.
	(Sichtbärä Durchbruch in derä värfaarnä Situazion.)
DRITTÄ:	- Abär i han z Gfühl, das äs das schon ämal gään hed.
ZWEITÄ:	- I au.
DRITTÄ:	- Vilicht...schtimmt...
VIÄRTÄ:	- Nei, miär chönntänd... miär chönntänd zum Bispiil gar nüd tuän.
DRITTÄ:	- Abär, das heds au schon gään.
ZWEITÄ:	- Äso chönntämr äswas tuän und so tuän, äswiä...
VIÄRTÄ:	- Miär müäständ äswas tuän, will mä nümä nüd tuän cha.
ZWEITÄ:	- Hmmh, das ischt scho so, abär...wemiär ünsch äswas abheglä tetänd?
DRITTÄ:	- Nei, das heds schon gään.
ZWEITÄ:	- Das heds schon gään, das gids schon, preziis.

How about dressing up as someone?

As everyone?

That's been done.

 Then maybe we could, like, do something and do something that would...

 How about distorting something?

 Maybe we could stuff a bird

Fourth:	-	Yeah, exactly. Cause we have to come up with something new.
Second:	-	Something. Like, something that hasn't been done before.
Fourth:	-	Yes.
Second:	-	Right.
		(Silence)
Third:	-	Maybe we could paint a kind of square, with a background...
Fourth:	-	No, that's been done already.
Second:	-	Ehmm... Cause we could paint a circle and a square....
Third:	-	Not that, what are you thinking?
Fourth:	-	No, a circle in a square... something next to the square maybe? Round the square...
Second:	-	Round?
Fourth:	-	Could there be something round the square?
Third:	-	Man! Round the square a triangle. And a circle.
Fourth:	-	Triangle round square!
First:	-	Maybe we could introduce three-dimensional figures?
Second:	-	A cone...
Fourth:	-	Well, that's been done.
Second:	-	A cone.
Fourth:	-	We could (he tries to get attention in the midst of the sudden excitement) we could do a sculpture too...
Third:	-	Oh! But a clay or a bronze one?
Fourth:	-	We could do a sphere!
Third:	-	A sphere...
Second:	-	On a base?
Fourth:	-	On a base.
Third:	-	On a pedestal.
Fourth:	-	On the basis of calculations one could...
Third:	-	On the basis of calculations. And a base without calculations?
Fourth:	-	Hmm, I don't know the formula for the base of a sphere.
Second:	-	I think that the base should... maintain proportions.
		(a visible breakthrough in the momentary stagnation)
Third:	-	But I get the impression that's been done before.
Second:	-	Me too.
Third:	-	Well, maybe... that's right...
Fourth:	-	No, because we could... we could do nothing, for instance.
Third:	-	But that's been done too.
Second:	-	Then maybe we could, like, do something and do something that would...
Fourth:	-	We have to do something because one can't do nothing anymore.
Second:	-	Hmm, that yes, of course but...if we cut off a piece of ourselves?
Third:	-	Noo, that's been done.
Second:	-	Done, done, that's right.

 I just thought about something symbolic.

 That's been done.

No, that's been done; I heard that one guy did just that. | Been done.. | But it's been done, for sure? Done? You've seen it?

VIERTER: - Ja eben. Wir müssen uns etwas Neues ausdenken.
ZWEITER: - Etwas. Na, etwas, das es noch nicht gegeben hat.
VIERTER: - Ja.
ZWEITER: - Genau.
(Schweigen)
DRITTER: - Vielleicht könnten wir ein Quadrat malen, vor einem Hintergrund.
VIERTER: - Nein, das gab's schon.
ZWEITER: - Ehmm... (nachdenklich) wir könnten ein Quadrat und einen Kreis malen...
DRITTER: - Nein, wo denkst du hin?
VIERTER: - Nein, einen Kreis in einem Quadrat... und um das Quadrat herum noch was?
ZWEITER: - Drum rum?
VIERTER: - Könnte um das Quadrat herum etwas sein?
DRITTER: - Ich hab's! Um das Quadrat herum ein Dreieck. Und ein Kreis.
VIERTER: - Ein Dreieck ums Quadrat!
ERSTER: - Vielleicht könnten wir dreidimensionale Figuren einfügen?
ZWEITER: - Einen Kegel...
VIERTER: - Nein, das gab's schon mal.
ZWEITER: - Einen Kegel.
VIERTER: - Man könnte (versucht in der plötzlichen Aufregung zu Wort zu kommen)
...man könnte auch eine Skulptur machen...
DRITTER: - Oh! Eine aus Ton oder eine aus Bronze?
VIERTER: - Eine Kugel könnte man machen!
DRITTER: - Eine Kugel...
ZWEITER: - Auf einer Grundlage?
VIERTER: - Auf einer Grundlage.
DRITTER: - Auf einem Unterbau?
VIERTER: - Aufgrund von Berechnungen könnte man sie...
DRITTER: - Berechnen aufgrund der Grundlage. Oder eine Grundlage ohne Berechnung?
VIERTER: - Hmmh, wie lautet die Formel der Grundlage einer Kugel?
ZWEITER: - Ich denke, die Grundlage sollte... die Proportionen einhalten.
(sichtbarer Durchbruch in der aufgetretenen Stagnation)
DRITTER: - Aber ich hab das Gefühl, daß es das schon mal gegeben hat.
ZWEITER: - Ich auch.
DRITTER: - Vielleicht... stimmt...
VIERTER: - Nein, denn wir könnten...wir könnten zum Beispiel gar nichts tun.
DRITTER: - Aber das hat's auch schon gegeben.
ZWEITER: - So könnten wir etwas tun und so tun, als ob...
VIERTER: - Wir müssen etwas tun, weil man nicht mehr nichts tun kann.
ZWEITER: - Hmmh, das ist schon so, aber... wenn wir uns etwas abschneiden würden?
DRITTER: - Nee, das gab's schon.
ZWEITER: - Das gab's schon, das gibt's, genau.

Vít Havránek, Sabine Schaschl-Cooper, Bettina Steinbrügge

Foreword

There has been an increasing turn to the documentary in contemporary art in recent years. Exhibitions such as Documenta11 or *True Stories* at Witte de With in Rotterdam, lecture series such as *Dokumentarische Strategien in der Kunst* at MUMOK in Vienna, and numerous biennials including *Manifesta 5* have presented a growing number of documentary works, the specific features of which have rarely been reflected upon. One the one hand, a large number of films and video installations, photographs and works of conceptual art, are oriented toward everyday life, attempting to capture socio-political and cultural-political events, historical reviews, as well as private moments permanently and with a claim to enlighten. In doing so, art focuses on the "testimonial" aspect, while taking on a position that reveals, points out, and makes determined comments. A second documentary trend examines its own means in a self-reflective manner, grasping the truth that images conveyed through media as constructed pieces of information situated at the interface of power and subjectivity, which Foucault calls "governmentality".

The recent political events that shook the world, the attack on the World Trade Center, the war in Iraq, the increasing shift to the Right of many European governments, the problems of asylum seekers, have newly stimulated the debates on a re-politicization of art that have been held since the 1990s. And, more than a decade after the fall of the Iron Curtain, many artists of the transforming Eastern European countries are remembering their own historical, art-historical, and socio-cultural roots and, based on these, establishing new connections to the present expressed with a documentary attitude.

The conceptual definition of the documentary springs from the legal discourse, that recognizes the document as an attestation or an evidence of truth. Similarly, what is behind contemporary documentary art production is a claim to objec-

Vorwort

In den letzten Jahren hat in der zeitgenössischen Kunst eine verstärkte Hinwendung zum Dokumentarischen stattgefunden. Ausstellungen wie die *Documenta11* oder *True Stories* am Witte de With in Rotterdam, Vortragsreihen, wie *Dokumentarische Strategien in der Kunst* am MUMOK in Wien und zahlreiche Biennalen, wie die *Manifesta 5*, präsentierten eine steigende Anzahl dokumentarischer Werke, über deren spezifischen Charakter nur selten reflektiert wurde. Zahlreiche Filme und Videoinstallationen, ebenso wie Fotografien und Werke der Konzeptkunst orientieren sich einerseits am Lebensalltag, versuchen sowohl sozial- und kulturpolitische Ereignisse, historische Rückblicke wie auch private Momente dauerhaft und mit einem Aufklärungsanspruch festzuhalten. Die Kunst fokussiert dabei auf „Zeugenhaftigkeit" und bezieht eine hinweisende und Stellung beziehende Position. Eine zweite Strömung des Dokumentarischen untersucht in selbstreflexiver Weise ihre eigenen Mittel als sozial konstruiert und versteht die medial vermittelten Wahrheitsbilder als konstruierte Informationen an der Schnittstelle von Macht und Subjektivität, bei Foucault bezeichnet als „Gouvernementalité".

Die jüngsten, die Welt erschütternden politischen Ereignisse, wie der Anschlag auf das World Trade Center, der Irak-Krieg, der zunehmende Rechts-Rutsch vieler europäischer Regierungen, die Problematik der Asylsuchenden, haben die seit den 90er Jahren geführten Debatten über eine Re-Politisierung der Kunst neuerlich angeheizt. Mehr als ein Jahrzehnt nach dem Fall des Eisernen Vorhangs besinnen sich zudem zahlreiche KünstlerInnen aus den sich transformierenden Ländern Osteuropas auf ihre eigenen historischen, kunsthistorischen und sozio-kulturellen Wurzeln und bilden, von diesen ausgehend, neue Verbindungen zur Gegenwart, die mit einer dokumentarischen Haltung zum Ausdruck gebracht werden.

Die begriffliche Bestimmung des Dokumentarischen entspringt dem juristischen Diskurs, wel-

tivity and faithfulness to truth, the attempt to come as close as possible to reality, and the intention to reveal how a work originated.

The project, *The Need to Document*, is a cooperation between Kunsthaus Baselland, Muttenz/Basel, Halle für Kunst eV, Lüneburg, and *tranzit*, Prague. Due to its specific form of cooperation, it simultaneously falls back upon several formats: two exhibitions, one round table in each of the three involved institutions, and this publication. The selection of the contributions shown in the two exhibitions – at Kunsthaus Baselland and Halle für Kunst eV – concentrated on works that demand a documentary approach to the formulation of their contents. Works in which the documentary merely depicts an action or a performance were not taken into consideration.

The publication with contributions by internationally renowned authors examines the backgrounds that determine the documentary and thematic focuses or concerns characterized by a documentary stance, and searches for the genuine documentary formulating itself as ontologically unalterable in terms of form. Short statements by individual panel participants and self-conceived contributions by artists involved in the project complete the book, which presents itself as an important compendium to situate the current discourse on documentarism.

cher im Dokument eine Beglaubigung bzw. ein Beweismittel für Wahrheit erkennt. Hinter der zeitgenössischen dokumentarischen Kunstproduktion steht in vergleichbarer Weise der Anspruch nach Objektivität und Wahrheitstreue; der Versuch, so nahe als möglich an die Realität heranzukommen und die Absicht, die Art und Weise der Entstehung eines Werkes offen zu legen. *The Need to Document* ist eine Kooperation zwischen Kunsthaus Baselland, Muttenz/Basel, Halle für Kunst eV, Lüneburg und tranzit, Prag.

Das Projekt greift aufgrund seiner spezifischen Form der Kooperation auf mehrere Vermittlungsformate zurück: Zwei Ausstellungen, ein Round-Table in jeder der drei beteiligten Institutionen und die hier vorliegende Publikation. Bei der Auswahl der in den beiden Ausstellungen – im Kunsthaus Baselland und in der Halle für Kunst eV – gezeigten Beiträge wurde der Schwerpunkt auf Werke gelegt, die nach einem dokumentarischen Zugang zur Formulierung ihrer Inhalte verlangen. Nicht berücksichtigt wurden Arbeiten, in denen das Dokumentarische lediglich Abbildung einer Aktion oder einer Performance ist.

Die Publikation mit Beiträgen international renommierter AutorInnen untersucht die Hintergründe, die das Dokumentieren bestimmen, benennt die Themenschwerpunkte bzw. Anliegen, welche eine dokumentarische Haltung auszeichnen und sucht nach dem genuin Dokumentarischen, das sich in seiner Form als ontologisch unveränderbar formuliert. Ergänzt von Kurzstatements einzelner Panel-TeilnehmerInnen und von selbst konzipierten Beiträgen der am Projekt beteiligten KünstlerInnen, präsentiert sich das Buch als wichtiges Kompendium zur Verortung des aktuellen Dokumentarismus-Diskurses.

Schwarz auf Weiss
Die Rückseite der Bilder

Klub Zwei
A / GB 2003, Beta SP, 4:3, b&w,
stereo, 5 min, englisch,
deutsch, polnisch, französisch,
bulgarisch, tschechisch, rumänisch

"Das Bild verstummt".

Eines der meist verwendeten Dokumente des Holocaust ist das Foto des kleinen Jungen mit erhobenen Händen im Warschauer Ghetto. Viele Reproduktionen dieses Bildes lassen den ursprünglichen Kontext aus oder verleugnen ihn. Sie konzentrieren sich nur auf den Jungen. Dadurch entfernen sie ihn aus jener Gemeinschaft, in die er eingebunden war und sie entfernen die Täter aus dem Blickfeld.

Das Bild war ursprünglich Teil des Berichts von SS-Gruppenführer und Generalmajor der Polizei Jürgen Stroop, dem Kommandanten der Operation zur Liquidierung des Warschauer Ghettos. Dieser Bericht von 1943 hatte den Titel „Es gibt keinen jüdischen Wohnbezirk in Warschau mehr!" und enthielt 54 Fotografien, die den Meldungen hinzugefügt und Himmler als Andenken präsentiert wurden.

Es verliert seine Aussagekraft,

Das Bild des Warschauer Jungen ist, wie alle TäterInnen-Bilder, in die fotografischen Praktiken der Nazis verstrickt. Wenn wir als BetrachterInnen mit diesen Fotos konfrontiert werden, sehen wir sie aus der Perspektive der impliziten Nazi-ZuschauerInnen. Wir sehen sie unter dem Ausrufungszeichen des Stroop-Berichts: „!"

L'image devient muette".

Il était formellement interdit de photographier dans les camps. Cette interdiction, formulée sur plusieurs panneaux placés le long des barbelés, est également rappelée par une circulaire du commandant d'Auschwitz, Rudolf Höss: „J'indique une fois encore qu'il est interdit de photographier dans le camp. Je punirai très sévèrement ceux qui ne se conformeront pas à cette ordonnance". [„Ich weise nochmals darauf hin, dass es verboten ist, im Lager zu fotografieren. Ich werde strengstens bestrafen, wer sich nicht an diesen Befehl hält"]

Pourtant, le nombre de photographies produites dans les camps peut être évalué à quelques millions, dont plusieurs dizaines de milliers ont été préservées de la destruction massive des archives. Comment expliquer un tel paradoxe?

Elle pert sa force d'expression,

La photographie ne fut pas totalement prohibée, au contraire, elle fut instrumentalisée par l'administration du camp, à son propre profit. À l'abri de tout regard étranger, l'administration des camps semble ainsi avoir fait de la photographie l'un des outils privilégiés de son fonctionnement en l'employant tour à tour comme un instrument bureaucratique, scientifique et de propagande. L'acte photographique était un droit exclusif de l'administration qui s'en servit dans certaines des ses structures centrales et, en premier lieu, dans la procédure d'enregistrement des détenus.

Obraz wycisza się.

The image is "silenced".

Traci siłę wymowy,

It loses its power to speak,

Welche Diskurse haben es diesem Bild ermöglicht, die Rolle der „berühmtesten Holocaust-Fotografie" einzunehmen? Fotos von Kindern eignen sich auf besondere Weise für Projektionen. Vor allem wenn sie ausgeschnitten und entkontextualisiert werden, evozieren sie einen BetrachterInnen-Blick, der sich zugehörig fühlt und einen beschützenden Blick; einen Blick, der Vergessen oder sogar Verleugnung befördert.

Oft werden Opfer infantilisiert. Diese Infantilisierung ist strukturell auch eine Feminisierung. Ist das Opfer infantilisiert, so ist der Täter hypermaskulinisiert, dargestellt als das übermenschliche Böse. Die Täter werden dadurch entwirklicht. Indem sich die BetrachterInnen durch den identifikatorischen Blick an die Stelle der infantilisierten und feminisierten Opfer imaginieren, nehmen sie an der Hypermaskulinisierung der Täter teil. Sie führt schließlich zu einer Depersonalisierung, zum Löschen der Frage nach konkreter TäterInnenschaft.

Es ist wahrscheinlich kein Zufall, dass das berühmteste Holocaust-Bild ein Bild aus dem Warschauer Ghetto ist. Der Name „Warschau" ist assoziiert mit Heldentum und Widerstand. Dieser Junge kann dadurch zugleich das ultimative Opfer und der klassische Held sein. Er kann im Bild verweiblicht und dennoch in der Erzählung für jene, die um seine Verbindung mit Warschau wissen, wieder vermännlicht werden.

Marianne Hirsch, „Täter-Fotografien in der Kunst nach dem Holocaust. Geschlecht als ein Idiom der Erinnerung", in: Insa Eschebach, Sigrid Jacobeit, Silke Wenk (Hg.), Gedächtnis und Geschlecht. Deutungsmuster in Darstellungen des nationalsozialistischen Genozids, Frankfurt am Main 2002

La photographie représentait, pour le prisonnier comme pour l'administration du camp, le franchissement d'un seuil autant symbolique que pratique: revêtu d'un uniforme, crâne rasé, marqué d'un insigne, le détenu pénétrait dans l'univers hiérarchisé du camp où son numéro, inscrit sur sa veste et son pantalon, prononcé en allemand, lui ferait désormais office de nom.

Le portrait signalétique participait à l'acquisition d'une nouvelle identité. L'inscription du visage dans un cadre, la contrainte du corps dans un système technique (la chaise pivotante, la tige métallique, les différentes numéro) faisait du „passage" à la photographie une véritable intronisation du détenu dans le monde du camp.

Par le biais de l'image photographique, l'administration concentrationnaire assurait ainsi la conformité du détenu à un type, à la fois physique et social. D'autres applications de la photographie, à la classification des types humains ou à des expérimentations médicales pratiquées sur les détenus, semblent, d'une manière différente, prolonger cette fixation photographique de la nouvelle identité des prisonniers des camps.

Ilsen About, „La photographie au service du système concentrationnaire nationalsocialiste (1933-1945)", dans: Mémoire des camps. Photographies des camps de concentration et d'extermination nazis (1933-1999), ouvrage publié sous la direction de Clément Chéroux, Paris 2001

swoją wartość jako dokument,

its historical value as a document,

dokument Holocaust.

as a document of the Holocaust.

www.klubzwei.at
www.sixpackfilm.com
www.wienerlibrary.co.uk

Sabine Schaschl-Cooper, Bettina Steinbrügge

The Need to Document

Pointing out the boom of the documentary in contemporary art is itself booming at present. There is hardly an article or an academic essay, starting with documenta X (1997) right up to current exhibitions, that fails to mention the increased move in current art production — by means of documentary languages — to social, political, ecological, and economic issues, and to the questioning of the effects of global network systems and their formulations. Accounts of the inordinate increase in documentary aesthetics that can frequently be heard lately prove that it is not the artists but rather certain critics accustomed to rapid thematic and formal changes in contemporary art who are again calling for new focuses in regard to contents and aesthetics. The tendency toward the documentary remains unimpressed by this, and contemporary art makes no secret of its need to document — reason enough to examine the motives.

Situations of Social Crisis and the Expanded Field of Culture

A recurring proposition establishes a connection between the increase in documentary practices and the increase in crisis situations. As Jan Verwoert already points out, Paul Arthur describes "the politicization of the documentary film in the 1930s in conjunction with the liberal New Deal program in opposition to the proliferation of the market economy — and the emergence of *Direct Cinema* in the context of the unrests of the 1960s"[1] as an historical example of the stepped-up development of documentary aesthetics.[2] Our present epoch reached a crisis climax with 9/11, the impact of which has led to a modern "liberation" and colonial war against Iraq, disguised as a "security war", and to a division between the Western and Muslim world, between the United States and parts of Europe. It has triggered general debates on security, border controls, methods of surveillance, and debates on the effects of international politics on local situations. In the face of global crises, the docu-

Das Bedürfnis, zu dokumentieren

Die Hochkonjunktur des Dokumentarischen in der zeitgenössischen Kunst zu konstatieren hat mittlerweile Konjunktur. In kaum einem Artikel oder einer wissenschaftlichen Abhandlung, ausgehend vom Wirkungskreis der documenta X (1997) bis zu gegenwärtigen Ausstellungen, wurde es versäumt, auf die verstärkte Hinwendung aktueller Kunstproduktionen zu sozialen, politischen, ökologischen, ökonomischen Problemstellungen, zur Hinterfragung der Auswirkungen globaler Netzwerksysteme und ihren Ausformulierungen mittels dokumentarischer Sprachmittel hinzuweisen. Verlautbarungen über ein Inflationär-Werden der dokumentarischen Ästhetik, die in jüngster Zeit häufiger zu hören sind, zeigen, dass nicht die KünstlerInnen, sondern manche KritikerInnen, gewohnt vom schnellen Themen- und Formwechsel der Gegenwartskunst, schon wieder nach neuen inhaltlichen und ästhetischen Schwerpunkten verlangen. Die Tendenz zum Dokumentarischen bleibt davon unbeeindruckt und die Gegenwartskunst macht keinen Hehl aus ihrem Bedürfnis nach dem Dokumentarischen, was Grund genug ist, die Beweggründe zu untersuchen.

Gesellschaftliche Krisensituationen und das erweiterte Feld der Kultur

Eine wiederkehrende These sieht einen Zusammenhang zwischen der Zunahme dokumentarischer Praktiken und verstärkt auftretenden Krisensituationen. Wie bereits Jan Verwoert anführt, nennt Paul Arthur „die Politisierung des Dokumentarfilms in den dreißiger Jahren im Rahmen des liberalen New-Deal-Programms gegen das Wuchern der Marktwirtschaft und die Entstehung des *Direct Cinema* im Kontext der Unruhen der sechziger Jahre"[1] als historische Beispiele für die Forcierung der Entwicklung dokumentarischer Ästhetiken.[2] Unsere gegenwärtige Zeitepoche hat mit 9/11 einen Krisenhöhepunkt erreicht, dessen Auswirkungen zu einem als „Sicherheitskrieg" getarnten, modernen „Befreiungs"- und Kolonialkrieg gegen den Irak führten, die eine

ment as an artistic means is used as visual, acoustic, or textual evidence and as a form of articulation in the "proceedings" against the bad state of the world. The artists' collective Raqs Media Collective working out of New Delhi writes: "The art space cannot keep the troubled world at bay, and in order to apprehend reality as it is, in all its disarray, it has to permit the entry of the document as a 'stable' referent of the chaotic world it inhabits."[3] In an article on the processes of cultural construction, Catherine David points out that art is currently characterized by extreme heterogeneity. "Contemporary aesthetics and the artists are dealing with highly complex themes, with physical, geographical, as well as mental and ideological correlations. They shift art to an [...] 'expanded field' of culture, to a space that until recently belonged exclusively to anthropology."[4] In her opinion, this results in a turning to contextualization, which again has to do with the representation of differences, the acknowledgment of conflicts, and the resulting necessary debates.[5] The fact is that the world is determined in an increasingly standardized way by a globalized political and economic system, and art cannot turn its back to this. Yet art cannot approach this state of affairs using conventional aesthetic means, either, since a contextualization can only be established in a limited way when using pure objects. Topical thematic complexes such as globalization, terrorism, construction of identity, feminism, and neoliberalism have entered into the context of art and seek an adequate form of expression. Non-linear interrelations and diverging attitudes are to be turned into a meaningful narrative that reveals the complexity of present-day representation. What frequently poses a problem here, is not that it cannot be ascertained what actually occurred, but how this reality can be related in such a way that it stands in a meaningful and comprehensible relationship to the present. A second important point is the fact that knowledge has been transformed into very many pieces of visual information, thus posing the problem of who possesses this information, who has access to it, and who is excluded from it. Due to its specific approach, the documentary has

Spaltung zwischen westlicher und muslimischer Welt, zwischen den USA und Teilen Europas sowie generelle Debatten um Sicherheit, Grenzkontrollen, Überwachungsmethoden und Auseinandersetzungen über die Auswirkungen internationaler Politik auf lokale Situationen hervorbrachten. Das Dokument als künstlerisches Mittel wird angesichts der globalen Krisen als visuelles, akustisches oder textuelles Artikulations- und Beweismittel im „Verfahren" gegen den schlechten Zustand der Welt eingesetzt. „Der Raum der Kunst kann die unruhige Welt nicht außen vor lassen, und um Realität als das wahrzunehmen, was sie in ihrer ganzen Unordnung ist, muss er den Einzug des Dokuments als einen ‚stabilen' Referenten der chaotischen Welt, in der er lebt, zulassen,"[3] schreibt das von Neu Delhi aus agierende Künstlerkollektiv Raqs Media Collective. In einem Artikel zu den Prozessen kultureller Konstruktion macht Catherine David deutlich, dass die Kunst derzeit von einer extremen Heterogenität geprägt ist: „Die zeitgenössische Ästhetik und die Künstler beschäftigen sich mit sehr komplexen Themen, mit physischen, geografischen und auch mentalen und ideologischen Zusammenhängen. Sie rücken die Kunst in ein [...] ‚erweitertes Feld' der Kultur, in einen Raum, der bis vor kurzem ausschließlich der Anthropologie gehörte."[4] Daraus resultiert ihrer Meinung nach eine Hinwendung zur Kontextualisierung, was wiederum mit der Darstellung von Gegensätzen, mit der Anerkennung von Konflikten und den daraus entstehenden notwendigen Debatten zu tun habe.[5] Fakt ist, dass die Welt immer einheitlicher von einem globalisierenden politischen und ökonomischen System bestimmt wird, dem sich auch die Kunst nicht entziehen kann. Dem sich aber die Kunst auch nicht allein mittels der herkömmlichen ästhetischen Mittel nähern kann, da eine Kontextualisierung nur bedingt mit reinen Objekten herstellbar ist. Derzeit aktuelle Themenkomplexe wie z.B. Globalisierung, Terrorismus, Identitätskonstruktionen, Feminismus oder Neoliberalismus sind in den Kunstkontext gewandert und suchen nun nach einer adäquaten Form des Ausdrucks. Nicht-lineare Zusammenhänge und divergierende Haltungen sollen zu einer sinnvollen Erzählung gemacht werden, die die Kom-

crystallized as a possible form of effectively addressing these issues in this context. The statement of the Raqs Media Collective also makes it clear that the connection between art and everyday life – as it was already examined by the avant-garde movements – must always be examined anew. This not only entails calling into question art's social function, but also drawing attention to the media-related conditions under which art is produced today – particularly in face of the mass media taking over the production of sense.

Representational Crises

It is not only the political crises that need to be addressed that have given impetus to documentarism in art. The visual reproduction of the world has itself entered into a crisis situation. The boom of reality-TV formats and the simultaneous loss of an historical image vocabulary stimulate the debates on documentarism and authenticity. Jean Baudrillard locates the crisis of representation as follows: "A wonderful model of [...] forced visibility is *Big Brother* and all similar programs, reality shows, docu-soaps etc. Just there; where everything is given to be seen there is nothing left to be seen. It is the mirror of platitude, of banality, of the zero degree of everyday life."[6] Here, the distinction between the image and the visual, as Catherine David formulated the topic at documenta X, is instructive. In *documenta documents 2*, Serge Daney stated. "When I wrote about the Gulf War, I found myself forced to distinguish between the image and the visual for the sake of clarity. The visual (which dominates television) is a powerful 'piece of evidence' that gets lost in a closed circuit. [...] The image is simply the opposite. It is that which constantly harbors a certain heterogeneity, reminding us that we are not alone in the world, even if we are the most powerful."[7] MTV is a synonym for the tendency to dissolve all contradictions and qualities of the image in a flow of the visual. The music station, founded in 1981, triggered something that meanwhile dominates all television stations and their programs. The artists working in a documentary manner today seem to want to

plexität heutiger Repräsentation deutlich werden lässt. Problematisch ist dabei häufig nicht, dass nicht zu ermitteln ist, was wirklich geschah, sondern wie diese Wirklichkeit so wiedergegeben wird, dass sie in einem sinnvollen und verständlichen Bezug zur Gegenwart steht. Ein zweiter wichtiger Punkt ist die Tatsache, dass Wissen in eine Vielzahl von visuellen Informationen umgewandelt wurde und sich damit das Problem stellt, wer über diese Informationen verfügt, wer Zugang zu ihnen hat und wer ausgeschlossen wird. Das Dokumentarische hat sich in diesem Kontext aufgrund der spezifischen Vorgehensweise als eine mögliche Form herauskristallisiert, diesen Fragestellungen wirkungsvoll zu begegnen. Und die Aussage des Raqs Media Collective macht auch deutlich, dass die Verbindung von Kunst und Alltagsleben, wie sie bereits von den Avantgarde-Bewegungen thematisiert worden ist, immer wieder neu gestellt werden muss. Damit ist an dieser Stelle nicht nur die Infragestellung der gesellschaftlichen Funktion gemeint, der Blick wird auch auf die medialen Bedingungen gerichtet, unter denen Kunst heute – gerade angesichts der Übernahme der Sinnproduktion seitens der Massemedien – entsteht.

Repräsentationskrisen

Die zu konstatierenden politischen Krisen sind es nicht allein, die dem Dokumentarismus in der Kunst Auftrieb gegeben haben. Ebenso ist die visuelle Reproduktion der Welt selbst in eine Krisensituation geraten. Der Boom von Reality-TV-Formaten und der gleichzeitige Verlust eines historischen Bildvokabulars stimulieren die Dokumentarismus- und Authentizitätsdebatte. Jean Baudrillard verortet die Repräsentationskrise folgendermaßen: „Dort, wo die Banalität des Bildes mit der Banalität des Lebens zusammentrifft, wie im Reality-TV, bei Doku-Soaps, *Big Brother* oder seiner französischen Version *Loft Story* etc. [...], dort beginnt jene integrale Sichtbarkeit, bei der alles gezeigt wird, und bei der man bemerkt, dass es nichts mehr zu sehen gibt."[6] Hier ist die Unterscheidung zwischen dem Bild und dem Visuellen aufschlussreich, wie sie auf der documenta X von Catherine David thematisiert wurde. Von Serge

counter this tendency, in the tradition of James Agee or Walker Evans, for example, usually by making use of cinematic and photographic means in a critical and reflective way. As early as 1936, the writer and film critic James Agee, in the context of the project, *Let Us Now Praise Famous Men*, that he realized together with Walker Evans in Alabama, spoke of a "corruption of seeing". The decisive fact in this photo essay is the attempt to do away with this corruption by attaching equal value to image and text. They do not comment on each other, but alternately overlap each other in order to create meaning. Joachim Koester's photo series *The Kant Walk* (2003) or *From The Travel of Jonathan Harker* (2003) present the artist's personal research work. He investigates the traces of the German national hero Immanuel Kant or the career of the Dracula myth in the form of classical photographs supplemented by the artist's written descriptions of the subjects of research. Image

Joachim Koester, *From the Travel of Jonathan Harker*, 2003

and text complement one another and jointly deconstruct social constructions: In his former place of residence, Königsberg, there are hardly any references to the philosopher Kant, who is immortalized in Germany in numerous monuments and dedications. Present-day Kaliningrad resembles a place marked by the Soviet politics of obliteration, where utopian social welfare housing, former elements of civilization directed against dilapidation and ruin, dominates the cityscape along with the historical Friedrichsburg. *From The Travel of Jonathan Harker* describes a journey through present-day Tran-

Daney ist in den *documenta documents 2* zu lesen: „Als ich über den Golfkrieg schrieb, sah ich mich um der Klarheit willen gezwungen, zwischen dem Bild und dem Visuellen einen Unterschied zu machen. Das Visuelle (das im Fernsehen dominiert) ist ein schlagkräftiger ‚Beweis', der sich in einem geschlossenen Kreislauf verliert. [...] Das Bild ist einfach das Gegenteil. Es ist das, was ständig eine gewisse Heterogenität beherbergt, was uns daran erinnert, dass wir nicht allein auf der Welt sind, selbst wenn wir die Stärksten sind."[7] MTV steht als das Synonym für die Tendenz, alle Widersprüche und Qualitäten des Bildes in einem Strom des Visuellen aufzulösen. Der 1981 gegründete Musiksender hat damit etwas ausgelöst, was mittlerweile beherrschend ist für alle Fernsehsender und ihre jeweiligen Programme. Die heute dokumentarisch arbeitenden KünstlerInnen scheinen, ganz in der Tradition von z.B. James Agee oder Walker Evans, dieser Tendenz etwas entgegensetzen zu wollen, zumeist durch einen kritisch-reflektierten Gebrauch filmischer und fotografischer Mittel. Der Schriftsteller und Filmkritiker James Agee sprach bereits 1936 im Kontext des Projekts *Let Us Now Praise Famous Men*, das er gemeinsam mit Walker Evans in Alabama durchführte, von einer „Korruption des Sehens". Das entscheidende Faktum an diesem Fotoessay ist der Versuch, die soeben zitierte Korruption durch die Gleichwertigkeit von Bild und Text aufzulösen. Bild und Text kommentieren sich hier nicht gegenseitig, sondern überlagern sich wechselseitig, um auf diesem Wege Sinn zu erzeugen. Joachim Koesters Fotoserien *The Kant Walk* (2003) oder *From The Travel of Jonathan Harker* (2003) präsentieren die persönlichen Recherchen des Künstlers, der den Spuren des deutschen Nationalhelden Immanuel Kant oder dem Werdegang des Mythos Dracula nachgeht, in Form von klassischen Fotografien, die durch schriftliche Schilderungen des Künstlers zum Untersuchungsgegenstand ergänzt werden. Bild und Text ergänzen sich und dekonstruieren gemeinsam gesellschaftliche Konstruktionen: In seinem ehemaligen Wohnort Königsberg gibt es kaum noch Hinweise, auf den in Deutschland in zahlreichen Denkmälern und Widmungen verewigten Philosophen Kant. Das heutige Kaliningrad gleicht einem

sylvania following the footsteps of Bram Stoker, where the ruins of post-communist reality and the traces of exploiting the landscape through a corrupt tourism industry have replaced Stoker's gloomy, romantic imagination. The film *Falls Burns Malone Fiddles* (2002) by the Glasgow-based artist Duncan Campbell portrays the youth scene in the working-class environment of

Duncan Campbell, *Falls Burns Malone Fiddles*, 2003

1980s Belfast. He presents the picture of a specific political situation, while simultaneously examining the possibilities and limits of the documentary. The starting point consists in material from photo and film archives assembled along with animations and also voids in such a way that the viewing habits of the audience are undermined. The pictures are reminiscent of images shot by surveillance cameras, but they are traversed by rebellious symbols, diagrams and geometrical shapes that break the representations in a destructive way. Only at the end of the film does the classical documentary film genre appear in the form of an interview sequence. But this genre is again recognized as fiction due to the underlying music.

The debate on the nature and functioning of contemporary images plays a significant role in the emergence of documentary forms in art. Here, the distinction is made between the undifferentiated flow of images of the visual, in which communication always only returns to itself, and the specific image that does not reveal everything but refers to "something else" that is not in the picture. In 1967, Guy Debord introduced his book, *The Society of the Spectacle*, with a quote by

von sowjetischer Auslöschungspolitik gekennzeichnetem Ort, an welchem utopisch anmutende Sozialbauten, dem Verfall entgegensteuernde Zivilisationselemente von einst, neben der historischen Friedrichsburg das Stadtbild prägen. *From The Travel of Jonathan Harker* beschreibt eine Reise durchs heutige Transsylvanien auf Bram Stokers Spuren, bei der die Ruinen postkommunistischer Realität und Spuren der Ausschlachtung der Landschaft durch eine korrupte Tourismusindustrie an die Stelle von Stokers düster-romantischer Imagination getreten sind. Der Film *Falls Burns Malone Fiddles* (2002) des in Glasgow lebenden Künstlers Duncan Campbell porträtiert die Jugendszene im Arbeitermilieu des Belfast der 80er Jahre. Er präsentiert das Bild einer konkreten politischen Situation, debattiert gleichzeitig aber auch die Möglichkeiten und Grenzen des Dokumentarischen. Ausgangspunkt ist fotografisches und filmisches Archivmaterial, das gemeinsam mit Animationen und auch Leerstellen derart montiert wird, dass die Sehgewohnheiten des Betrachters unterlaufen werden. Die Bilder erinnern an Aufnahmen von Überwachungskameras, die aber von rebellischen Symbolen, Diagrammen und geometrischen Formen durchzogen werden, welche die Darstellungen auf destruktive Art und Weise brechen. Nur am Schluss des Films taucht das klassische Dokumentarfilmgenre in Form einer Interviewsequenz auf, welches aber mittels der ihr unterlegten Musik wieder als Fiktion erkannt wird.

Die Debatte über das Wesen und Funktionieren der zeitgenössischen Bilder spielt eine große Rolle beim Aufkommen dokumentarischer Formen in der Kunst. Hier wird unterschieden zwischen der undifferenzierten Bilderflut des Visuellen, in der die Kommunikation immer nur zu sich selbst zurückkehrt, und dem spezifischen Bild, das nicht alles preisgibt und auf etwas „anderes" verweist, das nicht im Bild ist. 1967 leitete Guy Debord das Buch *Die Gesellschaft des Spektakels* mit einem Zitat von Feuerbach ein, welches exakt für die derzeitige Auseinandersetzung um die Frage von Bild und Visuellem bzw. um Dokumentation und Fiktion zu stehen scheint: „Aber freilich [...] diese Zeit, welche das Bild der Sache, die Kopie dem Original, die Vorstellung der

Feuerbach that appears to stand exactly for the current debate on the question of image and visual as well as documentation and fiction: "But certainly for the present age, which prefers the sign to the thing signified, the copy to the original, representation to reality, the appearance to the essence... *illusion* only is *sacred*, *truth* profane."⁸ This assertion is also visualized in the cinematic work of Dorit Margreiter, who adopts concepts and methods taken from the language of architecture and design, as well as from the film and TV genre, to use their content-related and formal elements for her description of the medial construction of reality. In *10104 Angelo View Drive* (2004), the focus is on a late-modernist, detached family house used in many Hol-

Dorit Margreiter, *10104 Angelo View Drive*, 2004

lywood productions as the location of "evil" (and which can be found at this excact address). Margreiter approaches the house from several perspectives by questioning the conventions of cinematic representation, naming the forms of use, plumbing different attributions of meaning, and differentiating between interior and exterior. Through these methods, she comes to deep insights into the mechanisms that make the reality of the media, of advertising, and of the world of commodities a structuring factor of everyday life.

Wirklichkeit, den Schein dem Wesen vorzieht [...]; denn *heilig* ist ihr nur die *Illusion*, profan aber die *Wahrheit*."⁸ Diese Aussage visualisiert sich ebenfalls im filmischen Schaffen von Dorit Margreiter, die Begriffe und Verfahren aus der Architektur- und Designsprache sowie dem Film- und TV-Genre aufnimmt, um deren inhaltliche und formale Bestandteile für ihre Beschreibung der medialen Konstruktion von Wirklichkeit zu nutzen. In *10104 Angelo View Drive* (2004) steht ein spätmodernistisches Einfamilienhaus im Vordergrund (welches unter genau dieser Adresse zu finden ist), das in zahlreichen Hollywood-Produktionen als Schauplatz des „Bösen" dient. Margreiter nähert sich diesem Haus aus mehreren Perspektiven, indem sie die Konventionen der filmischen Repräsentation hinterfragt, die Formen der Nutzung benennt, unterschiedliche Bedeutungszuschreibungen auslotet und Innen/Außen-Differenzierungen vornimmt. Durch diese Verfahren erzielt sie tiefe Einblicke in die Mechanismen, welche die Realität der Medien-, Werbe- und Warenwelt zum strukturierenden Faktor des Alltagslebens werden lassen.

Re-Politisierung und Medienrealitäten

Die Re-Politisierung des Kunstfeldes, die in den vorangegangenen Ausführungen ersichtlich wurde, setzte in den frühen 90er Jahren des 20. Jahrhunderts ein und hat entscheidend zum Aufkommen dokumentarischer Strategien beigetragen. Es entwickelten sich vielfältige kritische, emanzipatorische und politische Praxisformen, die hinreichend unter den Vorzeichen der Selbstorganisation, der Site Specificity oder des Archivierens besprochen worden sind. Ein derzeit etwas vernachlässigter aber durchaus interessanter Gesichtspunkt ist die These, dass die Re-Politisierung, wie dies Holger Kube Ventura anführt⁹, durch die Techno-Bewegung vorbereitet wurde. Die mit Techno verbundene Tanz- und Partykultur hegte den Anspruch politisch zu sein – zumindest wenn es darum ging „the right to party" gegenüber den Stadtverwaltern in getanzten „Demonstrationen", beispielsweise jener der *Love Parade*, einzuklagen. Oliver Marchart erklärt das Dreieck Techno-Politik-Kunst folgendermaßen: „Da Hip-

Re-politicization and Media Realities

The re-politicization of the art field that became evident in what was described above commenced in the early 1990s and contributed decisively to the emergence of documentary strategies. Many and varied critical, emancipatory and political forms of practice developed that have been sufficiently treated theoretically in terms of self-organization, site-specificity and archiving. An interesting aspect, which is currently a bit neglected, is the proposition that the techno movement paved the way for re-politicization, as Holger Kube Ventura points out[9]. The dance and party culture associated with techno claimed to be political – at least as far as asserting "the right to party" vis-à-vis town councilors in the form of dance "demonstrations" like the *Love Parade* is concerned. Oliver Marchart explains the triangle of techno-politics-art as follows: "Since the transfer of hipness is also the transfer of authenticity, the import of youth culture, in passing, also functions as the simulation of reality, of 'social practice'. A touch of the real outside world permeates the art institutions suffering from a chronic lack of 'reality impact' which must be compensated by constant legitimization work. Artist-DJs working as 'hipness scouts' are at the same time something like 'reality scouts' for the art system."[10] Even if there is hardly a direct relationship anymore between the dance and party culture of the early 1990s and today's documentary works – one can at most attribute to this culture an atmosphere that paved the way for an increased politicization – this form of expression also emulates the happenings of the 1950s and 1960s or the actions of ex-communards such as Theo Altenburg or Otto Mühl.

The techno movement was already based on new media realities that most likely fostered documentarism in various ways. The advanced technological means of media networks, the Internet, and, not least, the omnipresent "private" video camera play an important role in visualizing constructions of truth. When in March 1991 members of the Los Angeles Police Department beat the African-American Rodney King in front

of a running camera, and the filmed scenes were then shown around the world, a general awareness of video technology as a means of controlling and "looking back" at the people in power arose. It could not be overlooked that the image worlds and the processing of existing images gained increasing significance in formatting social roles and psychological dispositions, and, more generally, in the lifestyles of individuals. As surveillance systems, video technology allowed those in power to control the individual, who can, however, "turn around 180 social degrees to reveal the actions of power."[11] Without claiming technical perfection, video can capture and make people aware of things, it can act against turning a blind eye to things, and it thus became the most popular means of language in documentary art practices. For Oliver Ressler, for example, video is a central element used in wall and spatial installations. But he also emphasizes that videos are created independently of exhibitions in his creative work, videos "which can also be presented outside the immediate field of art. These videos move between art and political activism and deal with themes and practices of resistance in a non-institutionalized left."[12] An important aspect of creative documentary work within an artistic context is the rejection of the alleged neutrality of investigative journalism and the neutrality repeatedly claimed in television news reports. Ressler points out that he takes a clear stand in works such as *Disobbedienti* (2002), *This is what democracy looks like!* (2002), and *Venezuela from below* (2004), and that his videos are therefore to be

Video festhalten, ins Bewusstsein rücken und gegen das Ausblenden und Wegschauen vorgehen und wurde so zum beliebtesten Sprachmittel dokumentarischer Kunstpraktiken. Für Oliver Ressler z.B. bildet das Video ein zentrales Element, welches in Wand- und Rauminstallationen eingesetzt wird. Er macht aber auch deutlich, dass in seiner künstlerischen Arbeit unabhängig von Ausstellungen Videos entstehen, „die außerhalb des unmittelbaren Kunstfeldes präsentiert werden können. Diese Videos bewegen sich zwischen Kunst und politischem Aktivismus und greifen Themen und Praxen des Widerstandes einer nicht-institutionalisierten Linken auf."[12] Ein wichtiger Aspekt dokumentarischen Schaffens im künstlerischen Kontext ist die Abkehr von der angeblichen Neutralität des investigativen Journalismus und der behaupteten Neutralität, wie sie immer wieder in den Nachrichtenbeiträgen der Fernsehanstalten proklamiert wird. Ressler macht darauf aufmerksam, dass er in Arbeiten, wie *Disobbedienti* (2002), *This is what democracy looks like!* (2002) oder *Venezuela from below* (2004) eindeutig Position bezieht und seine Videos damit auch als politisches Statement zu verstehen sind.[13] Da diese Arbeiten aber dennoch primär in Kunstinstitutionen gezeigt werden, wird deutlich, dass diese derzeit die zentralen Freiräume bieten, um marginale politische und gesellschaftliche Themen zu artikulieren und auch zu diskutieren. Es scheint, als haben sich etliche Kunsträume zu den einzig verbliebenen Orten entwickelt, an denen frei von jeglicher Reglementierung streitbare Positionen gezeigt werden können, in denen Widersprüche ausgehalten werden und wo die Möglichkeit besteht, Diskussionen jenseits ökonomischer Interessen zu führen.

Neben dem Medium Video, welches die Aufnahmehoheit demokratisierte, öffnete das Internet ein breites Feld an Informations- und Bildmaterialien für die kunstdokumentarische Einflussnahme auf gesellschaftliche Vorgänge. Mit der Netzplattform „The Thing" initiierte Wolfgang Staehle bereits zu Beginn der 90er Jahre ein Mittel zum Informationsaustausch – nicht zuletzt mit einem sozio-politischen Anspruch – welches zunächst u.a. von KünstlerInnen frequentiert wurde und an dem KünstlerInnen wie John Cage,

Oliver Ressler and Dario Azzellini, *Venezuela from Below*, 2004

understood as political statements.¹³ But since these works are primarily shown at art institutions, it becomes evident that these institutions currently provide the freedom needed to articulate and also discuss marginal political and social topics. It seems as if quite a lot of art spaces have turned into the only remaining places where contestable positions can be presented free of any kind of regulation, where contradictions are endured, and where debates going beyond economical interests can be held.

Apart from the medium of video, which democratized the right to record, the Internet has opened up a wide field of information and image material for influencing social processes through documentary art. In the early 1990s, the network platform "The Thing", initiated by Wolfgang Staehle, was already a means of exchanging information – not least with a socio-political claim – that was initially frequented by artists and in which artists such as John Cage, Peter Halley, and Julia Scher were directly involved. At the start of its career, the Internet stood for the decentralization of information, for free communication, the de-hierarchizing of knowledge, and the entropic distribution of power. It thus became an important instrument for re-politicizing the world of art, as well as many others. Through its influence, the discourses of cultural studies, economy, sociology, art, the entertainment industry, and politics were increasingly linked. The Internet resisted *per se* authoritarian administration and monopolistic control, and thus raised the hopes in art circles, too, that new forms of collectivity and political counter-publics could be made possible. Politics turned into media politics and the dream of an "actually existing socialism"¹⁴ was revived. Regardless of the subsequent disillusionment, cyberspace established a political activism that characterized much of the 1990s. The net served as a space of resistance against any kind of economic co-option; political activism could be efficiently coordinated, avoiding long communication paths; and critics of globalization in particular acted via this medium, using it as a work space, a social center, and a project workshop.¹⁵ The

Peter Halley oder Julia Scher direkt beteiligt waren. Das Internet stand zu Beginn seiner Karriere für die Dezentralisierung von Information, für freie Kommunikation, für die Enthierarchisierung von Wissen und für die entropische Verteilung von Macht. Damit wurde es zu einem wichtigen Instrument der Re-Politisierung des Kunstbetriebs, aber nicht nur hier, wurden doch von nun an auch verstärkt die Diskurse in Cultural Studies, Ökonomie, Soziologie, Kunst, Unterhaltungsindustrie und Politik miteinander verquickt. Das Internet widersetzte sich per se der autoritären Verwaltung und monopolistischen Kontrolle und schürte damit auch in Kunstkreisen die Hoffnung, neue Formen der Kollektivität und politischen Gegenöffentlichkeiten zu ermöglichen. Politik wurde in Medienpolitik überführt und der Traum des „real existierenden Sozialismus"¹⁴ erlebte seine Wiedergeburt. Ungeachtet der darauf folgenden Desillusionierung etablierte der Cyberspace einen politischen Aktivismus, der große Teile der 90er Jahre bestimmte. Das Netz diente als Raum des Widerstands gegen jegliche Formen ökonomischer Vereinnahmung, im Netz konnte abseits langer Kommunikationswege politischer Aktivismus effizient koordiniert werden und besonders die GlobalisierungsgegnerInnen agieren über dieses Medium und benutzen es als Arbeitsraum, Sozialzentrum oder Projektwerkstatt.¹⁵ Der Utopieverlust der letzten Jahre ging damit einher, dass das Netz als strategisches Operationsfeld für kommerzielle NutzerInnen entdeckt wurde und die einzelnen Staaten darüber hinaus versuchten, ihren Einfluss auf das Internet zu verstärken. Es stellte sich heraus, dass auch das Cybernetz nicht vor Machtstrukturen gefeit ist, um so mehr diese dann wieder in den Mittelpunkt der Diskussion rückten. So diskutiert das *noborder*-Netzwerk die Zusammenhänge der Kontrolle von Grenzen im physikalischen und virtuellen Raum und lädt zur Beschäftigung mit *free movement* und *free communication* ein.¹⁶ Wie die Kulturwissenschaftlerin Marion Hamm schreibt: „Die permanente Anwesenheit von [...] Mediengerätschaften auf der Straße [...] bewirkt mehr als Berichterstattung – sie verändert die Form der politischen Artikulierung, kann Teil von Interventionen werden, beitragen zur permanenten Pro-

loss of utopias in the past few years was accompanied by the fact that the net was discovered as a strategic field of operation for commercial users and that individual nations additionally attempted to gain more influence on the Internet. It turned out that cyberspace was not immune to power structures either, which then became the focus of debates again. In this vein, the *no border* network discusses the conditions of controlling borders in physical and virtual space and invites people to debate about *free movement* and *free communication*.[16] The cultural scientist Marion Hamm writes: "The permanent presence of [...] media equipment on the street [...] affects more than reporting – it changes the form of political articulation, can become part of interventions, contribute to the permanent production of the public sphere, a public sphere [that] no longer has to distinguish between 'real' and 'virtual'."[17] Media networks, work with camcorders, and the Internet all live from creatively playing with their own means and rules and thus follow in the tradition of modern art. The fact that in the art field their technological possibilities allowed them to transgress the terrain of criteria originally directed toward art and to intervene in places where art usually does not occur, paved the way for today's documentaries.

The discussions of the net art community and its activist orientation provide a basis for examining a political form of documentary strategies that Søren Grammel calls participatory video practice in his contribution to this book. For Grammel, this means that the medium of video is used to intervene in certain environments and enable different persons and groups to work together. While the strategies of re-politicization in the 1990s primarily served to illustrate social relations, what is now emphasized is the creation of communities and communication. The common interest in social themes led to the formation of the artists' group Big Hope (Miklós Erhardt, Dominic Hislop and Elske Rosenfeld), for example, that pursues the goal of working together and communicating with people other than those interested in art. They view themselves in the role of mediators who, based on

duktion von Öffentlichkeit, die nicht trennen muss zwischen ‚wirklich' und ‚virtuell'".[17] Mediennetzwerke, die Arbeit mit Camcordern und das Internet leben davon, kreativ mit ihren eigenen Mitteln und Regeln zu spielen und stehen damit auch in der Tradition modernistischer Kunst. Dass sie im Kunstfeld aufgrund ihrer technischen Möglichkeiten das Terrain der ursprünglich an die Kunst gerichteten Kriterien überschreiten und dort intervenieren konnten, wo Kunst normalerweise nicht stattfindet, bereitete den Weg für heutige Dokumentarismen.

Die Diskussionen der Netzkunst-Community wie auch deren aktivistische Ausrichtung bieten eine Grundlage für die Betrachtung einer politischen Spielart mit dokumentarischen Strategien, die Sören Grammel in seinem Beitrag zu dieser Publikation als partizipative Videopraxis bezeichnet. Für Grammel bedeutet dies, dass das Medium Video verwendet wird, um in bestimmten Umgebungen zu intervenieren, und dort eine Zusammenarbeit zwischen verschiedenen Personen oder Gruppen herzustellen. Dienten die Re-Politisierungsstrategien der 90er Jahre primär der Darstellung gesellschaftlicher Zusammenhänge, so stehen jetzt Gemeinschaftsbildung und Kommunikation im Mittelpunkt. Die Künstlergruppe Big Hope (Miklós Erhardt, Dominic Hislop und Elske Rosenfeld) z.B. hat sich aus dem gemeinsamen Interesse für soziale Themen zusammengefunden und verfolgt das Ziel, mit weiteren Menschen zusammenzuarbeiten und zu kommunizieren als nur mit Kunstinteressierten. Sie sehen sich in der Rolle von Vermittlern, die auf Grundlage ihrer Ausbildung, ihrer Erfahrungen und ihres Status die ihnen zugänglichen Ressourcen mit anderen teilen. In dem Spiel *Commonopoly* werden die verschiedenen Varianten des Modells Kapitalismus systematisch marginalisiert. Es ist ein gemeinschaftsorientiertes, aber nicht gewinnorientiertes Spiel, das auf vorhergehenden Interviews in der ungarischen Industriestadt Dunaujvaros und in Berliner Arbeitervierteln basiert. Daraus ist ein Spiel entwickelt worden, welches auf Tauschökonomie und beiderseitigen Nutzen abzielt. An dieser Stelle geht es explizit nicht mehr um die „Wirklichkeitskulis-

their training, experience and status, can share with others the resources they have at their disposal. In the game *Commonopoly*, the different variants of the model of capitalism are systemat-

Big Hope: Miklós Erhardt & Dominic Hislop & Elske Rosenfeld, *Commonopoly*, 2004

ically marginalized. It is a game oriented toward a community and not profit. It is based on interviews that were held in the Hungarian industrial town of Dunaujvaros and in working-class districts of Berlin. They were developed into a game focusing on exchange economy and mutual benefit. Here, it is explicitly no longer about "reality backdrops"[18], which, according to Marius Babias, were created by the documentary trends of the 1990s, but about discussing the potentials of critical and political art projects. From the fact that aesthetic categories again play a more important role, one can conclude that a return to art's inherent qualities is taking place.

Postcolonialism Debates and Biennials

The thematic linking of postcolonialism debates with the question of globalization emerged in the mid-1990s and has since had a formative influence on current exhibitions of contemporary art. It transfers discussions originally held in other disciplines such as anthropology, ethnology or sociology to the field of art, thus considerably expanding its range of topics. As could be seen at documenta X and Documenta11, the current context can no longer be imagined without questions pertaining to migration, the "Other", Eurocentrism, and global culture. "A global view is inevitably a dispersed one"; in an

sen"[18], deren Aufbau Marius Babias den dokumentarischen Tendenzen der 90er Jahre unterstellt hat, sondern darum, die Potenziale von kritischen und politischen Kunstprojekten zu diskutieren. Dass dabei auch ästhetische Kategorien wieder eine verstärkte Rolle spielen, lässt den Schluss zu, dass eine Rückbesinnung auf die ureigenen Qualitäten von Kunst stattfindet.

Postkolonialismus-Debatten und Biennalen

Die thematische Verknüpfung der Postkolonialismus-Debatte mit der Frage der Globalisierung kam Mitte der 90er Jahre auf und prägt seither die aktuellen Ausstellungen von Gegenwartskunst. Sie überträgt die ursprünglich in anderen Disziplinen, wie der Anthropologie, Ethnologie oder Soziologie geführte Diskussion auf den Kunstbereich und hat die Themenpalette desselben entscheidend erweitert. Fragen der Migration, des „Anderen", des Eurozentrismus oder der Globalkultur sind, wie auch auf der documenta X und der Documenta11 zu sehen war, aus dem derzeitigen Kontext nicht mehr weg zu denken. „Eine globale Sicht ist zwangsläufig eine verstreute." Simon Njami macht in einem Interview mit Heike Munder deutlich, dass der globale Blick auf die Kunst unmöglich ist.[19] Diesem Diktum mögen auch viele KünstlerInnen gefolgt sein, die auf die diversen, in den letzten Jahren inflationär stattfindenden Biennalen eingeladen wurden. Diese dienen der Einbindung der Peripherie in den internationalen Kunstkontext, wobei westliche KünstlerInnen wie auch die jeweilige lokale Kunst-Community eingeladen werden. Wenn eine globale Sicht, die ja auch ein globales, einheitliches Wiedererkennen von Kunst bedeutet, nicht möglich ist, dienen dokumentarische Strategien als Türöffner für ein gegenseitiges Verstehen. Man kann dies als eine anthropologische Einstellung des Westens gegenüber dem Nicht-Westen auslegen, man kann Kunst in diesem Kontext aber auch als Möglichkeit der kritischen Reflexion von kulturellen, politischen und ideologischen Identitätsmustern verstehen. Die halbäthiopische, halbschwedische Künstlerin Loulou Cherinet inszeniert in ihren Videoarbeiten Geschichten, die den Betrachter in seiner gewohnten Sichtweise irritie-

interview with Heike Munder, Simon Njami stresses that the global view of art is impossible.[19] This dictum may have also been followed by many artists who were invited to the increasing number biennials over the past years. These biennials serve to integrate the periphery into the international art context, whereby both Western artists and the respective local art community are invited. If a global view, which also implies a global, uniform recognition of art, is not possible, then documentary strategies serve as a door-opener for mutual understanding. One can consider this as an anthropological attitude of the West toward the non-West, but one can also understand art in this context as an opportunity to critically reflect upon the cultural, political, and ideological patterns of identity. The half-Ethiopian, half-Swedish artist Loulou Cherinet stages stories in her video pieces that irritate the audience's accustomed ways of viewing. Against the background of her own life on different continents, the artist addresses issues of cultural identity in her work and, in they way she views Europe and the West, pursues the idea of an inverse ethnography with artistic means.

ren. Vor dem Hintergrund ihres eigenen Lebens auf unterschiedlichen Kontinenten thematisiert die Künstlerin in ihren Arbeiten Fragen kultureller Identität und verfolgt bei ihrer Sichtweise auf Europa bzw. den Westen mit künstlerischen Mitteln die Idee einer inversen Ethnografie. Im Film *White Women* (2002) sitzen neun afrikanische Männer, die alle in einem schwedischen Vorort leben, um einen runden Tisch. Die Kamera befindet sich in der Mitte des Tisches und dreht sich beständig, sodass die Männer ihr gegenüber nacheinander ins Blickfeld geraten. Sie tauschen ihre Erfahrungen im Spiel von Liebe und Partnerschaft zwischen schwarzen Männern in der Diaspora und einheimischen weißen Frauen aus. Das Thema und das Setting wurden von der Künst-

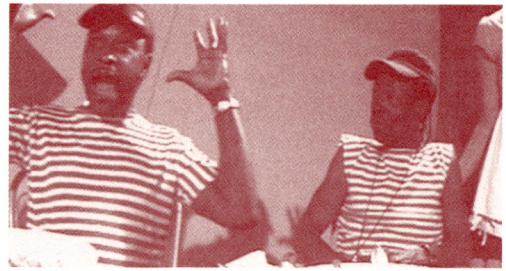

Loulou Cherinet, *White Women*, 2002

Loulou Cherinet, *White Women*, 2002

In the film *White Women* (2002), nine African men all living in a Swedish suburb sit at a round table. The constantly revolving camera is situated at the center of the table, so that the men, one after the other, are in the field of vision. They exchange the experiences they have made in regard to the game of love and partnership between black men living in the Diaspora and local white women. The theme and the setting were determined by the artist; the dialogues developed while shooting, lending the film its documentary character. Like many other artists

lerin vorgegeben; die Dialoge haben sich während des Drehs entwickelt, wodurch der Film seinen dokumentarischen Charakter erhält. Cherinet wie auch viele andere KünstlerInnen, die sich mit der Frage globaler Identität auseinandersetzen, begeben sich auf eine Suche nach Wahrheit, die mit dem Leben selbst untrennbar verbunden ist.

Diese kurze Untersuchung über die Beweggründe des Dokumentarischen in der zeitgenössischen Kunstproduktion muss notgedrungen lückenhaft bleiben. Es wird dennoch deutlich, dass die Öff-

dealing with the question of global identity, Cherinet searches for the truth that is inextricably connected with life itself.

This brief examination of the motives of the documentary in the production of contemporary art must, of course, remain incomplete. Yet it does become clear that art is opening up to every-day life in an extensive way and for good reasons. It must be pointed out that, especially at the moment, aesthetic issues are not being neglected, quite to the contrary: One can observe an inclination to link political and aesthetic issues that are even more important today than during the first half of the 1990s. In summary, one can perhaps bring into play Catherine David's proposed model: "It follows Jean-Luc Godard's intention, his special way of speaking about and from *Ici et ailleurs*, here and there, about the objectification of the conditions and production of works and exhibitions. It consists in making clear where one is located, what one is doing, and how one is doing it."[20]

nung der Kunst auf das alltägliche Leben breit gestreut stattfindet und auf guten Gründen basiert. Dabei sollte man nicht übersehen, dass gerade zurzeit die ästhetischen Fragestellungen nicht außer Acht gelassen werden; vielmehr ist eine Hinwendung zur Verquickung von politischen und ästhetischen Fragestellungen zu konstatieren, die heute stärker als noch in der ersten Hälfte der 90er Jahre von Belang ist. Zusammenfassend lässt sich vielleicht der Vorschlag eines Modells von Catherine David heranziehen: „Es folgt der Intention Jean-Luc Godards, seiner besonderen Weise, über und von *Ici et ailleurs*, von Hier und Dort, vom Objektivieren der Bedingungen, der Produktion, von Werken oder Ausstellungen zu sprechen. Sie besteht darin, deutlich zu machen, wo man ist, was man tut, und wie man es tut."[20]

---

1 Jan Verwoert, "Documentation as Artistic Practice," http://www.springerin.at/dyn/heft.php?id=36&pos=1&textid=1355&lang=en 2003 (04/10/05). Translated by Aileen Derieg.
2 See Paul Arthur, "Jargons of Authenticity (Three American Moments)," *Theorizing Documentary*, Michael Renov (ed.), New York/London 1993, p. 108–134.
3 Raqs Media Collective, "First Information Report," http://www.raqsmediacollective.net/texts3.html 2003 (04/10/05).
4 Catherine David, "Undurchsichtige Räume oder die Prozesse kultureller Konstruktion," *neue bildende kunst*, 4/5 (1995), p. 19. Translated by K.H.
5 Ibid.
6 Jean Baudrillard, "The violence of the image," http://www.egs.edu/faculty/baudrillard/baudrillard-the-violence-of-the-image.html 2003 (04/10/05).
7 Serge Daney, "Eine Geschichte über Unbeweglichkeit und Beweglichkeit," *documenta documents 2*, Ostfildern-Ruit 1996, p. 82. Translated by K.H.
8 Ludwig Feuerbach, Preface to the second edition of *The Essence of Christianity*, cited in Guy Debord, *The Society of the Spectacle* (1967), New York 1994, p. 11.
9 Holger Kube Ventura, *Politische Kunst Begriffe in den 1990er Jahren im deutschsprachigen Raum*, Vienna 2002.
10 Oliver Marchart, "Ambient im White Cube – Über Künstler-DJ's und Kuratoren-Club Hosts," *Springer* 3 (1996), p. 27.
11 John Fiske, "Videotech," *The Visual Culture Reader*, Nicholas Mirzoeff (ed.), London/New York 1998, p. 161.
12 Oliver Ressler, "Protesting Capitalist Globalization on Video," http://republicart.net/disc/representations/ressler01_en.htm 2003 (04/10/05). Translated by Aileen Derieg.

1 Jan Verwoert: Dokumentation als künstlerische Praxis, in: *springerin* (2003), Nr. 3, S. 29.
2 Vgl. Paul Arthur: Jargons of Authenticity (Three American Moments), in: Michael Renov (Hg.): *Theorizing Documentary*, New York/London 1993, S. 108-134.
3 Raqs Media Collective, in: *Texte zur Kunst*, 13. Jahrgang (2003), Nr. 51, S. 94.
4 Catherine David: Undurchsichtige Räume oder die Prozesse kultureller Konstruktion, in: *neue bildende kunst* (1995), Nr. 4/5, S. 19.
5 Ebd. S. 19.
6 Jean Baudrillard: *Die Gewalt am Bild*. (Ausst. Kat. Jean Baudrillard) Kunsthalle Fridericianum, Kassel 2003, S. 4–9.
7 Serge Daney: Eine Geschichte über Unbeweglichkeit und Beweglichkeit, in: documenta GmbH (Hg.): *documenta documents 2*, Ostfildern-Ruit 1996, S. 82.
8 Ludwig Feuerbach: Das Wesen des Christentums (Vorrede zur zweiten Auflage), in: Guy Debord: *Die Gesellschaft des Spektakels*, Berlin 1996 (1967), S. 11.
9 Holger Kube Ventura: *Politische Kunst Begriffe in den 1990er Jahren im deutschsprachigen Raum*, Wien 2002.
10 Oliver Marchart: Ambient im White Cube — Über Künstler-DJ's und Kuratoren-Club Hosts, in: *Springer* (1996), Nr. 3, S. 27.
11 John Fiske: Videotech, in: Nicholas Mirzoeff (Hg.): *The Visual Culture Reader*, London/New York 1998, S.161.
12 Oliver Ressler: Proteste gegen die kapitalistische Globalisierung auf Video, in: Gerald Raunig (Hg.): *Bildräume und Raumbilder*, Wien 2004, S. 140.
13 Ebd. S. 142.
14 Pit Schultz: Hybride Öffentlichkeiten. Netz-Aktivismus gegen Content-Industrie, in: Marius Babias und Achim Könnecke (Hg.): *Die Kunst des Öffentlichen*, Amsterdam/Dresden 1998, S. 140.
15 Vgl. Marion Hamm: Ar/ctivism in physikalischen und virtuellen Räumen, in: Gerald Raunig (Hg.): *Bildräume und Raumbilder*, Wien 2004, S. 34.
16 www.noborder.org (10.04.05).
17 Marion Hamm, a.a.O., S. 42.
18 Marius Babias: *Ware Subjektivität*, München 2002, S. 23.

13 Ibid.
14 Pit Schultz, "Hybride Öffentlichkeiten: Netz-Aktivismus gegen Content-Industrie," *Die Kunst des Öffentlichen*, Marius Babias and Achim Könnecke (eds.), Amsterdam/Dresden 1998, p. 140. Translated by K.H.
15 See Marion Hamm, "A r/c tivism in Physical and Virtual Spaces," http://republicart.net/disc/realpublicspaces/hamm02_en.htm 2003 [04/10/05]. Translated by Aileen Derieg.
16 http://www.noborder.org [04/10/05].
17 Marion Hamm, "A r/c tivism in Physical and Virtual Spaces."
18 Marius Babias, *Ware Subjektivität*, Munich 2002, p. 23. Translated by K.H.
19 Simon Njami, "Simon Njami im Interview mit Heike Munder," The African Sniper Reader, Fernando Alvim, Heike Munder and Ulf Wuggenig (eds.), Zurich 2005. Translated by K.H.
20 Catherine David, "Undurchsichtige Räume oder die Prozesse kultureller Konstruktion," p. 21. Translated by K.H.

19 Simon Njami im Interview mit Heike Munder, in: Fernando Alvim, Heike Munder und Ulf Wuggenig (Hg.): *Next Flag. The African Sniper Reader*, Zürich 2005 (im Erscheinen).
20 Catherine David, a.a.O., S. 21.

Microfiltration (a performance for two actors)
Jiří Skála and Mark Ther

The performance takes place in a space that is 20 to 30 metres square. There is a light carpet covering the entire space on the ground. In addition, there are sixteen vacuum cleaner bags, full of waste, acquired from families and public institutions. Each of them is a different size and probably has different contents. The last one is from the institution where this performance takes place.

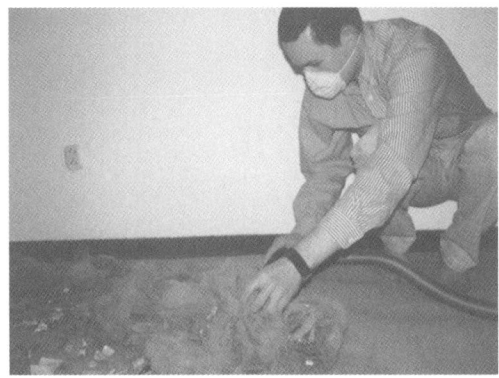

The second part of the performance follows. The actors no longer make records of the samples, but only refine the waste. They proceed as in the preceding part of the action. They open the individual bags, vacuum up one half of the waste and leave the other half on the carpet. At the end, they have four new bags. Each of them contains four samples.

The actors continue, making two new bags, containing eight types of waste, from four bags.

Both actors enter the surface defined by the size of the carpet and remain there for the entire time of the performance. They bring with them all the things and instruments needed. These are: a knife for opening the bags, a notebook and pen for noting the contents of the samples, stick-on labels, a vacuum cleaner, and finally fifteen new bags. Both actors are wearing ordinary clothing. For the whole time, they wear protective masks over their mouths. They do not wear shoes.

The Microfiltration action begins thus: One of the actors takes a bag, opens it with the knife, and dumps the entire contents on the carpet. Both actors then begin to examine the contents of the sample and to note them down in the notebook. Each record begins with the name of the family or institution that provided the bag. The actors also mark the sample on the carpet with a stick-on label. During the action, the records are stuck on the nearest wall, all at the same level.

After the record is finished, the actors vacuum up one half of the waste into a new bag. Subsequently, they study another sample and vacuum up half of it into the same bag that contains the waste from the previous sample. They proceed thus with all 16 samples. After the actors have opened and studied all the bags, there will be eight new ones lying on the ground in front of them, which contain a mixture of eight pairs of samples full of domestic or public waste.

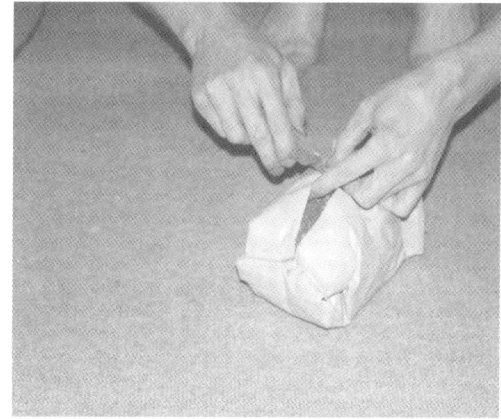

 These two bags yield the last one, which contains some waste from all the original samples.

This ends the performance and both actors can leave.

Vít Havránek

The Documentary — An Ontology of Forms in Transforming Countries[1]

The Wild East

In Central Europe, in the Balkans, in countries undergoing a transformation from the system of communist socialism, we have witnessed a historical turning point. This turning point can be illustrated metaphorically by the development of computer technologies. Imagine that you have never worked with a computer in your life. You discover computers in 2000. You learn to work with a computer, to use the internet, to receive and send emails. It is logical that you will have contemporary technology at your disposal: Pentium, Windows 2000, and the latest version of Office. This is, all in all, a banal situation. It is obvious that this kind of user (if he does not take up computers as his main field), will not investigate how technology arrived at its present state, how the old computers worked, how Commodore, Atari, Dos, or Windows 98 worked. It is as if history is fully included in the present. That is the situation in which the societies of "Eastern Europe" found themselves in 1989, after the fall of the Berlin wall. We were given the then relevant and functioning economic, artistic, social, and moral models of behavior. Naturally, we were already equipped with a certain type of performative and reactive behavior and experiences from the past. Reality, like technology, develops in jumps. The reality that we were suddenly exposed to was governed by laws about which we had no clue. We had experiences with a different type of reality and from the past we had virtual ideas about that reality, which originated in dreams dreamed in the past.

The rise of spectacularity and the "entertainment industry" in Eastern Europe was facilitated by film distribution, the creation of commercial television stations, advertising, and marketing. The entry of advertising into the public space was the most striking. Until 1989 there was virtually no advertising in these countries. Nor was there a statute of public space, as we know it

today. If you go from the Bucharest airport into the center today, or if you are driving through Czech towns or on the highways through the countryside, even a person from the West, accustomed to advertising at home, will be shocked at how much bigger, more visible, and intense the (unregulated) advertisements are in these new countries. Advertising (like the size of shopping centers), has flooded the space in leaps, to its present capacity.

Image taken on the way from the Otepeni Bucarest Airport to the City Center, 2004

Advertising and marketing have their own systems of rules. Their primary function is as a service to the seller or producer of goods or services. The aim of advertising is to awaken a need in a target group, which will be satisfied by the purchase of a product. The aim of advertising is to increase the sale of products by all possible means.

It seems that the unbridled entry of advertising into the public space of the transforming countries in the 1990s created a mental-visual code, the main but hidden particularity of which was an ethical vacuum. Advertising subordinates all media-visual means of communication and creativity to one postulate: to increase the sale of products. Advertising has at its disposal powerful economic means, but, aside from its position in the economic chain of functions, it has no firm ground in the area of ethics. In a loose polemic with the expansion of advertising, there developed, in the sphere of visual art, a concep-

den öffentlichen Raum das auffälligste Phänomen. Bis 1989 gab es in diesen Ländern so gut wie gar keine Werbung, noch existierten gesetzliche Regelungen für die Nutzung des öffentlichen Raums, wie wir sie inzwischen kennen. Fährt man heute vom Bukarester Flughafen in die Innenstadt oder durch tschechische Ortschaften oder auf der Autobahn übers Land, wird sogar ein Mensch aus dem Westen, der an Werbung gewöhnt ist, schockiert sein, wie viel größer, sichtbarer und dichter gesät die (unregulierten) Werbeplakate in diesen Ländern sind. Werbung (wie auch die riesigen Einkaufszentren) überflutete den Raum blitzschnell bis zu seiner völligen Auslastung.

Werbung und Marketing haben ihre eigenen Regeln. Ihre primäre Funktion besteht darin, den/die VerkäuferIn oder ProduzentIn von Waren bzw. Dienstleitungen zu unterstützen. Werbung soll bei einer Zielgruppe ein Bedürfnis wecken, das durch den Kauf des Produkts befriedigt wird; es geht darum, den Verkauf von Waren mit allen Mitteln zu steigern.

Es scheint, als hätte der ungezügelte Einzug der Werbung in den öffentlichen Raum der Transformationsländer in den 90er Jahren einen geistig-visuellen Code produziert, dessen wesentliches und doch verstecktes Merkmal ein ethisches Vakuum ist. Die Werbung unterwirft alle medialen, visuellen Kommunikationsmittel sowie die Kreativität einem einzigen Postulat: den Verkauf von Produkten zu steigern. Sie verfügt über enorme ökonomische Mittel, doch hat Werbung – abgesehen von ihrer Position in der ökonomischen Funktionskette – im ethischen Bereich keinen festen Boden unter den Füßen. Als eine Art Polemik gegen die Ausbreitung von Werbung entwickelte sich im Bereich der visuellen Kunst das Konzept einer gegenläufigen Position, die ich die „dokumentarische Position" nennen möchte.

Dokumentarismus in der zeitgenössischen visuellen Kunst

Im Bereich der Fotografie und des Films, mit denen wir den dokumentarischen Ansatz traditionell verbinden, lassen sich mühelos verschiedene

tion of its own position, which I call the "documentary position".

Documentarism in Contemporary Visual Art

In the area of photography and film, with which we have traditionally linked the documentary approach, we will easily find definitions of the various documentary genres. In the complexity of these genres it is rather difficult to find an essential definition of documentarism. But a notion of the discernable grammar of the documentary language runs through the debate.

Documentarism, in film and photography, could be described as a genre in which the director/artist carries out a transfer of his own or other people's knowledge, stances and experiences through his own articulation of the media and technology.

The decision to devote oneself to documentary is an acceptance of the condition to define one's creativity in direct connection with the complexes of social historical issues, which the artist documents; what permits us to call a work documentary is the relation between the documenting and the documented. Thus, the decision to work in a documentary manner primarily situates the not-I, other people, creators, works, social phenomena, and so on, at the center of the thinking and acting of the creative subject. All metaphysical horizons and aesthetic operations in documentary arise in connection with a real social historical matrix.

In the sphere of visual art, the documentary approach creates a causal connection between the social positions of the subject, and creative operations in specific media.[2] Aesthetic decisions and norms have a social-political dimension in documentarism and vice versa. In the documentary, it is impossible to look at form and aesthetics isolated, unconnected to the theme, and this relationship is defined in ethical categories.

dokumentarische Genres definieren. Es ist zwar etwas schwierig, in diesem Genrekomplex eine grundlegende Definition des Dokumentarismus zu finden, die Debatten sind jedoch von der Vorstellung einer erkennbaren Grammatik der dokumentarischen Sprache durchzogen.

In Film und Fotografie könnte man Dokumentarismus als ein Genre beschreiben, in dem der/die RegisseurIn/KünstlerIn sein Wissen, seine Haltungen und seine Erfahrungen – oder die anderer Menschen – mittels einer eigenen Artikulation der Medien und der Technologie transferiert.

Die Entscheidung, sich dem Dokumentarischen zu widmen, bedeutet, die Bedingung zu akzeptieren, dass die eigene Kreativität in einer direkten Beziehung zu den dokumentierten gesellschaftlich-historischen Themenkomplexen steht; aufgrund dieser Beziehung zwischen der Dokumentation und dem Dokumentierten können wir eine Arbeit dokumentarisch nennen. Daher rückt die Entscheidung, dokumentarisch zu arbeiten, vor allem das Nicht-Ich, d.h. andere Menschen, SchöpferInnen, Werke, soziale Phänomene etc., in den Mittelpunkt des Denkens und Handelns des kreativen Subjekts. Im Dokumentarismus entstehen sämtliche metaphysischen Horizonte und ästhetischen Operationen in Zusammenhang mit einer realen gesellschaftlich-historischen Matrix.

Im Bereich der visuellen Kunst stellt der dokumentarische Ansatz eine kausale Verbindung zwischen den sozialen Positionen des Subjekts und den kreativen Operationen in einem bestimmten Medium her.[2] Ästhetische Entscheidungen und Normen haben im Dokumentarismus eine gesellschaftspolitische Dimension und umgekehrt. Im Dokumentarischen ist es unmöglich, die Form und die Ästhetik isoliert, völlig unabhängig vom Thema zu betrachten. Diese Beziehung wird durch ethische Kategorien definiert.

Der Zusammenhang zwischen den einzelnen Komponenten zwingt den/die visuelle/n KünstlerIn, eine Ethik der formalen Herangehensweisen in seinen Arbeiten zu entwickeln. Dokumentarische Arbeiten definieren eine Ethik der Formen.

This interrelatedness of the individual components compels the visual artist to develop an ethic of formal approaches in his works. Documentary works define an ethic of forms. One cannot speak of the subordination of aesthetics to ethics, but what we are interested in is looking at the connection between them and understanding how ethical views are implemented in a specific aesthetic and vice versa. How visual art attributes an ethical value to certain forms.

Hito Steyerl, in his text *The Articulation of Protest*, compares two films, shot in different ways, about protest political movements.3 She concludes that the political message is included in the utterances of the actors, but it is articulated, first and foremost, in the very structure of the film. The media grammar employed by the film director and the degree of experimentation modify the political effectiveness of the testimony. In journalism, the *écriture* with which the journalist treats the political dimension is analogous. The ethical responsibility of the documentary approach also generates the retrospective application of ethical criteria in the outlook on the history of visual disciplines.

The Customer

In one of the first steps, which appear to be behind the above-mentioned polarity with advertising, the documentary approach logically turns to its own origins. It reflects the fact of who the "customer" is, who the initiator of a specific artwork or institution is, who the regulator of the entire system is. For these reasons, one group of documentary works concentrates on the business of art. On the basis of previous investigations mapping out the vectors of power and interests (Hans Haacke, Andrea Fraser), documentarism focuses on the subjective testimony. It analyses the relationships that the artist has with the producer, the administrator of artistic production. These works also concentrate on analysis of the positions taken up by specific institutions of contemporary art in the social field. The work of Pawel Althamer, Roman Ondák, Deimantas Narkevicius and a whole host

of other artists visualizes, thematizes, and problematizes the relationship between artists and the art business. Their operations are virtually always focused on tracing the subjective impacts and feelings of the actors. Therefore they often combine the documentary approach with directed actions, so their work connects fictive and documentary approaches. Their work was made according to scripts, but the absent public speaks about them in terms of documentary.

"Shooting Must Take Place Where the Film Takes Place"

In the famous manifesto, "The Vow of Chastity"4, of the Danish collective Dogma 95, one reads: "Shooting must be done on location, [...] shooting must take place where the film takes place. The film must not contain superficial action." The Dogma 95 manifesto was reacting to the systemic-economic situation in which cinematography found itself. It postulated (not for the first time in the history of film) important fundamentals: the return of cinematography to real space-time, and sound, and the naturalness of the action shot.

Roman Ondák, *Antinomads*, 2000

Roman Ondák, in his work *Antinomádi* (Antinomads, 2000), photographed portraits of his relatives and acquaintances who did not travel or did not like to travel. He photographed them in their domestic setting, in the rooms and apartments where they usually spent their time. He let them choose the places where they would be photographed and the gestures and positions

Roman Ondák, Deimantas Narkevicius und vielen anderen KünstlerInnen visualisieren, thematisieren und problematisieren das Verhältnis zwischen KünstlerInnen und Kunstbetrieb. Ihre Operationen greifen fast immer die subjektiven Gefühle der AkteurInnen und deren Auswirkungen auf. Sie kombinieren daher häufig den dokumentarischen Ansatz mit Regieanweisungen; ihre Arbeiten verbinden also fiktionale und dokumentarische Elemente. Sie führen ein Drehbuch aus, doch spricht die abwesende Öffentlichkeit über sie in einer dokumentarischen Sprache.

„Gedreht wird dort, wo die Szene spielt"

Im berühmten „Reinheitsgelübde"4 des dänischen Dogma 95-Kollektivs heißt es: „Gedreht wird nur on location. [...] gedreht wird dort, wo die Szene spielt. [...] Der Film darf keine oberflächliche Handlung zeigen." Das Dogma 95-Manifest reagierte auf die systembedingte ökonomische Situation, in der sich das Kino befand. Es postulierte (nicht zum ersten Mal in der Filmgeschichte) wichtige Grundsätze, wie die Rückkehr des Kinos zur realen Raum-Zeit und zum realen Ton sowie die Natürlichkeit des action shot.

In seiner Arbeit *Antinomádi* (Anti-Nomaden, 2000) machte Roman Ondák Porträtaufnahmen seiner Verwandten und Bekannten, die nicht oder nur ungern verreisen. Er fotografierte sie in ihrer häuslichen Umgebung, in den Räumen und Wohnungen, in denen sie sich meistens aufhalten. Sie durften die Orte bestimmen, an denen sie fotografiert wurden, sowie die Gesten und Positionen, die sie für die Porträts einnahmen. Die Fotos übertrug er dann auf Postkarten – die um die Welt reisen können, die viele Menschen sehen werden. Doch gleichzeitig demonstrieren Ansichtskarten, dass der reale Kontext der physischen Existenz nicht übertragbar ist – er ist dort, wo er ist.

Die zunehmende Mobilität ermöglicht es, diese Kontexte zu verändern und neue Kontexte des Reisens, die auf temporären Beziehungen beruhen, herzustellen. Bei NomadInnen führt die Mobilität zu dem Wunsch, an allen Orten, die sie kennen und schon besucht haben, gleichzeitig zu

they would adopt in the photographs. He then transferred the photographs onto postcards. The postcards can travel around the world and many people will see them, but they demonstrate that the real context of physical existence is non-transferable. It is where it is.

Ever increasing mobility means that it is possible to change these contexts and create new traveling contexts, based on instant relationships. Mobility creates, in nomads, a desire to be in all the places that they know and that they have visited, at once. In the CVs of contemporary artists and curators we often notice that they live in several places. This is not proof of success, but rather expresses their desire to be part of two, three, or more contexts at once. This is possible and, thanks to email and the mobile telephone, it is even possible to constantly exchange information with people in those places. Air travel has singularly heightened the incongruity in the flow of time. When we arrive in a distant foreign country after a flight of an hour and a half, our brain takes several hours to adapt. Thanks to the popularization of the theory of relativity, we know that time does not pass the same way everywhere; while we are in an airplane, we age more slowly.

The essence of a place, the multi-layered quality of its content and function, have been an important theoretical issues for some time now, in particular in the American milieu (historically suffering from the "non-site" syndrome).[5] In connection with visual art, "The Vow of Chastity" is important in its dogmatic definition of the inseparability of the theme of the documentary, and the language and grammar employed by the artist. Just as Hito Steyerl postulates the ontological basis and ethical canon for this relationship.

Context

In her texts, Marina Gržinić casts doubt on the "enterprized-up" genealogy, the practice of large (and probably also small) exhibitions cloning works from the second or third world into the international arena of art. A definition of this

sein. In den Lebensläufen von KünstlerInnen und KuratorInnen bemerken wir oft, dass sie an verschiedenen Orten leben. Dies ist kein Beweis des Erfolgs, vielmehr wird dadurch der Wunsch ausgedrückt, zu zwei, drei oder mehreren Kontexten gleichzeitig zu gehören. Das ist möglich; und dank E-Mail und Mobiltelefon kann man sogar ständig Informationen mit Menschen an anderen Orten austauschen. Flugreisen haben mehr als alles andere die Inkongruenz im Fluss der Zeit verstärkt. Wenn wir nach anderthalb Stunden in einem anderen Land ankommen, benötigt unser Gehirn dennoch mehrere Stunden um sich anzupassen. Dank des Bekanntheitsgrades der Relativitätstheorie wissen wir alle, dass die Zeit nicht überall gleich vergeht; im Flugzeug altern wir langsamer.

Das Wesen eines Ortes, die vielschichtige Qualität seines Inhalts und seiner Funktion, ist seit einiger Zeit zu einem wichtigen theoretischen Thema geworden, besonders im amerikanischen Milieu (das historisch am Syndrom des „Nicht-Ortes" leidet).[5] Für die visuelle Kunst ist das „Reinheitsgelübde" deswegen relevant, weil es auf dogmatische Weise die Untrennbarkeit des dokumentierten Themas von der Sprache und Grammatik, die der/die KünstlerIn verwendet, feststellt, so wie Hito Steyerl die ontologische Grundlage und den ethischen Kanon dieser Beziehung postuliert.

Kontext

Marina Gržinić kritisiert in ihren Texten die „enterprised-up"-Genealogie, die Praxis großer (und vermutlich auch kleiner) Ausstellungen, Arbeiten der Zweiten und Dritten Welt in die internationale Kunstarena hineinzuklonen. Die Tatsache, dass dies geschieht, muss definiert werden, doch Gržinić liefert hierfür keinen Ausgangspunkt. KünstlerInnen, die mit dokumentarischen Mitteln arbeiten und dieser Praxis gegenüber sensibel sind, scheinen ihren Ausgangspunkt gefunden zu haben. Sie wenden sich gegen den Prozess, ein künstlerisches Simulakrum zu erzeugen, gegen die Verflachung der Arbeit als begrenzte Reproduktion und gegen die Werte des Exotischen und die Political Correctness, zu der

fact is needed; Gržinić, however, does not offer any point of departure. It seems that documentary artists, sensitive to this practice, have found their point of departure and taken a stance against the process of creating an artistic simulacrum, flattening the work out into a limited reproduction, creating the values of the exotic and the political correctness to which it leads. For this reason, documentary approaches have included the local context (on its many levels) into the corpus of the work.

"Shooting must take place where the film takes place". The integration of real space-time, its physical and mental dimensions, means to have the local situation as a starting point. That sounds like a cliché, but in the age of nomadism, we have adopted approaches that enable us to enter local contexts, so that we are no longer condemned to represent the place where we were born. The penetration of a social-cultural matrix is an experience that can be repeated. The living, creative archaeology of context can even be an intoxicating and, for some, addictive obsession, connected in some way with the search for immortality.

History

In the transforming countries, the 1990s saw a fierce struggle for "success" in the new conditions, connected with a focus on the use and representation of success. This struggle was accompanied by a displacement of the past, leading, in the past fifteen years, to a kind of social amnesia. Society forced out historical memory as a negative stigma, which was useless in the new conditions. The past might disintegrate "market" competence and professionalism, that were demanded of economic actors. One of the new facts that the transforming countries have to deal with is the trend toward the economization of the individual as an instrument of production.[6] Functioning in the economic structures does not guarantee that the spiritual needs of the individual will be fulfilled; this happens separately from the secular economic role.[7]

diese führen. Daher beziehen dokumentarische Ansätze den lokalen Kontext (auf seinen vielen Ebenen) in den Korpus des Werks ein.

„Gedreht wird dort, wo der Film spielt." Die Integration der realen Raum-Zeit und ihrer physischen und geistigen Dimensionen bedeutet, die lokale Situation zum Ausgangspunkt zu machen. Dies klingt wie ein Klischee, doch im Zeitalter des NomadInnentums haben wir uns Herangehensweisen angeeignet, die es uns ermöglichen, in lokale Kontexte einzutreten. Wir sind also nicht mehr dazu verurteilt, den Ort, an dem wir geboren wurden, zu repräsentieren. Die Durchdringung einer soziokulturellen Matrix ist eine wiederholbare Erfahrung. Die lebendige, kreative Archäologie des Kontexts kann sogar berauschend sein und für manche zu einer süchtig machenden Obsession werden, die irgendwie mit der Suche nach Unsterblichkeit zu tun hat.

Little Warsaw, *Poster for Contra Monument Cathedral*, 2005

In the last few years, in reaction to the social amnesia, artists have begun to revoke the systematic and widespread forgetting of recent national history. Ján Mančuška, Zbyněk Baladrán, Little Warsaw, Deimantas Narkevicius, Tamás Szentjóby, subreal, and many other artists, offer, through individual reconstruction of the group memory, their own version of what most of their fellow citizens consider to be the "objective" domain of historical scholarship.

Zbyněk Baladrán, Jan Mančuška, *Vide*, 2003

IRWIN, in the project *East Art Map*, revises the political model of art history, based on the secularization of Eastern art from history.[8] IRWIN gave the term "Eastern art" an adequate content for the first time in its history. It thus carried out *de facto* an operation similar to that of the Trojan horse: it inserted its own "unknown" history of Eastern art into the originally empty political construction.

It is interesting how documentarism defines "professionalism" in opposition to the way in which spectacularity and the entertainment industry define professionalism. Many contemporary Czech artists earn a living by working on films.[9] For the most part, the artists work as decorators or apply finishing touches; they are one of the cogs of the film industry. They work there as professionals who know how to finish a freshly washed car so that it looks like "it drove 50 miles through a desert". They are actors in the mechanism of professionalization, which consists in implementing exactly what has been

Geschichte

Die Transformationsländer erlebten in den 90er Jahren einen erbitterten Kampf um „Erfolg" unter den neuen Verhältnissen, verbunden mit der Konzentration auf die Verwendung und Darstellung von Erfolg. Begleitet war dieser Kampf von einer Verdrängung der Vergangenheit, die in den letzten 15 Jahren zu einer gesellschaftlichen Amnesie geführt hat. Die historische Erinnerung wurde von der Gesellschaft als ein negatives Stigma, das unter den neuen Bedingungen nutzlos geworden war, verdrängt. Die Vergangenheit hätte ja die „Markt"-Kompetenz und den Professionalismus, die von den wirtschaftlichen Akteuren verlangt wurde, zersetzen können. Die Transformationsländer müssen sich damit auseinander setzen, dass die Tendenz zur Ökonomisierung des Individuums als Instrument der Produktion zur Tatsache geworden ist.[6] Das Funktionieren innerhalb ökonomischer Strukturen gewährleistet nicht, dass die spirituellen Bedürfnisse des Individuums erfüllt werden; dies geschieht säkularisiert von der ökonomischen Rolle.[7]

Als Reaktion auf diese gesellschaftliche Amnesie haben KünstlerInnen in den letzten Jahren damit begonnen, das systematische und weit verbreitete Vergessen der jüngsten nationalen Geschichte rückgängig zu machen. Jan Mančuška, Zbyněk Baladrán, Little Warsaw, Deimantas Narkevicius, Tamás Szentjóby, subreal und viele andere präsentieren mittels der individuellen Rekonstruktion des kollektiven Gedächtnisses ihre eigene Version dessen, was ihre MitbürgerInnen für den „objektiven" Gegenstandbereich historischer Gelehrsamkeit halten.

Ausgehend von der Verweltlichung der Kunst des Ostens in der Historie revidierte IRWIN mit dem Projekt *East Art Map* das politische Modell der Kunstgeschichte.[8] IRWIN füllte den Begriff „Kunst des Ostens" zum ersten Mal in dessen Geschichte mit einem adäquaten Inhalt. Dieser funktionierte de facto ähnlich wie das trojanische Pferd, indem er seine eigene „unbekannte" Kunstgeschichte des Ostens in die ursprünglich leere politische Konstruktion einfügte.

demanded. The professional, one of the links in the long production chain, has no influence on the final meaning of the whole to which he has contributed.

Depth of Focus

When we look at the work of artists winning back a lost or non-existent history, we see that this happens on the basis of emphasizing the individual position of the artists. History is always arbitrary and testifies to the position, the context, and the situation of the individual in history. The operation of focusing, familiar from the realms of photography and film, is characteristic of the documentary approach.

Focusing results in a so-called depth of focus, which is the depth in a photograph/film shot that remains sharp (it depends on the stopping-down). The process of focusing is fundamental to these media because they are fatally passive in mirroring the surroundings. The process of focusing singles out and marks what the photographer considers to be important in the totality of the shot; when he singles something out, he considers it necessary to separate it from the background. The act of focusing is an act of photographic filmic significance. Documentarism sets a small depth of focus. Beginning with Anri Sala's *Intervista* (1998), we have witnessed the process of focusing in historical time. In these works, art seeks and sets a small depth of focus; it is able to conquer history through the personal experience of friends, family or living figures. That means in a biased manner, with an awareness of the fact that bias and individualization have, as the other side of the coin, a soft focus on events, objects, and landscapes in the background. Documentarism is characterized by a distrust of the background, of de-subjectivized historical experience, and any kind of grand narration.

Omer Fast's work *Spielberg's List* (2003), about the shooting of the film *Schindler's List* (1993), is a documentary about fiction. Watching this documentary about the production of a simulacrum,

Interessant ist, wie der Dokumentarismus den Begriff des „Professionalismus" in genauer Umkehrung zum Spektakel und zur Unterhaltungsindustrie definiert. Viele zeitgenössische tschechische KünstlerInnen verdienen ihr Geld beim Film.[9] Meistens arbeiten sie als BühnenbildnerInnen oder RequisiteurInnen; sie sind Rädchen im Getriebe der Filmindustrie, wo sie als Professionelle arbeiten, die wissen, wie man ein frisch gewaschenes Auto so präpariert, dass es aussieht, als wäre es „50 Meilen durch die Wüste gefahren". Sie sind SchauspielerInnen im Apparat der Professionalisierung; es geht darum, genau das umzusetzen, was verlangt wird. Der/die Professionelle, ein Glied in der langen Produktionskette, hat keinen Einfluss auf den Sinn des Ganzen, zu dem er/sie beigetragen hat.

Tiefenschärfe

Betrachten wir die Arbeit von KünstlerInnen, die eine verlorene oder nicht-existente Vergangenheit zurückerobern, sehen wir, dass diese Rückeroberung durch die Betonung der individuellen Position des Künstlers/der Künstlerin geschieht. Geschichte ist immer willkürlich und zeugt von der Position, dem Kontext und der Situation des Einzelnen in der Geschichte. Die Tätigkeit des Fokussierens, die man aus dem Bereich der Fotografie und des Films kennt, ist charakteristisch für den dokumentarischen Ansatz.

Das Fokussieren stellt die so genannte Tiefenschärfe her, d.h. die Tiefe, die in der Foto- oder Filmaufnahme scharf bleibt (abhängig von der Abblende). Für diese Medien ist der Prozess des Fokussierens fundamental, denn sie sind, was die Widerspiegelung ihrer Umgebung angeht, auf fatale Weise passiv. Indem der/die FotografIn fokussiert, wählt er/sie das aus, was er/sie innerhalb des gesamten Bildes für wichtig hält; das, was er/sie herausgreift und markiert, soll sich vom Hintergrund abheben. Das Fokussieren ist eine in fotografisch-filmischer Hinsicht bedeutende Handlung. Der Dokumentarismus arbeitet mit einer flachen Tiefenschärfe. Angefangen mit Anri Salas *Intervista* (1998) haben wir erlebt, wie die historische Zeit fokussiert wurde. In diesen

there are times when we do not know if an actor is speaking about real events, such as how the Nazis treated deportees, or if he is describing a scene in the shooting of the film. Fiction has, thanks to its coverage and entertaining quality, a greater impact on reality than a true testimony does. Analysis of the constructed nature of fiction offers the instruments to address the question of how our individual or group awareness of events that we have not witnessed was actually formed.

The Ontology of Scholarship

Characteristic of the documentary approach is the fact that the artist approaches reality with an ethic of form and with a certain method. Like scholars, artists work with sources. Orientation in and classification of the sources, the choice of methodological approaches that cannot be avoided in work with sources, require at least a basic theoretical fundament. They require an approach to a suspended world and familiarity with the basics of scholarly methodology, which is demonstrated, for example, in Zbyněk Baladrán's text for this book. His text is purely theoretical; if we did not know the author, we would not be able to tell that he was an artist. The documentarist, as he is compelled to use a methodology in his work with sources, situates himself in a methodological field, whether implicitly or explicitly. He thus creates for himself and for his work the context in which they will be read.

One of the horizons that documentarism wants to establish itself in is the public media discourse. Pierre Huyghe's projects in the 1990s reintroduced scripts and the use of documentary in media (*Mobile TV*, 1995, *Rue Longvic*, 1994 among others). In the transforming countries, in some of its manifestations, documentarism has set itself the goal of filling the vacuum of subjectivity in the choice of themes and media articulation of the documentary in the milieu of the mass media.

The ontological rootedness of the documentary in the social sciences, politics and history cre-

Arbeiten sucht die Kunst eine flache Tiefenschärfe; sie kann sich die Geschichte durch die persönlichen Erfahrungen von FreundInnen, Familienmitgliedern und noch lebenden Personen aneignen, d.h. auf voreingenommene Weise, in dem Bewusstsein, dass Voreingenommenheit und Individualisierung – als Rückseite der Medaille – die Ereignisse, Objekte und Landschaften im Hintergrund weichzeichnen. Geprägt ist der Dokumentarismus dadurch, dass er dem Hintergrund misstraut, er misstraut der Entsubjektivierung historischer Erfahrung sowie jeglicher großen Erzählung.

Omer Fasts Arbeit *Spielberg's List* (2003) über die Dreharbeiten zu *Schindlers Liste* (1993) ist ein Dokumentarfilm, der sich mit Fiktion auseinander setzt. Beim Betrachten dieses Films über die Produktion eines Simulakrums gibt es Momente, in denen man nicht weiß, ob ein/e SchauspielerIn über reale Ereignisse spricht – z.B. darüber, wie die Nazis mit den Deportierten umgingen – oder über eine Szene, die bei den Dreharbeiten stattfand. Die Fiktion hat auf Grund ihrer Verbreitung und ihres Unterhaltungswerts eine größere Wirkung auf die Realität als die wahren Zeugnisse. Die Analyse der konstruierten Natur der Fiktion stellt die Instrumente zur Verfügung, die notwendig sind, um zu fragen, wie unser individuelles oder kollektives Bewusstsein von Ereignissen, die wir nicht erlebt haben, tatsächlich geformt wurde.

Die Ontologie der Gelehrsamkeit

Der dokumentarische Ansatz ist dadurch bestimmt, dass der/die KünstlerIn mit einer Ethik der Form und einer bestimmten Methode an die Realität herantreten muss. KünstlerInnen arbeiten, wie Gelehrte, mit Quellen. Um sich in den Quellen zu orientieren und diese zu klassifizieren und um den methodologischen Ansatz zu wählen, den die Arbeit mit Quellenmaterial erfordert, ist theoretisches Grundwissen unerlässlich. Die KünstlerInnen benötigen einen Zugang zu einer abgehobenen Welt und müssen mit den Grundlagen wissenschaftlicher Methodologie vertraut sein, wie sie z.B. in Zbyněk Baladráns Text in diesem Buch dargelegt werden. Sein Text ist reine

ates a main axis of the "documentary attitude". This, it would seem, is one of the reasons behind the development and success of this approach in contemporary art. In rich countries, contemporary art ended up with an excess supply and solved the problem of how to defend the quantitative and territorial expansion of its institutions in the social debate by means of politically relevant arguments. In this debate, socially engaged art (urbanism, the socio-territorial crisis, racism, minorities, feminism, etc.) became an instrument of argumentation. In some instances, this resulted in the dangerous identification of political engagement with moral or political correctness.

In the end, or maybe right from the beginning, on the basis of our experience, art should not fulfill a social commission; rather, it should have the conditions to create a space in which to define its social validity on its own.

Even today the *Laboratorium* (laboratory) seems like a pertinent metaphor for artistic creativity; for the needs of documentarism, it should be democratized in a certain manner.[10] The process of the ever increasing accessibility of scientific devices and methods, and the fact that the documentary is situated in the space of the social sciences, transform the idea of the laboratory into a barrier-free online office, a production office with an archive. In its openness and emphasis on the method of classification of information, Kosuth's model *Information Room* is close to documentarism. It was institutionalized and de-aestheticized (Manifesta Archive, etc.). In the project *Re:route*, 2002, by the group Big Hope, recent immigrants living in Torino, in Italy, documented the subjective geography of the city. Big Hope decided to visualize the mix of diverse materials that came out of meetings with the actors in the form of a complex, but still amateur, spatial collage. The method of this spatial presentation polemicizes with the conceptualist aesthetic of the purely library or gallery form.

As I have said, the documentary introduces, on the one hand, a firm link between contemporary visual art and social processes; on the other

Theorie; würden wir den Autor nicht kennen, wüssten wir nicht, dass er Künstler ist. Da er sich gezwungen sieht, bei seiner Arbeit mit Quellen eine Methodologie anzuwenden, platziert sich der Dokumentarist, ob implizit oder explizit, in ein methodologisches Feld. Er schafft auf diese Weise für sich und seine Arbeit einen Kontext, in dem beide interpretiert werden.

Der Dokumentarismus will sich u.a. vor dem Horizont eines öffentlichen Mediendiskurses etablieren. Pierre Huyghes Projekte aus den 90er Jahren führten wieder Drehbücher und die Verwendung des Dokumentarischen in die Medien ein (u.a. *Mobile TV*, 1995, *Rue Longvic*, 1998, 1994). In den Transformationsländern haben sich einige Spielarten des Dokumentarismus zum Ziel gesetzt, mit ihrer Wahl der Themen und der Medienartikulation des Dokumentarischen das Vakuum, das durch die Subjektivität im Milieu der Massenmedien erzeugt wurde, zu füllen.

Die ontologische Verwurzelung des Dokumentarischen in den Sozialwissenschaften, der Politik und der Geschichte schafft eine Hauptrichtung der „dokumentarischen Haltung". Dies scheint einer der Gründe für die Weiterentwicklung und den Erfolg dieser Herangehensweise in der zeitgenössischen Kunst zu sein. In den reichen Ländern gab es ein Überangebot an zeitgenössischer Kunst. Die Notwendigkeit, die quantitative und territoriale Ausdehnung ihrer Institutionen im Rahmen der gesellschaftlichen Debatten zu verteidigen, wurde mittels politisch relevanter Argumente gelöst. In diesen Auseinandersetzungen wurde sozial engagierte Kunst (Urbanismus, die sozio-territoriale Krise, Rassismus, Minderheiten, Feminismus etc.) argumentativ eingesetzt. In manchen Fällen führte dies zu einer gefährlichen Identifikation des politischen Engagements mit moralischer oder politischer Korrektheit.

Am Ende – oder vielleicht von Anfang an – sollte eine auf Erfahrung basierende Kunst keinen gesellschaftlichen Auftrag erfüllen; sie sollte über die Bedingungen verfügen, einen eigenständigen Raum herzustellen, in dem ihre gesellschaftliche Berechtigung definiert wird.

hand, because of its essence, it views them through strongly subjective matrices. It establishes a unity of time and place for action, thereby getting rid of the fault of global nomadism. The context of the milieu through various approaches becomes the artwork, so global exhibition strategies can continue to function without the threat of power manipulation of the context. The documentary is, in the visual sphere, a newly constituted metaphor, the fulfillment of which is also an opportunity for us.

---

1 I use the term ontology in the sense of the following definition: "Ontologies as a specification mechanism. A body of formally represented knowledge is based on a conceptualization: the objects, concepts, and other entities that are assumed to exist in some area of interest and the relationships that hold among them [...]. A conceptualization is an abstract, simplified view of the world that we wish to represent for some purpose. Every knowledge base, knowledge-based system, or knowledge-level agent is committed to some conceptualization, explicitly or implicitly. An ontology is an explicit specification of a conceptualization. The term is borrowed from philosophy, where an Ontology is a systematic account of Existence. For AI systems, what 'exists' is that which can be represented. When the knowledge of a domain is represented in a declarative formalism, the set of objects that can be represented is called the universe of discourse. This set of objects, and the describable relationships among them, are reflected in the representational vocabulary with which a knowledge-based program represents knowledge. Thus, in the context of AI, we can describe the ontology of a program by defining a set of representational terms. In such an ontology, definitions associate the names of entities in the universe of discourse (e.g., classes, relations, functions, or other objects) with human-readable text describing what the names mean, and formal axioms that constrain the interpretation and well-formed use of these terms." Thomas R.Gruber, *Toward Principles for the Design of Ontologies Used for Knowledge Sharing*, Stanford 1993.
2 By position I mean a complex of rational and irrational motives.
3 Hito Steyerl, "The Articulation of Protest," http://republicart.net/disc/mundial/steyerl02_en.htm 2002 [04/10/05].
4 http://www.dogme95.dk/menu/menuset.htm (under "Manifesto, The Vow of Chastity") [04/10/05].
5 Of the many books and articles I would mention, for example, Lucy Lippard, *The Lure of the Local: Senses of Place in a Multicultural Society*, New York 1998.
6 This is manifest on an intuited level in the monologues of employees from the Hungarian Dunaujvaros in Big Hope's project *Talking About Economy*, 2003.
7 This observation has interesting connections with a new trend in an economy that overcomes this duality. The idea is popularized in books such as David Brooks, *Bobos In Paradise: The New Upper Class and How They Got There*, New York 2001. They note the growth of new types of enterprises in the tertiary sector, in which the founders implement production or services based on contemporary opinion trends (ecological agriculture, multiculturalism in dress, entertainment, food, and drinks, etc.).

Noch heute ist das *Laboratorium* eine relevante Metapher für künstlerische Kreativität, die für die Bedürfnisse des Dokumentarismus auf gewisse Weise demokratisiert werden sollte.[10] Die zunehmende Verfügbarkeit wissenschaftlicher Geräte und Methoden und die Tatsache, dass das Dokumentarische sich im Feld der Gesellschaftswissenschaften befindet, transformiert die Idee des Labors in ein Online-Büro ohne Grenzen, in ein Produktionsbüro samt Archiv. Mit seiner Offenheit und der Betonung auf der Klassifizierung von Information steht Kosuths Modell des *Information Room* dem Dokumentarismus sehr nahe. Es wurde institutionalisiert und entästhetisiert (*Manifesta Archive* etc.). Das Projekt *Re:route* (2002) der Gruppe Big Hope, die jüngst nach Turin in Italien emigriert ist, dokumentierte die subjektive Geografie der Stadt. Big Hope visualisierte die Mischung unterschiedlichster Materialien, die bei Treffen mit den AkteurInnen entstanden sind, in Form einer komplexen, doch nach wie vor amateurhaften Raumcollage. Die Methode dieser räumlichen Präsentation polemisiert gegen die konzeptuelle Ästhetik der reinen Bibliothek- oder Galerieform.

Wie bereits gesagt, stellt der Dokumentarismus einerseits eine feste Verbindung zwischen der zeitgenössischen visuellen Kunst und gesellschaftlichen Prozessen her; anderseits betrachtet er diese Prozesse aufgrund seines Wesens durch äußert subjektive Matrizen. Er stellt eine für Handlungen geeignete raumzeitliche Einheit her und reagiert so auf die Unzulänglichkeiten des globalen Nomadentums. Unterschiedliche Ansätze machen den Kontext des Milieus zum Kunstwerk. Globale Ausstellungsstrategien können also weiter funktionieren ohne Gefahr zu laufen, durch den Kontext manipuliert zu werden. Im visuellen Bereich ist der Dokumentarismus eine neu konstituierte Metapher, deren Erfüllung uns auch eine Chance bietet.

THE DOCUMENTARY — AN ONTOLOGY OF FORMS IN TRANSFORMING COUNTRIES

8 IRWIN, ed. "East Art Map. A (Re)construction of the History of Art in Eastern Europe," *New Moment Magazine* 20 (2002), p. 28. "New East Art Map," http://www.eastartmap.org/ [04/10/05].
9 The Czech Republic was a favorite shooting site for dozens of foreign productions, for example the films *Alien 5*, *Hart's War*, *Triple X*, *Blade 2*, *From Hell*, *Zoo Keeper*, *Mists of Avalon*, *The League of Extraordinary Gentlemen*, *The Diary of Anne Frank*, *Charles II*, the serial *Commissar Maigret*, and many others.
10 Hans Ulrich Obrist and Barbara Vanderlinden, eds., *Laboratorium*, Cologne 2001.

DAS DOKUMENTARISCHE — EINE ONTOLOGIE DER FORMEN IN DEN TRANSFORMATIONSLÄNDERN

1 Ich benutze den Begriff Ontologie gemäß der folgenden Definition: „Ontologien als Spezifikationsmechanismus. Ein Komplex formal repräsentierten Wissens basiert auf einer *Begriffsbildung*: die Objekte, Konzepte und andere Entitäten, von denen angenommen wird, sie existieren in einem Interessensbereich, sowie die zwischen ihnen bestehenden Relationen [...]. Eine Begriffsbildung ist eine abstrakte, vereinfachende Sichtweise auf eine Welt, die wir zu einem bestimmten Zweck repräsentieren wollen. Jede Wissensbasis, jedes wissensbasierte System oder jeder Agent auf der Wissensebene unterliegt implizit oder explizit einer Begriffsbildung. Eine Ontologie ist eine explizite Spezifikation einer Begriffsbildung. Der Ausdruck ist der Philosophie entlehnt, in der eine Ontologie eine systematische Darstellung der Existenz ist. Für Künstliche-Intelligenz-Systeme kann das, was ‚existiert', repräsentiert werden. Wenn das Wissen eines Gegenstandsbereichs in einem deklarativen Formalismus repräsentiert wird, nennt man die Menge derjenigen Objekte, die dargestellt werden können, das Universum des Diskurses. Diese Menge von Objekten und die beschreibbaren Relationen zwischen ihnen werden in dem Vokabular der Repräsentation, durch das ein wissensbasiertes Programm Wissen repräsentiert, widergespiegelt. Im Kontext der Künstlichen Intelligenz können wir folglich die Ontologie eines Programms dadurch beschreiben, dass wir eine Menge repräsentierender Termini definieren. In einer solchen Ontologie verbinden Definitionen die Namen der Entitäten im Universum des Diskurses (z.B. Klassen, Relationen, Funktionen oder andere Objekte) mit einem von Menschen lesbaren Text, der beschreibt was die Namen bedeuten, und mit formalen Axiomen, die die Interpretation und den korrekten Gebrauch dieser Termini einschränken", aus: Thomas R. Gruber: *Toward Principles for the Design of Ontologies Used for Knowledge Sharing*, Stanford 1993, Übersetzung K.H.
2 Mit Position meine ich einen Komplex bestehend aus rationalen und irrationalen Motiven.
3 Hito Steyerl: Die Artikulation des Protestes, in: Gerald Raunig (Hg.): *TRANSVERSAL. Kunst und Globalisierungskritik*, Wien 2003, S. 19-28.
4 Vgl. http://www.dogme95.dk/menu/menuset.htm (unter Manifesto, The Vow of Chastity) [10.04.05].
5 Man könnte viele Bücher und Artikel in diesem Zusammenhang erwähnen, z.B. Lucy Lippard: *The Lure of the Local. Senses of Place in a Multicultural Society*, New York 1998.
6 Dies zeigt sich auf einer intuitiven Ebene in den Monologen der Arbeiter aus dem ungarischen Dunaujvaros in: Big Hopes Projekt: *Talking About Economy*, 2003.
7 Diese Beobachtung steht in einer interessanten Beziehung zu einem neuen Trend in der Ökonomie, der diese Dualität überwindet. Die Idee wurde verbreitet u.a. in: David Brooks: *Die Bobos. Der Lebensstil der neuen Elite*, München 2001. Es wird auf das Wachstum eines neuen Firmentypus im tertiären Bereich hingewiesen. Die Firmengründer bieten Produkte oder Dienstleistungen an, die auf aktuellen Trends beruhen (ökologische Landwirtschaft, multikulturelle Kleider, Unterhaltung, Lebensmittel und Getränke etc.).
8 IRWIN: East Art Map. A (Re)construction of the History of Art in Eastern Europe, in: *New Moment Magazine* (2002), Nr. 20, S. 28. New East Art Map auf: http://www.eastartmap.org/ [10.04.05].
9 Die Tschechische Republik war ein beliebter Drehort für Dutzende ausländische Filme, z.B.: *Alien 5*, *Hart's War*, *Triple X*, *Blade 2*, *From Hell*, *Zoo Keeper*, *Nebel von Avalon*, *Die Liga der außergewöhnlichen Gentlemen*, *Das Tagebuch der Anne Frank*, *Charles II*, die Serie *Kommissar Maigret* u.v.a.
10 Hans Ulrich Obrist und Barbara Vanderlinden (Hg.): *Laboratorium*, Köln 2001.

Re:route www.bighope.hu/reroute

A project by Big Hope: Miklós Erhardt & Dominic Hislop

A participative project to create an alternative map of the city of Turin, Italy, illustrated with photographs, sketches, and text, based on the view and experiences of recent immigrants. Between December 2001 and April 2002, around 30 migrants (see list) who had arrived in Turin in the last few years were approached and asked to participate. Through a series of dialogues, each participant was asked to sketch a 'mental map', illustrating how they perceive and experience the city, then subsequently given a camera to illustrate their maps with photographs.

Participants

Akinyi (Kenya)
Cosmin (Romania)
Dalena (Romania)
Emmanuel (Democratic Republic of Congo)
Evelyn (Nigeria)
Gringo (Roma/Bosnia)
Ismael (Somalia)
James (Nigeria)
Jefferson (Democratic Republic of Congo)
Larry (Sierra Leone)
Li (China)
Lidia (Moldova)
Luke (Nigeria)
Mariana (Ecuador)
Mergjan (Roma/Bosnia)
Mirella (Romania)
Mahmoud (Morocco)
Mohammed (Bangladesh)
Mohamed (Morocco)
Mustapha (Morocco)
Nali (Kurdistan)
Oleg (Moldova/Russia)
Papa Lo (Senegal)
Prince Will (Sierra Leone)
Rachid (Morocco)
Robdu (Ethiopia)
Robert (Romania)
Stefano (Roma/Yugoslavia)
Stephen (Nigeria)
Valter (Roma/Italy)
Yasine (Tunisia)

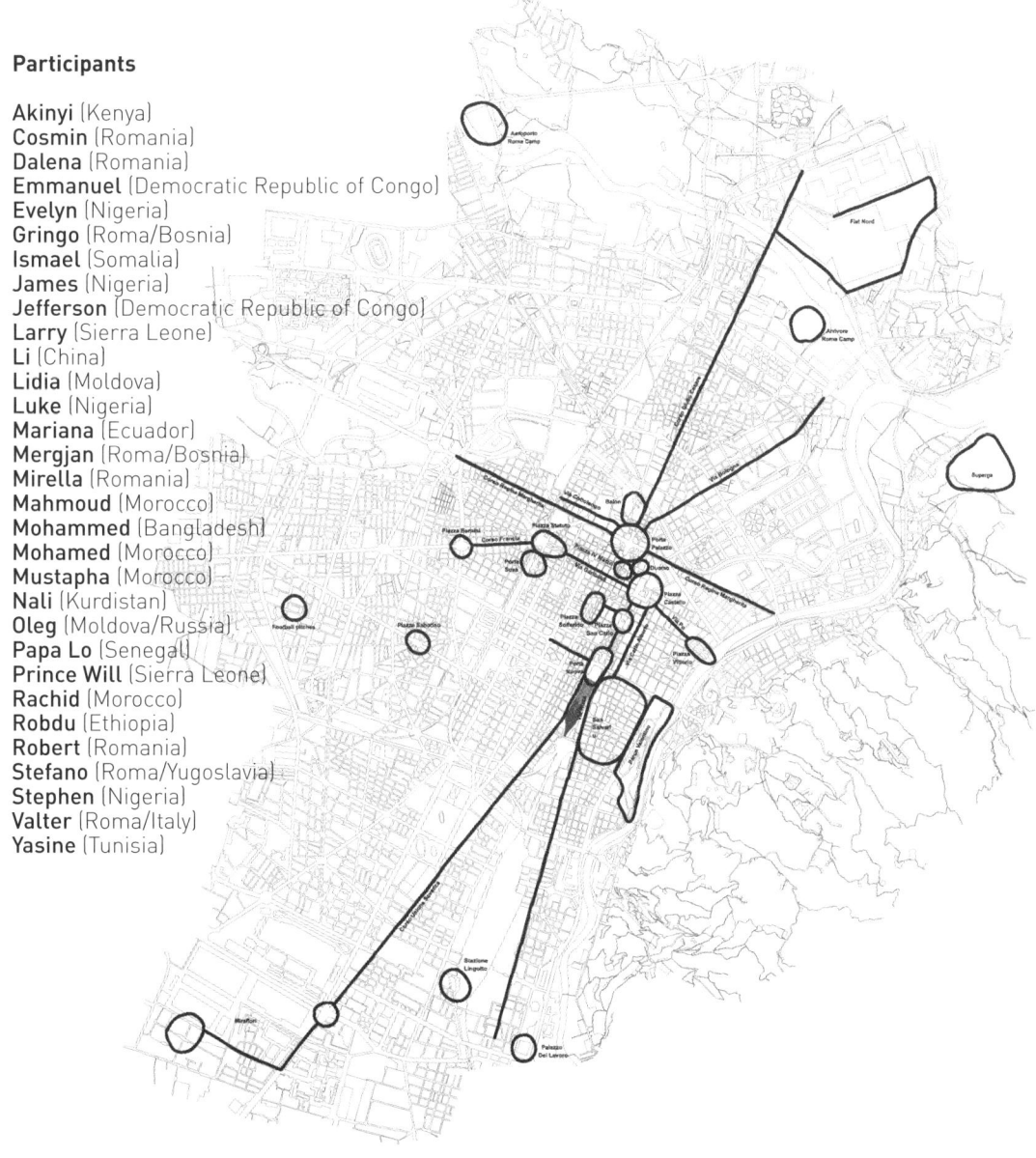

The mental maps, photographs, and comments by each of the participants have previously been presented as an installation and website in Turin, Bologna, and Budapest. This is the installation view at Kunsthaus Baselland, Muttenz/Basel.

Having examined much of the body of sociological writing about the city, a part of contemporary artistic research has singled out the urban context, and its rapid mutations, as an important source of information with which to read the transformation of a complex territory, and interpret the thick web of visual perceptions that city inhabitants are subjected to on a daily basis.

In his writings the sociologist Max Weber theorized a history of the urban context as a sequence of discontinuities, a continuous retracing, implying a work in progress particularly evident in the social geographical contexts of many contemporary cities.

Likewise, according to the anthropologist Ulf Hannerz, the urban experience is consumed by the subject through a continous accumulation of images that change rapidly and thus produce a discontinuity.

Starting from a similar state of disorientation which inevitably follows from a loss of reference points, *Re:route*, a project by Big Hope: Miklós Erhardt & Dominic Hislop, investigates the perception of a specific urban space from the point of view of recent imigrants. *Re:route* is a modular project, composed of a series of mental maps, photographs of Turin, and short, written comments. All the material was produced by foreigners who had arrived in this specific urban environment not more than two years ago. Initiated in December 2001 and presented at the Big Torino Biennial, 2002: 'Big Social Game', the project developed through the involvement and active participation of immigrants originating from different parts of the world: Africa, Eastern Europe, South America, the Middle East, and Far East, and the collaboration of public institutions and intercultural associations. In the realization of the project, the two artists used a participative methodology based on dialogue, relationship and the view of the 'other', all means that engender respect for the subjectivity of the individual, while at the same time emphasizing the plurality of gazes and experiences consumed in one urban landscape.

Taking a specific geographic location, a city whose social fabric has been altered considerably in the last decade by the presence of 'citizens' originating from other countries, Big Hope initiated an anomalous retracing of the urban context. Over the 'ordinary' vision of the city, as perceived by Italian inhabitants, the artists laid the 'extraordinary' vision of those who have lived there for a short time, but are not tourists. Through this reversal, the urban context inevitably presents itself with unfamiliar spaces, alternative routes, different centres, and generates processes that make the experience of 'place' clearly visible as an inner, subjective gaze from which to find the coordinates, determine the reference points, and remap the space within which we position ourselves.

Lisa Parola (curator, art critic, and founding member of Turin based public art collective, 'a.titolo'.)

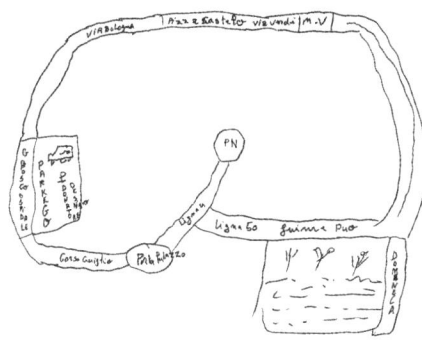

Through a series of dialogues, each participant was asked to sketch a 'mental map', illustrating how they perceive and experience the city, then given a camera with which to represent images and locations that had become significant for them.

The above map, sketched by Mahmoud from Morocco, reveals his perception of the city and it's spaces as a linear path that passes through each of the places that are significant for him in the city. Starting from Porta Nuova (PN), a central point established on each person's map, he has drawn the route he takes through the central street market, to the car park where he sleeps in an abandoned car every night. The path then leads on to show the police station where he has to register every three months, the river, and finally the park where he goes every Sunday.

Mahmoud (Morocco)

This is where I sleep. It's near to the hospital car park. I don't have a flat, or a job to pay the rent.
I haven't had a residence permit for years now. I had one before but they took it away. I can't do anything else now so I sleep in one of the cars that are just left there. They could be stolen cars. They're just left there.
Do you always sleep in the same car?
I have to change cars because they take them away, so I have to find another.
Don't the police disturb you here?
They know me in fact, there's no problem.

Evelyn (Nigeria)
People that work by the road here. They are working on the streets. You can only see the people there at night. Most of them, if they could get a job, they would leave the streets.
This is a place where, if it is cold during the night, she can make a fire. They collect bits of wood, paper, or clothes that they find lying around and try to burn it to make a fire. She can stay there to warm up. A lot of the prostitutes back home in my country work in hotels, and not outside like this. I don't know why it's like this here. Just imagine, somebody who comes from a hot country and they have to stand outside like this. She could stay in a house that is warm instead of standing outside like this. Apart from this, the work is dangerous.
Sometimes the girls get serious burns on their legs on these fires, just so they can stay warm. I saw that they made a fire here and I asked the girl, 'why did you make a fire here, why don't you wear more clothes?'. she said that you have to show your legs to get the customers. Some of them have some wounds, bad injuries because they stand by the fire with bare legs, because this country is very cold in winter.
One day we were coming from outside Turin and we saw this place full of girls. I asked one Nigerian girl why she does this job, why she doesn't go looking for another job. She told me that she didn't have documents. She was crying. I told her that there is a place where there are some sisters who are helping people. I gave her the address so that if she decides to leave that job she can go there and ask for help. I asked her 'why don't you go to the sisters and ask for help', she said 'no, if I don't pay back the money, the madama will give me problems'. I met her some time later and she had got a bad injury, because of the fire, so she tried to leave the streets. Now she's moving from one hospital to another trying to cure the burns that she has on her legs.

Jefferson (Democratic Republic of Congo)
This is the garden of Sermig (dormitory). If foreigners leave in the morning, then they come here. You have to leave at 7 am, even if it's raining, if it's snowing, or it's sunny, for them it doesn't matter. At seven there's the alarm, at seven thirty you're out already. You can only come back at 7 pm. I had spent two months like this. This is the park where foreigners gather in the morning; there's nothing to do, so, you may as well just walk.
What did you do with so much free time?
What could I do? I was walking around, that's it.
Then you must know Turin well?
I was walking withouth noticing what's there around me, just like that. You know, when you have problems, then you can only think about them. They throw you out at seven and immediately you start thinking about what kind of life you're living here, and that you would never have expected to do anything like that. Before I had never had such a heavy situation.

Nali (Kurdistan/Iraq)
The markets in my country are very similar to this. The stalls. It reminds me of my country. But there are many immigrants in Porta Palazzo, some are good people, and some are bad people, but the Italians tend to see all of the immigrants as evil. I don't like this. They think that most of the people in this area are taking drugs and stealing. That's not true. Sometimes I can see it in they way that they look at me, that they are discriminate against me and think that I'm bad just because they can see that I'm a foreigner. But they don't know my reasons for coming here. That I am a political refugee.

Hito Steyerl

The Politics of Truth — Documentarism in the Art Field

The most important development in contemporary art in the past decade can be subsumed under the term "documentary turn". Particularly in the 1990s, one can witness a revival of the working methods of research, archiving, and journalistic documentation techniques, which since the 1930s have cyclically recurred in the art field. Concepts such as context, archive, and knowledge production played an important role in this development. Initially conceived as strongly social-critical and more or less marginalized practices, documentary working methods were integrated into the world of mainstream art through large-scale exhibitions such as the documenta X and Documenta11. At the same time, documentary essay films were also incorporated in the field of art. Hence, an experimental field was established in which various documentary techniques and rhetorical forms permeated and intersected with each other. In the 1990s, although there has so far been little theoretical treatment of it, a zone emerged of an overlapping of video art, documentary film, reportage, essay, and other forms, in which various existing genres and formats intersect and constantly change their stylistic devices in the form of film, video, and installation works.

Despite their increasing significance, however, documentary approaches at first hardly provoked further debate. Instead, they were often perceived as natural representations, as it were, of social or political reality. A debate on the specific formal features of documentary art practices commenced just a few years ago. Many exhibitions examined certain documentary styles in phenomenological terms and highlighted their interaction with mass-media formats, political developments such as globalization, and earlier documentary practices.[1] A large variety of individual samples was thus engendered, processed by the specific aspects of the "documentary turn" of the 1990s. At the same time, a

heated debate took place in the field of art criticism – usually inspired by a culturally conservative stance – as to whether documentarism can even be considered art.

The field in which documentary practices face the greatest challenges, however, does not relate to the question of their inclusion in or exclusion from different concepts of art. The path to be taken leads precisely in the opposite direction. If documentary practices as such are to be taken seriously, the debate automatically finds itself situated in the field of philosophy. Especially those documentary forms that are all to often held in low regard or misunderstood[2] raise questions that are fundamental to the concepts of reality, truth and ethics. It seems as if the dimension of these genuinely philosophical issues is hardly perceived anymore in the art field, while in the field of documentary film theory the philosophical dimension has been discussed for decades. Every discussion on documentary forms, "invokes philosophy"[3], as one documentary film theorist says. The documentary field, another dramatically claimed, is the "battlefields of epistemology"[4], where the fundamental debates on the production and status of knowledge are fought out.

But these debates, too, often got stuck in theoretical dead ends. Generations of theorists have already failed trying to answer the question: "What is the documentary?" All definitions of this term – e.g., by distinguishing it from fiction, by attributing to it a privileged relation to reality, by describing certain forms of behavior on the side of the documentarist or modes of reception on the side of the audience – ultimately proved to be hopeless attempts to provide a binding definition of a practice that is as nimble and variable as life itself.[5] Instead of answers, the question as to what documentarism is merely produced more questions. What guarantees documentarism's seemingly so privileged access to the world in the first place? How do documentary works relate to reality and truth? How do we understand these concepts? Is reality, in this case, an "effect" or an "object"? How is documen-

durch die Einzelaspekte des „Documentary Turn" der 90er Jahre bearbeitet wurden. Parallel dazu entbrannte im Bereich der Kunstkritik auch eine – meist kulturkonservativ inspirierte – Debatte darüber, ob Dokumentarismus überhaupt Kunst sei.

Der Bereich, in dem sich dokumentarische Praxen den größten Herausforderungen zu stellen haben, bezieht sich jedoch nicht auf die Frage ihrer Ein- oder Ausgrenzung aus verschiedenen Kunstbegriffen. Der einzuschlagende Weg verläuft vielmehr genau in die andere Richtung. Wenn nämlich dokumentarische Praxen als solche ernst genommen werden, findet sich die Untersuchung wie von selbst auf dem Gebiet der Philosophie wieder. Denn ausgerechnet dokumentarische Formen, die allzu häufig als simpler und kunstloser Abklatsch des Bestehenden gering geschätzt und missverstanden werden[2], werfen umgekehrt die fundamentalsten Fragen über Begriffe wie Wirklichkeit, Wahrheit und Ethik auf. Es scheint, als seien die Ausmaße dieser genuin philosophischen Problematik im Kunstfeld noch kaum erkannt worden. Im Gegensatz dazu wird die philosophische Dimension auf dem Gebiet der Dokumentarfilmtheorie seit Jahrzehnten diskutiert. Bei jeder Diskussion um dokumentarische Formen werde „die Philosophie auf den Plan" gerufen[3], so ein Dokumentarfilmtheoriker. Der Bereich des Dokumentarischen sei sogar – so deklamiert ein anderer in dramatischer Überspitzung – das „Schlachtfeld der Epistemologie"[4], auf dem grundsätzliche Debatten über die Produktion und den Status von Wissen ausgefochten würden.

Auch diese Debatten verrannten sich allerdings oft in theoretische Sackgassen. An der Frage: „Was ist Dokumentarismus?" sind schon Generationen von TheoretikerInnen gescheitert. Alle Definitionen dieses Begriffs – etwa durch die Abgrenzung von der Fiktion, durch ein privilegiertes Verhältnis zur Realität, durch bestimmte Verhaltensweisen der DokumentaristInnen oder Rezeptionsweisen des Publikums – erwiesen sich letztendlich als der aussichtslose Versuch, eine Praxis zu fixieren, die fast ebenso beweglich und veränderlich ist wie das Leben selbst.[5] Statt Antworten produziert die Frage danach was Doku-

tarism's understanding of social conventions influenced by the status and production of truth? How is its interconnection with power relations and the production of subjectivities to be understood? Which technologies, practices, and rhetorics of truth are developed in the process? What is its connection with institutions, political discourses, and social or biopolitical technologies? What impact does it therefore have on the intersections between power and subjectivity that Foucault called "Gouvernementalité" – i.e. as forms of governing?[6] And, are there documentary forms of visualization that can, in analogy to this, be designated as "documentality"[7]?

Just as documentary practices can function like nodes of power/knowledge, it is also possible to describe them as moments of sudden change, in which this power/knowledge begins to waver. Documentary practices can also focus on that which is unexpected within the relations of power – the inconceivable, the discreet, the unknown, and even the monstrous – and thus create the possibility of change. As Jean-Luc Godard says, "even terminally scratched, a small square of 35mm is capable of redeeming the honor of the whole of reality."[8] Documentary practices can just as easily serve as the media of government as they can be tools to undermine it – in the extreme case, even to suspend it. They do not represent politics but are themselves political actions.

From the Solution to the Problem

Perhaps one reason for the lacking theoretical reflection on documentary practices lies in a further surprising circumstance: Especially in the art field, documentary practices have turned from being a solution to posing a problem. At first, documentary working methods appeared to be a practice-oriented solution to an institutional problem, which, in turn, had to do with the delimitations of the art field. In the early 1990s, the problem consisted in the widespread loss of a sense of reality in art and the fact that it cut itself off from all external worlds except from

mentarismus sei, nur noch mehr Fragen. Denn was garantiert eigentlich den anscheinend so privilegierten Zugang des Dokumentarismus zur Welt? Auf welche Weise beziehen sich dokumentarische Arbeiten auf Wirklichkeit oder Wahrheit? Was verstehen sie darunter? Ist die Wirklichkeit darin „Effekt" oder „Objekt"? Wie wird ihr Verständnis von gesellschaftlichen Konventionen über den Status und die Produktion von Wahrheit beeinflusst? Wie ist dessen Verschaltung mit Machtverhältnissen und der Produktion von Subjektivitäten zu verstehen? Welche Technologien, Praxen und Rhetoriken der Wahrheit werden in dokumentarischen Praxen entwickelt? In welcher Verbindung stehen sie mit Institutionen, politischen Diskursen und sozialen Technologien? Inwiefern wirken sie also an jener Schnittstelle zwischen Macht und Subjektivität, die Foucault als Gouvernementalität – also als Formen der Regierung – bezeichnet hat?[6] Und gibt es dokumentarische Formen der Sichtbarmachung, die wir analog dazu als „Dokumentalität"[7] bezeichnen können?

Ebenso wie dokumentarische Praxen als Knotenpunkte von Macht-Wissen wirken können, ist es aber auch möglich, sie als Momente eines Umschlags darzustellen, in dem dieses Macht-Wissen ins Wanken gerät. Dokumentarische Praxen können auch dasjenige in den Mittelpunkt stellen, was innerhalb herrschender Machtverhältnisse unvorhergesehen ist – das Unvorstellbare, Verschwiegene, Unbekannte, Rettende und sogar Ungeheuerliche – und somit die Möglichkeit zur Veränderung schaffen. Denn, so Jean-Luc Godard: „selbst tödlich zerkratzt vermag ein kleines Rechteck von 35 Millimetern die Ehre der gesamten Wirklichkeit zu retten."[8] Dokumentarische Praxen eignen sich als Medien der Herrschaft ebenso wie als Werkzeuge ihrer Aushöhlung – im Extremfall sogar ihrer Aussetzung. Sie bilden Politik nicht ab, sondern stellen an sich politische Handlungen dar.

Von der Lösung zum Problem

Ein Grund für die mangelnde theoretische Reflexion dokumentarischer Praxen ist möglicherweise

that of the art market. In the market-fixated 1980s, the relation to social and political reality – which was still a fundamental aspect of many art practices in the 1970s – was to a large extent displaced by an obsessive preoccupation with the cynical and often silly ornamental art of postmodernism. In contrast to this, the documentary gesture held the promise of a new transparency toward a world expanding at breathtaking speed. The white cubes turned into dark side aisles of documentary cathedrals into which the colorful light of the world seemed to shine through digital glass windows. Documentary practices, as realistic as possible, were considered to be the escape route leading away from the exploitation and subject-oriented mythologies of the art market, an enlightened rebellion against everything private, formalistic, provincially garbled, and tensely ironic. Especially in the first half of the 1990s, a new interest in social realism forms arose. Methods of institutional criticism and analysis came to the fore in the form of sociological self-reflections of artistic working conditions, or dealing with social fringe groups. The combination of concept, research, archive, documentation, and intervention work[9] led to a concept of art that strongly, or even insistently, placed its trust on the didactical effects of enlightenment.[10] Documentary representation was grasped as a power-critical instrument, as a form of protest against the power relations inherent to the art field. By applying it, the borders between art and the world, social reality and elitist ivory tower, were to be torn down. The political field was thus stylized as the art field's big Other, to be re-conquered, as it were, by means of the documentary.

The supposed solution to the problem turned out to be a problem itself. Precisely the attempt to focus on contents defined as "political", or even on "reality itself", produced a huge number of new formal questions. Documentary forms by no means convey a universal truth of the political but, conversely, a very specific politics of truth. This concept, adopted from Michel Foucault[11], refers to an all but banal condition: the fact that documentary forms are not a transparent win-

in einem weiteren überraschenden Umstand zu suchen: Speziell im Kunstfeld verwandelten sich dokumentarische Praxen von einer Lösung in ein Problem. Zunächst schienen dokumentarische Arbeitsweisen eine praktische Lösung für ein institutionelles Problem darzustellen, das wiederum mit der Eingrenzung und Abgrenzung des Kunstbereichs zu tun hat. Das Problem war Anfang der 90er Jahre dessen grassierender Realitätsverlust und seine Abschottung von jeder anderen Außenwelt als dem Kunstmarkt. Der Bezug auf soziale und politische Wirklichkeit – in den 70ern noch grundlegender Bestandteil vieler Kunstpraxen – war in den marktfixierten 80ern weitgehend von einer obsessiven Beschäftigung mit der zynischen und oftmals läppischen Ornamentkultur der Postmoderne verdrängt worden. Im Gegensatz dazu verhieß die dokumentarische Geste eine neue Transparenz gegen eine sich in atemberaubendem Tempo erweiternde Welt. Aus den White Cubes wurden dunkle Seitenschiffe dokumentarischer Kathedralen, in die durch digitale Glasfenster das bunte Licht der Welt hineinzuschimmern schien. Möglichst realistische dokumentarische Praxen erschienen als Ausweg aus den verwertungs- und subjektfixierten Mythologemen des Kunstmarkts, als aufklärerische Rebellion gegen alles Privatistische, Formalistische, provinziell Verquaste und verkrampft Ironische. Vor allem in der ersten Hälfte der 90er Jahre erwachte ein neues Interesse an sozialrealistischen Formen. Verfahren der Institutionskritik bzw. -analyse traten in Form soziologistischer Selbstreflexionen künstlerischer Arbeitsbedingungen oder als Beschäftigung mit sozialen Randgruppen in den Vordergrund. Aus der Kombination von Konzept-, Recherche-, Archiv-, Dokumentations- und Interventionsarbeit[9] entstand ein Kunstbegriff, der mitunter stark, um nicht zu sagen penetrant, auf didaktische Aufklärungseffekte setzte.[10] Die dokumentarische Darstellung wurde als herrschaftskritisches Instrument begriffen, als Protest gegen die internen Machtverhältnisse des Kunstfelds. Durch ihren Gebrauch sollten die Grenzen zwischen Kunst und Welt, zwischen sozialer Realität und elitärem Elfenbeinturm eingerissen werden. So wurde das Feld des Politischen zum großen Anderen des Kunstbe-

dow to reality but, quite to the contrary, articulate complex power relations. The document is a traditional historical coordinating point of knowledge and power. When Walter Benjamin wrote that each document of culture is simultaneously a document of barbarism, this also implied that each cultural document carries with it the trace of suppression and domination. This is also true of the way in which these documents are created, distributed, and passed on.[12] Benjamin's verdict on the complicity of the document and power does not only apply to individual documents, though, but also to the more complex documentary articulations through which documents are organized and interpreted.

The documentary form that was understood in terms of content as an instrument of the critique of power, thus transformed itself — in terms of form — into an instrument of power saturated with power/knowledge. Due to their dissemination in the field of art, the "discourses of sobriety" (Bill Nichols)[13], e.g., science, economy, education, etc., whose affinity to documentary forms was meant to ensure their proximity to social reality, now began exercising the same governmental, administrative, regimenting, and regulating functions of power/knowledge as in the other social spheres.

A problem that was to be solved on the level of making conscious a political issue, thus returned as a problem of an unconscious politics of form. And the attempt to tear down the borders of the art field and change its power relations now saw itself confronted with two surprising results: On the one hand, the import of new forms of power/knowledge into the art field, and on the other, a general aestheticizing of social discourses.

And this is not all: This osmotic exchange of functions between the field of art and other social spheres was accompanied by an almost tragicomical development. As opposed to what was desired, the art field did not once and for all depart from the elitist terrain of the white cube — so as to permanently anchor itself as a part of

reichs stilisiert, das auf dokumentarischem Wege gewissermaßen zurückerobert werden sollte.

Die vermeintliche Lösung des Problems stellte sich jedoch selbst als Problem heraus. Denn gerade der Versuch, einen als „politisch" definierten Inhalt — oder gar die „Wirklichkeit selbst" in den Mittelpunkt zu stellen, erzeugte umgekehrt eine Vielzahl neuer formaler Fragen. Denn dokumentarische Formen vermitteln keineswegs eine allgemeine Wahrheit des Politischen — sondern im Gegenteil eine jeweils ganz besondere Politik der Wahrheit. Dieser von Michel Foucault entlehnte Begriff[11] bezeichnet einen fast schon banal zu nennenden Umstand — dass dokumentarische Formen kein transparentes Fenster zur Realität darstellen, sondern ganz im Gegenteil komplexe Machtverhältnisse artikulieren. Das Dokument ist eine traditionelle historische Schaltstelle von Wissen und Macht. Wenn Walter Benjamin schreibt, dass jedes Dokument der Kultur zugleich ein Dokument der Barbarei sei, bedeutet das auch, dass jedes kulturelle Dokument die Spur von Unterdrückung und Herrschaft in sich trägt. Dies gilt auch für die Art und Weise, in der diese Dokumente erzeugt, verbreitet und weitergegeben werden.[12] Benjamins Verdikt über die Komplizität von Dokument und Herrschaft trifft jedoch nicht nur auf einzelne Dokumente, sondern auch auf jene komplexeren dokumentarischen Artikulationen zu, durch die Dokumente organisiert und interpretiert werden.

Die dokumentarische Form, die in der Perspektive des Inhalts als Instrument der Herrschaftskritik verstanden wurde, verwandelte sich somit aus der Perspektive der Form in ein von Macht-Wissen saturiertes Instrument der Herrschaft. Jene „discourses of sobriety" (Bill Nichols)[13] — wie etwa Wissenschaft, Ökonomie, Politik, Bildung etc., deren Verwandtschaft zu dokumentarischen Formen deren Nahverhältnis zur sozialen Realität garantieren sollten — begannen nun durch ihre Verbreitung im Kunstbereich auch dort jene gouvernementalen, verwaltenden, reglementierenden und regulierenden Funktionen des Macht-Wissens auszuüben, wie in anderen gesellschaftlichen Bereichen.

the world of political negotiation and participation. Precisely the white cube, which was to be abandoned for good, turned into one of the last spaces in which a genuinely critical political practice was able to resist the onslaught of the neo-liberal, conservative elimination of the political public sphere. The "political reality", along with its notions of a participatory public and criticism, seemed to be integrated into the field of art to such an extent that there was hardly anything left of this reality on the outside.

Of course, the gradual disappearance of the political public and its retreat to the reservation of the art field are not the result of the documentary practices that emerged, but rather the effect of a large-scale conservative, cultural, political, and economic revolution. The return of documentary forms is to be regarded more as a symptom of this development. But this return is also situated in a context in which art and society increasingly permeate each other, thus calling into question the field of aesthetic autonomy, and in which the entire social sphere is, in turn, aestheticized.

History of Truth or Truth of History?

Conclusion: Documentary practices create more problems than they claim to solve. As if in defiance, they transform themselves into genuinely philosophical questions. And these then point to a further paradoxical situation which now affects the level of theory production. For decades, the universal concepts of truth and reality have been dismantled and questioned on a theoretical level. In the wake of the linguistic turn, and later with deconstructivist and poststructuralist thought, a nominalistic view of the world gained hegemony in this field. According to these views, we cannot speak about the truth but at most about truth effects, not about reality but only about the discourses in which they are constructed, not about facts but only about the narratives through which they are articulated. It is not the question of truth that is decisive, according to Michel Foucault, but truth's history as a history of its forms, modes of production, and

Ein Problem, das auf der Ebene der Bewusstmachung eines politischen Inhalts bekämpft werden sollte, kehrte damit als Problem einer unbewussten Politik der Form zurück. Und der Versuch, die Grenzen des Kunstfelds einzureißen und dessen Machtverhältnisse zu ändern, sah sich nun mit zwei überraschenden Resultaten konfrontiert: auf der einen Seite mit dem Import neuer Formen von Macht-Wissen ins Kunstfeld, auf der anderen Seite mit einer generellen Ästhetisierung gesellschaftlicher Diskurse.

Damit nicht genug, ging dieser osmotische Austausch von Funktionen zwischen Kunstfeld und anderen gesellschaftlichen Bereichen mit einer fast schon tragikomischen Entwicklung einher. Der Kunstbereich wanderte nicht wie erhofft ein für alle Mal aus dem elitären Bereich des White Cube aus – um sich fest als Bestandteil der Welt politischer Aushandlung und Partizipation zu verankern. Denn ausgerechnet jener White Cube, der eigentlich endgültig verlassen werden sollte, verwandelte sich in einen der letzten Räume, in dem eine genuin kritische politische Praxis dem Ansturm eines neoliberalen konservativen Abbaus politischer Öffentlichkeit noch standhalten kann. Die „politische Wirklichkeit" mitsamt ihren Vorstellungen von partizipativer Öffentlichkeit und Kritik scheint so gründlich in den Kunstbereich integriert worden zu sein, dass außerhalb kaum etwas davon übrig geblieben ist.

Natürlich ist das Schwinden der politischen Öffentlichkeit und ihr Rückzug ins Reservat des Kunstbereichs keine Folge des Aufkommens dokumentarischer Praxen, sondern vielmehr Effekt einer groß angelegten konservativen, kulturellen, politischen und ökonomischen Revolutionierung. Die Wiederkehr dokumentarischer Formen ist eher als Symptom dieser Entwicklung zu betrachten. Sie ist aber auch verortet in einem Kontext, in dem Kunst und Gesellschaft sich zunehmend durchdringen und somit sowohl der Bereich der Autonomie des Ästhetischen in Frage gestellt wird, als auch umgekehrt der gesamte Bereich des Gesellschaftlichen ästhetisiert wird.

But if truth is grasped historically, then what is there left to say in terms of whether a history is true? Nothing — according to the historian Hayden White, who uses the rhetorics and fictitiousness of historiography as a starting point and comes to the conclusion that historiography does not discover and describe its objects, but rather constructs them through narration.[15] His meta-historiography starts from the assumption that history is not anchored in real events or facts, but originates in the rhetorical tropes in which they are narrated.[16] The documentary film theorist Noël Carroll countered this concept convincingly by asking whether the German *Luftwaffe* was also constructed by means of a documentary film dealing with their airplanes.[17]

At this point, the extreme constructivist approach turns into obvious nonsense, if not into relativization and revisionism.[18] And it appears as if the theoretical debate on truth — which is at stake — has reached an impasse, here, which was already described in the so-called paradox of Epimenides. A Cretan himself, he claimed that all Cretans were liars. But if he, as a Cretan, lied, then the Cretans as such spoke the truth. But if they spoke the truth, this must also be true of Epimenides. In this case, it cannot be denied that all Cretans lie. No matter how you look at it, — there is no solution to the circular argument. Put briefly, something similar applies to the constructivist concepts of truth. If each truth is a construction, why should that one construction claiming this assertion to be true be believed?

Although in the past years, after a longer span of time, fundamental questions pertaining to truth have again been raised in philosophy, e.g., Alain Badious' concept of the truth process[19], the field of art, in particular, is a place where these issues have been articulated in the form of reflective documentary works. For this reason, we can also understand these articulations as a form of philosophical practice, orchestrating an increasingly resounding silence in the field of theory. In

Geschichte der Wahrheit oder Wahrheit der Geschichte?

Fazit: Dokumentarische Praxen schaffen mehr Probleme als sie zu lösen vorgeben. Wie zum Trotz verwandeln sie sich in genuin philosophische Fragen. Und diese wiederum verweisen auf eine weitere paradoxe Situation — die diesmal jedoch die Ebene der Theorieproduktion betrifft. Denn auf theoretischer Ebene werden seit Jahrzehnten universale Begriffe von Wahrheit und Wirklichkeit demontiert und in Frage gestellt. Mit dem Linguistic Turn und später auch dekonstruktivistischen und poststrukturalistischen Denkweisen eroberte eine nominalistische Weltsicht in diesem Bereich die Hegemonie. Und dieser zufolge können wir nicht über Wahrheit sprechen, sondern allenfalls über Wahrheitseffekte, nicht über Realität, sondern nur über die Diskurse in denen sie konstruiert, nicht über Fakten, sondern nur über die Narrative durch die sie artikulierbar werden. Nicht die Frage der Wahrheit sei entscheidend — so Michel Foucault — sondern ihre Geschichte, als Geschichte ihrer Formen, ihrer Produktionsweisen und der Dispositive und Regimes in denen sie als Realität erzeugt wird.[14]

Aber wenn Wahrheit geschichtlich begriffen wird, was können wir dann noch darüber sagen, ob eine Geschichte auch wahr ist? Nichts — meint etwa ein Historiker wie Hayden White, der von der Rhetorizität und Fiktivität von Geschichtsschreibung ausgeht und zu dem Schluss kommt, dass die Geschichtsschreibung ihre Objekte nicht entdecke und beschreibe, sondern durch die Narration erst konstituiere.[15] Seine Metahistoriographie geht davon aus, dass Geschichte nicht in realen Ereignissen oder gar Fakten verankert sei, sondern durch die rhetorischen Tropen entsteht, in denen sie erzählt wird.[16] Eine überzeugende Replik auf diese Konzeption gab der Dokumentarfilmtheoretiker Noël Carroll, der sich fragte, ob auch die deutsche Luftwaffe durch einen Dokumentarfilm konstituiert worden sei, der sich mit ihren Flugzeugen befasse.[17]

An diesem Punkt verwandelt sich der extrem konstruktivistische Ansatz in offensichtlichen Unfug,

many cases, their work on truth expresses a deep dissatisfaction with the contingent and relativistic concepts that are preferably summarized under the unclear term of "postmodernism" and are often merely the mirror images of totalizing and authoritarian concepts of truth in modernity. In other cases, they retrace the dilemmas of these concepts in a descriptive manner. But apart from that, documentary practices also trigger a debate on ethical issues that problematize the specific and presumptuously Eurocentric concepts of truth in modernism, and reject the arrogant renunciation of any kind of concept of truth.

Work on Truth

Documentary forms in the art field are currently primarily assuming two contrary functions. First, they represent a strategy of authenticity, which is intended to ensure the claim of artistic works to establish contact with an auratized field of the social or the political. The formal devices employed here are often social-realistic and attempt to remain as transparent as possible. Examples are art documentation, in which performances or interventions are depicted and which illustrate certain effects in the social field. Here the documentary moment is used as proof of social relevance and evidence of an "organic" relationship to the field. In this perspective some forms of art documentation represent one of the currently most widespread strategies of authentication in the art field by cultivating the Rousseauian myth that there is an art actively embedded in local practices and communities, which is absolutely uncorrupted by any art market that first produces it through its demand. In their function of structuring and intervening in the social field, these documentary forms assume biopolitical tasks.

Authenticity becomes a vitalistic ideology here, which is chosen as the desired raw material of difference, particularly also in the context of globalization. It is nourished from the myth of the genuine and different local, which is currently reproduced in post-ethnographic and neo-cul-

wenn nicht gar in Relativierung und Revisionismus.[18] Und es scheint, als habe sich an diesem Punkt die theoretische Diskussion von Wahrheit – denn um diese geht es dabei – in einer Sackgasse verrannt, die schon im so genannten Paradoxon des Epimenides beschrieben wird. Epimenides – der selbst ein Kreter ist – sagt aus, dass alle Kreter lügen. Wenn er aber – als Kreter – lügt, sagen die Kreter als solche die Wahrheit. Wenn sie jedoch die Wahrheit sagen, muss dies auch für Epimenides gelten. In diesem Fall kann wiederum nicht bestritten werden, dass alle Kreter lügen. Egal wie man es dreht und wendet – es gibt keinen Ausweg aus dem Zirkelschluss. Verkürzt gesagt, verhält es sich mit konstruktivistischen Wahrheitsbegriffen ähnlich. Denn wenn jede Wahrheit eine Konstruktion ist, weshalb sollte man dann ausgerechnet jener Konstruktion, die dies als wahr behauptet, Glauben schenken?

Obwohl auch in der Philosophie in den letzten Jahren, etwa mit Alain Badious Begriff des Wahrheitsprozesses[19], nach langer Zeit wieder grundsätzlichere Fragen nach Wahrheit gestellt werden, ist vor allem auch der Kunstbereich ein Ort, an dem diese Fragen in Form reflexiver dokumentarischer Arbeiten artikuliert werden. Wir können diese Artikulationen daher auch als eine Form philosophischer Praxis begreifen, die ein immer dröhnenderes Schweigen auf dem Gebiet der Theorie orchestriert. Ihre Arbeit an der Wahrheit drückt in vielen Fällen ein tiefes Ungenügen an den kontingenten und relativistischen Konzepten aus, die gern unter dem diffusen Sammelbegriff „Postmoderne" zusammengefasst werden, und oftmals nur negative Spiegelbilder totalisierender und autoritärer Wahrheitskonzeptionen der Moderne darstellen. In anderen Fällen vollziehen sie deren Dilemmata deskriptiv nach. Darüber hinaus setzen dokumentarische Praxen aber auch eine Auseinandersetzung mit ethischen Fragen in Gang, die sowohl die zum Teil partikularen und anmaßend-eurozentrischen Wahrheitskonzepte der Moderne problematisieren, als auch den überheblichen Verzicht auf jeglichen Wahrheitsbegriff überhaupt ablehnen.

tural exhibitions.[20] The documentary is intended to depict a certain truth of the political here, an authentic and "genuine" core of the social. This style forms a template with which given local situations can be fed into the global art field: through an ambivalent procedure that makes authenticity ripe for global serial production. Here the myth of the authentic that forms the vitalistic fetish of documentary discourse proves to be a sophisticated, hybrid, and artificial product of palatable difference and repetition.

In contrast to this, there is another, more reflected current of the documentary, which perceives its own devices as socially constructed epistemological tools. In these works there is no intention at all of depicting the authentic truth of the political, but rather of changing the "politics of truth" on which its representation is based. The visual and epistemological formations of the documentary themselves are thus defined as functions of the political.

An example of the problematization of the status of historical documents is the short video *Schwarz auf Weiß* (Black on White) by the artist group Klub Zwei. *Schwarz auf Weiß* concentrates on the question of the photographic document – specifically by means of a radical withdrawal of the images of the Shoah that are spoken of in the voice-over. While the supervisor of a photo archive raises questions of memory, image, and history, all we see are written plaques on black and white. Despite their principle technical reproducibility, images change according to the thesis. Gray tones disappear with every generation of the photographic print; what remains in the end are the hard contrasts of black and white. It is particularly by withdrawing the pictures that are spoken of, however, that a reflection is set off about what distinguishes their status as historical documents. It is not exclusively the face of the pictures of obliteration, which are often used purely symbolically, but rather the inconspicuous backs with their stamps and remarks, that first give the pictures their historical context and thus also their significance, as Klub Zwei argues. The use of pictures as icons,

Arbeit an der Wahrheit

Dokumentarische Formen im Kunstbereich übernehmen gegenwärtig vor allem zwei gegenläufige Funktionen. Erstens stellen sie eine Authentizitätsstrategie dar, die den Anspruch künstlerischer Arbeiten auf Kontakt mit einem auratisierten Feld des Sozialen bzw. Politischen gewährleisten soll. Die formalen Mittel, die hier eingesetzt werden, sind oft sozialrealistisch und versuchen möglichst transparent zu bleiben. Beispiele sind etwa Kunstdokumentationen, in denen Performances oder Interventionen abgebildet werden, und die bestimmte Effekte im sozialen Feld veranschaulichen. Hier wird das dokumentarische Moment als Beweismittel sozialer Relevanz und als Beleg eines „organischen" Verhältnisses zum sozialen Feld eingesetzt. In dieser Perspektive stellen einige Formen von Kunstdokumentation eine der derzeit verbreitetsten Authentisierungsstrategien im Kunstfeld dar, indem sie den rousseauistischen Mythos nähren, es gäbe eine in lokalen Praxen und Communities aktiv eingebettete Kunst, die absolut unkorrumpiert von jenem Kunstmarkt sei, der sie durch seine Nachfrage erst hervorbringt. In ihrer Funktion als Strukturierung und Eingriff ins soziale Feld übernehmen diese Dokumentarformen biopolitische Aufgaben.

Authentizität wird dabei zur vitalistischen Ideologie, die gerade auch im Kontext von Globalisierung zum begehrten Rohstoff der Differenz erkoren wird und vom Mythos jenes echten und differenten Lokalen zehrt, der gegenwärtig in postethnographischen und neokulturalistischen Ausstellungen reproduziert wird.[20] Hier soll das Dokumentarische eine bestimmte Wahrheit des Politischen abbilden, einen authentischen und „echten" Kern des Sozialen. Dieser Stil bildet eine Schablone, mit der gegebene lokale Situationen in den globalen Kunstbetrieb eingespeist werden können: durch ein ambivalentes Verfahren, das Authentizität zur globalen Serienreife bringt. Hier erweist sich jener Mythos des Authentischen, der den vitalistischen Fetisch dokumentarischer Diskurse bildet, als ausgeklügeltes, hybrides und artifizielles Produkt aus genießbarer Differenz und Wiederholung.

on the other hand, frequently leads to their use as mere illustrations of authenticity. In contrast, *Schwarz auf Weiß* insists on perceiving photographs as something we have given up "reading" (Walter Benjamin).[21] The video is positioned within a debate that attempts to carry out a critical reading of pictures — yet without rejecting every representation altogether as a purely social or media construction containing no truth. Unlike many media-critical approaches of recent years, this reflection therefore does not lead to an endless, circular and narcissist self-reflexivity, but rather to an ethical-political stance.

By importing documentary forms to the field of art, classical problems of the documentary are newly raised there, too — the connection between documentary forms and political and social power relations as well as the major power and knowledge complexes of law, science and journalism. But the gaze regimes of the documentary, its links to forms of control, objectivization, and categorization, are also imported into the space of art. Between biopolitical realism and idle reflectivity, between documentary conceptualism and a precise reading of gazes and images and the ethical-political negotiation of their claims to truth, there do exist various documentary approaches that not only articulate themselves by means of various documentalities, but also represent different forms of the politics of truth. So it is precisely the questions pertaining to truth, ethics, and reality, that were increasingly banned from theory in the past 20 years, that are now raised in a new form in the art field through the emergence of documentary works.

---

1 Just to mention a few exhibitions: *True Stories* (Witte de With, Rotterdam, 2002), *Es ist schwer das Reale zu berühren* (Kunstverein Munich, 2003), Documenta11 (Kassel, 2002), Manifesta 5 (San Sebastian, 2004), *Experiments with Truth* (Philadelphia, Fabric Workshop and Museum, 2004), or the Taipei Biennial 2004 with the indicative title: *Do You Believe in Reality?*
2 Not always wrongly.
3 Noël Carroll, "Nonfiction Film and Postmodernist Skepticism," *Post-Theory: Reconstructing Film Studies*, David Bordwell and Noël Carroll (eds.), Madison, Wisconsin 1996, p. 283.
4 Brian Winston, *Claiming the Real*, London 1995, p. 242.

Dementgegen steht eine andere, reflektiertere Strömung des Dokumentarischen, die ihre eigenen Mittel als sozial konstruierte epistemologische Werkzeuge wahrnimmt. In diesen Arbeiten soll mitnichten die authentische Wahrheit des Politischen abgebildet werden, sondern umgekehrt die Politik der Wahrheit verändert werden, die ihrer Darstellung zugrunde liegt. Die visuellen und epistemologischen Formationen des Dokumentarischen werden somit selbst als Funktionen des Politischen bestimmt.

Ein Beispiel für die Problematisierung des Status historischer Dokumente ist das kurze Video *Schwarz auf Weiß* der Künstlerinnengruppe Klub Zwei. *Schwarz auf Weiß* konzentriert sich auf die Frage des fotografischen Dokuments — und zwar mittels eines radikalen Entzugs jener Bilder der Shoah, von denen im Off die Rede ist. Während die Leiterin eines Fotoarchivs Fragen zu Gedächtnis, Bild und Geschichte aufwirft, sehen wir nur Texttafeln auf Schwarz und Weiß. Trotz ihrer prinzipiellen technischen Reproduzierbarkeit ändern sich Bilder, so die These. Mit jeder Generation des fotografischen Abzugs verschwinden Grautöne — was letztlich bleibt, sind die harten Kontraste von Schwarz und Weiß. Gerade durch den Entzug der Bilder, von denen die Rede ist, wird jedoch die Reflektion über das, was ihren Status als historische Dokumente ausmacht, in Gang gesetzt. Es sei nicht ausschließlich die Vorderseite der Bilder der Vernichtung, die oftmals rein symbolisch eingesetzt werde, sondern die unscheinbare Rückseite mit ihren Stempeln und Vermerken, die Bildern erst ihren historischen Kontext verschaffe und somit auch ihre Bedeutung, argumentiert Klub Zwei. Die Verwendung von Bildern als Ikonen führe hingegen oft genug dazu, sie als bloße Illustrationen der Authentizität zu verwenden. *Schwarz auf Weiß* insistiert demgegenüber darauf, Fotografien als etwas, was zu lesen aufgegeben sei (Walter Benjamin)[21], wahrzunehmen. Das Video positioniert sich innerhalb einer Debatte, die versucht, eine kritische Lektüre von Bildern zu betreiben — ohne jedoch jegliche Repräsentation in Bausch und Bogen als rein soziale bzw. mediale Konstruktion ohne Wahrheitsgehalt zu verwerfen. Anders als in vielen medienkritischen Ansätzen

5 A good overview can be found in Eva Hohenberger, "Dokumentarfilmtheorie: Bilder des Wirklichen," *Texte zur Theorie des Dokumentarfilms*, Hohenberger (ed.), Berlin 1998, p. 8–35.
6 See e.g. Toby Miller, *Technologies of Truth: Cultural Citizenship and the popular Media*, Minneapolis 1998, p. 14–18.
7 See also Hito Steyerl, "Framing Globalities," *Gouvernementalität: Ein sozialwissenschaftliches Konzept in Anschluss an Foucault*, Encarnación Gutiérrez-Rodriguez and Marianne Pieper (eds.), Frankfurt a. M. 2003. Steyerl, "Politik der Wahrheit," *Springerin* 3, (2003). Steyerl, "Dokumentarismus als Politik der Wahrheit," *Raumbilder und Bildräume*, Gerald Raunig (ed.), Vienna 2004. Steyerl, "Dokumentarismus und Dokumentalität," *Theorie der Visua-lität, Visualität der Theorie*, Nina Möntmann and Dorothee Richter (eds.), Cologne 2004. Steyerl, "Die Farbe der Wahrheit," *Spuren des Realen: Dokumentarische Strategien im Kunstbereich*, Karin Gludovatz (ed.), Vienna 2005.
8 Jean-Luc Godard, *Histoire(s) du Cinéma*, Paris 1998, p. 86. Cited in Georges Didi-Huberman, "Bilder trotz allem: Über ein Stück Film, das der Hölle entrissen wurde," unpublished manuscript of a lecture held at the Academy of Fine Arts Vienna 12/14/02. Translated by Aileen Derieg.
9 Gerald Raunig, *Charon: Eine Ästhetik der Grenzüberschreitung*, Vienna 1999. Stella Rollig, "Das wahre Leben," *Die Kunst des Öffentlichen*, Marius Babias and Achim Könneke (eds.), Amsterdam/Dresden 1998, p. 12–27.
10 Holger Kube Ventura, *Politische Kunst Begriffe in den 1990er Jahren im deutschsprachigen Raum*, Vienna 2001, p. 69.
11 Michel Foucault, "Truth and Power: Interview by Alessandro Fontana and Pasquale Pasquino," *Power/Knowledge: Selected Interviews and Other Writings 1972-1977*, Colin Gordon (ed.), New York 1980, p. 132.
12 Walter Benjamin, *Geschichtsphilosophische Thesen: Zur Kritik der Gewalt und andere Aufsätze*, Frankfurt a. M. 1978, p. 83.
13 Bill Nichols, *Representing Reality*, Bloomington/Indianapolis 1991, p. 3–4: "Documentary has a kinship with those other nonfictional systems that together make up what we may call the discourses of sobriety. Science, economics, politics, foreign policy, education, religion, welfare — these systems assume that they have instrumental power; they can and should alter the world, they can affect action and entail consequences [...] Discourses of sobriety are sobering because they regard their relation to the real as direct, immediate, transparent. Through them power exerts itself. Through them, things are made to happen. They are the vehicles of domination and conscience, power and knowledge, desire and will."
14 See Foucault, "Truth and Power," p. 132.
15 In the context of a discussion on documentarism: Michael Renov, *Theorizing Documentary*, London/New York 1993, p. 7.
16 Hayden White, *Tropics of Discourse: Essays in Cultural Criticism*, Baltimore/London 1978.
17 Carroll, "Nonfiction Film and Postmodernist Skepticism," p. 290–291. On the problem of relativism see Saul Friedländer, ed., *Probing the Limits of Representation: Nazism and the "Final Solution,"* Cambridge, Massachusetts 1992.
18 For more detail see Friedländer, *Probing the Limits of Representation*.
19 Alain Badiou, *Theoretical Writings*, London 2004, p. 97–160.
20 See Boris Buden, "Da bumst der Wahnsinnige den Verwirrten," *springerin* 2 (2003).
21 Walter Benjamin, *Das Kunstwerk im Zeitalter seiner technischen Reproduzierbarkeit*, Frankfurt a. M. 1966, p. 64.

der letzten Jahre führt diese Reflexion daher keineswegs zu endloser, zirkulärer und narzisstischer Selbstreflexivität, sondern zu einer ethisch-politischen Haltung.

Mit dem Import dokumentarischer Formen in den Kunstbereich werden auch dort die klassischen Probleme des Dokumentarischen neu aufgelegt — die Verknüpfung dokumentarischer Formen mit politischen und sozialen Machtverhältnissen sowie mit den großen Macht-Wissenskomplexen von Recht, Wissenschaft und Journalismus. Aber auch die Blickregimes des Dokumentarischen, ihre Verknüpfung mit Formen der Kontrolle, Objektivierung und Kategorisierung werden in den Kunstraum importiert. Zwischen biopolitischem Realismus und leer laufender Reflexivität, zwischen dokumentarischem Konzeptualismus und einer genauen Lektüre von Blicken und Bildern und der ethisch-politischen Verhandlung ihrer Wahrheitsansprüche existieren also die verschiedenen dokumentarischen Ansätze, die sich nicht nur durch verschiedene Dokumentalitäten artikulieren, sondern auch verschiedene Formen von Wahrheitspolitik darstellen. Somit sind es gerade die Fragen nach Wahrheit, Ethik und Realität, die zunehmend aus der Theorie der letzten 20 Jahre verbannt wurden und die sich nun durch das Auftauchen dokumentarischer Arbeiten im Kunstraum in neuer Form stellen.

1 Um nur ein paar Ausstellungsbeispiele zu nennen: *True Stories* (Witte de With, Rotterdam, 2002), *Es ist schwer das Reale zu berühren* (Kunstverein München, 2003), Documenta11 (Kassel, 2002), manifesta 5 (San Sebastian, 2004), *Experiments with truth* (Philadelphia, Fabric Workshop and Museum, 2004) oder die Taipei Biennale 2004 mit dem bezeichnenden Titel: *Do you believe in reality?*
2 Nicht in jedem Fall zu Unrecht.
3 Noël Carroll: Der nicht-fiktionale Film und postmoderner Skeptizismus. Bilder des Wirklichen, in: Eva Hohenberger (Hg.): *Texte zur Theorie des Dokumentarfilms*, Berlin 1998, S. 35.
4 Brian Winston: *Claiming the real*, London 1995, S. 242–250. ÜdV.
5 Einen guten Überblick über die Debatte etwa bei Eva Hohenberger: Dokumentarfilmtheorie. Bilder des Wirklichen, in: Dies. (Hg.): *Texte zur Theorie des Dokumentarfilms*, Berlin 1998, S. 8–35.
6 Mediale Formen als Formen der Gouvernementalität werden etwa von Toby Miller beschrieben, in: Toby Miller: *Technologies of Truth. Cultural Citizenship and the popular Media*, Minneapolis 1998, S. 14–18.
7 Siehe auch Hito Steyerl: Framing Globalities, in: Encarnación Gutiérrez-Rodriguez und Marianne Pieper (Hg.): *Gouvernementali-*

tät. Ein sozialwissenschaftliches Konzept in Anschluss an Foucault, Frankfurt a. M. 2003. Steyerl: Politik der Wahrheit, in: *springerin* (2003), Nr. 3. Steyerl: Dokumentarismus als Politik der Wahrheit, in: Gerald Raunig (Hg.): *Raumbilder und Bildräume*, Wien 2004. Steyerl: Dokumentarismus und Dokumentalität, in: Nina Möntmann und Dorothee Richter (Hg.): *Theorie der Visualität, Visualität der Theorie*, Köln 2004. Steyerl: Die Farbe der Wahrheit, in: Karin Gludovatz (Hg.): *Spuren des Realen. Dokumentarische Strategien im Kunstbereich*, Wien 2005.

8 Jean-Luc Godard: *Histoire(s) du Cinéma*, Paris 1998, S. 86. Zit. nach Georges Didi-Huberman: *Bilder trotz allem. Über ein Stück Film, das der Hölle entrissen wurde*. Unveröffentlichtes Vortragsmanuskript, gehalten an der Akademie der Bildenden Künste Wien, 14.12.02, Wien 2003.

9 Gerald Raunig: *Charon. Eine Ästhetik der Grenzüberschreitung*, Wien 1999. Stella Rollig: Das wahre Leben, in: Marius Babias und Achim Könneke: *Die Kunst des Öffentlichen*, Dresden 1998, S. 12–27.

10 Holger Kube Ventura: *Politische Kunst Begriffe in den 1990er Jahren im deutschsprachigen Raum*, Wien 2001, S. 69.

11 Michel Foucault: Wahrheit und Macht. Interview von Allessandro Fontana und Pasquale Pasquino, in: Ders.: *Dispositive der Macht. Über Sexualität, Wissen und Wahrheit*, Berlin 1978, S. 51.

12 Walter Benjamin: *Geschichtsphilosophische Thesen. Zur Kritik der Gewalt und andere Aufsätze*, Frankfurt a. M. 1978, S. 83.

13 Bill Nichols: *Representing Reality*, Bloomington/Indianapolis 1991, S. 3f.: „Documentary has a kinship with those other non-fictional systems that together make up what we may call the discourses of sobriety. Science, economics, politics, foreign policy, education, religion, welfare — these systems assume that they have instrumental power; they can and should alter the world, they can affect action and entail consequences. [...] Discourses of sobriety are sobering because they regard their relation to the real as direct, immediate, transparent. Through them power exerts itself. Through them, things are made to happen. They are the vehicles of domination and conscience, power and knowledge, desire and will."

14 Michel Foucault, a.a.O., S. 51.

15 Siehe dazu im Kontext einer Diskussion um Dokumentarismus: Michael Renov: *Theorizing documentary*, London/New York 1993, S. 7.

16 Hayden White: *Auch Klio dichtet oder die Fiktion des Faktischen. Studien zur Tropologie des historischen Diskurses*, Stuttgart 1986.

17 Noël Carroll, a.a.O., S. 44–46. Zum Problem des Relativismus s.a. Saul Friedländer (Hg.): *Probing the limits of representation. Nazism and the „final solution"*, Cambridge, Mass. 1992.

18 Genauer dazu Saul Friedländer a.a.O.

19 Alain Badiou: *Theoretical writings*, London 2004, S. 97–160.

20 Siehe z.B. Boris Buden: Da bumst der Wahnsinnige den Verwirrten, in: *springerin* (2003), Nr. 2.

21 Walter Benjamin: *Das Kunstwerk im Zeitalter seiner technischen Reproduzierbarkeit*, Frankfurt a.M. 1966, S. 64.

Untitled #76

Untitled #99

Untitled #118

Untitled #127
Kaucylia Brooke, from *Vitrinen in Arbeit*, 2002–2005, color photograph, 76,2 x 76,2 cm

Christoph Behnke

The Documentary Method

After decades of representation-critical reading about the constructedness of social reality, there seems to be a need in the field of art in recent years – indicated by the theme of *documentarism* – to turn one's back on the discourse-analytical or deconstructive technique of second-order observation that dismantles everything, and, *against one's better judgment*, to leave the commanding post and become politically committed, in the lowly realms of reality – for example with the help of *documents*. However, the tailoring of *documentarism* for the world of art is not to be had without the effect of refraction that Bourdieu considered one of the *laws of art*: In the world of advanced art, the *document* is transformed into an *art-specific document*, just like concepts of everyday life are assigned specific meanings in science that can only be understood in the scientific world. At the Documenta11, one could witness 90-minute documentary films being *exhibited*, obviously to create the *effect of the documentary* (Tom Holert). But the turn to documentary representation on the occasion of Documenta11 was at the same time an opportunity to tie on to the discourse of Postcolonialism, because it justified focusing on a method of representation in art that was already dismissed by Brecht and Benjamin (Brecht's famous assertion: "A photograph of the Krupp works or AEG tells us next to nothing about these institutions [...]"). Moreover, what might play a role in art's interest in the document is that the *politics of truth*, as Foucault called it, is increasingly based on documentarisms (this was Catherine David's starting point at documenta X), whereby the standards of the economy of attention set by the system of advertising function as the *currency* determining the value of the document; in the world of art, the issue is therefore to render this *currency of the spectacle* invalid. The fact that documentary photos, especially those of a social-documentary photographic practice (e.g. the exhibition *The Social Scene*, MOCA, Los Angeles, 2000), cannot lay claim to any objectivity, no matter how it is defined (*arbitrariness of*

the photographic image); that the camera reproduces the *field of vision of the Cyclops* and not that of the human (Pierre Francastel), meaning that from the retinal perspective reality is not doubled through the photo; that photos, then, are socially appropriated like surprisingly effective fetishes — all these insights belong to the common sense of the advanced critique of photography in the past decades and should make a naive use of photographic documents impossible. Yet they have not been able to prevent them from becoming successful at the center of the art world.

The photography critics would indeed have to communicate their message like prophets if they seriously wanted to call into question the *naturalistic creation of illusions* through documents. The *initiated* have no ambition in this respect, though: the art system cultivates a *privileged gaze*, also as a feature of social distinction, making certain questions uninteresting. It is not surprising, then, that questions pertaining to *reception* in the field of advanced art are not met with interest, because the viewers of art are simultaneously perceived as producers of art, and so production and consumption are described as one and the same process. What remains are questions like: *What is an image?* etc. Little is known about the process of reception in the case of documentary photography. The relevant studies of Bourdieu et al. deal with amateur photography and stem from the 1960s. If it is correct that the meanings of photographs are produced by the viewers, that every photo is poly-semantic, and that, as a result, the social use is to be conceived as heterogeneous, then one would at least like to know in which social realms the craftiness of ideological image politics can do its mischief especially well and which specific means it applies to this end. Along these lines, it ought to be examined whether the intellectual approach to the analysis of photography documents, as is the case in advanced photography criticism, fosters universalism of explanation that deems the concrete process of reception outside the world of art insignificant. The issue here is by no means to reiterate the thesis of John Fiske and other exponents of *cultural studies*, who — contrary to con-

tarfotos — gerade auch solche aus der sozialdokumentarischen Fotopraxis, die sich zum Teil der Sozialkritik verbunden fühlen (vgl. z.B. die Ausstellung *The Social Scene* im MOCA, Los Angeles 2000) — keinen Anspruch auf eine wie immer auch definierte Objektivität haben können (*Arbitrarität des photographischen Bildes*), dass die Kamera *das Gesichtsfeld des Zyklopen* und nicht das des Menschen wiedergibt (Pierre Francastel), also auch aus retinaler Sicht keine Verdoppelung der Wirklichkeit durch Fotos stattfindet, dass Fotos also eigentlich wie erstaunlich wirksame *Fetische* sozial angeeignet werden — all diese Einsichten gehören zum Common Sense der avancierten Fotokritik der letzten Jahrzehnte und machen einen naiven Gebrauch von z.B. Fotodokumenten eigentlich unmöglich, haben es aber nicht verhindern können, dass diese im Zentrum der Kunstwelt reüssierten.

Allerdings müssten Akteure der Fotokritik ihre Botschaft schon wie religiöse Propheten kommunizieren, wenn sie denn die *naturalistische Illusionsbildung* durch Dokumente ernsthaft in Frage stellen wollten. Die *Eingeweihten* haben diesbezüglich jedoch keinen Ehrgeiz: Das Kunstsystem kultiviert sich einen *privilegierten Blick* auch als soziales Unterscheidungsmerkmal, womit bestimmte Fragestellungen uninteressant werden. So ist es nicht überraschend, dass Fragen der *Rezeption* im avancierten Kunstfeld nicht auf Interesse stoßen, weil die Rezipienten von Kunst hier zugleich als Produzenten von Kunst gedacht werden und also Produktion und Konsumtion ein und denselben Vorgang beschreiben. Es bleiben dann Fragen wie: *Was ist ein Bild?* etc. Im Fall der Dokumentarfotografie weiß man über den Prozess der Rezeption wenig. Die einschlägige Untersuchung von Bourdieu et al. beschäftigt sich mit Amateurfotografie und stammt aus den 60er Jahren. Wenn es denn richtig ist, dass die Bedeutungen der Fotos durch die Rezipienten hervorgebracht, dass jedes Foto polysem und dass infolgedessen der soziale Gebrauch heterogen zu denken ist, dann würde man zumindest gern wissen, in welchen sozialen Bezirken die Raffinesse der ideologischen Bildpolitik ihr Unwesen besonders konsequent betreiben kann und welche spezifischen Mittel sie dafür einsetzt. In diesem Sinne

vincing empirical evidence — were enthused about *oppositional readings* of popular culture: as alleged *messages without a code* (Roland Barthes), recodings come up to other limiting factors in the medium of photography anyway.

In his iconographic method of interpreting images under the influence of the sociology of knowledge in his three-stage classification (pre-iconographic, iconographic, iconological), Erwin Panofsky also spoke of *the sense of document* that can reveal the *historical truth* of images. The method with which Panofsky intended to establish a specific canon of art history can also be used in a modified form as a model for examining recent image interpretations, namely when the *highest stage* of interpretation is understood as an activity produced by incorporated knowledge, habitual practice, and the relation to *conjunctive spaces of experience* (Karl Mannheim). In this context, it would be interesting to bring the concept of *documentary method* into play, as it was particularly developed in ethno-methodology: For the sake of establishing social order, the argument goes, humans are forced to accept linguistic (and visual) enunciations in everyday communication as *documents* — they use a *documentary method* to relate a concrete event to a *pattern*; otherwise, communication would become hopelessly unraveled. This necessity of the *sense of document* also prevails in the reception of photographs; an instrument of everyday communication is thus used as a matter of course, also where the agenda is to confirm social worlds as *hyper-ritualization* (Erving Goffman). No more than we (are allowed to) answer the greeting *How are you?* extensively in everyday life, but instead register it as a *document* of the *greeting* event, do we reflect upon the *naive realism* of photography. We instead understand it as a self-evident *document* of reality. And this *sense of document* manifests itself socially in different ways. This touches on the real desideratum of research: to show that something like documentary photography cannot only not count on being *correctly* understood (or becoming ideologically effective) in all strata of society on the level of the iconic doubling of reality and the narratives associated

müsste überprüft werden, ob nicht der intellektualistische Zugang zur Analyse des Foto-Dokuments, wie er in der avancierten Fotokritik betrieben wird, einen Universalismus des Erklärens befördert, der den konkreten Rezeptionsvorgang vor allem außerhalb der Kunstwelt für unbedeutend hält. Es geht hier keineswegs um die Wiederholung der These von John Fiske und anderen Exponenten der *Cultural Studies*, die — entgegen überzeugender empirischer Evidenz — von *oppositionellen Lesarten* der Populärkultur geschwärmt haben: als vermeintliche *Botschaft ohne Code* (Roland Barthes) sind im Medium Fotografie Rekodierungen ohnehin andere Grenzen gesetzt.

Erwin Panofsky hat beim Entwurf seiner ikonologischen Methode der Bildinterpretation unter dem Einfluss der Wissenssoziologie innerhalb seiner dreistufigen Klassifikation (vorikonografisch, ikonografisch, ikonologisch) auch vom *Dokumentsinn* gesprochen, der die *geschichtliche Wahrheit* von Bildern aufweisen könne. Das Verfahren, mit dem Panofsky einen bestimmten Kanon der Kunstgeschichte festschreiben wollte, lässt sich in abgewandelter Form auch als Modell für die Erforschung rezenter Bildinterpretationen verwenden, dann nämlich, wenn man die *höchste Stufe* der Interpretation als eine durch inkorporiertes Wissen, durch habituelle Praxis, durch Bezug auf *konjunktive Erfahrungsräume* (Karl Mannheim) zustande kommende Aktivität versteht. Dabei dürfte es interessant sein, den Begriff der *dokumentarischen Methode* ins Spiel zu bringen, wie er insbesondere in der Ethnomethodologie entwickelt wurde: Um soziale Ordnung herzustellen, so die Überlegung, sind Menschen gezwungen in der Alltagskommunikation sprachliche (und visuelle) Ausdrücke als *Dokument* zu nehmen — sie benutzen die *dokumentarische Methode* um ein konkretes Ereignis auf ein *Muster* zu beziehen, da Kommunikation sonst hoffnungslos ausfransen würde. Diese Notwendigkeit des *Dokumentsinns* herrscht auch bei der Rezeption von Fotografien vor; es wird also ein Instrument der Alltagskommunikation wie selbstverständlich auch dort verwendet, wo die Bestätigung sozialer Welten als *Hyper-Ritualisierung* (Erving Goffman) Programm ist. So wenig wie wir die Begrüßungsformel *wie geht's* im Alltag ausführlich beantwor-

with it, but that a further hurdle in the social use of documentary photography consists in *how* it is appropriated. *The sense of document* can be professionally shaped, it can be furnished with the filter of *aestheticizing*, it can give preference to questions of *ethos*, and it can also wither away like an undeveloped faculty of language. In any case, the reception of the document cannot be assigned to a specific interpretation. Therefore, *The Need to Document* should also be understood as a return to the *minor* issues. The crushing deconstruction of Dorothea Lange's *Migrant Mother* ought to be supplemented by the question of what the *reality* of this photograph was in sociological terms?

ten (dürfen), sondern sie als *Dokument* für das Ereignis *Begrüßung* verbuchen, so wenig reflektieren wir den *naiven Realismus* der Fotografie und verstehen sie stattdessen als selbstverständliches *Dokument* der Wirklichkeit. Und eben dieser *Dokumentsinn* ist sozial unterschiedlich ausgeprägt; hier liegt das eigentliche Forschungsdesiderat, zu zeigen, dass so etwas wie Dokumentarfotografie nicht nur nicht damit rechnen kann auf der Ebene der ikonischen Verdoppelung der Realität und der damit verbundenen Erzählungen durch alle Schichten hindurch *richtig* verstanden zu werden (auch: ideologisch wirksam zu werden), sondern dass eine weitere Hürde im sozialen Gebrauch der Dokumentarfotografie im *Wie* der Aneignung liegt. Der *Dokumentsinn* kann professionell geformt, kann mit dem Filter der *Ästhetisierung* ausgestattet sein, kann Fragen des *Ethos* bevorzugen, kann schließlich auch verkümmern, wie ein nicht ausgebildetes Sprachvermögen. In jedem Fall wird die Rezeption des Dokuments sich keineswegs einer bestimmten Lesart zuordnen lassen können. Deshalb sollte *The Need to Document* auch als eine Rückkehr zu den *kleinen* Fragen verstanden werden: Der alles zermalmenden Dekonstruktion der *Migrant Mother* von Dorothea Lange müsste nun die Frage beigestellt werden, was denn die *Wirklichkeit* dieses Fotos in soziologischer Hinsicht war?

JORGE LUIS BORGES

Borges is forever commenting on the style of the stories or the entire volume, preparing the reader for what is to come stylistically as well as thematically

- he at times will draw attention to his "plain style" as opposed to his earlier "baroque."

- "without astonishment" a double negative of sorts that acts as a device in the sentence that stands out / pronounced because of it's odd wording sequence.

"He examined his wounds and saw, without astonishment, that they had healed."
(THE CIRCULAR RUINS)

- Quietness, subtlety, and laconic terseness

↓   ↓
FREE OF SUPERFLUOUS WORDS   USING FEW WORDS,
CONCISE, SUCCINCT   CONCISE

- Borges style is intellectual and dense w/ allusions to literature, philosophy, religion or theology, to myth, to the culture and history of Buenos Aires and Argentina, and the Southern Cone of South America. ☆ ☆ ☆
(this is phone!!!)

- In "Versions of Homer" 1932 he makes it clear that every translation is a version and not a definitive translation, because that cannot be. Lyotard shared this idea in the "effigy to memory" essay in which he describes the memorial as not a recreation of alluding to the past event, but an entirely new event all together. The anti-memorial.   TRIVIUM →

— Borges acknowledges the fictive nature of his stories — but the "UNIVERSAL NATURE OF INIQUITY". this volume is a series of biographies of reprehensible evil doers, but as a biography — the book might seem to rely heavily upon "Historical sources" the changing and distorting of the characters and stories (-sometimes without aesthetic justification) motives are to produce a work singularly his own.

↑ ↑ ↑

← ROOTLESSN
← (THIRD MANIF
  RUTHLESS & 1

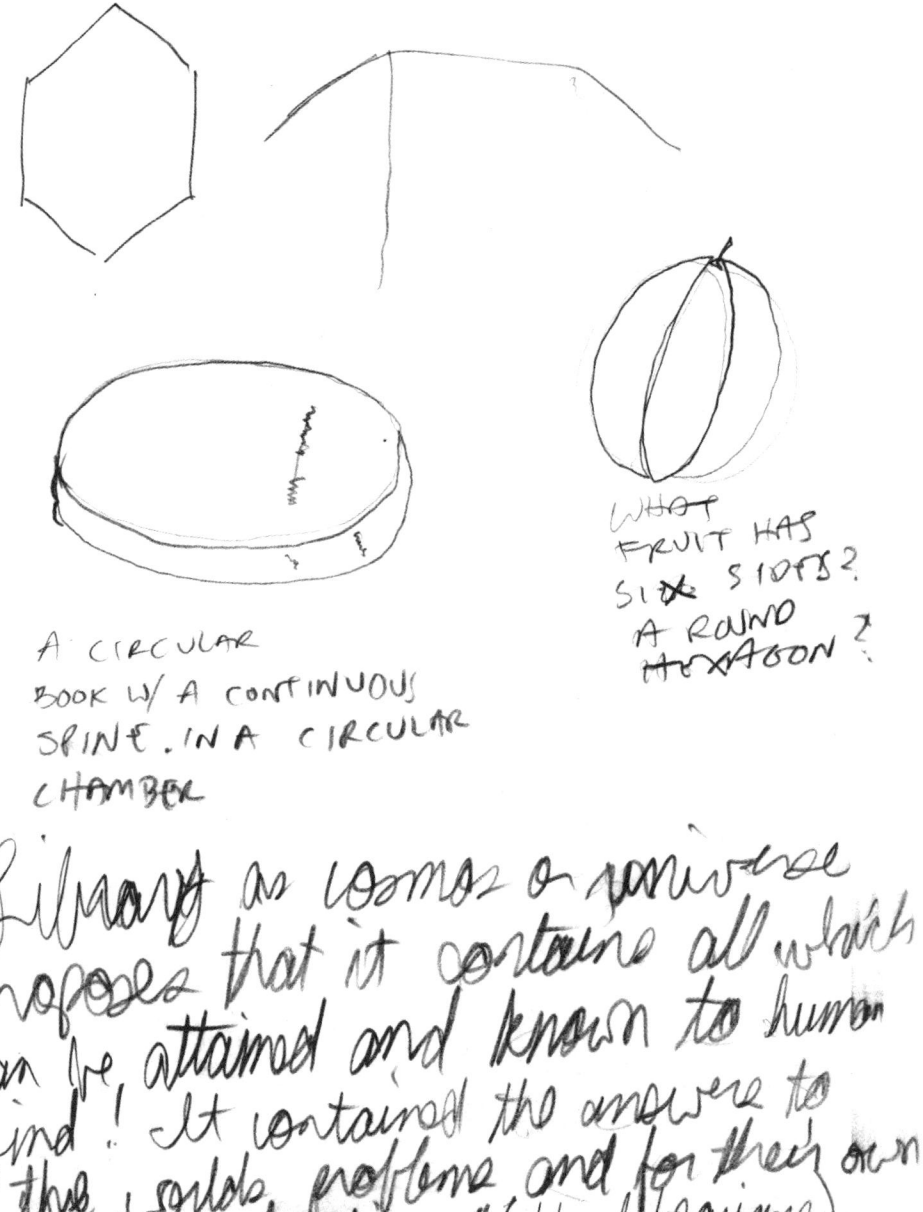

A CIRCULAR BOOK W/ A CONTINUOUS SPINE. IN A CIRCULAR CHAMBER

WHAT FRUIT HAS SIX SIDES? A ROUND HEXAGON?

Library as cosmos or universe proposes that it contains all which can be attained and known to human kind! It contained the answers to all the worlds problems and for their own personal "Vendications." (the librarians) It also contained prophecies and writings of all people yet to be as well as all lies and fantasies. Proposing that there is a truth contained in its infinite bounds.

These notes are taken from Jorge Luis Borges, *Selected Non-Fictions*, (ed.) Elliot Weinberger, New York 1999.

Jan Verwoert

The Expanded Working Field of Documentary Production

As a genre rich in tradition, documentary film in cinema, television, and at festivals has produced its own formats and accompanying discourses in film studies. In the past years, however, documentary forms of presentation have also gained increasing significance in the field of art. Currently, documentary aesthetics substantially characterizes the appearance of biennials and thematic shows claiming to depict, in art, the social realities of different societies, and to create a global political awareness in this way. In this context, documentary aesthetics has become a sort of *lingua franca* in that it promises to relate specific local realities in a globally comprehensible visual language. That this aesthetics is indeed able to keep its promise to a certain degree can be discerned in the profundity and above all the specificity that the debates on global issues have attained through the specificity of documentary images.

There are certainly reasons to be skeptical. The routines of the present-day exhibition business occasionally foster a naive form of social realism: Nonfiction is misunderstood as information, and art in a documentary format is judged merely by its content. Artists are treated as informants, and one expects to learn, through their art, things about the situation in their respective countries of origin. But this objection does not mean devaluating documentary practices in art across the board. Whether a work or an exhibition sheds light on the problems inherent to the documentary form of presentation in an appropriately complex manner or not, is a question that these practices formulate themselves, insofar as they create a need for debate and provide both the material and the criteria for this debate. The increase in documentary practices is one reason why delving in issues related to representational critique and identity politics is no longer a marginal phenomenon in art. Instead, it is at the center of contemporary exhibition practices, without becoming a matter of course. (The heated debate on the meaning

and purpose of the documentary in art is, after all, continuing.) To take this development seriously implies examining and discussing, time and again, whether and to what extent certain artistic positions or shows treat the potentials and problems of the documentary in a subtly differentiated way, or whether they just hawk topics and identity claims in a negative sense.

It is decisive, in this respect, not to grasp the increase in documentary approaches in art, as the frequently used and utterly tendentious term "documentarism" suggests, in the sense of a tendency, as a symptom of the zeitgeist, but as a positive expansion of the field of action of artistic practice. The art magazine *Texte zur Kunst* does not acknowledge the discourse-based power of artistic practice in the preface to its thematic issue "Documentarisms"[1]. It is seriously claimed here that the only reason artists choose documentary media is to evade their responsibility for the message of their work: the documentary image ultimately gives the enticing impression that reality was speaking for itself. This over-subtle interpretation of documentary practice as a naive strategy ignores a simple but crucial finding: The medium of documentary presentation has always been characterized precisely by bringing with it (to a certain extent) its own media-critical discourse. In this context, Paul Arthur has convincingly shown that, in the public sphere of Western media societies, the documentary traditionally functions as a forum for a recurring debate on the truth content of the respectively dominant mass media. (Just as the New Deal documentary appeared as a corrective to Hollywood movies in the United States in the 1930s, direct cinema of the 1960s reflected the new dispositive of television, while today's documentations correspond to and compete with the current dispositive of reality TV and the consumer culture of digital image production methods.)[2]

Documentary presentation is thus overcoded in a positive sense: The need for discussion is inscribed in it. Even when it turns into an empty gesture when exploited by the mass media, documentary presentation demands the critical judgment of its truth value. Today, the

weshalb die Auseinandersetzung mit Fragen der Repräsentationskritik und Identitätspolitik in der Kunst kein marginales Phänomen mehr darstellt, sie steht vielmehr im Mittelpunkt zeitgenössischer Ausstellungspraxis, ohne dabei selbstverständlich zu werden. (Der Streit um Sinn und Zweck des Dokumentarischen in der Kunst dauert schließlich an.) Diese Entwicklung ernst zu nehmen, heißt, immer wieder neu zu untersuchen und zu diskutieren, ob und inwiefern bestimmte künstlerische Positionen oder Ausstellungen differenziert mit den Potentialen und Problemstellungen des Dokumentarischen umgehen, oder ob sie im negativen Sinne einfach Themen und Identitätsbehauptungen kolportieren.

Entscheidend ist dabei, die Zunahme dokumentarischer Ansätze in der Kunst nicht, wie es der oft verwendete, von Grund auf tendenziöse Begriff „Dokumentarismus" nahe legt, im Sinne einer Tendenz als Symptom des Zeitgeistes zu begreifen, sondern als eine positive Erweiterung des Handlungsfeldes künstlerischer Praxis. Ebendiese Anerkennung der Diskurs-begründenden Kraft künstlerischer Praxis verweigert beispielsweise die Redaktion der Zeitschrift *Texte zur Kunst* im Vorwort ihres Themenheftes zu „Dokumentarismen"[1]. Allen Ernstes wird hier die Behauptung aufgestellt, KünstlerInnen wählten dokumentarische Medien nur, um sich aus der Verantwortung für die Aussage ihrer Arbeit zu stehlen: Das dokumentarische Bild erwecke schließlich auf verlockende Weise den Anschein, hier spräche die Realität für sich selbst. Diese spitzfindige Deutung dokumentarischer Praxis als naive Strategie übergeht einen einfachen aber wesentlichen Befund: Das Medium der dokumentarischen Darstellung zeichnet sich seit jeher genau dadurch aus, dass es seinen eigenen medienkritischen Diskurs (bis zu einem gewissen Grad) immer schon mit sich bringt. Paul Arthur hat in diesem Kontext überzeugend dargelegt, dass dem Dokumentarischen in der Öffentlichkeit westlicher Mediengesellschaften traditionell die Funktion zukommt, das Forum einer immer wieder neu erfolgenden Diskussion über den Wahrheitsgehalt des jeweils dominanten Massen-Mediums zu bilden. (So wie in den USA in den 30ern die New-Deal-Documentary als Korrektiv zum Hollywood-Kino auftrat,

ability and the need to discuss the authenticity of an image communicated as "real" is part of the media competence of every TV consumer. It is rather absurd to insinuate that artists choose precisely this medium because they shrink from responsibility and media-critical debate. The contrary conclusion is far more obvious: The increased examination of documentary means of presentation is not to be understood as an attempt to import the genre of documentary film into art, but as the will to tap the critical sensitivity inherent to the current media competence in dealing with documentary material for artistic practice.

Nevertheless, typical questions pertaining to the transgression of genre borders are inevitably raised: Is the debate on the documentary in art sufficiently profound? Does it not ack the required background, the knowledge that only the genre-specific discourse in the classical tradition of documentary film can provide? This may be true. But the lack of binding conventions can equally be grasped as a precondition for taking on new perspectives. Hence, the historically over-coded concept of the documentary is provocatively underdetermined the moment it is transferred to the context of art, especially because, as opposed to cinema, there is no institutionally founded authority that could prescribe an official definition of this concept. In a positive sense, this effects a *de-disciplining* of documentary practice. In a situation in which no one can say for sure what the notion of the documentary ultimately means, everyone is principally invited to propose what it could mean. Unsettled framework conditions *per se* do not guarantee innovative developments, but they do provoke more than unambiguously delimited and institutionally anchored discourses.

In this sense, arguments can be found in favor of the framework conditions of the art field.[3] Certain constraints that the more strongly conventionalized production conditions in the "professional" sphere of documentary film bring with them do not exist here. A film or video neednot have the format of a full-length cinema or TV film and result from a year-long production to comply with the standards. Therefore,

reflektiert das Direct Cinema der 60er das neue Dispositiv Fernsehen, so wie heute Dokumentationen mit dem aktuellen Dispositiv des Reality-TVs und der Konsumentenkultur digitaler Bildgenerierungsverfahren korrespondieren und konkurrieren.)[2]

Die dokumentarische Darstellung ist somit im positiven Sinne übercodiert: Der Diskussionsbedarf ist ihr eingeschrieben. Selbst dann noch, wenn sie in ihrer medialen Massenverwertung zur leeren Geste wird, verlangt die dokumentarische Darstellung nach der kritischen Beurteilung ihres Wahrheitswerts. Die Fähigkeit dazu und das Bedürfnis danach, die Authentizität eines als „echt" vermittelten Bildes zu diskutieren, gehört in diesem Sinne heute zur medialen Kompetenz jedes TV-Konsumenten. Die Unterstellung, KünstlerInnen wählten gerade dieses Medium aus Scheu vor Verantwortung und medienkritischer Diskussion, ist also denkbar absurd. Die gegenteilige Schlussfolgerung liegt weitaus näher: Die vermehrte Auseinandersetzung mit dokumentarischen Darstellungsmitteln wäre demnach nicht so sehr als Versuch zu verstehen, das Genre des Dokumentarfilms in die Kunst zu importieren, sondern als das Anliegen, die kritische Sensibilität, die der aktuellen Medien-Kompetenz im Umgang mit dokumentarischem Material innewohnt, für die künstlerische Praxis zu erschließen.

Dennoch stellen sich unweigerlich die für die Überschreitung von Genre-Grenzen typischen Fragen: Hat die Diskussion des Dokumentarischen in der Kunst die nötige Tiefe? Fehlt ihr dazu nicht der notwendige Hintergrund, das Wissen, das nur der Genre-spezifische Diskurs der klassischen Dokumentarfilmtradition bereitstellen kann? Das mag sein. Gerade das Fehlen verbindlicher Konventionen kann ebenso gut als Voraussetzung für die Erschließung neuer Perspektiven begriffen werden. Der historisch übercodierte Begriff des Dokumentarischen ist so im Moment seiner Übernahme in den Kunstkontext auf provokative Weise unterbestimmt, und zwar insbesondere deshalb, weil es im Gegensatz zum Kino in der Kunst keine Instanz gibt, die mit institutionell begründeter Autorität eine offizielle Definition dieses Begriffs vorgeben könnte. Im positiven Sinne bewirkt dies

short, sketchy and inexpensively produced videos can also be regarded as contributions of equal value in the art field. The art public is to a large extent sensitive toward conceptual points and thus acknowledges works as being worthy of discussion that are primarily concerned with taking concepts to an extreme and not with complying with production standards. The fact that in the art discourse, ever since the decisive transformations of the 1960s, the general examination of conceptual issues is given preference over more narrowly grasped genre and media-specific discourses, may also be a reason why the concept of the documentary in the art sphere is not necessarily associated with the medium of film alone. What characterizes the discourse on the documentary in art is, instead, the huge variety of media in which artists work in a documentary way. Multimedia installations with the characteristic of archives or other forms of spatially displaying researched material stand equally next to the classical media of photography, film, and video as formats of documentary presentation. As an alternative to cinema-like single projections, other forms of spatial staging also offer themselves when presenting film or video, e.g. multi-channel projection installation situations or monitor arrangements. In art, then, the concept of the "documentary" designates less a genre than a mixture of the most various practices. What they have in common is a shared media-critical sensitivity. Comparable approaches of methodically questioning documentary presentation are realized in different media. Therefore, the shared critical sensitivity in art forms the basis of an expanded discourse on the potentials and problems of the documentary. And precisely because of the wide variety of media, this discourse has become highly differentiated within a comparatively short period of time.

The positive expansion of the space of action in the working field of documentary practice outlined here, however, is hardly recognized in an adequate way in the theoretical treatment of this development (as the example of the denigrating analysis in *Texte zur Kunst* demonstrates). This mainly has to do with the fact that

eine *Entdisziplinierung* dokumentarischer Praxis. In einer Situation, in der niemand mit Sicherheit sagen kann, was der Begriff des Dokumentarischen letztlich bedeutet, steht im Prinzip jedem die Möglichkeit offen, einen Vorschlag zu machen, was er denn bedeuten könnte. Ungeklärte Rahmenbedingungen garantieren zwar nicht von sich aus innovative Entwicklungen, provozieren sie aber vielleicht eher als klar abgesteckte und institutionell verankerte Diskurse.

In diesem Sinne lassen sich auch Argumente für die Vorteile der Rahmenbedingungen des Kunstbereichs finden.[3] Bestimmte Zwänge, die die stärker konventionalisierten Produktionsbedingungen im „professionellen" Dokumentarfilmbereich mit sich bringen, existieren hier nicht. Ein Film oder Video muss kein abendfüllendes Kino- oder Fernsehformat besitzen und Ergebnis einer mehrjährigen Produktion sein, um dem Standard zu entsprechen. Auch kurze, skizzenhaft und unaufwendig produzierte Videos können deshalb im Kunstbereich als vollwertige Beiträge gelten. Die Kunstöffentlichkeit ist in weiten Bereichen für konzeptuelle Pointen sensibilisiert und erkennt infolgedessen auch Arbeiten als diskussionswürdig an, bei denen es primär um die Zuspitzung des Konzepts und nicht um die Erfüllung von Produktionsstandards geht. Der Umstand, dass im Kunstdiskurs seit den einschneidenden Transformationen der 60er Jahre den allgemeinen Auseinandersetzungen mit konzeptuellen Fragestellungen der Vorzug gegenüber enger gefassten Genre- oder medienspezifischen Debatten gegeben wird, mag zudem auch der Grund dafür sein, dass der Begriff des Dokumentarischen im Kunstbereich nicht notwendig allein mit dem Medium Film verbunden wird. Bezeichnend für den Dokumentardiskurs in der Kunst ist ja vielmehr gerade die große Bandbreite der Medien, in denen KünstlerInnen dokumentarisch arbeiten. Multimediale Installationen mit Archivcharakter oder andere Formen des räumlichen Displays von Recherche-Material stehen als Formate dokumentarischer Darstellung gleichberechtigt neben den klassischen Medien Fotografie, Film oder Video. Als Alternative zur Kinoähnlichen Einzelprojektion bieten sich bei der Präsentation von Film oder Video darüber immer

the significance of documentary film and video works is usually only discussed in terms of the conditions of their reception in the art context, and seldom in regard to the conditions of their production and circulation. It is certainly necessary to ask how the different viewing habits and expectations in the cinema and art contexts influence the perception of a film when a change of context occurs. The contextual analysis of the horizon of reception is based to a certain degree on the validity of traditional borders and framework conditions of two allegedly clearly distinguishable fields of cultural production (cinema and art), exactly that which interdisciplinary practice calls into question. Contextual analyses of context-expanding practices stand in their own way with their own concepts, when the issue is to describe the decisive dynamics of opening up the discourse, which is produced by the approach of working with documentary means of presentation in a genre-independent manner. From the viewpoint of the conditions of production and circulation, on the other hand, one quickly comes to the simple and fundamental diagnosis that, today, more is possible in the field of documentary practice than in earlier times. More works are circulating, and the increased interest prompts increased production.

One theoretical finding regarding the conditions of production and the production aesthetics of circulating documentary works is a *becoming-practical* of representation critique. Categorical representation critique (for example, Appropriation art of the 1980s or neo-conceptual institutional criticism of the early 1990s) has now turned into an immanent component of documentary practice, due to a widespread sensitivity of artistic producers toward the political quality of forms of representation, a practice in which assertions, images, displays, and cartographies relating to reality are methodically questioned while being produced. So this critique is no longer model-like and categorical, but immanent and practical. It risks making reference to social, political and historical reality, while simultaneously raising questions as to the ideological implications of the methods that allow this reference, and making an effort to for-

auch andere Formen der räumlichen Inszenierung, wie etwa installative Mehrkanalprojektions-Situationen oder Monitor-Arrangements, an. Der Begriff des „Dokumentarischen" benennt in der Kunst also weniger ein Genre als vielmehr eine Gemengelage unterschiedlichster Praktiken. Was diese verbindet, ist eine geteilte medienkritische Sensibilität. Vergleichbare Ansätze der methodischen Befragung dokumentarischer Darstellung werden in verschiedenen Medien realisiert. Somit wird die geteilte kritische Sensibilität in der Kunst zur Grundlage eines erweiterten Diskurses über die Potentiale und Problematiken des Dokumentarischen. Und gerade auch aufgrund der medialen Vielfalt hat sich dieser Diskurs innerhalb einer vergleichsweise kurzen Zeitspanne hochgradig ausdifferenziert.

Die hier skizzierte positive Erweiterung des Handlungsraums im Arbeitsfeld dokumentarischer Praxis findet jedoch in der theoretischen Aufarbeitung der Entwicklung kaum eine angemessene Anerkennung (wie das Beispiel der abwertenden Analyse von *Texte zur Kunst* zeigt). Dies liegt wohl vor allem daran, dass die Bedeutung dokumentarischer Film- oder Videoarbeiten zumeist nur in Bezug auf die Bedingungen ihrer Rezeption im Kunstkontext diskutiert wird und kaum je in Bezug auf die Bedingungen ihrer Produktion und Zirkulation. Sicherlich ist es notwendig, danach zu fragen, auf welche Weise die unterschiedlichen Sehgewohnheiten und Erwartungshaltungen im Kino- und Kunstkontext die Wahrnehmung eines Films im Falle eines Kontextwechsels beeinflussen. Die kontextuelle Analyse des Rezeptionshorizonts setzt dabei jedoch stets bis zu einem gewissen Grad die Gültigkeit der traditionellen Grenzen und Rahmenbedingungen zweier vermeintlich klar unterscheidbarer Felder kultureller Produktion (Kino und Kunst) voraus, auf deren Infragestellung interdisziplinäre Praxis ja gerade abzielt. Kontextuelle Analysen kontexterweiternder Praktiken stehen sich so mit ihren Begrifflichkeiten unter Umständen selbst im Weg, wenn es darum geht, die entscheidende Dynamik der Diskursöffnung zu beschreiben, die der Ansatz eines Genre-ungebundenen Arbeitens mit dokumentarischen Darstellungsmitteln produziert. Vom Standpunkt einer Betrachtung der

mulate alternatives. In order to reconstruct this development in an adequate way, then, one would have to learn to understand whether and how the parameters of artistic representation critique have changed and are still changing in the process of becoming practical.

1 Karin Gludovatz and Clemens Krümmel, "Nichts als die Wahrheit," *Texte zur Kunst* 51 (2003), p. 4–5.
2 See Paul Arthur, "Jargons of Authenticity (Three American Moments)," *Theorizing Documentary*, Michael Renov (ed.), New York/London 1993, p. 108–134.
3 I have attempted, in various contexts, to formulate arguments that justify and highlight the productive character of dealing with documentary practices in art. As a firm foundation for the interdisciplinary and cross-genre treatment of the documentary image, I regard a certain representation-critical sensitivity informed by critical theory as a common denominator in the practice of representatives of different disciplines and genres. See Jan Verwoert, "Dokumentation als künstlerische Praxis," *springerin* 3 (2003), p. 26–29. In addition, I see the debate on the concept of the archive in late 1980s art and the redefinition of the archive as a personal, pragmatic medium to organize documents in the art of the 1990s, e.g. the installations of Renée Green, as standing in a positive tradition of the debates on the politics of truth of the documentary, which in the past years has developed from delving in (archive-like) installations to an examination by means of filmic media. See Verwoert, "Research and Display. Of Transformations of Documentary Practice in Recent Art," *Untitled (Experience of Place)*, Gregor Neuerer (ed.), London 2003, p. 9–22.

Produktions- und Zirkulationsbedingungen kommt man dagegen schnell zu dem so einfachen wie grundlegenden Befund, dass im Bereich dokumentarischer Praxis heute mehr möglich ist als zuvor. Es zirkulieren mehr Arbeiten und das gesteigerte Interesse fördert eine vermehrte Produktion.

Ein theoretischer Befund, der sich dabei sowohl in Bezug auf die Produktionsbedingungen als auch mit Blick auf die Produktionsästhetik der zirkulierenden dokumentarischen Arbeiten feststellen lässt, ist ein *Praktischwerden* der Repräsentationskritik. Die kategorische Repräsentationskritik (etwa der Appropriation Art der 80er und der neokonzeptuellen Institutionskritik der frühen 90er) ist so durch eine allgemeine Sensibilisierung künstlerischer ProduzentInnen für die Politizität der Darstellungsform heute zum immanenten Bestandteil einer dokumentarischen Praxis geworden, in der realitätsbezogene Aussagen, Bilder, Displays und Kartografien im Vollzug ihrer Produktion methodisch befragt werden. Die Kritik ist somit nicht mehr modellhaft und kategorisch, sondern immanent und praktisch. Sie riskiert die Bezugnahme auf die soziale, politische und historische Wirklichkeit, fragt jedoch gleichzeitig nach den ideologischen Implikationen der Methoden, die diese Bezugnahme erlauben und bemüht sich, Alternativen zu formulieren. Um diese Entwicklung angemessen nachzuvollziehen, müsste man also vor allem verstehen lernen, ob und wie sich die Parameter der künstlerischen Repräsentationskritik im Prozess ihres Praktischwerdens verändert haben und noch verändern.

1 Karin Gludovatz und Clemens Krümmel: Nichts als die Wahrheit, in: *Texte zur Kunst* (2003), Nr. 51, S. 4–5.
2 Vgl. Paul Arthur: Jargons of Authenticity (Three American Moments), in: Michael Renov (Hg.): *Theorizing Documentary*, New York/London 1993, S. 108–134.
3 Ich habe in verschiedenen Zusammenhängen versucht, Argumente für die Berechtigung und den produktiven Charakter der Auseinandersetzung mit dokumentarischen Praktiken in der Kunst zu formulieren. Als eine tragfähige Grundlage für die Disziplinen und Genres übergreifende Beschäftigung mit dem dokumentarischen Bild sehe ich dabei eine bestimmte, durch kritische Theorie informierte repräsentationskritische Sensibilität, die bei VertreterInnen der verschiedenen Disziplinen und Genres den gemeinsamen Nenner ihrer Praxis bildet. Vgl. Jan Verwoert: Dokumentation

als künstlerische Praxis, in: *springerin* (2003), Band IX Heft 3, S. 26–29. Darüber hinaus sehe ich in der Auseinandersetzung mit dem Archivbegriff in der Kunst der späten 80er und der Neubestimmung des Archivs als persönlich pragmatischem Medium zur Organisation von Dokumenten in der Kunst der 90er, etwa in den Installationen von Renée Green, eine positive Tradition der Auseinandersetzung mit der Wahrheits-Politik des Dokumentarischen, die sich in den letzten Jahren zunehmend aus dem Bereich der (Archiv-ähnlichen) Installationen hin zu einer Beschäftigung mit filmischen Medien entwickelt hat. Vgl. Jan Verwoert: Research and Display. Of Transformations of Documentary Practice in Recent Art, in: Gregor Neuerer (Hg.): *Untitled (Experience of Place)*, London 2003, S. 9–22.

Domingo 1, 2001
color photograph, 80 x 80 cm

Domingo 2, 2001
color photograph, 80 x 80 cm

Vivre à Rio, je trouve que c'est un rêve. C'est si beau que même si tu es triste, tu ne t'effondres jamais en vivant à Rio. Il y a toujours quelque chose qui te fait vibrer. Voir et d'écouter la mer, c'est déjà merveilleux. Si tu viens ici à cinq heures du matin voir le soleil se lever, tu en restes émerveillée pour toute la journée…pour le reste de l'année, je trouve. Ca compense tout ce qui se passe ici, tout. Une fois, je revenais du collège, j'avais environ 14 ans. J'ai été violée et je suis tombée enceinte. J'ai eu une fille mais elle est née avec un problème. A huit mois elle est décédée. Tout ça c'est à cause de la violence: j'ai été violée, je suis tombée enceinte, je n'ai pas voulu avorter. Au septième mois sept mois de grossesse, j'ai de nouveau été violée, ça m'a causé des troubles et ma fille est morte. Je suis devenue stérile. J'ai seulement 20 ans et je ne peux plus avoir d'enfant. C'est pour ça que je veux être infirmière et faire des études de pédiatrie, pour voir. A la station-service où on travaille, on est inutiles. On est comme des prostituées. Moi, par exemple, j'ai deux filles, j'ai 17 ans et je dois payer mon loyer et toutes les factures. Je suis l'homme de la maison. Alors j'ai été obligée de travailler, pour ne pas tomber dans la prostitution, ne pas avoir de mauvaises fréquentations. Mais celles qui sont mentalement faibles et qui travaillent dans une station-service finissent par se prostituer. Elles se font des illusions. Elles pensent qu'un homme va s'arrêter avec une grosse voiture et va s'intéresser à elles. Il va rester avec elle un ou deux mois et va la quitter. Les gens disent: «C'est une jolie femme», mais ce n'est pas si facile, c'est difficile. Quand tu es riche, tu es raciste envers le pauvre. Tu penses n'avoir rien en commun avec lui, être meilleur. La majorité des gens pensent qu'il faut écraser ceux qui sont pauvres, qu'il faut les humilier. Ici, la discrimination est de 10% envers le noir, mais du riche envers le pauvre elle est de 90%. Ici, c'est très bien pour vivre mais tu dois faire très attention. Je pars travailler à cinq heures du matin. Quand je descends, il y a parfois des contrôles de police. Ils te mettent la main sur les seins, dans ton vagin pour pouvoir te fouiller. Parfois ils fouillent dans ton sac, prennent ton argent et disent qu'ils n'en ont pas vu. Même s'il ne fait que te toucher, c'est la pire des choses: tu te sens humiliée. Un type qui passe ses mains sur ta poitrine comme ça ! Tu es dégoûtée et tu ne peux rien dire. Une femme c'est sentimental, c'est sensible. Un homme non, il va te toucher intimement. Mais pour une femme, son corps c'est tout. Une femme ne supporte même pas qu'on lui effleure la jambe. Aujourd'hui, il y a beaucoup de femmes qui sont trafiquantes. J'ai une amie qui l'est, je n'ai pas honte de le dire. Je vois des amis avec qui j'étais à l'école et qui sont trafiquants et qui passent parfois à la télévision pour des histoires d'enlèvement. Je les vois en prison, je les vois morts. Alors tu perds ton innocence. Tu n'as rien à voir avec tout ça mais tu apprends. Tu n'as pas peur parce que tu as grandi avec eux, tu les connais, tu sais qu'ils sont comme toi. Le bandit est toujours celui qui a tort. Mais pour ceux qui vivent dans la favela et les connaissent...

La femme est sentimentale, 2001
10 min. video

... Le bandit, s'il te vole ta voiture, il ne va te tirer dessus que si tu réagis. Si tu le laisses prendre la voiture, il ne va rien te faire. D'accord, il vole ta voiture et ce n'est pas juste. Mais qu'il ne te tue pas, c'est déjà beaucoup. Si tu voles près d'une favela, tu meurs. Tu ne peux pas car tu dois respecter l'endroit où tu vis. Tu ne peux pas voler le pauvre qui est ton égal. Ceux qui habitent dans la favela ont la protection des bandits. Si tu te fais braquer et que tu en parles là-haut, ils vont descendre pour tuer la personne ou lui faire mal. Ils disent: «Volons, mais volons une banque ou alors faisons un rapt! Nous ne volerons pas nos semblables, les pauvres, mais volons ceux qui possèdent». Si tu voles dans une favela, tu meurs, tu prends une raclée. Tu perds la main. De la même manière qu'ils nous protègent, nous leur offrons une certaine protection. Si la police se pointe en bas, ça va arriver jusqu'en haut: «La police est là!». Ils sont immédiatement avertis. Mais quand la police arrive en haut, ils estiment que tout les habitants sont des bandits. Alors ils frappent, prennent les femmes par les cheveux. C'est comme ça, la police d'ici est violente. Et ils sont corrompus aussi. Dans la favela tu ne peux rien avoir de valeur. Tu ne peux pas avoir une chaîne hi-fi, un magnétoscope ou une télévision. un canapé neuf, tout ça tu ne peux pas l'avoir. Particulièrement si tu as perdu les factures. Et si tu ne les as pas, ils prennent tout ce qu'ils peuvent prendre. Ils mangent, fouillent dans tes affaires, cassent tout, même si tu n'as rien à voir avec tout ça. Alors ton mari se révolte: «Pourquoi ils prennent toutes ces choses que j'ai acheté pour ma femme? Alors je vais devenir bandit et ils auront affaire à moi». C'est une des choses qui fait la violence. Ils montent la favela vers 3 ou 4 heures du matin: «Allons tuer tout le monde!». Et si il y a quelqu'un à tuer, ils tuent. Dans certaines favela, il n'y a pas d'échanges de tirs. Ils tirent des feux d'artifice, les mecs s'enfuient dans les collines, où il y a beaucoup d'arbres où se cacher. Ils fuient mais ne tirent pas, car ils pensent aux habitants et aux amis avec qui ils ont grandi et sur qui ils ne voudraient pas qu'on tire. Le policier tire de loin, même s'il ne voit pas de bandit. Il tire même si personne ne lui tire pas dessus, et après il dit que ça a été un échange de tirs. Mais toi qui vis dans la favela, tu n'as vu aucun tir descendre, mais seulement monter, et tu retrouves le mur de ta maison troué. L'unique différence entre le policier et le bandit, c'est que le bandit s'assume: «Je suis bandit, je suis mauvais, ne t'approche pas de moi». Le policier: «Je suis bien gentil, si tu as un problème, tu m'en parles». Mais en réalité, tu vois qu'il n'est rien de tout ça, qu'il ne vaut rien, qu'il ment, qu'il est corrompu. Il est faux, il a deux visages. Chacun a son mauvais côté. Un bon policier, ça existe, il y aura un moment où il t'aidera. Le bandit, il y a un moment ou il t'aide, un autre ou il te piège. Le policier, c'est la même chose. Si tu n'es pas la femme d'un bandit et si tu vis en ville, il te traitera bien. Dans la favela, on est défendus par les bandits et en ville, par la police.

La femme est sentimentale, 2001
10 min. video

Gerald Raunig

The Document as Present Becoming

I. Exploitation and Devaluation of the Political

The general eagerness to archive and the compulsion to document are not exactly new elements in art (history). What is necessarily associated with this are the problematic moments of identification (of the Other, for example, in the different periods of European colonial rule), of exclusion (e.g., of female artists from the canon of the museum), and of the affirmation of power, property, and discipline. For several centuries the issue in the delicate field of artistic documentation and commentary of political movements has also been the decontextualization, historization, appropriation, and neutralization of the political.

As Michel Foucault and Gilles Deleuze have emphasized in their elaborations on the concepts of disciplinary societies and the society of control, there is no linear, historical movement from the first phenomenon to the second. The functions and effects of documentation mentioned above still prevail to a certain extent today, but they are intermingled with new aspects. If, in earlier times, the practice of documenting was used as a means of identification, archiving, and discipline, the "ideal" future subject of control no longer needs to be identified, disciplined, and documented from the outside; control is internalized within the setting of a governmental society of control. In this context, the present boom in (artistic) documentation could also be misunderstood as the death throes of a genre coming to an end and soon no longer required. With her theorem of "documentality", however, Hito Steyerl has shown how the document increasingly functions as an aspect of governing by means of truth; the documentary production of truth can even turn into rule.[1] So, in the logic of the governmental spectacle, what is at stake is by no means the disappearance of documentation as an instrument of rule, but rather an increasingly rapid exploitation of the political as well as its simultaneous devalua-

tion through critical strategies in artistic documentation.

The video, *Get Rid of Yourself* (2002), by the Bernadette Corporation (who are in their own words a "fictitious corporation") is an example of this simultaneity of exploitation and devaluation of the political in documentation. As an intelligently constructed, formally extremely attractive game of confusion concerned with the issues of violence, improvisation, chaos, opacity, body politics, black blocs, and riots during the G8 summit in Genoa in the summer of 2001, *Get Rid of Yourself* on the one hand presents scenes of the unrepresentable event of post-national insurrection in Genoa[2], and on the other, the critical self-reflection of – well, whose?

Bernadette Corporation, *Get Rid of Yourself*, 2003

After a long and varied series of accounts, reflections, theorizations, and documentary reports from the perspective of militant protesters, the next sequence depicts the actress Chloë Sevigny rehearsing a text apparently written as a script for an anti-globalization activist. Following the propaganda and over-affirmation of autonomous-militant poetry, it is not the activists of Genoa who self-critically discuss the problems of their practice, which was undoubtedly plunged into a deep crisis after Genoa and 9/11, but instead an actress who, as the mouthpiece of the Bernadette Corporation, problematizes the language of Genoa with her attempts to learn the text. First, the affirmation of militancy without comment, then, the critique of the language of militancy as stereotyped, well-rehearsed, and adhering to a script: both are

mentation als Herrschaftsinstrument, sondern eher um eine immer schnellere Verwertbarkeit des Politischen wie zugleich auch um dessen Entwertung durch kritizistische Strategien im künstlerischen Dokumentarismus.

Das Video *Get rid of yourself* (2002) der Gruppe Bernadette Corporation (Selbstbezeichnung „fiktives Unternehmen") ist neben vielem anderen auch ein Beispiel für diese Gleichzeitigkeit von Verwertbarkeit und Entwertung des Politischen in der Dokumentation. Als intelligent konstruiertes, formal äußerst attraktives Verwirrspiel um die Fragen von Gewalt, Improvisation, Chaos, Opazität, Körperpolitik, Black Blocs und Riots während des G8-Gipfels in Genua im Sommer 2001, präsentiert *Get rid of yourself* einerseits Szenen des unrepräsentierbaren Ereignisses der postnationalen Insurrektion in Genua[2], andererseits die kritische Selbstreflexion des – ja wessen eigentlich?

Nach einer langen und abwechslungsreichen Reihe von Beschreibungen, Reflexionen, Theoretisierungen und dokumentarischen Berichten aus der Sicht militanter DemonstrantInnen wird in der darauf folgenden Sequenz die Star-Schauspielerin Chloë Sevigny gezeigt, wie sie versucht, einen Text einzuüben, der offenbar als Skript für eine Antiglobalsierungsaktivistin geschrieben wurde. Nach Propaganda und Überaffirmation autonom-militanter Lyrik kommen nicht die AktivistInnen von Genua zur Sprache, um selbstkritisch die Probleme ihrer Praxis zu diskutieren, die zweifelsohne mit Genua und 9/11 in eine schwere Krise geraten sind. Als Sprachrohr von Bernadette Corporation problematisiert stattdessen eine Schauspielerin mit ihren Versuchen der Aneignung des Textes die Konstruktion der Sprache von Genua. Kommentarlose Affirmation von Militanz, dann Kritik der Sprache der Militanz als formelhaft, einstudiert, einem Skript folgend: Beides ist für sich stehend interessant, wird aber als völlig voneinander getrennte Strategie verfolgt, und genau diese Trennung führt zum parallelen Effekt der Ver- und Entwertung des Politischen.

Eine sinnvolle Funktion von ästhetischer Kritik im Zusammenhang politischer Bewegungen kann darin bestehen, dass durch Brüche, Ver-

interesting on their own, but they are pursued as entirely independent strategies – and precisely this separation results in the parallel effect of utilizing and devaluing the political.

Breaks, alienation, and distancing, which make it possible to pose questions to the movement, can make sense in the context of political movements. However, where these and similar means are used in the field of art to criticize the alleged substantialisation of authenticity in political movements or the stereotypical nature of their languages, for example, and where this criticism of the activists comes *from the outside*, the method obtains a strange cultural-pessimistic touch. At a presentation of the video in Vienna, Antek Walczak emphasised that the Bernadette Corporation was not interested in an external viewpoint. But in the end, this view from the outside reproduces the common dichotomous clichés: in the case of *Get Rid of Yourself,* not the totally hackneyed dichotomy of Robocops on the one side and the Tute Bianche[3] on the other, but of rioting autonomous squatters (good) and 1968-inspired peace activists (bad). The borders of these identities seem like communities or generations sealed off to the outside.

If one thing has characterized the practice of post-national insurrection in the anti-globalization protests of this decade, it is the tendency to dissolve such identities. Against the background of utilizing the political, however, this strategy of dichotomisation is successful: by linking documentation and fiction, the Bernadette Corporation succeeds in translating the radical chic of the construction called black bloc into their video and thus bringing it to the (alternative) art market in order to be exploited. At the same time, an endless loop is created that critically devaluates political activism. Perhaps it is also this devaluation of the political that allows it to be exploited in the first place.

II. Representation of the Unrepresentable

Also within the context of the G8 summit in Genoa, the Tute Bianche lead to the Disobbedienti. Oliver Ressler's video, *Disobbedienti* (2002),

fremdung und Distanzierung eine Öffnung von Fragen an die Bewegung erreicht wird. Wo allerdings im Feld der Kunst mit diesen oder ähnlichen Mitteln Kritik geübt wird, etwa an der vermeintlichen Substanzialisierung von Authentizität in politischen Bewegungen oder eben an der Formelhaftigkeit ihrer Sprachen, und wo diese Kritik *von außen* gegen die AktivistInnen gewendet wird, bekommt die Methode auch einen eigenartig kulturpessimistischen Touch. Wie Antek Walczak bei einer Präsentation des Videos in Wien betonte, ging es Bernadette Corporation um eine externe Sicht, doch am Ende reproduziert dieser Blick von außen die gängigen und dichotomen Klischees: im Fall von *Get rid of yourself* zwar nicht jenes völlig abgedroschene zwischen Robo-Cops und Tute Bianche[3], sondern das von randalierenden, autonomen HausbesetzerInnen (gut) auf der einen, und friedensbewegten 1968er-PazifistInnen (schlecht) auf der anderen Seite. Die Grenzen dieser Identitäten scheinen wie Communities oder Generationen zu sein, die nach außen abgeschlossen sind.

Wenn eines die Praxis der postnationalen Insurrektion in den Antiglobalisierungsprotesten dieses Jahrzehnts prägt, dann ist es die Tendenz zur Auflösung solcher Identitäten. Im Zeichen der Verwertung des Politischen ist diese Strategie der Dichotomisierung aber erfolgreich: Bernadette Corporation gelingt es bei aller Qualität der Verkettung von Dokumentarischem und Fiktionalem, den Radical Chic des Konstrukts namens Black Bloc in ihr Video zu übersetzen und damit der Verwertung im (alternativen) Kunstmarkt zuzuführen. Zugleich entsteht eine kritische Endlosschleife, die den politischen Aktivismus kritizistisch entwertet. Und vielleicht ist es auch gerade diese *Ent*wertung des Politischen, die jene *Ver*wertung erst möglich macht.

II. Repräsentation des Unrepräsentierbaren

Ebenfalls im Umfeld des G8-Gipfels in Genua gingen aus den Tute Bianche die Disobbedienti hervor. Oliver Resslers Video *Disobbedienti* (2002) thematisiert die Entstehungsgeschichte, die politischen Grundlagen und die Aktionsformen dieser Bewegung anhand von Gesprächen mit sieben

deals with the origin, the political principles, and the forms of action of this movement, based on conversations with seven people involved. It thus documents the collective practice of civil resistance and disobedience that — originating in the sensational appearances of the Tute Bianche — propagated an opening of the strategy of spectacularity and effected an increase from just a few protagonists to a broad movement of resistance. For a period of time and despite government repression, this opening seemed to succeed, if one takes the successful action of dismantling a deportation camp in Bologna in January 2002 shown in the video as an example. But it remains unclear, how the "unrepresentable multitude" conjured up in such contexts is to be created, when predominantly male self-representations of brute force intrude into all the images, thus underpinning an identitarian historiography in which the Disobbedienti and their past as Tute Bianche are staged as the roots of an arising broader movement.

Oliver Ressler and Dario Azzellini, *Disobbedienti*, 2002

The video as such, however, to a certain extent reproduces the (self-)representation of that which claims to be unrepresentable. The strategy, which Oliver Ressler already deployed in his earlier works, is mainly that of counter-information: experts of a little-known minority practice present themselves and their political objectives. In the case of the Disobbedienti, five men and two women make a very convincing appearance and seem to master the complex concepts of post-operaism, post-Fordism, post-

Beteiligten. Es dokumentiert damit eine kollektive Praxis des zivilen Widerstands, des Ungehorsams, die — aus den aufsehenerregenden Auftritten der Tute Bianche hervorgegangen — eine Öffnung der Strategie der Spektakularität und der Forcierung einiger weniger ProtagonistInnen hin zu einer breiten Bewegung des Widerstands propagierte. Diese Öffnung schien trotz staatlicher Repression einige Zeit zu gelingen, betrachtet man etwa die im Video dargestellte gelungene Aktion der Demontage des Abschiebelagers in Bologna im Jänner 2002. Unklar bleibt jedoch, wie die in solchen Zusammenhängen beschworene „nicht repräsentierbare Multitude" entstehen soll, wenn sich vor allem männliche Brachial-Selbstrepräsentationen in alle möglichen Bilder drängen, die eine identitaristische Geschichtsschreibung forcieren, in der die Disobbedienti sich und ihre Vergangenheit als Tute Bianche als Wurzel breiterer Bewegungsansätze inszenieren.

Das Video als solches doppelt allerdings in gewisser Weise das Problem der (Selbst-)Repräsentation dessen, was sich selbst als nicht repräsentierbar wähnt. Die Strategie, die Oliver Ressler schon in früheren Arbeiten wählte, ist hauptsächlich die der Gegeninformation: ExpertInnen einer wenig bekannten, minoritären Praxis präsentieren sich selbst und ihre politischen Ziele. Im Fall der Disobbedienti sind es fünf Männer und zwei Frauen, die sehr überzeugend auftreten und die komplexen Konzepte des Postoperaismus, Postfordismus, Poststrukturalismus und „Empireismus" und deren Popularisierung noch besser zu beherrschen scheinen als deren Miterfinder Antonio Negri selbst. Genau diese Strategie der Klarheit von ideologischen Standpunkten ist manchmal sicherlich notwendig, sowohl auf der Bühne des politischen Aktivismus wie auf der Bühne der dokumentarischen Repräsentation. Im Fall einer Praxis, die sich auf zapatistische und deleuzianische, also nicht-repräsentationistische Hintergründe beruft, wären komplexere, formal wie inhaltlich heterogenere Ansätze jedoch adäquater. Wo *Get rid of yourself* zu sehr als Blick von außen angelegt ist, hätte *Disobbedienti* eine gewisse Distanzierung und damit implizite oder explizite Problematisierung von Fragen der Repräsentation nicht schaden können.

structuralism, and Empire-ism as well as their popularization even better than the co-inventor of these concepts, Antonio Negri. This strategy of clarifying ideological standpoints is certainly necessary at certain points in time, both on the stage of political activism and on that of documentary representation. In the case of a practice referring to Zapatist and Deleuzian, i.e. non-representational, backgrounds, more complex and heterogeneous approaches in terms of form and content would be more adequate. While the approach of *Get Rid of Yourself* is dominated too much by a view from the outside, *Disobbedienti* could have done with a certain distance and thus an implicit or explicit problematization of issues relating to representation.

At this point, a difference in terms of the "target groups" of the two videos must be mentioned: while the Bernadette Corporation produces for the field of art, albeit for persons in this field who are interested in politics, Oliver Ressler's aim is to disseminate his counter-information in the political field, where complicated aesthetic issues deriving from expert debates come up against limiting factors. In activist contexts, the effect of the video could indeed be that through Ressler's strategy of affirmation, of emphatic visualization without commentary, and of the reduction of complexity, the *actual weakness* of the *Disobbedienti* in terms of representation is brought up: the fact that they do not, although they claim otherwise, question the movement terms of to necessary failure and ever new becoming. Outside the field of art, the double impossibility of representing the unrepresentable, both terms of to the political representation of the multitude and its visual representation in the video, may have been even more recognizable for the audience of *Disobbedienti*.

III. Becoming-activism of the Documentary

In her essay, *The Articulation of Protest*[4], Hito Steyerl addressed a similar twofold problem: the meaning of "articulation" is ambiguous. On the symbolic level, it designates the verbalization and visualization of political protest, but also refers to the concatenation, internal organiza-

An dieser Stelle ist allerdings eine Differenzierung in Bezug auf die „Zielgruppen" der beiden verschiedenen Videos festzuhalten: Während Bernadette Corporation für das Kunstfeld produzieren, wiewohl für politisch interessierte AkteurInnen desselben, will Oliver Ressler seine Gegeninformation auch ins politische Feld verbreiten, wo vertrackte Fragen aus ästhetischen Fachdiskussionen an ihre Grenzen stoßen. Zugleich könnte in aktivistischen Zusammenhängen durchaus der Effekt entstehen, dass durch Resslers Strategie der Affirmation, des kommentarlosen und dennoch empathischen Sichtbarmachens, ja der Komplexitätsverengung, in der Repräsentation per Video gerade die *reale Schwäche* der Disobbedienti aufgeworfen wird: ihr Nichtentsprechen in Bezug auf das notwendige Scheitern und immer aufs neue Werden der von ihnen selbst betonten andauernden Selbstbefragung der Bewegung. Die doppelte Unmöglichkeit, das Unrepräsentierbare zu repräsentieren, sowohl in der – politischen – Vertretung der Multitude, als auch in ihrer visuellen Darstellung im Video, mag gerade außerhalb des Kunstfeldes für das Publikum von *Disobbedienti* besser erkennbar geworden sein.

III. Aktivismus-Werden des Dokumentarischen

In ihrem Essay zur *Artikulation des Protestes*[4] hat Hito Steyerl ein ähnlich zweifach gelagertes Problem aufgeworfen: „Artikulation", vor allem in seiner englischen Wortbedeutung zweideutig, meint auf der Ebene der Symbole die Verbalisierung und Verbildlichung des politischen Protests, andererseits aber auch Verkettung, innere Organisation und Gliederung der Bewegung. Steyerl beschreibt beide Ebenen als Montagen, als Zusammenstellungen in Form inhaltlicher Ein- und Ausschließungen, von Prioritäten und blinden Flecken. Genau diese blinden Flecken analysiert sie anhand der Indymedia-Produktion *Showdown in Seattle* (1999), die anlässlich der Proteste gegen die WTO in Seattle noch während der Manifestationen gedreht und geschnitten wurde. Produktionsweise wie auch Ergebnis entsprächen paradoxerweise der Fertigungskette der kritisierten Corporate Media, der Mythos der Information in

tion and structure of the movement. Steyerl describes both levels as montages, as compilations in the form of content-related inclusions and exclusions, of priorities and blind spots. She analyzes precisely these blind spots using the Indymedia production, *Showdown in Seattle* (1999), shot and edited during the protests against the WTO in Seattle. Both the mode of production and the result correspond — paradoxically — to the criticized chain of production of corporate media; the myth of information in mainstream media correlates with Indymedia's counter-information. The result is a strange "voice of the people", an addition of voices that "in part contradict each other in a radical way, e.g., those of environmentalists and unionists, various minorities, feminist groups, etc."[5]

As the first two video examples have already revealed, it is certainly a recurring challenge, when representing movements and forms of protest, to neither capture and thus bring to a halt their flowing heterogeneity in filmic representation, nor to conceal their contradictions in the form of a pseudo-synergetic addition. Steyerl rightly criticizes the naïve attitude of the pioneers of the globalization-critical protests and the beginnings of Indymedia's media activism. By juxtaposing the two-and-a-half-hour Seattle documentary with the self-critical (and, in my opinion, narcissistic) strategy of Godard and Mieville in *Ici et ailleurs* (1974), Steyerl asks whether the addition of the Deleuzian AND is not totally blind and therefore instead a process of subtraction in which contradictions and oppositions are by no means mediated but rather exclude each other.

But a differentiation needs to be made here. Firstly, between political movement and moving pictures: what Steyerl presents as intertwined — the montage of the film and the montage of the movement — does not function as analogously as it may seem. Insofar as it insists on an oppositional truth as unbroken counter-information, the filmic representation of heterogeneity indeed threatens to homogenize this heterogeneity, to create a filmic totality that, despite of its opposite intention, generates effects resembling those of the attacked spectacle machine. In

Mainstream-Medien korreliere mit der Gegeninformation bei Indymedia. Und heraus käme eine seltsame „Stimme des Volkes" (*the voice of the people*), die Addition von Stimmen, die „einander politisch teilweise radikal widersprechen, etwa die von Umweltschützern und Gewerkschaften, verschiedenen Minderheiten, feministischen Gruppen etc."[5]

Wie schon die ersten beiden Videobeispiele zeigen, ist es zweifellos eine wiederkehrende Herausforderung bei der Darstellung von Bewegungen und Protestformen, weder ihre fließende Heterogenität in filmischer Repräsentation auf zu bestimmte Weise *fest-*, und damit *an*zuhalten, noch ihre Widersprüche als pseudo-synergetische Addition zu verschleiern. Steyerl kritisiert zu Recht die naive Haltung der PionierInnen der globalisierungskritischen Proteste und der Anfänge des Medienaktivismus bei Indymedia. In Gegenüberstellung der zweieinhalbstündigen Seattle-Doku und der selbstkritischen (wie für meinen Geschmack auch selbstverliebten) Strategie von Godard und Mieville in *Ici et ailleurs* (1974) fragt Steyerl, ob die Addition des Deleuze'schen UND nicht völlig blind und daher eher ein Vorgang der Subtraktion wäre, in der Widersprüche und Gegensätze mitnichten vermittelt, sich vielmehr gegenseitig ausschließen würden.

Hier muss aber in der Tat unterschieden werden; zunächst zwischen politischer Bewegung und bewegten Bildern: Was bei Steyerl ineinander verflochten präsentiert wird, die Montage des Films und die Montage der Bewegung, funktioniert nicht ganz so analog, wie es scheint. In der filmischen Repräsentation der Heterogenität besteht — so sie als ungebrochene Gegeninformation auf einer oppositionellen Wahrheit insistiert — tatsächlich die Gefahr einer Homogenisierung dieser Heterogenität, der Erzeugung einer filmischen Totalität, die trotz gegensätzlicher Intention ähnliche Effekte erzeugt wie die angegriffene Spektakelmaschine. In Bezug auf das aktivistische Indymedia-Beispiel von Seattle wäre allerdings darauf hinzuweisen, dass gegenhegemoniale Bilder von Wider- und Aufständen nicht fundamentalkritisch abgekanzelt werden können, nur weil sie CineastInnen zu wenig reflektiert sind. Die notwendigerweise ebenso spontane wie prekäre

terms of the activist Indymedia example of Seattle, it should be pointed out that counter-hegemonic images of resistance and riots cannot simply be denigrated in a fundamentally critical way, just because they are not reflected enough for cineastes. The necessarily spontaneous and precarious production of images of an uprising is a form that engenders specific and structurally-dependent problems, albeit in a totally different way, as does the auteur film, no matter how reflected and aesthetically ambitious it is. In this respect, Steyerl's criticism draws a comparison between things that cannot be compared; it can, however, be made constructive in that it can be used to advance the development of documentary practices and the media-activist discourse. In terms of the concatenation of the movement, though, it is at best a current in which there is nothing a montage could be created of and therefore nothing that can be added together. Just like the Deleuzian AND sweeps away all relations, the issue, here, is not that of an arbitrary addition (or subtraction), but of a movement whose parts can only be depicted, that is represented, as such *ex post*. On the levels of organization and representation Hito Steyerl's question emerges to ask what one would think, "if nationalists, protectionists, anti-Semites, conspiracy theorists, Nazis, religious persons, and reactionaries joined the chain of equivalencies at the anti-globalization protests"[6].

I do not want to play down this evident problem most contemporary protests are faced with, but the question of certain positions possibly joining in, and, even before that, the question of mediating contradictions, only poses itself within the rigid frame of a dialectical method intent on bringing existing elements of a movement into a relationship — but not in the Deleuzian sense of concatenation. The fact that anyone with or without a (revolutionary or reactionary) banner can march along in a demonstration does not necessarily have to do with what Deleuze called *becoming* revolutionary. Deleuze's philosophy attempts to set against the EST (French for "is" as a placeholder for "being") an ET (French for "and" as a reference to "becoming"), and this is not philosophical — and certain-

Produktion von Bildern des Aufstands ist eine Form, die genauso spezifische und strukturell bedingte Probleme erzeugt wie – in ganz anderer Weise – die des AutorInnenfilms, sei er noch so reflektiert und ästhetisch anspruchsvoll. Dementsprechend vergleicht Steyerls Kritik zwar Unvergleichbares, ist aber als konstruktiv insofern brauchbar zu machen, als damit eine Weiterentwicklung der dokumentarischen Praxen und des medienaktivistischen Diskurses befördert werden kann.

Bei der Verkettung der Bewegung handelt es sich dagegen im besten Fall um einen Strom, bei dem es nichts zu montieren, und daher auch nichts zu addieren gibt. Wie das Deleuze'sche UND alle Relationen mit sich fortreißt, geht es auch hier nicht um beliebige Addition (oder Subtraktion), sondern um eine Bewegung, deren Glieder erst *ex post* als solche dargestellt, also repräsentiert werden können. Erst auf den Ebenen der Organisation und Repräsentation stellt sich Hito Steyerls Frage, was davon zu halten sei, „wenn sich auf den Antiglobalisierungsdemos Nationalisten, Protektionisten, Antisemiten, Verschwörungstheoretiker, Nazis, Religiöse und Reaktionäre problemlos in die Kette der Äquivalenzen einreihen"[6]. Nicht dass ich dieses evidente Problem der meisten kontemporären Proteste nivellieren wollte, aber die Frage eines möglichen Ausschlusses gewisser Positionen und, vorher noch, der Vermittlung von Widersprüchen, stellt sich eben nur im festen Rahmen einer dialektischen Methode, die vorhandene Bewegungselemente in eine Beziehung bringen will, nicht aber im Deleuze'schen Denken von Verkettung. Dass irgendwer mit oder ohne (revolutionärem oder reaktionärem) Plakat in einer Demo mitmarschiert, muss nicht notwendigerweise mit dem, was Deleuze revolutionär *werden* nennt, zu tun haben. Deleuzes Philosophie versucht dem EST (franz. für „ist" als Platzhalter für „sein") ein ET (franz. für „und" als Hinweis auf ein „Werden") entgegenzustellen, und das ist keine philosophische – und schon gar keine mathematische – Spielerei, sondern ein Konzept, das die Logik von Identität und Repräsentation durch ein Spiel von Differenz und Wiederholung ersetzen will. „Das UND ist weder das eine noch das andere, es ist

ly not mathematical — frivolity, but a concept aimed at replacing the logic of identity and representation with a play of difference and repetition. "AND is neither one thing nor the other, it's always in-between, between two things; it's the borderline, there's always a border, a line of flight or flow, only we don't see it, because it's the least perceptible of things. And yet it's along this line of flight that things come to pass, becomings evolve, revolutions take shape."[7]

On the other hand, the difference between movement and mass, the lack of explicit and coordinated political demands, as well as resolved and unresolvable contradictions, are not only ingredients of spontaneous political movements, but also the basics of a long refined technique of denying these movements' legitimacy and seriousness. The shapeless and formless mass has been an element of reactionary propaganda for centuries: the chaotic-anarchic aspect was the object of theoretical-polemical aggression in Hegel's interpretation of the French Revolution, as it was in the many bourgeois and dogmatically Marxist writers who branded the Parisian Commune as "Hetzmasse" (hunting mass) — to use a term from Elias Canetti, who was one of the few capable of countering the negative concept of mass with a positive one.

To describe the mass less as a "hunting mass" than as a flow and a line of flight, less as *form*less than noncon*form*ist, means to not constantly threaten the war machine with re-territorialization, not to let it become an instrument of the state apparatus, and at the same time to welcome the unruliness of its deterritorializations.[8] The issue cannot be a "trouble-free addition of political desires", but it can also not be the concept of movement that makes an underlying and fundamental sense its prerequisite, a sense fitting together all its components to an identity and thus making it coherent and representable.

Only by asserting a new paradigm can that of representation be broken. Instead of the paradigm of identity and representation in a striated space, the paradigm of event and muliplicity unfolds in a smooth space. Here, the images, signs, and statements do not serve to represent or document objects and the world, but to make

immer zwischen den beiden, es ist die Grenze, es gibt immer eine Grenze, eine Flucht- oder Stromlinie, nur sieht man sie nicht, weil sie das Unsichtbarste ist. Und doch spielen sich die Dinge, die Werden auf dieser Fluchtlinie ab, zeichnen sich hier die Revolutionen ab."[7]

Andererseits: Uneinheitlichkeit von Bewegung und Masse, das Fehlen von expliziten und abgestimmten politischen Forderungen, nicht aufgehobene und nicht aufhebbare Widersprüche, das sind nicht nur die Ingredienzien spontaner politischer Bewegungen, sondern auch die Grundlagen einer lange verfeinerten Technik, diesen Bewegungen vor allem die Legitimität und Seriosität abzusprechen. Die gestalt- und formlose Masse ist schon seit Jahrhunderten Bestandteil reaktionärer Propaganda: Das Chaotisch-Anarchische war ebenso schon Gegenstand theoretisch-polemischer Aggression bei Hegels Interpretation der Französischen Revolution wie bei den vielen bürgerlichen wie auch dogmatisch-marxistischen Autoren, die die Pariser Commune als *Hetzmasse* brandmarkten — um hier den Begriff Elias Canettis zu übernehmen, der als einer unter Wenigen dem negativen Begriff der Masse einen positiven entgegenzusetzen hatte.

Masse weniger als Hetzmasse denn als Strom und Fluchtlinie, weniger als *formlos* denn als nonkon*form* zu beschreiben, heißt, die Kriegsmaschine nicht ständig mit Reterritorialisierung zu bedrohen, sie nicht zum Instrument eines Staatsapparats werden zu lassen und gleichzeitig die Wildheit ihrer Deterritorialisierungen zu begrüßen.[8] Es kann sich nicht um eine „problemlose Addition politischer Begehren" drehen, genau so wenig aber auch um ein Konzept von Bewegung, das ihr einen grundgelegten und grundlegenden Sinn voraussetzt, der alle ihre Teile in eine Identität zusammenspannt und damit auch kohärent und repräsentierbar macht.

Erst durch die Forcierung eines neuen Paradigmas wird jenes der Repräsentation durchbrochen. Statt des Paradigmas von Identität und Repräsentation im gekerbten Raum entfaltet sich im glatten Raum das Paradigma von Ereignis und Mannigfaltigkeit. Hier fungieren die Bilder, Zeichen und Aussagen nicht, um Objekte, um die Welt zu repräsentieren oder zu dokumentieren,

the world happen. Maurizio Lazzarato highlighted the strategic role of images, signs and statements in the context of Seattle 1999, addressed by Hito Steyerl, as follows: "They contribute to making that which is possible evolve and to its realization."[9] The arrangement of signs does not have the effect of solving problems (also not the problem posed by the addition of contradictions), but of opening up possibilities. By inventing and enunciating the slogan, "Another world is possible", a possibility is opened up that can become a reality.

In this context, *Showdown in Seattle* becomes a line in an event that actualizes itself in the concatenation of the bodies as well as the slogans, the Internet communication, the images, and the enunciations of the Indymedia video.[10]

Another concept of documentation is thus also created within the frame of a type of media activism that no longer limits its function to the documentation of political movements, but takes place in the becoming-activism of the documentary. The need to document within this paradigm can no longer be denigrated as the compulsion to document or as documentality; it is, instead, the need to document as present becoming.

---

[1] Hito Steyerl, "Documentarism as Politics of Truth," http://republicart.net/disc/representations/steyerl03_en.htm 2003 [04/10/05].
[2] On the concept of "post-national insurrection" see Gerald Raunig, *Kunst und Revolution. Künstlerischer Aktivismus im langen 20. Jahrhundert*, Vienna 2005, p. 51–55.
[3] "Tute Bianche" was the name of the Italian activists dressed in white who used their bodies protected with foam material, tires, helmets, gas masks, and home-made shields as weapons of civil disobedience during direct actions and protests.
[4] Steyerl, "The Articulation of Protest," http://republicart.net/disc/mundial/steyerl02_en.htm 2002 [04/10/05].
[5] Ibid.
[6] Ibid.
[7] Gilles Deleuze, *Negotiations*, New York 1995, p. 45.
[8] On the concept of the "nonconformist mass" see Raunig, *Kunst und Revolution. Künstlerischer Aktivismus im langen 20. Jahrhundert*, Vienna 2005, p. 51–55.
[9] Maurizio Lazzarato, "Struggle, Event, Media," http://republicart.net/disc/representations/lazzarato01_en.htm 2003 [04/10/05].
[10] See also Marion Hamm, "A r/c tivism in Physical and Virtual Spaces," http://republicart.net/disc/realpublicspaces/hamm02_en.htm 2003 [04/10/05].

sondern dazu, die Welt sich ereignen zu lassen. Maurizio Lazzarato hat gerade am von Hito Steyerl aufgegriffenen Kontext Seattle 1999 die strategische Rolle der Bilder, Zeichen und Aussagen betont: „Sie tragen dazu bei, das Mögliche entstehen zu lassen, und sie tragen zu seiner Verwirklichung bei."[9] Das Gefüge der Zeichen wirkt nicht als Lösung des Problems (auch nicht des Problems der Addition von Widersprüchen), sondern als Eröffnung des Möglichen. So wird etwa durch das Erfinden und Aussprechen des Slogans „Eine andere Welt ist möglich" eine Möglichkeit eröffnet, die damit gewissermaßen auch zur Wirklichkeit werden kann.

In diesem Kontext wird *Showdown in Seattle* eine Linie im Ereignis, das sich in der Verkettung der Körper, aber auch der Slogans, der Internet-Kommunikation, der Bilder und Aussagen des Indymedia-Videos aktualisiert.[10] Und damit entsteht auch ein anderer Begriff von Dokumentation im Rahmen des Medienaktivismus, der seine Funktion nun nicht mehr auf das Dokumentieren von politischen Bewegungen beschränkt, sondern sich im Aktivismus-Werden des Dokumentarischen ereignet. Die Notwendigkeit zu dokumentieren, lässt sich in diesem Paradigma nicht mehr auf Dokumentierungszwang oder Dokumentalität zurückführen, sondern wird zur Notwendigkeit des Dokuments als gegenwärtiges Werden.

---

[1] Hito Steyerl: Dokumentarismus als Politik der Wahrheit, in: Gerald Raunig (Hg.): *Bildräume und Raumbilder. Repräsentationskritik in Film und Aktivismus*, Wien 2004, S. 165–174.
[2] Vgl. zum Begriff der „postnationalen Insurrektion" Gerald Raunig: *Kunst und Revolution. Künstlerischer Aktivismus im langen 20. Jahrhundert*, Wien 2005, S. 51–55.
[3] „Tute Bianche" war die Bezeichnung für jene weiß gekleideten AktivistInnen aus Italien, die ihre durch Schaumstoff, Reifen, Helme, Gasmasken und selbst gemachten Schilde geschützten Körper bei direkten Aktionen und Demonstrationen als Waffe des zivilen Ungehorsams einsetzten.
[4] Hito Steyerl: Die Artikulation des Protestes, in: Gerald Raunig (Hg.): *TRANSVERSAL. Kunst und Globalisierungskritik*, Wien 2003, S. 19–28.
[5] Ebd., S. 23.
[6] Ebd., S. 25.
[7] Gilles Deleuze: *Unterhandlungen*, Frankfurt a. M. 1993, S. 68.
[8] Zum Begriff der „nonkonformen Masse" vgl. Gerald Raunig: *Kunst und Revolution. Künstlerischer Aktivismus im langen 20. Jahrhundert*, Wien 2005, S. 51–55.

9 Maurizio Lazzarato: Kampf, Ereignis, Medien, in: Gerald Raunig (Hg.): *Bildräume und Raumbilder. Repräsentationskritik in Film und Aktivismus*, Wien 2004, S. 176.
10 Vgl. dazu auch Marion Hamm: Ar/ctivism in physikalischen und virtuellen Räumen, in: Gerald Raunig (Hg.): *Bildräume und Raumbilder. Repräsentationskritik in Film und Aktivismus*, Wien 2004, S. 34–44.

Hotelroom

Ort / *Location*:	Ramada Hotel, Hamilton, Kanada / *Ramada Hotel, Hamilton, Canada*
Datum / *Date*:	Juni 2004 / *June 2004*
Material / *Material*:	Verpackungsmaterial / *packages*
Beteiligte / *Participants*:	—

Ich wohne eine Woche im Ramada Hotel in Hamilton, Ontario im Zimmer 714. *I live for one week in room 714 at the Ramada Hotel in Hamilton, Ontario.*

Mein Hotelzimmer 714, im Ramada Hotel, Hamilton. In dem Hotelzimmer befindet sich unter der Garderobe ein Safe. *My hotel room 714 at the Ramada Hotel, Hamilton. In this room you can find a safe under the wardrobe.*

Ich rekonstruiere das Hotelzimmer in dem Safe. Am Tag meiner Abreise schließe ich den Safe und gebe den Schlüssel kommentarlos an der Rezeption ab. *I reconstruct the hotel room in the safe. Before I leave I close the safe and return the keys of the safe and the room without comment back to the reception.*

Lean on

Ort / *Location*:	Prenzlauer Allee, Berlin / *Prenzlauer Allee, Berlin*
Datum / *Date*:	Dezember 2001 / *December 2001*
Material / *Material*:	Fahrrad / *Bycicle*
Beteiligte / *Participants*:	Christoph Meierhans, unbekanner Passant / *Christoph Meierhans, unknown passer-by*

Ich fahre mit dem Fahrrad langsam an eine rote Ampel und lege meine Hand auf die linke Schulter einer mir fremden Person. Ich stütze mich an der Person ab solange die Fußgängerampel rot ist. *I drive by bycicle slowly to the red traffic lights and put my right hand on the left shoulder of an unknown passer-by. I lean on a foreign person who is waiting at the red traffic lights.*

Die Fußgängerampel wird grün. Ich stoße mich von der fremden Schulter ab und fahre weiter. *The traffic lights changes. I push off the foreign shoulder and drive away.*

o.T. (Heft) / *Untitled (Exercise Book)*

Ort / *Location*:	»Kaufhof«, Halle/Saale / *Shopping Center »Kaufhof«, Halle/Saale*
Datum / *Date*:	August 1999 / *August 1999*
Material / *Material*:	Schulheft A4, blanko, Lineal, Bleistift / *Exercise book A4 unlined, pencil*
Beteiligte / *Participants*:	—

Ich gehe zu »Kaufhof« und kaufe ein Schulheft A4, blanko. *I go to the shopping center »Kaufhof« and buy an unlined A4 exercise book.*

Zuhause liniere ich das Heft anhand des Linienblattes, einem Lineal und einem Bleistift. Das dauert 3 Stunden. *At home I use the sheet with lines, a ruler and a pencil for drawing lines in the blank exercise book. It takes 3 hours.*

Zum Schluß ist das ganze Heft liniert. Es sieht wie ein liniertes Heft aus. *In the end the whole exercise book looks like a A4 exercise book with lines.*

Ich bringe das Heft zu »Kaufhof« zurück und lege es unbemerkt zu den linierten A4 Heften. *Then I bring this exercise book back to the shopping center and put it back in the partition where you can find the exercise books with lines.*

Fontäne / *Fountain*

Ort / *Location*:	Wallauer Weg, Wiesbaden / *Wallauer Weg, Wiesbaden*
Datum / *Date*:	28.6.2002 - 6.8.2002
Material / *Material*:	Wasser / *Water*
Beteiligte / *Participants*:	Hr. Wegerle und Hr. Hasselbach der ESWE Wasserversorgung AG / *Mr. Wegerle and Mr. Hasselbach from ESWE Versorgungs AG*

Während meiner Recherche im Archiv der Stadt Wiesbaden bin ich auf zahlreiche Thermalquellen, die sich unter der Stadt Wiesbaden befinden, aufmerksam geworden. *While researching in the Archives of Wiesbaden I found numerous thermal springs which exist underground in the city of Wiesbaden.*

28.6.2002 Ich stelle bei der ESWE Versorgungs AG einen Antrag für die kontrollierte Öffnung eines Hydranten im Stadtgebiet Wiesbaden. Der Antrag wird bewilligt. *I asked the company ESWE water supply AG if it would be possible to open one of the hydrants in the city of Wiesbaden. They agreed to do this.*

6.8.2002 Ich treffe Hr. Wegerle und Hr. Hasselbach von der ESWE Versorgungs AG. Wir öffnen einen Hydranten hinter dem Theater in der Paulinenstraße, Wiesbaden. *I met Mr. Wegerle and Mr. Hasselbach from ESWE Versorgungs AG. We open a hydrant at Paulinenstraße in the city centre of Wiesbaden.*

Georg Schöllhammer

A Question of Display

In the early 1990s, it was quite fashionable in the art world to claim that the cultural world was a political one. Young artists again referred to the interrupted, non-canonized, or exhausted motifs of political conceptual art of the late 1960s and early 1970s and sought to think them out further in formal terms.

Toward the end of the 1990s, this practice seemed to have lost its momentum. The reason for its ossification was not that its belief in its own ideological arguments was too strong, but that the practice appeared in the form of an enormous confidence in the linguistic power of certain aesthetic displays that were misunderstood as ideological phrases.

If, since then, many involved in the art world – as opposed to the beginning of the 1990s – have difficulties conceiving categories such as institutional significance and political interpretation as the key problems of cultural analysis, this is probably one of the reasons. A certain historical irony lies in the fact that a new generation of artists has addressed and further worked on the many political motifs of this art all too rashly in terms of formats and methods of representation in a new, equally formalistic genre: that of documentary videos, documentary installations, etc.

In the classical art world, these concepts themselves soon became code words for relatively easily predictable positions that negotiated ideas of social transformation, historical agency and the disposition of the self – no matter how it was understood –, the heterogeneity of cultures, and brief post-Empire globalization analyses in montages of interviews and real-site material. The artists who made use of these were already cast aside the moment they appeared, along with the preceeding neo-conceptual generation. The criticism of their work, claiming that they followed a blind and aesthetically amateurish realism, disavows an entire genre and basically makes an accusation that is blind to method.

The classical art world must free itself from conceiving documentation as a trivial and

Displayfragen

Anfang der 90er Jahre war es im Kunstbetrieb recht modisch, zu sagen, die kulturelle Welt sei eine politische. Junge KünstlerInnen bezogen sich wieder auf abgebrochene, nicht kanonisierte oder ausagierte Motive politisch-konzeptueller Kunst der späten 60er und frühen 70er und suchten diese auch formal weiterzudenken.

Gegen Ende der 90er erschien diese Praxis ihre Kraft verloren zu haben. Der Grund für ihre Erstarrung lag nicht an einem zu starken Glauben an die eigenen ideologischen Argumente, sondern sie erschien in Form eines ungeheuren Vertrauens in die Sprachkraft gewisser ästhetischer Displays, die als ideologische Wendungen missverstanden wurden.

Wenn viele im Kunstbetrieb seit damals – und eben ganz anders als Anfang der 90er Jahre – Schwierigkeiten damit haben, sich Kategorien wie institutionelle Bedeutung und politische Interpretation als die Schlüsselprobleme kultureller Analyse vorzustellen, hängt das wohl damit zusammen. Es liegt eine gewisse historische Ironie darin, dass viele der politischen Motive dieser Kunst in einer Art Genrewechsel von einer neuen Generation von KünstlerInnen in allzu kurzen Schlüssen in Bezug auf Formate und Methoden von Repräsentation in einem neuen ebenso formalistischen Genre weiterbehandelt wurden: dem des dokumentarischen Videos, der Doku-Installation etc.

Im klassischen Kunstbetrieb wurden diese Begriffe selbst bald wieder zu Codewörtern für relativ leicht vorhersagbare Positionen, in denen Ideen von sozialer Transformation, historischer Agency und die – wie immer verstandene – Disposition des Selbst, die Heterogenität von Kulturen und knappe Post-Empire-Globalisierungsanalysen in Interview- und Realsite-Material-Montagen verhandelt wurden. Die KünstlerInnen, die sich ihrer bedienten, wurden gewissermaßen zeitgleich mit ihrem Erscheinen zusammen mit der neokonzeptuellen Vorgängergeneration schon wieder aufs Abstellgleis geschoben. Die Kritik an ihrer Arbeit, sie folge einem blinden und ästhetisch dilettantischen Realismus, desavouiert ein ganzes Genre

rigid method. What we are instead faced with is a modular technology in which representations differ from the minimalism of self-interpretation of many other forms of contemporary art precisely through their modes of projection. They welcome otherness, yes, they strive to achieve it. It has often been said that their plots are nothing more than the necessary element of representation and communication.

As Gilles Deleuze said of the films of Straub/Huillet, the aesthetics of the visual image takes on a new trait here. Its "pictorial" and "sculptural" features are dependent on the quasi-tectonic power of the real which they document. What Maurizio Lazzarato, referring to Dziga Vertov's concept of cinema, calls "time crystallization machines", can also be said of these new practices: they are machines in which new forms of subjectivization occur; they allow us to see the movements and time, and they work on the duration of images.

und erhebt einen im Grunde methodenblinden Vorwurf.

Der klassische Kunstbetrieb muss sich von der Vorstellung befreien, das Dokumentarische als eine banale und starre Methode zu denken. Vielmehr handelt es sich um eine modulare Technologie, in der die Repräsentationen sich gerade durch ihre Projektionsweisen vom Minimalismus der Selbstinterpretation vieler anderer Spielarten der Gegenwartskunst unterscheiden. Sie begrüßen Andersheit, ja, sie streben sie an. Ihre Plots sind – das ist oft beschrieben worden – nichts mehr als das notwendige Element der Vergegenwärtigung, der Verständigung.

Ähnlich wie Gilles Deleuze über das Kino von Straub/Huillet gesagt hatte, nimmt hier die Ästhetik des visuellen Bildes einen neuen Zug an. Seine „piktoralen" und „skulpturalen" Eigenschaften sind von der quasi-tektonischen Kraft des Realen, das sie dokumentieren, abhängig. Was Maurizio Lazzarato in Bezug auf Dziga Vertovs Konzept des Kinos „Zeitkristallisationsmaschinen" nennt, lässt sich auch für diese neuen Praktiken sagen: Sie sind Maschinen, in denen sich neue Formen von Subjektivierungen ereignen; sie lassen uns die Bewegung und die Zeit sehen, und sie arbeiten an der Bilder-Dauer.

SO YOU GOTTA LET ME KNOW

SHOULD I STAY OR SHOULD I GO?

IF I GO THERE WILL BE TROUBLE

IF I STAY IT WILL BE DOUBLE

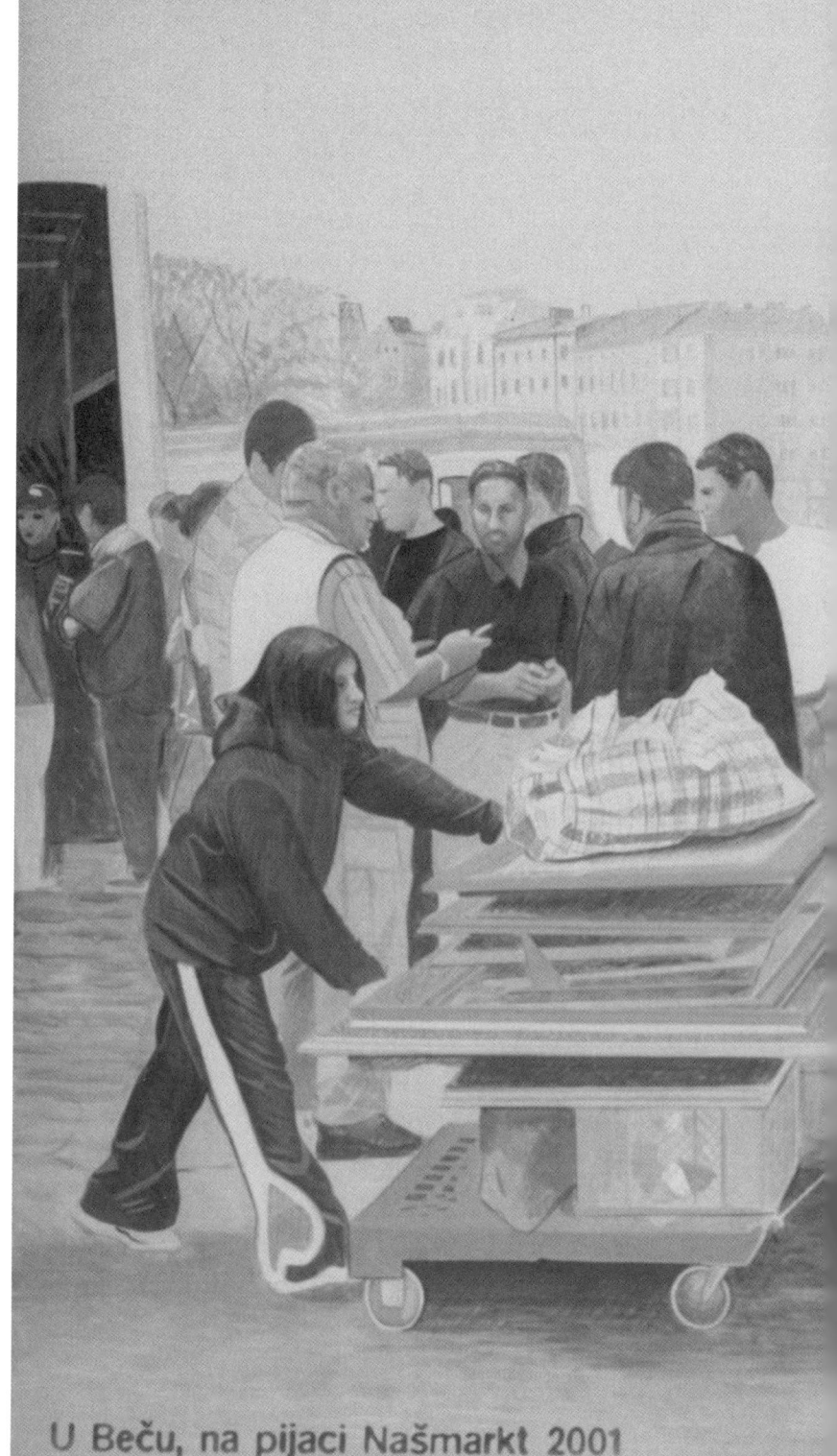

U Beču, na pijaci Našmarkt 2001
Viyana Naschmarktdaki büyük Pazar 2001

Søren Grammel in collaboration with Gerhard Zarbock

Worktop Video

What characterizes current video productions? First, I would like to briefly retrace the perspective conceived by the protagonists of the 1968 movement from a diachronic point of view in order to then structure the models and methods of a participatory video practice more clearly and to bring out specific media-related features in their social context in a more distinct way.

At the time, super 8 film, and then to an increasing degree video, were regarded as an adequate medium for a revolutionary remodeling of social conditions, because these innovations made image production affordable. Video equipment cost merely a fraction compared to 16-mm film or television productions. This was considered an indication that the progressing technological development would more or less automatically place the means of production in the hands of the proletariat and that these radical changes would become paradigmatically discernable precisely in the progress of video technology. These assumptions were based on the theories of Eisenstein, Kracauer, Brecht, and Benjamin, and placed their hopes in the idea that the documentation of social conditions would make the proletarians aware of their situation like in a mirror, thus making a revolutionary spark conceivable or even historically inevitable – provided that the means of production for such documentation were in the hands of *those deprived of their rights*. These theories were soon connected with theories that can be summed up using a term propagated by François Lyotard, the "patchwork of minorities", and which started from the notion that especially in social fringe groups, a strong potential for changing the system could be found.

How do these *video utopias* appear today? Indeed, video in current art production has increasingly become a means to interact with social reality. Video is used to intervene in certain environments, e.g., to create situations in

Arbeitsfläche Video

Was kennzeichnet aktuelle Videoproduktionen? In einer diachronen Sicht will ich zunächst die Perspektive in aller Kürze nachzeichnen, wie sie von den Protagonisten der 68er Bewegung entworfen wurde, um, davon ausgehend, Modelle und Verfahren einer partizipativen Video-Praxis sowohl übersichtlicher zu strukturieren, als auch spezifische mediale Merkmale in ihrem sozialen Kontext deutlicher herausarbeiten zu können.

Erst Super-8, dann zunehmend Video galten damals deshalb als geeignete Medien für eine revolutionäre Umgestaltung der gesellschaftlichen Verhältnisse, weil mit diesen Innovationen die Bildproduktion erschwinglich wurde. Ein Video-Equipment kostete nur noch einen Bruchteil im Vergleich zum 16mm-Film oder zur Fernsehproduktion. Dies wurde als Indiz dafür gewertet, dass mit der fortschreitenden technologischen Entwicklung dem Proletariat die Produktionsmittel mehr oder weniger automatisch in die Hände gespielt würden und gerade am Fortschritt der Video-Technologie diese Umwälzungen paradigmatisch ablesbar seien. Diese Annahmen stützten sich auf Theorien von Eisenstein, Kracauer, Brecht oder Benjamin, und bauten auf die Hoffnung, dass mit der Dokumentation der gesellschaftlichen Verhältnisse dem Proletarier seine Lage wie in einem Spiegel bewusst und auf diese Weise eine revolutionäre Initialzündung denkbar, oder sogar historisch unausweichlich werden würde – vorausgesetzt, die Produktionsmittel für solche Dokumentationen lägen in der Hand der *Entrechteten*. Verknüpft wurden diese Theorien bald mit denjenigen, die sich unter dem von François Lyotard propagierten Ausdruck vom „Patchwork der Minderheiten" zusammenfassen lassen und die an der Vorstellung ansetzen, dass gerade bei sozialen Randgruppen ausgeprägte systemverändernde Potenziale zu finden seien.

Wie stellen sich diese *Video-Utopien* heute dar? Tatsächlich ist Video in der aktuellen Kunstproduktion zunehmend zu einem Mittel der Interak-

which different persons or groups can collaborate. The aim of these interventions can consist in joint actions, the creation of a community, or communication. During the course of these projects, documentary video images are frequently produced that depict the concrete living contexts of those involved. So has the slogan, "the revolution is over, we won", come true in the field of video? For a number of reasons, the situation is indeed not clear enough to be pressed into such a sloppily formulated scheme. This also has to do with the fact that the development of the electronic media has fundamentally dissolved the seemingly firm relationship between reality and fiction and that this "caesura of the media"[1] has triggered a storm tide of, to a large extent, contradictory media theories, from Marshall McLuhan to Paul Virilio, from Friedrich Kittler to Régis Debray or Jean Baudrillard.

Today, one can describe video practices that are not primarily aimed at producing recordings. In these cases, the video images are often just by-products or parallel products of video-based practices – picture material that accumulated during the creation of a moment of self-constituting reality. In this context, the medium functions as a *work surface* on which people come together for the duration of a certain production. Less a medium (through which a practice is communicated) than a tool (utilized by a practice), video turns into a catalyst of social interaction, e.g., in the public reading seminars organized by Rainer Ganahl since the mid-1990s.[2] The permanent presence of the running video camera initially leads to an enhanced perception of the situation

tion mit sozialer Realität geworden. Video wird verwendet, um in bestimmten Umgebungen zu intervenieren, beispielsweise um dort Situationen der Zusammenarbeit zwischen verschiedenen Personen oder Gruppen herzustellen. Das Ziel dieser Interventionen kann in gemeinsamen Handlungen, in der Gemeinschaftsbildung und Kommunikation bestehen. Im Verlauf dieser Projekte entstehen oft dokumentarische Videobilder, die konkrete Lebenszusammenhänge der Beteiligten zeigen. Hat sich also im Bereich Video der Slogan bewahrheitet: *Die Revolution ist vorbei, wir haben gesiegt?* Tatsächlich ist die Situation aus mehreren Gründen unübersichtlicher, als dass sie sich in ein solch flapsig formuliertes Schema fügen würde. Das liegt auch daran, dass mit der Entwicklung der elektronischen Medien ein bis dahin scheinbar festgefügtes Verhältnis von Realität und Fiktion grundsätzlich aufgelöst wurde und diese *Zäsur der Medien*[1] eine Sturmflut neuer, sich größenteils widerstreitender Medientheorien ausgelöst hat: von Marshall McLuhan bis Paul Virilio, von Friedrich Kittler bis Régis Debray oder Jean Baudrillard.

So lassen sich heute Video-Praktiken beschreiben, bei denen die Produktion der Aufnahmen nicht mehr das primäre Ziel des Projektes darstellt. In diesen Fällen sind die Videobilder oft nur Neben- oder Parallelprodukte videogestützter Praktiken – Bildmaterial, das während der Entstehung eines Momentes selbstkonstituierter Realität angefallen ist. Das Medium erhält in diesem Zusammenhang die Funktion einer *Arbeitsfläche*, auf der man sich für die Dauer einer bestimmten Produktion zusammenfindet. Weniger Medium (über das sich eine Praxis vermittelt) als Werkzeug (dessen sich eine Praxis bedient), wird Video zum Katalysator sozialer Interaktion. Ein Beispiel bieten die öffentlichen Leseseminare, die Rainer Ganahl seit Mitte der 90er Jahre veranstaltet.[2] Die permanente Anwesenheit der laufenden Videokamera führt anfangs zu einer gesteigerten Wahrnehmung der Situation durch die gemeinsam Lesenden. Später verschwindet die Kamera aus dem Bewusstsein und wird zum rein indexikalischen Dokument. Die Bänder werden nicht produziert, um später abgespielt zu werden. Sie werden nicht als Repor-

Rainer Ganahl, *A Reading Seminar...*, 1995

by those reading together. Later, one is no longer aware of the camera, which then becomes a purely indexical document. The tapes are not produced to be shown afterward as a reportage of the reading seminar, but are stored. Through aging and the increasing loss of analogue picture information they instead document structures of appropriation and memory processes on a metaphorical level. The camera does record a number of activities, but hardly anyone views them because already during the course of a one-week seminar the quantity of the video material reaches almost absurd dimensions. The function of the camera lies more in initiating these activities. The objectives and meanings of such working contexts are formulated by the producers themselves on the personal and interpersonal level. They cannot necessarily be visualized and, for the producers, they do not have to be. Philippe Parreno provided a nice picture of this with his project *While...* Visitors found what was left over of a working situation. They could inform themselves of it, if they were willing to take some of the video tapes, which were produced and as it seemed carelessly thrown away, out of the paper baskets and play them.[3] Perhaps we can call this model of a collaborative video practice the *initializing model*, because the use of video technology only serves to initiate social interaction.

There are video practices that differ fundamentally from the *initializing model* and, in a methodological respect, follow earlier, practice-oriented models. They are oriented toward a more or less direct political-aesthetic aim; their results consequently consist in the direct change of a (local) political situation, like with the project *Participation* (2001) of the PTTL collective. After a questionable invitation by the job center of Sint-Joost sent to unemployed artists, asking them to participate in "brightening up" the job center, PTTL was established in 1998 as an initiative of five of the invited artists. Instead of "brightening up", discussions about the sense and nonsense of such activities between artists and authority officials led to the foundation of PTTL as a basis for artistic and political practice

tage über das Leseseminar gezeigt, sondern gelagert. Durch ihr Altern und den ständig fortschreitenden Verlust der analogen Bildinformation dokumentieren sie stattdessen auf einer metaphorischen Ebene Strukturen von Aneignungs- und Gedächtnisprozessen. Die Kamera hält zwar eine Anzahl von Handlungen fest, aber kaum jemand schaut sie an, weil die Quantität an Videomaterial schon während eines einwöchigen Seminars fast absurde Ausmaße annimmt. Die Funktion der Kamera liegt eher darin, zum Anlass für diese Handlungen zu werden. Die Ziele und Bedeutungen eines solchen Arbeitszusammenhangs werden auf der persönlichen und zwischenmenschlichen Ebene von den Produzierenden selber formuliert. Sie sind so nicht unbedingt visualisierbar und müssen es für die Produzierenden auch nicht sein. Ein schönes Bild dafür hat Philippe Parreno mit dem Projekt *While...* geliefert: Besucher fanden die Überreste einer Arbeitssituation vor, über die sie sich informieren konnten, insofern sie bereit waren, einige der entstandenen und scheinbar achtlos weggeworfenen Videotapes aus den Papierkörben neben den Arbeitstischen zu entnehmen und abzuspielen.[3] Wir können dieses Modell einer kollaborativen Video-Praxis vielleicht das *Initialmodell* nennen, weil der Einsatz der Videotechnik dabei nur noch als Auslöser für eine soziale Interaktion dient.

Grundsätzlich unterschieden von diesem *Initialmodell*, und im Verfahren an frühere praxisorientierte Modelle anschließend, sind Video-Praktiken, die sich an einem mehr oder weniger direkten politisch-ästhetischen Ziel orientieren, deren Ergebnisse also in der direkten Veränderung einer (lokal-)politischen Situation liegen, wie bei dem Projekt *Participation* (2001) des Kollektivs PTTL. Nach einer fragwürdigen Einladung des Arbeitsamtes von Sint-Joost an arbeitslose Künstler, an der „Verschönerung" des Arbeitsamtes teilzunehmen, formte sich PTTL 1998 als Initiative durch fünf der eingeladenen KünstlerInnen. In den Diskussionen über Sinn und Unsinn solcher Unternehmungen zwischen Künstlern und Behördenleitern wurde anstelle der Verschönerung PTTL als eine Basis für künstlerische und politische Praxis im sozialen Raum (konkret: des

in the social sphere (here specifically: the job center). An initial question of those involved was: Why should they let their own situation be managed by an authority instead of becoming active themselves in – or rather *as* – the institution? PTTL consists of various, in part temporary work groups, including a video group.[4] In the project, the critical dealing with one's own living conditions and the attempt to transform them become the object of a political-aesthetic practice. The primary goal of the producers is to actively intervene in social space or social reality, and the dividing line which activism is blurred. In the case of PTTL, job offers were actually made. They did not lead to the reintegration into the wage labor market, however, but to working on individual situations. Such projects are hardly representative to others because they are situation-related. Their power lies in the impact they can have on a group of people.[5]

A comparable approach, but as opposed to PTTL targeting as much public media attention as possible, is taken by the American collective, Paper Tiger TV[6], which empowered a large group of people to produce an alternative television program concerned with the Iraq crisis, and publicly broadcast it via satellite (slogan: "Smashing the Myths of the Information Industry"). The program, *Manufacturing the Enemy,* was produced in November 1990 as part of *Gulf Crisis TV* and broadcast as a Paper Tiger TV program for the first time the night the bombing of Baghdad began (January 1991). The focus of attention is on how the media utilize racist (image) languages to demonize Iraq and *the Arabs*. In this initiative, video becomes a catalyst allowing different people to act together and change a situation through their active participation.

Whereas in approaches that are more oriented toward producing a video as an end product of a work process the aim of video as a work surface is usually to either leave the process of image production entirely to other individuals or to involve them to different degrees. How can people or groups to be represented in the video image be involved in its production? This open

concept of a documentary practice adopts methods of the workshop principle. The advantages of an uncomplicated and affordable use of video and the possibilities of using the medium in a spontaneous and playful way are obvious in this context. The principle of this strategy can be discerned in the early practices of Stephen Willats, for example. Willats distributed cassette recorders and later disposable cameras to the inhabitants of urban problem zones and asked them to record their living environment in sound and vision for a certain period of time. While the tasks are still defined by the artists here, there are approaches that reverse the "you press the button" of Conceptual photography of the 1960s. Here, the artist operates the camera while others select the theme and direct (a striking example of this was provided by Nasrin Tabatabai in *Old House* from 1999, dealt with in more detail below). In such cases, the artists turn themselves into service providers. The competence of image production is passed on: the author becomes the producer who makes this competence available to enable other persons to communicate aesthetically. One of several examples is the project Marion von Osten organized with the Sans Papiers office in Antwerp, Belgium, titled *nordreise-südreise* (2000)[7]. The artist deliberately placed herself at the *service* of, or in a collaborative relationship to, the Sans Papiers to produce a promotion video according to their ideas. The artist makes her medium available for others in a targeted way as a means of communication, and simultaneously offers her abilities to

eines Arbeitsprozesses ausgerichtet sind, besteht das Ziel von Video als Arbeitsfläche zumeist darin, anderen Subjekten den Prozess der Bildproduktion entweder ganz zu überlassen oder diese in verschiedenen Abstufungen einzubinden: Wie können die Personen oder Gruppen, um deren Darstellung es im Videobild gehen soll, an dessen Produktion beteiligt werden? Diese offene Konzeption dokumentarischer Praxis macht sich Methoden des Workshop-Prinzips zu eigen. Dabei sind die Vorteile der unkomplizierten und preiswerten Verwendung von Video und die Möglichkeiten der spontanen und spielerischen Handhabung des Mediums offensichtlich. Das Prinzip dieser Strategie kann zum Beispiel in frühen Praktiken von Stephen Willats nachvollzogen werden. Willats teilte Kassettenrecorder und später auch Einwegkameras an Bewohner urbaner Brennpunkte aus und forderte sie auf, über eine bestimmte Zeit ihren Lebensraum in Tönen und Bildern festzuhalten. Während hier die Aufgabenstellung noch vom Künstler definiert wird, gibt es Ansätze, die das „you press the button" der konzeptuellen Fotografie der 60er Jahre umkehren: Nun hält der Künstler die Kamera, während andere das Thema auswählen und Regie führen (ein prägnantes Beispiel dafür liefert die weiter unten noch ausführlich besprochene Arbeit *Old House*, 1999, von Nasrin Tabatabai). In solchen Fällen machen sich Künstler zu Dienstleistern. Die Kompetenz der Bildproduktion wird weitergereicht: Der Autor wird zum Produzenten, der diese Kompetenz zur Verfügung stellt, um anderen Personen Formen ästhetischer Kommunikation zu ermöglichen. Als eines von mehreren Beispielen wäre das von Marion von Osten zusammen mit dem Sans-Papiers-Büro in Antwerpen, Belgien, erarbeitete Projekt *nordreise-südreise* (2000)[7] zu nennen, für das sich die Künstlerin bewusst in den *Dienst* bzw. in ein Verhältnis der Zusammenarbeit mit den Sans-Papiers gestellt hat, um eine Art Promotion-Video nach deren Vorstellungen zu produzieren. Die Künstlerin stellt hier ihr Medium gezielt als Sprachrohr für andere bereit und bietet zugleich ihre Fähigkeiten bei der Erarbeitung und Umsetzung an. Hintergründe und Bedingungen der politischen Realität der Sans-Papiers werden aus deren eigener Perspektive dargestellt. Das Pro-

Marion von Osten and Sans Papiers Belgium, *nordreise-südreise*, 2000

work out and implement the project. The backgrounds and conditions of the political reality of the Sans Papiers are shown from their own perspective. The product is thus the result of the communication between the artist and the "clients". It becomes especially clear in this case how strategies of empowerment can become involved in negotiating and making productive the artistic-experimental aim of abandoning control and authorship.

The video objects of Hilary Lloyd (from the second half of the 1990s) are examples of models of a distinct division of labor that, on the one hand, give those represented complete freedom within the frame they are to fill out, but on the other hand, clearly define this frame by controlling the camera. For Lloyd, video is a medium for establishing contact. She addressed people she saw somewhere in the city (London), in clubs, pubs, or other public places; after getting to know them a bit she then asked them to stage an action important for their personality in front of the camera. Lloyd let the actors define the space of the performance in front of the fixed camera, i.e. the subsequent image space of the video, entirely on their own. At the same time, she contrasted this openness with shots that were controlled up to the tiniest detail and with an increasingly sophisticated material fetishism in terms of the presentation/installation. One could also mention works by Annika Eriksson in this context, e.g., *Collectors* (1998). Different collec-

Hilary Lloyd, *Colin #2*, 2000

tors present themselves along with the objects of their passion in front of the camera for a period of time they determine themselves and speak about the various aspects of collecting. The form

dukt ist somit Ergebnis der Kommunikation zwischen Künstlerin und „Auftraggebern". In diesem Fall wird besonders deutlich, wie Strategien der Ermächtigung die künstlerisch-experimentell angestrebte Aufgabe von Kontrolle und Autorenschaft mitverhandeln und produktiv machen können.

Modelle einer klaren Arbeitsteilung, die den Abgebildeten einerseits völlige Freiheit in dem für sie zu füllenden Rahmen geben, diesen aber klar durch die Kontrolle über die Kamera definieren, wären zum Beispiel die Videoobjekte (zweite Hälfte der 90er) von Hilary Lloyd. Für sie ist Video ein Medium der Kontaktaufnahme. Menschen, die sie irgendwo in der Stadt (London) gesehen hatte, in Clubs, Pubs oder an öffentlichen Orten, sprach sie auf eine Zusammenarbeit an und bat sie nach einiger Zeit des Kennen lernens darum, eine für ihre Persönlichkeit wichtige Handlung vor der Kamera zu inszenieren. Dieser Raum der Performance vor der fixen Kamera, also später der Bildraum des Videos, wurde den Agierenden von Lloyd vollständig überlassen. Zugleich kontrastiert sie diese Offenheit durch eine bis in das Detail kontrollierte Aufnahme und dem immer ausgeklügelten Materialfetischismus der Präsentation/Installation. Hier wären auch einige Arbeiten Annika Erikssons zu nennen, beispielsweise *Collectors* (1998): Verschiedene Sammler präsentieren sich vor der laufenden Kamera für die Dauer eines selbstbestimmten Zeitraums mit den Objekten ihrer Leidenschaft und sprechen über verschiedene Aspekte des Sammelns. Die Form der Arbeit ist dadurch bestimmt, dass sie einerseits einen bestimmten Entscheidungs- oder Auftrittsraum an andere abgibt, zugleich aber immer auch dessen Rahmung durch konzeptuelle und formale Entscheidungen vorgibt, beispielsweise durch Perspektive und Kamerabewegungen. Es lassen sich erstaunlich viele und verschiedene Spielformen solcher Ansätze ausmachen. In *Sarajevo Guided Tours* (2001) befragt Isa Rosenberger eine Reihe von Einwohnern der Stadt Sarajevo zu ihren Kriegserinnerungen. Zwar bestimmt die Künstlerin das Thema und die Kamera bleibt in ihren Händen, die Befragten wählen aber den Aufnahmeort, für den sie sich nach persönlichen Vorstellungen und Erinnerungen entscheiden. Mitunter

of the work is determined, one the one hand, by leaving a certain space for decision and presentation to others, while on the other, its framing is defined by conceptual and formal decisions in terms of the perspective and camera movements, for example. One can distinguish a surprising variety of such approaches. In *Sarajevo Guided Tours* (2001), Isa Rosenberger questions a number of inhabitants of Sarajevo about their memories of the war. While the artist chooses the theme and operates the camera, those questioned select the location according to their personal ideas and memories. While shooting, those being questioned at times give spontaneous stage directions regarding the camera movements.

If one wanted to simplify, one could distinguish between two different tendencies:

— On the one hand, participatory practices can result from the producer's examination of his or her own self-conception as an image producer. In this case, the search for complex and collective concepts of authorship determine the working approach. The attempt to counter the one-dimensional representation of others is linked to the search for anti-subjectivist concepts of coming up with images. This tendency can be understood as still standing in the tradition of documentary representation in video (and film), since the product and its form, through which it aesthetically communicates contents, are at the center of attention. Here, interaction and participation open up new possibilities of exploring alternative strategies of depiction and finding images.

— On the other hand, there are approaches that primarily deal with the relations and processes within a situation catalyzed by video and with the empowerment of those participating. Video creates work surfaces, the occasion, purpose, and result of which can be viewed independently of the image production.

So, one can roughly distinguish between two strategic models of participation and empower-

kommt es während der Aufnahme zu spontanen Regieanweisungen der Befragten für die Kamerabewegungen.

Isa Rosenberger, *Sarajevo Guided Tours*, 2001

Wollte man hier vereinfachen, ließen sich zwei unterschiedliche Tendenzen feststellen:

— Zum einen können partizipatorische Praktiken Resultat der Auseinandersetzung des Produzenten mit seiner eigenen Selbstkonzeption als Bildproduzierender sein. Hier bestimmt die Suche nach komplexen oder kollektiven Konzeptionen von Autorschaft den Arbeitsansatz. Der Versuch, der eindimensionalen Repräsentation anderer entgegenzuwirken, ist hier mit der Suche nach antisubjektivistischen Konzepten von Bildfindung verknüpft. Diese Tendenz kann weiterhin als in der Tradition der dokumentarischen Darstellung in Video (und Film) stehend verstanden werden, weil das Produkt und dessen Form, mittels derer es Inhalte ästhetisch kommuniziert, im Mittelpunkt stehen. Interaktion und Partizipation eröffnen hier neue Möglichkeiten zur Erkundung von alternativen Strategien der Abbildung und Bilderfindung.

— Zum anderen können Ansätze ausgemacht werden, in denen es primär um die Beziehungen und Prozesse innerhalb der durch Video katalysierten Situation geht und die Ermächtigung derer, die an ihnen teilnehmen. Video bildet Arbeitsflächen, deren Anlass, Zweck und Ergebnis unabhängig von der Bildproduktion gesehen werden können. So können zwar grob zwei Modelle von Strategien der Partizipation und Ermächtigung im Umgang

ment in dealing with video as a work surface, but on the level of practice one usually finds both tendencies to various degrees in one and the same project. What appears important here, is the observation that new claims to reality in cultural practice are always formulated the sharpest when aesthetic and situation-related objectives permeate each other. Below, several projects will be presented in which different facets of such approaches can be observed.

1. Video as a Service, or: Passing On the Symbolic Power to Define

Nasrin Tabatabai, *Old House* (1999)

Nasrin Tabatabai, *Old House*, 1999

Old House is a so-called travelogue shot by Nasrin Tabatabai from the window of a traveling car. But this is where the artist's authorship already ends, since the travel route was defined by someone else. The route becomes the shooting plan. The car travels through the center of Rotterdam, one sees buildings, streets, and bridges. The camera movements and the images they capture are determined by the driver. One can hear Turkish music from the car radio. A perfume card and prayer beads are hanging from the rear-view mirror. Once in a while the male voice of the driver points out special features of the architecture passing by. One learns that there are four Turkish banks in the center of Rotterdam. They are mentioned by name. The voice repeats the request to film everything. An historical building is passed by, followed by the remark: "old house".

mit Video als Arbeitsfläche unterschieden werden. Auf der Ebene der Praktiken lassen sich aber meist beide Tendenzen unterschiedlich proportioniert innerhalb ein und desselben Projektes finden. Hier scheint die Beobachtung wichtig, dass neue Wirklichkeitsansprüche in der kulturellen Praxis immer dann am schärfsten formuliert werden, wenn es zu einer gegenseitigen Durchdringung ästhetischer und situationsbezogener Zielsetzungen kommt. Im Folgenden sollen einige Projekte vorgestellt werden, in denen sich verschiedene Facetten solcher Ansätze betrachten lassen.

1. Video als Dienstleistung, oder: symbolische Definitionsmacht weiterreichen

Nasrin Tabatabai, *Old House* (1999)

Bei *Old House* handelt es sich um einen so genannten Travelogue, der von Nasrin Tabatabai aus dem Fenster eines fahrenden Autos heraus aufgenommen wird. Aber schon hier hört die Autorschaft der Künstlerin auf. Denn die Fahrtroute wurde durch jemanden anders festgelegt. Die Strecke wird zum Drehplan. Das Auto fährt quer durch das Zentrum Rotterdams. Man sieht Häuser, Straßen, Brücken. Die Bewegungen der Kamera und die Bilder, die sie festhält, werden durch den Fahrer gelenkt. Es ist türkische Musik zu hören, die aus dem Autoradio kommt. Duftbäumchen und Gebetsperlen baumeln am Rückspiegel. Bisweilen erläutert eine männliche Stimme, die zu der Person des Fahrers gehört, besondere Punkte der vorbeiziehenden Architektur. Man erfährt, dass es im Zentrum Rotterdams vier türkische Banken gibt. Sie werden beim Namen genannt. Die Stimme wiederholt die Aufforderung, alles zu filmen. Ein historisches Gebäude zieht vorüber. Es folgt die Bemerkung „altes Haus".

Der Fahrer des Autos ist Haci Cyhan, ein türkischer Ladenbesitzer, der in der Nähe von Nasrin Tabatabais Wohnung oder Atelier in Rotterdam lebt. Das Video *Old House* ist für seine Verwandten in der Türkei entstanden. Als er erfuhr, dass Tabatabai als Künstlerin mit Video arbeitet, bat er sie um ihre Mithilfe bei der Aufnahme. Haci

The driver of the car is Haci Cyhan, a Turkish shop-owner living near Nasrin Tabatabai's flat or studio in Rotterdam. The video *Old House* was shot for his relatives in Turkey. When he found out that Tabatabai works with video as an artist, he asked her to help with the shooting. Haci Cyhan wanted a video in which they would view Rotterdam through his eyes. He acts as the director, like on a sight-seeing tour of the city, by deciding which route to take and what Tabatabai should film. His specific perception of the urban space becomes the video's script. His comments direct the viewer's attention, and he even chooses a CD for the soundtrack that plays continuously throughout the drive.

The topography of Rotterdam created in this manner corresponds with Haci Cyhan's individual perspective. His own perception is also determined by the future viewers for whom the video is meant and whom he addresses with his explanations during the trip. At one point, his mobile phone rings – it's someone from his shop. He is needed there for a short while. Is it a coincidence or was it staged to show his relatives his everyday life? They drive past the Turkish consulate to his shop, where they drink tea. The journey is then continued across the newly built Erasmus Bridge to a Turkish bakery, where the video ends with the words: "Now we will eat with pleasure. Now stop!" Marking urban space by means of video is also a tourist strategy. Applied to one's own living environment in the city which is increasingly characterized by the conditions of migration and globalization, the video displays an iconography that establishes correlations within the personal documentation.

Old House is the product of a collaboration between Tabatabai and Cyhan, or rather his utilization of her services. The two also collaborated in post-processing and editing the video, which was primarily produced for his relatives in Turkey. Nasrin Tabatabai deliberately accepts the role of a service provider reacting to Cyhan's wishes and depicting his specific view of the city. Beyond the portrayal of Rotterdam thus created, she also gives him the opportunity to introduce himself. The video becomes a document

Cyhan wollte ein Video, in dem sie Rotterdam durch seine Augen sehen würden. Wie bei einer touristischen Stadtrundfahrt führt er die Regie, indem er über die Route entscheidet und durch kurze Anweisungen auch darüber, was Tabatabai filmt. Seine spezifische Wahrnehmung des Stadtraums wird zum Drehbuch des Videos. Seine Kommentare lenken die Aufmerksamkeit des Betrachters und sogar der Soundtrack entspricht seiner Wahl, da es sich um eine von ihm ausgewählte CD handelt, die während der Fahrt durchgehend läuft.

Die so entstehende Topografie Rotterdams entspricht der individuellen Perspektive Haci Cyhans. Dabei ist auch seine eigene Wahrnehmung durch die zukünftigen Betrachter geprägt, für die das Video entsteht und an die er sich während der Fahrt mit seinen Erläuterungen wendet. Während der Fahrt klingelt das Mobiltelefon. Jemand aus Cyhans Geschäft ruft an. Man braucht ihn kurz im Laden. Zufall oder Inszenierung für die Verwandten, um ihnen seinen Alltag zu vermitteln? Die Fahrt führt nun am türkischen Konsulat vorbei zu seinem Geschäft. Dort wird Tee getrunken. Anschließend führt die Fahrt über die neugebaute Erasmus-Brücke zu einer türkischen Bäckerei. Hier endet das Video mit der Feststellung: „Jetzt werden wir mit Freude essen. Now stop!" Die Markierung von Stadtraum mittels Video ist auch eine touristische Strategie. Angewendet auf den eigenen urbanen Lebensraum, der zunehmend durch die Bedingungen von Migration und Globalisierung geprägt ist, zeigt das Video eine Ikonografie, die innerhalb der persönlichen Dokumentation entsprechende Zusammenhänge herstellt.

Old House ist das Produkt einer Zusammenarbeit zwischen Tabatabai und Cyhan bzw. vielmehr der Inanspruchnahme ihrer Dienste durch ihn. Auch die Nachbearbeitung und der Schnitt des Videos fanden in Zusammenarbeit zwischen Tabatabai und Cyhan statt. Das Video wurde primär für seine Verwandten in der Türkei erstellt. Nasrin Tabatabai nimmt bewusst die Rolle einer Dienstleisterin an, die auf die Wünsche Cyhans reagiert und seine spezifische Sicht der Stadt abbildet. Über die so entstehende Darstellung von Rotter-

guided by a non-art-specific interest. What is also interesting is that Tabatabai does not even retain control in a programmatic respect, as an artistic strategy, but that the initiative comes from Cyhan. Video and its use were the occasion for an encounter. Although Cyhan does need Tabatabai's practical assistance, the concern and the conception of the image production remain in his hands.

Here, the documentary coup does not lie in working on a situation, but in entering into a situation and being able to lose oneself to it. When Tabatabai shows the video in an art context afterwards, her work is mainly to be understood as a conceptual decision to exhibit this video. She does not display the product of her own artistic expression, but a piece of visual culture, a document she encountered as a participant in the process of its origination.

2. Video as Workshop, or: Playing with Self-representation

2.1 Esra Ersen, *Om du kunde tala svenska...* (If you could speak Swedish...) (2001)

Esra Ersen, *Om du kunde tala svenska...*, 2001

The starting point of the project *Om du kunde tala svenska...* was Esra Ersen's three-month stay in Stockholm. In order to find out more about the state-run language schools within the context of Swedish immigration policies, Ersen enrolled for a language course directly at *Infokomp*. This working method is characteristic of almost all of Ersen's projects. Investing an enormous amount of time, she enters into situations in which she

dam hinaus gibt sie ihm die Möglichkeit, sich selbst vorzustellen. Das Video wird zu einem Dokument, in dem ein nicht kunstspezifisches Interesse Regie führt. Interessant ist auch, dass Tabatabai ihre Kontrolle nicht einmal programmatisch, als künstlerische Strategie, beibehält, sondern dass die Initiative hierfür von Cyhan ausgeht. Video und sein Gebrauch wurden zum Anlass für die Begegnung. Cyhan braucht zwar Tabatabais praktische Hilfe – Anliegen und Konzeption der Bildproduktion bleiben aber in seinen Händen.

Der dokumentarische Coup liegt hier also nicht darin, über oder zu einer Situation zu arbeiten, sondern in eine Situation zu geraten und sich ihr überlassen zu können. Wenn Tabatabai das Video später im Kunstkontext zeigt, ist ihre Arbeit vor allem als die konzeptuelle Entscheidung zu verstehen, dieses Video auszustellen. Sie zeigt nicht das Produkt ihres eigenen künstlerischen Ausdrucks, sondern ein Stück visueller Kultur, ein Dokument, auf das sie als Beteiligte im Entstehungsprozess gestoßen ist.

2. Video als Workshop, oder: Spiele mit Selbstrepräsentation

2.1 Esra Ersen, *Om du kunde tala svenska...* (If You Could Speak Swedish...) (2001)

Den Ausgangspunkt für das Projekt *Om du kunde tala svenska...* bildet ein dreimonatiger Aufenthalt Esra Ersens in Stockholm. Um mehr über die staatlichen Sprachschulen im Kontext der schwedischen Einwanderungspolitik zu erfahren, schreibt sich Ersen direkt am *Infokomp* für einen Sprachkurs ein. Diese Arbeitsweise ist spezifisch für fast alle Projekte Ersens. Mit großem Zeitaufwand begibt sie sich in Situationen, in denen sie über lange Zeiträume mit bestimmten Gruppen eng zusammenarbeitet. Die Teilnehmer am Sprachkurs teilen eine gemeinsame Erfahrung: Für sie ist das Erlernen der neuen Sprache nicht Nebenprodukt einer Reisetätigkeit, hinter der sich touristische oder geschäftliche Interessen verbergen. Für ImmigrantInnen steht die Aneignung der neuen Sprache für einen Prozess der Integration in die Koordinaten eines komplett neuen kulturellen

closely collaborates with certain groups over longer periods of time. The participants of the language course share a common experience: learning a new language is not the by-product of travels abroad motivated by tourist or business interests. For immigrants, learning the new language is a process of integration into the coordinates of a completely new cultural system. In very few cases is the process based on a voluntary decision. By developing *Om du kunde tala svenska...*in one of the municipal language schools, Ersen locates the work directly in a situation with the greatest potential for conflict.

*Om du kunde tala svenska...*is available as a 23-minute video that can be presented independently, but it mainly documents the process of the project that took place in autumn of 2001 based on the collaboration between Ersen and the course participants. This collaboration can be described as a kind of "workshop". On Ersen's suggestion, the course participants wrote down what they would say in Swedish once they could speak it well enough. Of course, they did so in their respective native languages, since their Swedish was not that good yet. There were no guidelines regarding the content and length of the texts – only that the statements had to be personally important. The quite different answers – some were emotional, others more political, some short and some long – were translated into Swedish by a language teacher (from, among others, Chinese, Arabic, Russian, Spanish, and Bengali).

In the second phase of the project, which is documented in the video, one sees the individual course participants practicing the correct pronunciation of their texts with the help of the teacher. The voice of the female teacher is off-screen. Only the respective course participants can be seen speaking in the direction of the camera, which thus takes on the possible perspective of the teacher. The personal texts turn into didactic material. In the process, the video unfolds an iconography of the institute by showing the speaking students in different places in the school, along with details of its furnishing.

Systems. In wenigen Fällen beruht der Prozess auf einer freiwilligen Entscheidung. Indem Ersen *Om du kunde tala svenska...* in einer der kommunalen Sprachschulen entwickelt, lokalisiert sie die Arbeit so direkt in einer Situation mit dem größten Konfliktpotenzial.

Om du kunde tala svenska... liegt als Video (23 Minuten) vor, das zwar eigenständig präsentiert werden kann, aber vor allem den Prozess des Projektes dokumentiert, der im Herbst 2001 stattfand und auf der Zusammenarbeit zwischen Ersen und den TeilnehmerInnen des Kurses basiert. Die Zusammenarbeit kann als eine Art „Workshop" beschrieben werden. Auf Ersens Anregung hin schreiben die KursteilnehmerInnen auf, was sie auf Schwedisch sagen würden, wenn sie die Sprache hinreichend sprechen könnten. Natürlich müssen sie dies in ihren jeweiligen Muttersprachen tun, da ihr Schwedisch nicht weit genug ausgebildet ist. Es gibt keine Vorgaben hinsichtlich des Inhaltes oder der Länge der so entstehenden Texte – nur, dass die Aussage eine persönlich empfundenc Wichtigkeit hat. Die sehr unterschiedlichen Antworten, teilweise emotional, teilweise eher politisch, manche kurz, manche lang, werden von einer Sprachlehrerin ins Schwedische übersetzt (unter anderem aus dem Chinesischen, Arabischen, Russischen, Spanischen, Bengalischen).

In der zweiten Phase des Projektes, die in dem Video dokumentiert wird, sieht man die einzelnen KursteilnehmerInnen, wie sie mit der Hilfe der Lehrerin die richtige Aussprache ihrer Texte einstudieren. Die Stimme der Lehrerin kommt aus dem Off. Dabei werden nur die jeweiligen KursteilnehmerInnen gezeigt, wie sie frontal in Richtung der Kamera sprechen. Diese übernimmt so die mögliche Perspektive der Lehrerin. Die persönlichen Texte werden zum didaktischen Material. Das Video entfaltet dabei eine Ikonografie des Instituts, in dem es die vor laufender Kamera sprechenden SchülerInnen an unterschiedlichen Orten der Schule, zusammen mit Details der Einrichtung und ihrer Ausstattung zeigt. Die für AsylantInnen und EinwanderInnen konzipierte, d.h. die vor einem konkreten Hintergrund einge-

In Ersen's video, the school which was conceived for asylum-seekers and immigrants, i.e. furnished against a specific background, becomes readable like a picture that constantly produces a dichotomy of "exotic" and "native". At the intersection of the video's two levels – the statements of the course participants on the one hand and the framing of their articulation through the interior of the school on the other – it becomes clear how the individual perspectives of the course participants enter into a relationship to the social and ideological context of the institution. The problem discernable in the video is also that of translation. The aspect that the personal narrations of the course participants must be translated into Swedish mirrors the gap existing between one's own biography and the new context of life. This becomes evident when the translated text suddenly appears strange to the course participants, and when they have trouble pronouncing it. The problem of translation is symbolically juxtaposed with the situation of the immigrants: can the identity and world of an individual simply be "translated" into a new cultural context? Can one go on living elsewhere under entirely new conditions?

It is also interesting that Ersen does not shoot a pure documentary addressing these circumstances and questions, but incites the course participants, through the workshop, to deal with this topic. The work treats the problem very directly, without constructing *victims*. Practicing in front of the camera imports a theatrical element into the situation, something which is not unusual in coaching situations. What is special about the process Ersen stimulates is that the learning material was elaborated by the students themselves and thus stands in a relationship to the personal life and immigration experiences of those concerned. It is different to the lessons usually found in the curriculum. The re-contextualization of the formulated wishes appears impossible within the context of the course and points to a moment of loss. The significance of the project primarily lies in the effects that the situation has for the participants in terms of their self-perception in the workshop situation.

richtete Schule, wird in Ersens Video wie ein Bild lesbar, das beständig eine Dichotomie von „exotisch" und „heimisch" produziert. Im Schnittpunkt zwischen den beiden Ebenen des Videos – zum einen der Äußerungen der KursteilnehmerInnen und zum anderen der Rahmung ihrer Artikulationen durch das Interieur der Schule – wird deutlich, wie die individuellen Perspektiven der KursteilnehmerInnen mit dem sozialen und ideologischen Kontext der Institution in Beziehung treten. Das im Video erkennbare Problem ist auch eines der Übersetzung. Der Aspekt, dass die persönlichen Erzählungen der KursteilnehmerInnen in die schwedische Sprache umgeschrieben werden müssen, spiegelt den Graben wider, der zwischen eigener Biografie und dem neuen Lebenskontext besteht. Dies wird deutlich, wenn der übersetzte Text den KursteilnehmerInnen plötzlich fremd erscheint und sich der eigenen Aussprache widersetzt. Das Übersetzungsproblem steht bildhaft der Situation der ImmigrantInnen gegenüber: Lassen sich Identität und Lebenswelt eines Individuums so einfach in einen neuen kulturellen Kontext „übersetzen"? Kann man an einem anderen Ort unter komplett neuen Vorzeichen weiterleben?

Interessant ist, dass auch Ersen keine pure Dokumentation über diese Umstände und Fragen dreht, sondern die KursteilnehmerInnen durch den Workshop vielmehr zu der Erarbeitung des Themas anregt. Die Arbeit nähert sich sehr direkt dem Problem, ohne dabei *Opfer* zu konstruieren. Die Übung vor der Kamera importiert dabei ein theatrales Element in die Situation, was in Coaching-Situationen erstmal nicht außergewöhnlich ist. Die Besonderheit in dem von Ersen angeregten Prozess liegt darin, dass das Lehrmaterial von den Lernenden selber erarbeitet wurde und so in einem anderen Verhältnis zu den jeweiligen persönlichen Lebens- und Immigrationserfahrungen der Betroffenen steht, als es die normalerweise im Lehrplan vorgesehenen Lektionen tun. Dabei erscheint die Rekontextualisierung der selbstformulierten Wünsche im Kontext des Unterrichts nicht möglich und zeigt einen Verlustmoment auf. Die Bedeutung des Projekts liegt vor allem in den Effekten, welche die Situation für die Teilnehmen-

At the same time, the situation interrupts the usual procedures at language school. The teachers are also prompted to reflect upon the role they play.

2.2 Annika Eriksson, *Arbeitswelt* (Working World) (2003)

Annika Eriksson, *Arbeitswelt — Martin Hartmann*, 2003

Another example of video as an instrument of interaction in an institutional situation is Annika Eriksson's project *Arbeitswelt* (2003).[8] The artist uses the camera as a means of communicating with a large part of the staff of the Munich branch of Swiss Re, one of the world's largest reinsurance firms. Over a period of several weeks, the artist and her assistant, Phillip Metz, stayed in a room provided by the company. An invitation was sent via inter-office mail to all employees, asking them to take part in an art project and to register with Eriksson for this purpose. The interested employees (more than 50, from the caretaker to members of the executive floor) were asked to select a place in the building that was important for them personally or with regard to their function in the company (see Isa Rosenberger's project described above). The place was then determined as the shooting location where the employees discussed three topics: their position and tasks, what security means for them, and what they associate with the location they had selected. The individual contributions are neither edited, nor are the questions posed in the form of a dialogue. The result is a series of small talks that the speakers declare ended at the moment they deem appropriate.

den in Bezug auf ihre Selbstwahrnehmung in der Situation des Workshops hat. Zugleich unterbricht die Situation das übliche Prozedere der Sprachschule. Auch den Lehrkräften wird die Reflexion ihrer eigenen Rolle abverlangt.

2.2 Annika Eriksson, *Arbeitswelt* (2003)

Ein weiteres Beipiel für Video als Instrument der Interaktion in einer institutionellen Situation ist Annika Erikssons Projekt *Arbeitswelt* (2003).[8] Die Künstlerin nutzt die Kamera als Mittel der Kommunikation mit einem breiten Teil der Belegschaft der Münchener Niederlassung der Swiss Re, einem der weltweit größten Rückversicherer. Über einen Zeitraum von mehreren Wochen hielt sich die Künstlerin mit ihrem Helfer Phillip Metz in einem von der Firma zur Verfügung gestellten Raum auf. Gleichzeitig ging mit der Hauspost eine Einladung an alle MitarbeiterInnen, an einem Kunstprojekt teilzunehmen und sich dafür bei Eriksson anzumelden. Die interessierten MitarbeiterInnen (mehr als 50 Personen, vom Hausmeister bis in die Chefetagen) wurden gebeten, einen Ort im Gebäude auszuwählen, der ihnen persönlich oder in Bezug auf ihre Funktion im Konzern wichtig ist (vgl. oben das Projekt von Isa Rosenberger). Dieser wurde als Drehort festgelegt, an dem der jeweilige Mitarbeiter, die jeweilige Mitarbeiterin, auf drei Themenstellungen eingingen: ihre Position und Aufgaben, was Sicherheit für sie bedeutet und was sie mit dem ausgewählten Ort verbinden. Die einzelnen Beiträge sind weder geschnitten, noch durch Fragen dialogisch angelegt. Es handelt sich um eine Reihe kleiner Vorträge, die von den Sprechenden im für sie geeigneten Moment für beendet erklärt werden. Diese Form ist ohne Regie möglich, weil alle TeilnehmerInnen vorher durch Einzelgespräche mit Eriksson auf die inhaltlichen Fragen und den Ablauf der Aufnahmen vorbereitet wurden. Dabei haben die MitarbeiterInnen auch Einfluss auf die meist statisch ausgerichtete Kameraperspektive nehmen können. In einzelnen Fällen kommt es dabei zu spontanen Anweisungen für Kamerabewegungen bis hin zu kleinen dramaturgischen Inszenierungen. Diese Entscheidungsmöglichkeiten werden von Eriksson an die Teilnehmer weiterge-

This form is possible without directing, because all participants were informed beforehand of the content-related questions and the style of shooting in preliminary discussions with Eriksson. The employees were also allowed to influence the mostly static camera perspective. In some cases, spontaneous instructions for camera movements are given, up to small dramaturgical stagings. Eriksson passes these possibilities to decide on to the participants. The concept of *Arbeitswelt* offers the employees the opportunity to reflect upon and especially to communicate their own position within the company. Afterwards, all contributions, edited sequentially, were shown to all employees in the cafeteria of Swiss Re. As with Ersen, the range of individual contributions and perspectives unfolds parallel to a view of the architecture and the way it is furnished. One can discern different relations between the individual and the overall staging of the company along with the ideas (the company philosophy) it communicates: identification, criticism, pride, defiance, enthusiasm, and soberness, etc. The employees become visible as parts of a micro-society accumulated piece by piece from personal knowledge, observations, views, reflections, as well as the different attitudes toward them.

In order to make the project possible within the frame of a strongly controlled, semi-public situation of the firm, a long series of preliminary discussions with the management of Swiss Re's art department were necessary, who were then able to communicate the concern of the project to the decision-making board and the employees, until an agreement was finally reached. This aspect is important, because often a large proportion of work required to communicate an endeavor and win over the partner subsequently remains invisible in art projects; it is not to be marginalized as nerve-racking preliminary work, but to be acknowledged as an import part of the projects themselves. To convince an authority (as in the case of PTTL, see above) or a firm, that art is not exclusively there to "brighten things up", is already the result of a dialogue between totally different artistically and politically motivated viewpoints. The processes of

reicht. Das Konzept von *Arbeitswelt* bietet den MitarbeiterInnen die Möglichkeit, ihre eigene Position innerhalb des Konzerns zu reflektieren und vor allem auch zu kommunizieren. Sämtliche Beiträge wurden anschließend hintereinander geschnitten in der Kantine der Swiss Re gezeigt, wo sie für alle MitarbeiterInnen sichtbar waren. Wie bei Ersen entfaltet sich das Spektrum der individuellen Beiträge und Perspektiven parallel zu einer Sicht auf die Architektur und die Art ihrer Einrichtung. Unterschiedliche Verhältnisse des Einzelnen gegenüber der Gesamtinszenierung der Firma und der durch sie kommunizierten Ideen (Firmenphilosophie) werden erkennbar: Identifikation, Kritik, Stolz, Trotz, Begeisterung oder Nüchternheit etc. Die MitarbeiterInnen werden als Teile einer Mikrogesellschaft sichtbar, die sich stückchenweise aus dem persönlichen Wissensschatz, den Beobachtungen, Sichtweisen, Reflexionen sowie den unterschiedlichen Haltungen ihr gegenüber akkumuliert.

Damit das Projekt im Rahmen der stark kontrollierten, halböffentlichen Situation des Konzerns möglich werden konnte, bedurfte es zuvor einer langen Reihe von Gesprächen mit der Leitung der Kunstabteilung der Swiss Re, die wiederum in der Lage war, das Anliegen des Projektes dem Vorstand bzw. Mitarbeitern mit Entscheidungsbefugnissen zu kommunizieren, bis es zur Einwilligung kam. Dieser Aspekt ist wichtig, weil häufig ein großer Anteil der Arbeit, der für die Vermittlung eines Vorhabens und das Gewinnen des Partners benötigt wird, in Kunstprojekten später unsichtbar bleibt. Dieser Aspekt der Projekte ist nicht als nervenraubende Vorarbeit zu marginalisieren, sondern als wichtiger Teil ihrer selbst zu bewerten. Allein die Behörde (wie bei PTTL, s.o.) oder die Firma für eine Sichtweise zu gewinnen, dass Kunst nicht ausschließlich der „Verschönerung" dienen muss, ist bereits das Ergebnis eines Dialogs zwischen völlig unterschiedlichen künstlerisch und politisch begründeten Ansichten. Die durch solche Projekte in Gang gesetzten Bewusstseinsprozesse oder Effekte wie die Bildung von gegenseitigem Vertrauen und Interesse und gemeinsamem Spaß, sind kaum objektiv evaluierbar, aber dadurch nicht weniger wichtig.

consciousness triggered by such interactions or effects, such as confidence building, arousing interest, and having fun together, can hardly be evaluated objectively, but they are no less important for this reason.

3. Video as a Work Surface, or: The Creation of thematic work contexts

3.1 Ruth Kaaserer in collaboration with Andrea Beutel, Fatuma Juma, Anna Fleischmann, Shirow Muriuki, Ute Schön, and Venta Seifu-Mulubrhan, *mädchen sind.* (girls are.) (2004)

Ruth Kaaserer's work is based on the collaborative relationship that is built up as part of the work process between the artist and the actors. Similar to Nasrin Tabatabai, she is interested in the aspect of documentation geared to cooperation, in which the medium – entirely or in part – is at the service of the self-representation of others, as in her video *Balance* (2000) that deals with the way in which girls position themselves in public space. Magda Karwat, Andrea Ozabalova, and Ewa Rogal, emigrants living in Austria, speak about their future. Ruth Kaaserer chose a working method for *Balance* that is characterized by a large amount of freedom for the girls. When working with Magda, Andrea, and Ewa, it was important for her "[...] that the girls could

Ruth Kaaserer, *Balance*, 2000

themselves determine how much they wanted to reveal in the conversations." The shooting locations were also chosen together. The girls were given the opportunity to stage themselves in the way in which they wanted to see themselves in

3. Video als Arbeitsfläche, oder: Herstellung thematischer Arbeitszusammenhänge

3.1 Ruth Kaaserer in Zusammenarbeit mit Andrea Beutel, Fatuma Juma, Anna Fleischmann, Shirow Muriuki, Ute Schön und Venta Seifu-Mulubrhan, *mädchen sind.* (2004)

Ruth Kaaserers Arbeit beruht auf dem kollaborativen Verhältnis, das sich als Teil des Arbeitsprozesses zwischen ihr und den Darstellenden aufbaut. Ähnlich wie bei Nasrin Tabatabai (s.o.) interessiert sie beispielsweise in dem Video *Balance* (2000) der Aspekt der auf Zusammenarbeit angelegten Dokumentation, in der das Medium – ganz oder teilweise – in den Dienst der Selbstrepräsentation anderer gestellt wird. *Balance* ist eine Videoarbeit, die die Positionierung von Mädchen im öffentlichen Raum thematisiert. Die in Österreich lebenden Emigrantinnen Magda Karwat, Andrea Ozabalova und Ewa Rogal sprechen über ihre Zukunft. Ruth Kaaserer hat für *Balance* eine Arbeitweise gewählt, die sich durch das hohe Maß an Raum charakterisiert, der für die Mädchen offen gehalten wird. In der Umsetzung mit Magda, Andrea und Ewa war es ihr wichtig, „[...] dass die Mädchen selber bestimmen konnten, wie viel sie in den Gesprächen von sich hergeben wollten". Auch die Auswahl der Drehorte fand in gemeinsamer Absprache statt. Zugleich wurde den Mädchen die Möglichkeit gegeben, die eigene Inszenierung dabei so vorzunehmen, wie sie sich in der jeweiligen Situation gerne sehen wollten. Sowohl diese Arbeitsmethode als auch ihr thematischer Fokus auf die mediale Repräsentation von Mädchen und jungen Frauen in der Öffentlichkeit erfahren mit dem Projekt *mädchen sind.* (2004)[9] eine spannende Weiterentwicklung.

Von Februar bis September 2004 arbeitete die Künstlerin in München zusammen mit einer Gruppe von sechs jungen Frauen – Andrea Beutel, Fatuma Juma, Anna Fleischmann, Shirow Muriuki, Ute Schön und Venta Seifu-Mulubrhan, alle zwischen 16 und 20 Jahren. Gemeinsam entwickelten sie das Anliegen, die Situation von Frauen und Mädchen zum Gegenstand einer Gameshow zu machen bzw. das Format Game-

the respective situations. Both this working method and the thematic focus on the media representation of girls and young women in public are further pursued in an exciting way with the project *mädchen sind.* (2004).⁹

Ruth Kaaserer, *mädchen sind.*, 2004

From February to September 2004, the artist worked in Munich together with a group of six young women – Andrea Beutel, Fatuma Juma, Anna Fleischmann, Shirow Muriuki, Ute Schön, and Venta Seifu-Mulubrhan, all between 16 and 20 years old. They jointly developed the idea of making the situation of women and girls the subject of a game show, or rather artistically distorting the game show format for their own purposes and points of view. Kaaserer did not meet the girls as a group: "When I started looking for young women for the project, it was very important for me not to bring together an homogenous group – I wanted young women who had made different experiences due to their varying backgrounds or living conditions, but who were open and curious enough to get involved with each other" (Kaaserer).¹⁰ She visited numerous youth centers and various institutions and organizations in Munich to find participants for the project in talks. During these encounters, many of the girls' questions and points of criticism already became pivotal for the concept and the further course of the project.

The widespread game-show or talk-show format offers an interesting medium for dealing with the subject. In TV shows, gender roles are established through repetitive and typified represen-

show für ihre eigenen Zwecke und Sichtweisen künstlerisch zu verfremden. Die Mädchen traf Kaaserer nicht als zusammenhängende Gruppe: „Als ich mich für das Projekt auf die Suche nach jungen Frauen gemacht habe, war es mir sehr wichtig, eine nicht homogene Gruppe zusammenzustellen – es sollten junge Frauen sein, die aufgrund ihrer unterschiedlichen Herkunft oder Lebensumstände verschiedene Erfahrungen gemacht hatten, jedoch Offenheit und Neugierde besaßen, um sich aufeinander einzulassen" (Kaaserer).¹⁰ Hierzu besuchte sie zahlreiche Jugendzentren und verschiedene Einrichtungen und Organisationen in München, um in Gesprächen Teilnehmerinnen für das Projekt zu finden. Bereits in diesen Begegnungen bekamen viele der Fragen oder Kritikpunkte der Mädchen eine zentrale Bedeutung für das Konzept des Projekts sowie seines weiteren Verlaufs.

Das weit verbreitete Sendeformat der Game- bzw. Talkshow bietet für die Auseinandersetzung mit dem Thema eine interessante Arbeitsfläche an. In Fernsehshows werden Geschlechterrollen durch repetitive und typologisierte Darstellungen von Männern und Frauen festgeschrieben. Publikum und Moderation haben dabei Normalisierungsfunktion. Geschlechterrollen werden nicht neu ausgehandelt, sondern lediglich als Klischees affirmiert. Im gemeinsamen Arbeitsprozess von *mädchen sind.* wurden solche Zusammenhänge und ihre medialen Bedingungen diskutiert und über Möglichkeiten ihrer spielerischen Umkehrung und Brechung nachgedacht. Die für den Video-Mitschnitt produzierte Show *mädchen sind.* eignete sich formale Ähnlichkeiten und Elemente von Gameshows an, wie Studioraum, Studiogäste, Moderation, Videoprojektionsfläche für Zuspielungen, Telefonspiel und Interviews. Mittels einer clipartigen Animation und einem von den Teilnehmerinnen selbst geschriebenen und eingesungenen Song¹¹ sowie Vor- und Abspann erfahren die Show und die eingespielten Reportagen eine medial versierte Rahmung. Zugleich werden die genutzten Darstellungsmittel laufend mit abweichenden Inhalten oder neuen Kommunikationsmustern konfrontiert: Die Interviews mit PassantInnen („[...] soll es mehr nackte Männer in der

tations of men and women. Audience and presenters have a normalizing function. Gender roles are not renegotiated, but merely affirmed as clichés. In the joint working process of *mädchen sind.*, such relations and their media-related conditions, as well as possibilities to reverse and break them in a playful way, were discussed. The show *mädchen sind.* produced for the video adopted formal similarities and elements of game shows such as studio, studio guests, presenters, video projection screen for remote contribution inserts, telephone games, and interviews. The show and the inserted reportages are framed in a media-experienced way by a clip-like animation and a song[11] written and sung by the participants themselves, as well as opening and end credits. At the same time, the utilized means of representation are constantly confronted with deviating contents or new communication patterns: The interviews with passers-by ("[...] should there be more nude men in advertising?") or with one of the coordinators of youth work with young girls in Munich, are conducted in such a way that enough time is given for the answers, thus avoiding clichés; the game of telephone scrabble deals with words like "respect" and "self-confidence" and what they personally mean for the caller; the round-table talk addresses topics such as the representation of women in advertising; and an animated sweepstake is about the critical interpretation of advertising images. The program is produced in a casual and professional way. Watching it raises interesting questions pertaining to the public image of young women and the media construction of these images, and is at the same time fun (a declared goal of one of the female presenters at the beginning of the show). The entire atmosphere is unaffected and playful, e.g., when the producers of the show dance through a pedestrian underpass to the self-produced jingle at the beginning. Or when three of the participants can be recognized as icon graphics on the logo developed for the project, which is also distributed as a sticker in public space. The girls are in control of all the details of their self-produced program and maintain their own media space according to the motto: "[...] if some guy on the under-

Werbung geben?") oder mit einer der Koordinatorinnen der Münchner Mädchenarbeit werden so geführt, dass genug Zeit besteht um nicht laufend in Klischees antworten zu müssen; im Telefonscrabble geht es um Wörter wie „Respekt" und „Selbstvertrauen" und was diese den Anrufern persönlich bedeuten, in der Talkrunde werden Themen wie Frauendarstellungen in der Werbung besprochen und bei einem animierten Gewinnspiel geht es um die kritische Interpretation der Werbebilder. Die Sendung ist ungezwungen und professionell gemacht. Sie anzusehen wirft interessante Fragen bezüglich des öffentlichen Bildes junger Frauen bzw. ihrer medialen Konstruktion auf und macht zugleich Spaß (ein erklärtes Ziel einer der Moderatorinnen zu Beginn der Show). Die gesamte Atmosphäre ist zwanglos und spielerisch, zum Beispiel wenn die Macherinnen der Sendung im Vorspann locker zum selbstproduzierten Jingle durch einen Fußgängertunnel tanzen. Oder wenn im eigens für das Projekt entwickeltem Logo, das zugleich als Sticker im öffentlichen Raum verteilbar ist, drei der Beteiligten als Icon-Grafiken wiederzuerkennen sind. Die Mädchen kontrollieren alle Details der von ihnen selbstproduzierten Sendung und behaupten ihren eigenen medialen Raum, Motto: „[...] if some guy on the underground sits himself beside me and tries to make more space for himself then I'll respond in a similar vein. I have no intention of being driven into a corner."[12]

Video wird in dem Projekt für Kaaserer und die Mädchen zu einer gemeinsamen Arbeitsfläche. Alle können in diesem Prozess voneinander lernen und ihre jeweils unterschiedlichen Erfahrungen einbringen. Das Projekt wird von Kaaserer initiiert und begleitet, den Mädchen steht offen, wie sie es sich aneignen. Die Annäherung an das Thema beginnt von Anfang an als Austausch untereinander. Die Erzählungen und Eindrücke der Mädchen aus ihrem Alltag und ihren eigenen medialen Rezeptionsgewohnheiten formen die Inhalte und Methoden des gemeinsamen Vorhabens. Zugleich werden die Klischees medialer Repräsentationsformen analysiert um später selbst damit spielen zu können. Auch muss jede von ihnen in der Gruppe Stück für Stück ihre

ground sits himself beside me and tries to make more space for himself then I'll respond in a similar vein. I have no intention of being driven into a corner."[12]

In the project, video becomes a common medium for Kaaserer and the girls. They can all learn from each other in this process and contribute in the different experiences. The project is initiated and accompanied by Kaaserer, and the girls can decide how they want to adopt it. From the very start, the theme is approached in the form of mutual exchange. The girls' narrations and impressions from their everyday life and their own media reception habits form the content and the methods of the joint endeavor. At the same time, the clichés of the forms of media representation are analyzed in order to be able to play with them later. Each girl must gradually learn to test her possibilities and abilities within the group: Who prefers conducting interviews in the street? Or who would rather take care of the technological and visual aspects, e.g., the stage decoration? Then there is the question of the dimensions (time, inclination) of their own commitment, and how the decisions are made within the group: How are competences negotiated and determined?[13] Hence, the project places those involved in a permanent working context for a relatively long period of time, offering intense social experiences going beyond the thematic issues and the acquisition of media competence. The personal effects this situation has on the participants can at most be reflected on the level of the video, meaning that the video alone is not enough for the reception of such a project. Next to the video, the practice itself is a product that for a certain time-span has become an integral part of the concrete living situation of a group of young women who had very little to do with art or video production beforehand.[14] On a further level, the complex decision-making procedures, and the actions they are based on, must also be considered. There is a possibility that some of the girls will now present the video and its process to people of the same age at different schools, and that *mädchen sind.* will be contiued in this manner.[15]

Möglichkeiten und Fähigkeiten ausprobieren lernen: Wer führt lieber Interviews auf der Straße? Oder, wer kümmert sich lieber um technische und visuelle Aspekte, zum Beispiel bei der Dekoration der Bühne? Dazu kommt die Frage nach den Dimensionen (Zeit, Lust) des eigenen Engagements und danach, wie Entscheidungen in der Gruppe getroffen werden: Wie werden Kompetenzen ausgehandelt und erkannt?[13] So bringt das Projekt die Beteiligten über einen relativ langen Zeitraum in einen festen Arbeitszusammenhang, der über thematische Fragestellungen und die Aneignung medialer Kompetenz hinaus eine intensive soziale Erfahrung bietet. Die persönlichen Effekte dieser Situation für die Teilnehmerinnen lassen sich auf der Ebene des Videos allenfalls spiegeln. Das bedeutet, für die Rezeption eines solchen Projektes kann das Video allein nicht genügen. Als Produkt steht neben dem Video die Praxis selbst, die über einen bestimmten Zeitraum fester Teil der konkreten Lebenssituation einer Gruppe von jungen Frauen geworden ist, die vorher wenig mit Kunst- oder Videoproduktion zu tun hatten.[14] Auf einer zusätzlichen Ebene müssen die komplexen Entscheidungsvorgänge und die ihnen zu Grunde liegenden Handlungen mitgedacht werden. Eventuell kommt es nun dazu, dass einige der Mädchen das Video und seinen Prozess selber in verschiedenen Schulen Gleichaltrigen präsentieren und *mädchen sind.* auf diese Weise fortsetzen.[15]

3.2 kpD (kleines postfordistisches Drama), *Kamera läuft!* (2004)

kpD, *Kamera läuft!*, 2004

3.2 kpD (small post-Fordist drama), *Kamera läuft!* (Camera running!) (2004)

kpD, *Kamera läuft!*, 2004

In the project *Kamera läuft!*, the documentation of a specific social reality also forms the starting point for further cultural examinations, in which video becomes a decisive, joint instrument and in a certain respect also a *meeting point* for those involved. kpD – Marion von Osten, Katja Reichard, Brigitta Kuster and Isabell Lorey – jointly worked out the exhibition and research project *Atelier Europa* (Studio Europe) (2004)[16] initiated by Marion von Osten, in the context of which the video *Kamera läuft!*[17] was also shot. The way in which the video originated demonstrates how the medium can become a tool within a thematic and collective work context. The aim of *Atelier Europa* was to investigate the precarious working and living conditions of cultural producers from individual point of view. The objective consisted not least in developing requests for change and possibilities to take action and/or establish concrete associations in order to produce a new reality. A special starting point was the observation that unpaid or underpaid activities and creative professions – formerly assumed to be exceptions to wage labor – have been stylized in post-Fordist societies to models of self-determined work [by politics and business].[18] The project began by conducting interviews on this topic with 15 cultural producers living in Berlin. They were all asked the same questions: "1) What does your working life look like? /// 2) What do you like about it and what

Auch in dem Projekt *Kamera läuft!* bildet die Dokumentation einer bestimmten sozialen Realität den Ausgangspunkt für eine weiterführende kulturelle Auseinandersetzung, in der Video maßgeblich zum gemeinsamen Instrument und in gewisser Hinsicht auch zum *Treffpunkt* für die Beteiligten wird. „kpD" – Marion von Osten, Katja Reichard, Brigitta Kuster und Isabell Lorey – erarbeiteten gemeinsam das von Marion von Osten initiierte Ausstellungs- und Forschungsprojekt *Atelier Europa* (2004)[16], in dessen Kontext auch das Video *Kamera läuft!*[17] gedreht wurde. Die Entstehung des Videos führt vor, wie das Medium zum Instrument innerhalb eines thematischen und kollektiven Arbeitszusammenhangs werden kann. *Atelier Europa* hatte das Ziel, die prekären Arbeits- und Lebensverhältnisse von KulturproduzentInnen aus eigener Perspektive zu untersuchen. Das Ziel dabei war nicht zuletzt, Veränderungswünsche und Handlungsmöglichkeiten bzw. konkrete Zusammenschlüsse für die Herstellung einer neuen Realität zu entwickeln. Einen besonderen Ausgangspunkt spielt dabei die Beobachtung, dass un- oder unterbezahlte Tätigkeiten und kreative Berufe – ehemals als Ausnahmetätigkeiten zur Lohnarbeit angenommen – in postfordistischen Gesellschaften zu Modellen selbstbestimmter Arbeit [von Seiten der Politik und der Wirtschaft] stilisiert worden sind".[18] Zu Beginn des Projekts wurden zu dieser Thematik Interviews mit 15 hauptsächlich in Berlin lebenden KulturproduzentInnen geführt. An alle wurden die gleichen Fragen gerichtet: „1. Wie sieht dein Arbeitsleben aus? /// 2. Was gefällt dir daran und was sollte sich ändern? /// 3. Wann und warum wird dir alles zuviel, und was machst du dann? /// 4. Was stellst du dir unter einem ‚guten Leben' vor? /// 5. Sollten KulturproduzentInnen sich auf Grund ihrer gesellschaftlichen Vorzeigerolle mit anderen sozialen Bewegungen zusammentun, um an neuen Formen der Organisierung zu arbeiten?"

Interessant war, dass zu diesem Zeitpunkt noch nicht eindeutig geklärt war, wie genau mit dem so gesammelten Textmaterial verfahren werden würde. Fest stand nur, dass es nicht um eine Dokumentation der Interviews allein gehen sollte, also um die Abbildung der Situation, sondern dass das

should change? /// 3) When and why does it get too much for you and what do you then do? /// 4) What's your idea of a 'good life'? /// 5) Should cultural producers, due to their social model role, join other social movements to work on new forms of organization?"

It is interesting that at this point in time there was no definite decision on what to do with the collected text material. It was only clear that it should not merely consist in documenting the interviews, i.e. in depicting the situation, but that the material should be further translated or contextualized. This was then done by staging a casting session that was publicly advertised at places where young actors are trained or meet in Zurich, as well as by personally addressing them. The actors willing to take part in the casting session were given edited versions of the interview texts beforehand, which were then to be played or scenically interpreted during the casting session. As is customary for a casting situation, video was used in its function as a medium of (self-)observation (recording) and evaluation. But as opposed to what is usually the case with castings, the video shots already provided the material out of which *Kamera läuft!* was then edited. The casting itself became a film. The aesthetic strategy lies in primarily utilizing material that in commercial productions only has a secondary function within a certain work step, where it serves to actually control and select, i.e. to further develop the product – in the case of casting, testing the aptitude as far as acting is concerned and selecting the candidates. Reversed, this principle is no longer concerned with achieving an end product, but instead with visualizing the underlying working strategies and the contents that they convey in terms of the essence of the product itself. Now, this initially critical strategy has long been recognized as being commercially exploitable and has become a mainstream broadcasting format of the entertainment industry. Due to *Deutschland sucht den Superstar* (Germany Searches for the Superstar) and numerous similar programs and casting shows, the production of culture is tightly linked to techniques of the self and of self-marketing

Material eine weitere Übersetzung bzw. Kontextualisierung erfahren sollte. Diese wurde dann mit der Inszenierung eines Castings hergestellt, das öffentlich an Ausbildungs- oder Aufenthaltsorten von jungen Schauspielern in Zürich ausgeschrieben oder über persönliche Ansprachen beworben wurde. Den Schauspielern, die an dem Casting teilnehmen wollten, wurden zuvor editierte Versionen der Interviewtexte ausgehändigt, die während des Castings aufgeführt bzw. szenisch interpretiert werden sollten. Wie für die Situation des Castings üblich, wurde Video in seiner Funktion als Medium der (Selbst-)Beobachtung (Aufnahme) und Auswertung genutzt. Anders als bei Castings normalerweise der Fall, lieferten die so entstandenen Aufnahmen aber bereits die Videobilder, aus denen *Kamera läuft!* geschnitten ist. Das Casting wurde selber zum Film. Die ästhetische Strategie liegt darin, ein Material primär zu benutzen, das in kommerziellen Produktionszusammenhängen nur eine sekundäre Funktion innerhalb eines bestimmten Arbeitsschrittes hat. Dieser würde im eigentlichen Sinn der Kontrolle und Auswahl dienen, also der Weiterentwicklung des Produkts – im Casting also der Kontrolle schauspielerischer Eignung und der Auswahl der Kandidaten. In seiner Umkehrung geht es bei diesem Prinzip nicht mehr um das Erreichen des Endproduktes, sondern vielmehr um die Visualisierung der ihm zugrunde liegenden Arbeitsstrategien und den Gehalten, die diese über das Wesen des Produktes selbst vermitteln. Mittlerweile ist diese anfangs kritische Strategie längst als kommerziell verwertbar erkannt und im Mainstream der Unterhaltungsindustrie selbst zum Sendeformat geworden. Durch *Deutschland sucht den Superstar* und zahlreiche andere verwandte Sendungen und Casting-Shows wird die Produktion von Kultur eng mit Techniken des Selbst und der Selbstvermarktung unter ökonomischen und kompetitiven Gesichtspunkten verknüpft. Als „Künstler" werden die vorgeführt, welche die Regeln am optimalsten auszufüllen wissen. *Kamera läuft!* begreift die soziale Realität des Castings als ästhetisierte Form des Wettbewerbs, in dem das durch die Interviews gewonnene Material unter den Bedingungen dieser Realität zum Sprechen gebracht wird. Das Paradox dabei ist, dass die Forderung

under economic and competitive aspects. Those who can best comply with the rules are presented as "artists". *Kamera läuft!* grasps the social reality of casting as an aesthetic form of competition that lets the voice of the material acquired through the interviews be heard under the conditions of this reality. The paradox is that the demand and the desire for flexible, self-designed living and working contexts, as they are voiced in the interviews, and the productivity-oriented theatricalization of work under neoliberal conditions of production, appear inextricably linked to each other in casting.

This variant of video practice can be compared in one respect to the strategy exemplified by Tabatabai. The issue is passing on the act – a certain ability or a certain material, a certain *subject matter* – to others. Through the way in which the others deal with it, e.g., the way in which the interview material is performed, it becomes independent and undergoes a change. Marks of appropriation are inscribed on its aesthetic surface. Only through the difference to itself, which is created by further processing, does it become detached from itself as purely factual or phenomenological information. The quality of this form of documentary practice lies in that it takes into account the non-identity of representation and object by activating the dialectical nature of all interpretations of factual material through participative strategies. In this sense, the well-meant *Need to Document* alone does not suffice – the aesthetic *shift* or *diffusion* of the representing format itself is needed. The practices dealt with above do not accomplish this as an expression of an artist-self, but by means of numerous forms and possibilities of playing that are offered through collaboration, participation and empowerment in the process of a cultural production understood as open and anti-disciplinary. Instead of working on people, they work with people, and instead of documenting social reality, they are dedicated to producing a new reality.

The models of current video practices presented here by no means exhaust the field of possibili-

und das Begehren nach flexiblen, selbstgestalteten Lebens- und Arbeitszusammenhängen, wie sie in den Interviews vorkommen, und die produktivitätsorientierte Theatralisierung von Arbeit unter neoliberalen Produktionsbedingungen, im Casting auf unlösbare Weise miteinander verknüpft erscheinen.

Diese Spielart der Praxis mit Video lässt sich in einem Punkt mit der am Beispiel Tabatabais (s.o.) veranschaulichten Strategie vergleichen. Es geht dabei um den Akt, etwas – eine bestimmte Fähigkeit oder ein bestimmtes Material, einen bestimmten Stoff – an andere weiterzureichen. Durch die Art und Weise des Umgangs anderer damit, also zum Beispiel, wie das Material der Interviews aufgeführt wird, erfährt es eine Verselbständigung und Veränderung. Auf seiner ästhetischen Oberfläche schreiben sich Spuren der Aneignung ein. Erst in dieser durch Verarbeitung entstandenen Differenz zu sich selbst löst es sich von seinem Dasein als rein faktische oder phänomenale Information. Die Qualität dieser Spielart dokumentarischer Praxis liegt darin, dass sie der Nichtidentität von Darstellung und Sache Rechnung trägt, indem sie durch partizipative Strategien den dialogischen Charakter jeder Deutung faktischen Materials aktiviert. In diesem Sinn ist das gut gemeinte Need to Document allein nicht genug – es braucht die ästhetische Verschiebung oder Diffusion des darstellenden Formates selbst. Diese wird durch die weiter oben besprochenen Praktiken nicht als Ausdruck eines Künstler-Ichs hergestellt, sondern mittels zahlreicher Formen und Spielmöglichkeiten, die sich durch Zusammenarbeit, Beteiligung und Ermächtigung im Prozess einer offen und antidisziplinär verstandenen kulturellen Produktion anbieten. Anstatt über Leute zu arbeiten, arbeiten sie mit Leuten und anstelle der Dokumentation sozialer Realität, widmen sie sich der Produktion neuer Realität.

Mit den hier vorgestellten Modellen einer aktuellen Videopraxis ist das Feld der Möglichkeiten keineswegs erschöpft. Es liegt auf der Hand, dass in allen emanzipatorischen Modellen die Frage nach der Repräsentation auftaucht, bzw. geklärt werden muss, wer das *Sagen* hat, ob Entscheidun-

ties. It is obvious that in all emancipatory models the question of representation arises, and it must be settled who is in the *driver's seat*, whether decisions are made collectively or through traditional stage directions, whether those concerned can use video to document their reality autonomously or whether they are subject to heteronomous conditions. The many and diverse possibilities already made use of in the presented models are surprising, from a service only providing technological competence to diverse moderator models, up to thematically oriented projects in which themes are jointly elaborated. Further hybrid forms are conceivable. The issue is an overall development that can be characterized using the title of an essay by Roland Barthes, *The Death of the Author*[19]. One has the impression that the question as to whether the video artist completely disappears behind his or her work and merges with the other, with those involved, with the audience, or instead continues to insist on his or her competence regarding direction, is constantly being negotiated anew – the results are correspondingly open and varied.

This open situation refers to a discontinuity when comparing the approaches of 1968, which were outlined above, with those of today. The works are placed in a political context more seldom nowadays and instead in an aesthetic one. One needn't lament over this shift as a sign of an affirmative depoliticization, but can indeed regard it as a turn to the specific conditions of the medium: playing with the material does remain immanent, but the results are convincing precisely for this reason, they often owe their charm to the absence of abstract, a priori ideas.

gen kollektiv herbeigeführt werden oder in traditioneller Regieanweisung, ob die Betroffenen ihre Wirklichkeit per Video autonom dokumentieren können oder ob sie heteronomen Bedingungen unterliegen. Gerade dabei überraschen die vielfältigen Möglichkeiten, die bereits in den vorgestellten Praxismodellen zum Tragen kommen, von der reinen Dienstleistung, bei der gerade noch die technische Kompetenz angeboten wird über diverse Moderatoren-Modelle bis hin zu thematisch ausgerichteten Projekten der gemeinsamen Erarbeitung von Themen. Weitere Mischformen sind denkbar. Es geht dabei um eine Entwicklung, die zusammenfassend mit dem Titel des Aufsatzes von Roland Barthes *Der Tod des Autors*[19] charakterisiert werden kann. Man gewinnt den Eindruck, dass die Frage, ob der Video-Künstler vollends hinter seinem Werk verschwindet und im anderen, im Betroffenen, im Zuschauer aufgeht oder weiterhin auf einer Regiekompetenz besteht, ständig neu verhandelt wird – entsprechend offen und vielfältig sind die Ergebnisse.

Diese offene Situation verweist auf eine Diskontinuität im Vergleich der eingangs skizzierten Ansätze von ´68 und heute: Entschieden seltener als früher werden die Arbeiten in einen politischen als vielmehr in einen ästhetischen Kontext gestellt, und diese Verschiebung muss nicht als Anzeichen einer affirmativen Entpolitisierung beklagt werden, sondern kann durchaus als eine Hinwendung zu den spezifischen Bedingungen des Mediums betrachtet werden: Das Spiel mit dem Material bleibt zwar immanent, aber gerade deshalb werden die Ergebnisse überzeugend, ihren Charme verdanken sie oft der Abwesenheit abstrakter, apriorischer Vorstellungen.

---

1 Georg Christoph Tholen, "Die Zäsur der Medien," *Kulturphilosophische Konturen*, Frankfurt a. M., 2002.
2 see http://www.ganahl.info [04/10/05].
3 While ... , Kunstverein Hamburg, 1995. See also Søren Grammel, "The Reader is the Extended Author. Or: Does putting a watercooler and some teabags into an exhibition space really cause a change in the hierarchy between artist and audience?" *Revisiting the Show*, Vector Association and Matei Bejenaru (eds.), Iasi (Romania) 2003.

1 Georg Christoph Tholen: *Die Zäsur der Medien. Kulturphilosophische Konturen*, Frankfurt a. M. 2002.
2 Vgl. http://www.ganahl.info [10.04.05].
3 *While...*, Kunstverein Hamburg, 1995. Vgl. auch Søren Grammel: The Reader is the Extended Author. Or: Does putting a watercooler and some teabags into an exhibition space really cause a change in the hierarchy between artist and audience?, in: Matei Bejenaru (Hg.): *Revisiting the Show*, Vector Association, Iasi (Rumänien) 2003.
4 Vgl. das Programm der Gruppe unter http://www.pttl.be/nl/07.html [10.04.05].

4 See the group's program at http://www.pttl.be/nl/07.html [04/10/05].

5 Thomas Hirschhorn also attempted to work with these means during his *Bataille-Monument* project (2003) by setting up a local TV studio enabling youths to independently produce videos. The studio, which was led by Hirschhorn as a permanently available, competent caretaker, soon became of meeting place for young people from the area. The opportunity to work with video was a magical point of attraction and functioned as a catalyst for the "studio" situation, in which video production and the formation of a community corresponded with each other on the same level. The difference between Hirschhorn's project and PTTL of course lies in the fact that the latter neither originated in an art context (even though it was based on the commitment of artists), nor ended up in any significant way in this context. Moreover, PTTL originated in the personal experience made in the context of the producers, while Hirschhorn came to Kassel as a "guest" of Documenta11 and installed the project in a targeted way in a part of the city characterized by social conflicts—a place he had previously never been involved with. Precisely for this reason, the project is frequently criticized as lacking credibility and being calculating. But those who spent several days there are aware of the great intensity and importance that the situation had for the youths in the immediate neighborhood—how they accepted it and the interesting productions that were created there.

6 See http://www.papertiger.org [04/10/05]. Since 1981, Paper Tiger TV has been producing a committed and humorous magazine for the public channels in New York and San Francisco on a weekly basis. Their counter-reportages on the Gulf War received attention in Europe as well.

7 See also http://www.eurovision2000.net [04/10/05].

8 See http://www.kunstverein-muenchen.de (under Archiv, 2003, Dispositiv Workshop, Arbeitswelt) [04/10/05].

9 See http://www.kunstverein-muenchen.de (under Archiv, 2004, Dispositiv Workshop, mädchen sind.) [04/10/05].

10 Ruth: Why did you decide to take part in *mädchen sind.*? // Ute: I think this project can change the way many people regard young women. In addition, I was able to show with this project that a disability needn't reduce one's joy of life and change one's attitude toward life. // Andrea: It wasn't a decision that had to do with weighing, considering, and doubting, which had to be overcome first. When you presented the project to me, I really noticed that you were nervous—you talked so much! I was already sure that I wanted to do it, that it would be good for me, because it all seemed so important. I also had time, I knew it would be exactly the right thing for me this year—those were my thoughts. // Venta: I was very eager to get to know the other girls. It's great what this project led to! // Shirow: I participated in a similar project beforehand, in which we dealt with the rights of girls. We also published a Web site at the time through which you contacted me. I thought I had nothing to lose, maybe I could even learn something. (The excerpt is taken from an exchange of ideas via email after the shooting of mädchen sind.) Translated by K.H.

11 Lyrics of *mädchen sind.*:CHORUS // it's about women / it's about rights / it's about girls / it's about equal rights // it's about / whatever you want / what moves you / and how things will go on // it's about rebellion / emancipation / gender roles / and old traditions // if you don't agree with something / then say so / take action / and don't give up // CHORUS // never stop asking / why things are / the way they are / only because they were always that way / doesn't mean / that they must remain that way / whether you like it or not // CHORUS // start doing it / try it out / take your time and you will see / what you want, what you want / what you want / what you really

want / for yourself / just start / just start now / just start / just start // CHORUS. Translated by K.H.

12 Ruth Kaaserer, "feminist dress codes," http://www.fabrics.at/modules.php?name=Sections&op=printpage&artid=14 [04/10/05].

13 Venta: There were so many suggestions at the beginning that I didn't know where we should start. It became more concrete when we worked with each other. I had a lot of fun during the entire preparation phase, especially with the interviews. (The excerpt is taken from an exchange of ideas via email after the shooting of *mädchen sind.*) Translated by K.H.

14 Andrea: I had no idea at the beginning where the journey would lead to, what *mädchen sind.* could really mean. Even now I still experience our project as very dynamic and still changing, they way we are to at our age. Where the journey will lead to — I have no idea. In any case we have grown stronger and have been enriched by what we experienced and created together — a bit further, each one in her direction. *mädchen sind.*, through dealing with the outside, with public space, has become a journey to the inside, to the self. *mädchen sind.* is a development and an impetus to self-initiative, self-determination and a journey of discovery of undreamt of possibilities and capabilities, and it thus enormously expands the personal freedom of everyone involved! To use Shirow's words: I can do it — and if not, at least I tried it. Translated by K.H.

15 Venta: We want to strengthen particularly young women by speaking about concrete subjects that affect us. We create a new form of public that stands out against the usual representation of young women in the media. We thus support the consciousness that young woman can move about in public space in a self-confident way. // Shirow: By publishing our project we can set examples. One person or another hears the signal and carries it on. It may be just a small step, but it can have a huge impact. // Andrea: Beuys' definition of art and his "social sculpture" comes to my mind. Art is where joint social activity, creation and shaping take place. These were also our ideas, right? From a social point of view our project was a beginning for all of us. And it is our task to pass this new thing, this knowledge on to others and to give an impetus from which others can profit. (see above). Translated by K.H.

16 The Atelier Europa project was shown from April to May 2004 at Kunstverein München, see http://www.kunstverein-muenchen.de (under Archiv, 2004, Atelier Europa), or directly http://www.atelier europa.com [04/10/05].

17 This first provisional version was followed by a final, revised version, the Berlin premiere of which was on September 7, 2004, at NGBK. This text refers to the first, provisional version, which is more interesting in terms of the addressed issues, because the post-production of the video led to an increased fictionalization and construction, which can, in turn, be interesting in other respects.

18 kpD in the text announcing the Berlin premiere (see above).

19 Roland Barthes, "The Death of the Author," *Image, Music, Text*, New York 1977.

dann sag das auch / mach dich dran / und gib nicht auf // CHORUS // hör nicht auf zu fragen / warum etwas so ist / wie es ist // nur weil es immer schon so war / heißt das noch lange nicht / dass es auch so bleiben muss / ob du willst oder nicht // CHORUS // fang doch an / probier es aus / nimm dir Zeit und du wirst sehn / was du willst, was du willst, / was du willst / was du wirklich willst / für dich // fang doch an / fang jetzt doch an / fang doch an, fang doch // CHORUS //

12 Ruth Kaaserer, *feminist dress codes*, http://www.fabrics.at/modules.php?name=Sections&op=printpage&artid=14 [10.04.05].

13 Venta: Am Anfang kamen so viele Vorschläge, dass ich nicht mehr wusste, wo wir anfangen sollten. Das ist dann im Laufe der Zusammenarbeit konkreter geworden. Die ganze Vorbereitung hat mir großen Spaß gemacht, vor allem die Interviews. (Der Auszug ist einem Gedankenaustausch entnommen, der nach den Dreharbeiten zu *mädchen sind.* per E-Mail geführt wurde).

14 Andrea: Wohin die Reise gehen sollte, was *mädchen sind.* wirklich mal bedeuten könnte, wusste ich am Anfang nicht. Auch jetzt erfahre ich unser Projekt als immer noch sehr dynamisch und im Wandel begriffen, wie wir das auch alle aufgrund unseres Alters sind. Wohin die Reise geht — keine Ahnung. Auf jeden Fall sind wir gestärkt und durch das gemeinsam Erlebte und Geschaffene bereichert — ein Stückchen weiter, jede in ihrer Richtung. *mädchen sind.* ist durch die Auseinandersetzung mit dem Äußeren, dem öffentlichen Raum, eine Reise ins Innere, ins Selbst, geworden. *mädchen sind.* ist Entwicklung und Anstoß zur Eigeninitiative, Selbstbestimmung und zu einer Entdeckungsreise in ungeahnte Möglichkeiten und Fähigkeiten und vergrößert damit den ganz persönlichen Spielraum einer jeden ganz gewaltig! Mit Shirows Worten: Ich kann das — und wenn nicht, habe ich es wenigstens probiert. (s.o.)

15 Venta: Wir wollen vor allem junge Frauen bestärken, indem wir konkret über Themen sprechen, die uns betreffen. Da schaffen wir eine neue Form von Öffentlichkeit, die sich von der gängigen Darstellung junger Frauen in den Medien abhebt. So unterstützen wir das Bewusstsein, dass sich junge Frauen selbstsicher im öffentlichen Raum bewegen können. // Shirow: Durch die Veröffentlichung unseres Projektes können Zeichen gesetzt werden. Die eine oder andere Person nimmt die Signale auf und trägt sie weiter. Das ist zwar nur ein kleiner Schritt, aber er kann große Auswirkungen zur Folge haben. // Andrea: Da fällt mir die Kunstdefinition von Beuys und seiner „sozialen Plastik" ein. Kunst ist demnach da, wo gemeinsam sozial gehandelt, geschaffen und gestaltet wird. Und das waren doch auch unsere Ideen, oder? Unser Projekt ist gesellschaftlich gesehen ein Anfang für jede von uns. Und es ist unsere Aufgabe, dieses Neue, dieses Wissen weiterzugeben und damit Anstöße zu geben, von denen auch andere profitieren können. (s.o.)

16 Das Projekt *Atelier Europa* wurde von April bis Mai 2004 im Kunstverein München gezeigt, vgl. http://www.kunstverein-muenchen.de (unter Archiv, 2004, Atelier Europa) oder direkt http://www.ateliereuropa.com [10.04.05].

17 Dieser ersten, provisorischen Version folgte noch eine endgültige, überarbeitete Version, deren Berliner Premiere am 7. September 2004 in der NGBK stattfand. Der vorliegende Text bezieht sich auf die erste, d.h. provisorische Version, die für die hier aufgeworfenen Fragen interessanter ist, weil die Postproduktion des Videos eher zu einer zunehmenden Fiktionalisierung und Konstruktion geführt hat, die wiederum in anderer Hinsicht interessant sein kann.

18 kpD im Ankündigungstext für die Berliner Premiere (s.o.).

19 Roland Barthes: Der Tod des Autors (La mort de l´auteur), erschienen in der Zeitschrift Manteia 1968. Deutsch in: *Texte zur Theorie der Autorschaft*, Stuttgart 2000, S. 181–197.

Dóra Hegyi

The Slaves Freely Choose their Masters[1]

A Few Strategies of Representation Through the Use of the Documentary Form

In the following, a few examples of works will show in which form the documentary was used as a critical strategy by artists in Hungary in two very different political-economic situations. The examples are grasped as key works utilizing the documentary to create situations in which public speech acts are made possible. These are very different in the culture of the "second public sphere"[2] in socialism of the 1970s and after the political change of the socialistic system in 1989 and in the second half of the 1990s, when a direct, critical, socio-political commentary emerged, as well as in the past years in which the consequences of globalization have been perceived in a more conscious way.

"Whatever happened beyond that, reality was the director"[3]

In the wake of the change of the political system of 1989 in Hungary, a vacuum existed[4] in the field of political and critical commentaries by artists, and only in the mid-1990s did some address the current social situation of a society in transition. Until today, there is a lack of artistic positions dealing with the most recent past and the consequences of the previous political system. Neither personal approaches like the film *Intervista* (1998) by the Albanian filmmaker Anri Sala, nor projects like the "work in progress" *Transaction* (since 2000) by the Lithuanian artist duo Nomeda and Gediminas Urbonas that deals with the collective unconscious, are to be found here. It would be worthwhile to examine how this general amnesia in Hungary – not only in the field of contemporary art – can be explained.

It is no coincidence that the work *Inside Out* by Big Hope – Miklós Erhardt and Dominic Hislop – from 1997–1998 was often mentioned as a rare

example of social sensibility in Hungary. With their project, the artists commented on the situation of the losers of the system change, the constantly increasing number of destitute persons and the homeless excluded from the social security net. In cooperation with social workers, disposable cameras were distributed to homeless people. Those involved in the project were to document, without content-related guidelines, what appeared important in their life. After the photos were developed, the participants were asked to comment on them. The photos, along with the comments, were then exhibited in an art context and in a hostel for the homeless.[5] As a result of this contact with the homeless, a film was additionally shot in cooperation with a community of homeless. The documentary feature

Big Hope: Miklós Erhardt & Dominic Hislop, *Inside Out*, László Hudák, 1997–1998

You see even if we find an ugly thing, that's what I wanted to express: a valueless thing, like this guy finds this piece of bread and this guy knows this thing has value, listen here, he knows why it has value, and it has value. And he starts to clean the coffee grounds from it, he beats the dirt off it. So this picture shows that value still exists on earth, you just have to beat the dirt off it, and then you've got it. This bread-beating man shows that there are people in this life — because the bread itself, man is bread as well — so, there are people who still have value. You see he took this bread out, he beat it and he increased its value. In the same way there are people who at some stage, will take us out of the bin (because we are in a bin, we are thrown out of society), and they're going to take us out and increase our value. This is what it's about.

film, *Tequila Gang* (1998), produced by the Balázs Bela Studio,[6] was "realized according to the ideas and the instructions of the members of the Tequila Gang, in which they acted out what

den Jahren 1997–1998 oft zitiert und als seltenes Beispiel für soziale Sensibilität in Ungarn aufgezeigt. Die Künstler kommentierten mit dem Projekt die Situation der Verlierer des Systemwechsels, die stetig zunehmende Zahl der Heruntergekommenen, der aus dem sozialen Netz ausgeschlossenen Obdachlosen. In Zusammenarbeit mit Sozialarbeitern wurden Einwegkameras an Obdachlose verteilt. Die am Projekt Beteiligten sollten ohne inhaltliche Vorgaben dokumentieren, was ihnen in ihrem Leben als wichtig erscheint. Nachdem die Bilder entwickelt waren, wurden die Teilnehmer gebeten, sie zu kommentieren. Die Fotos wurden dann zusammen mit den Kommentaren im Kunstkontext und in einem Obdachlosenheim gezeigt.[5] Aus dem Kontakt mit den Obdachlosen wurde in Zusammenarbeit mit einer Obdachlosengemeinschaft außerdem ein Film gedreht. Der Dokumentarspielfilm *Tequila Gang*

László Hudák, Imre Lénárt, *The Tequila Gang*, 1999

(1998), produziert vom Balázs Béla Studio,[6] wurde „nach den Vorstellungen und nach den Instruktionen der Mitglieder der Tequila-Gang realisiert, wo sie spielten, was sie über ihr Leben denken". Und weiter heißt es im Abspann des Films: „In allem was darüber hinaus passierte, führte die Wirklichkeit Regie." Die Beziehungen der Vierergruppe werden vor der Kamera schonungslos und ohne auf verbale und physische Aggressionen und Frustrationen zu verzichten, gezeigt. Die Mitwirkenden spielen ihr eigenes Leben, die Kontrolle der Kamera beeinflusst ihr Verhalten kaum. Die Bilder des Filmes lassen die Frage offen, ob man einen Dokumentarfilm oder Fiktion sieht. Zwi-

they think of their lives." The end titles of the film stated: "Whatever happened beyond that, reality was the director." The relationships among the group of four are depicted mercilessly in front of the camera, without shrinking from showing physical aggression and frustration. The participants play their own lives; the control of the camera hardly has an effect on their behavior. The film images keep the question open as to whether one is viewing a documentary film or a feature film. Staged scenes are inserted between the real events, video, and super 8 shots alternate, and since the homeless also directed the camera, their reality actually becomes visible. This tension prevails throughout the film and challenges the viewer's ethical stance and feelings.

"if the economy is well, humans are well"[7]

A more recent joint project by Big Hope points out that the impact of the globalized economy is being perceived in an increasingly conscious way.

In *Talking about Economy* (2003), people are shown within the context of their work. They are players in today's globalized economy, practicing classic professions, such as factory worker, teacher, or car mechanic, but also engaged in

Big Hope: Miklós Erhardt & Dominic Hislop, *Talking About Economy*, 2003

jobs newly created by the current economic situation, such as EU advisor, real estate agent and businessman. Representatives of the individual professions are visited in two cities, in

schen die realen Geschehnisse werden inszenierte Szenen gemischt, Video- und Super 8-Aufnahmen wechseln sich ab und da die Kameraführung ebenfalls von Obdachlosen übernommen wurde, wird tatsächlich deren Realität sichtbar. Diese Spannung durchzieht den gesamten Film und fordert die ethische Stellungnahme bzw. das ethische Empfinden des Zuschauers heraus.

„wenn die Wirtschaft in Ordnung ist, geht es den Menschen gut"[7]

Ein neueres Gemeinschaftsprojekt von Big Hope weist darauf hin, dass der Einfluss der globalisierten Wirtschaft immer bewusster wahrgenommen wird.

Im Projekt *Über Ökonomie sprechen* (2003) werden Menschen im Zusammenhang mit ihrer Arbeit gezeigt. Die Dargestellten sind Mitspieler der heutigen globalisierten Wirtschaft, die klassische Berufe, wie Fabrikarbeiter, Lehrer oder Automechaniker, ausüben, oder aber Jobs, die aufgrund der heutigen wirtschaftlichen Lage entstanden sind, wie EU-Berater, Immobilienmakler und Geschäftsmann. In zwei Städten werden RepräsentantInnen der einzelnen Berufe aufgesucht. In Dunaújváros, einem Musterbeispiel sozialistischer Städtegründung in Ungarn (1949 als Stalinstadt gegründet), das heute den Zusammenbruch und Ausverkauf der lokalen Schwerindustrie erlebt, und in Berlin, einer Weltstadt im ökonomischen Umbruch, werden die gleichen Fragen gestellt: „Wie würden Sie die Rolle der Wirtschaft in der Gesellschaft beschreiben? Was ist Ihre persönliche Beziehung zur Arbeit? Was macht für Sie gute Wirtschaft aus? Was macht für Sie schlechte Wirtschaft aus?"[8] Die Interviews wurden im Ausstellungsraum auf Bildschirmen präsentiert und aus den jeweiligen Filmen wurde ein Standbild als farbige Illustration an die Wand gemalt.[9] Überraschenderweise wird die Macht der Wirtschaft in den meisten Fällen unkritisch und affirmativ als notwendig angesehen, „wenn die Wirtschaft in Ordnung ist, geht es den Menschen gut". Dabei wird nicht reflektiert, warum das Nachdenken über Ökonomie relevant sein kann. Es bleibt den BetrachterInnen überlassen, sich darüber klar zu werden, inwieweit sie ein Bewusstsein für ihre

Dunaújváros, a perfect example of a socialist city founded in 1949 as Stalin City, which is today experiencing the collapse and sell-out of its local heavy industry, and in Berlin, a cosmopolitan city undergoing constant economic change. In both cities, the same questions are posed: "How would you describe the role of the economy in society? What is your personal relation to work? What is a good economy in your opinion? And what is a bad economy?"[8] The interviews were presented on monitors in the exhibition space, and a still picture from each film was painted on the wall as a color illustration.[9] It is surprising that in most cases the power of the economy is viewed in an uncritical and affirmative manner as something necessary, "if the economy is well, humans are well." It is not reflected why it can be relevant to give the economy more consideration. It is up to the viewers to get clear in their minds to what extent they possess an awareness of their situation which is determined by the increasingly less controllable world power of private economy. The project *Talking about Economy* does not point to alternatives, it presents and takes stock of attitudes.

At this point, it is worth looking back at a work that was created in the years of socialism, with the full awareness that the tarnished language takes a stand against the existing power relations and must therefore reckon with being silenced. The comparison is also interesting because in Tamás Szentjóby's film *Kentaur* from 1975[10], people are also shown within the context of their work, but their relationship to leisure time is dealt with in a completely different sociopolitical situation.

"what may be said and what is worthwhile saying"[11]

"Newest edition of *No Grass Grows Here*!", the paperboy shouts in a smoky café in Tamás Szentjóby's film *Kentaur*. The ironic name of the newspaper reporting on world events in an alleged objective way undoubtedly refers to the devastating impact of ideology. *Kentaur* was immediately censored after its official screening

Lage haben, die von der immer weniger kontrollierbaren Weltmacht der Privatwirtschaft bestimmt wird. Das Projekt *Über Ökonomie sprechen* zeigt keine Alternative auf, es stellt lediglich dar und inventarisiert die Meinungen.

An diesem Punkt lohnt sich der Rückblick auf ein Werk, das in den Jahren des Sozialismus entstanden ist, im vollen Bewusstsein darüber, dass die angeschlagene Sprache gegen die existierenden Machtverhältnisse Stellung nimmt und damit zu rechnen hat, dass sie zum Schweigen gebracht wird. Der Vergleich ist auch deshalb interessant, weil im Film *Kentaur* von Tamás Szentjóby[10] aus dem Jahr 1975 Menschen ebenfalls im Kontext ihrer Arbeit gezeigt werden, ihre Beziehung zur Freiheit aber in einer ganz anderen gesellschaftspolitischen Situation behandelt wird.

Tamás Szentjóby, *Kentaur*, 1975

„was man sagen darf und was sich lohnt zu sagen"[11]

„Neuste Ausgabe von *Hier wächst kein Gras*!", ruft der Zeitungsjunge in einem verrauchten Cafe im Film *Kentaur* von Tamás Szentjóby. Der ironische Name des Presseorgans, das von den Ereignissen der Welt objektiv berichten soll, weist zweifellos auf die verwüstende Wirkung der Ideologie hin. *Kentaur* wurde gleich nach seiner offiziellen Werkpräsentation in der Budapester Filmfabrik zensiert und für 15 Jahre der Öffentlichkeit vorenthalten.[12] Der Film benutzt die Methoden des Dokumentarfilms, unterläuft aber gleichzeitig die objektive Darstellungsweise. Der Titel weist auf

at the Budapest Film Factory and withheld from the public for 15 years.[12] The film utilizes documentary film methods, while simultaneously undermining the objective form of representation. The title refers to the montage of images and sound; the dialogues were added to the images afterwards by the artist and appear as a deliberately disturbing, shifted dub recording. This kind of audio-visual montage is a familiar method in the genre of propaganda films and newscasts, where the images illustrate the interpreting commentaries. In *Kentaur*, however, image and sound do not support each other; instead, a tension is created between both levels. The documentary-style shots depict scenes of socialist everyday life between factory and planning office, from the canteen to the waiting room of a railway station. Szentjóby makes use of a distanced and objectifying method. In each scene, the camera approaches the speakers from a total view, and after the dialogue ends, looks back at the site from a distance. This distance of

Tamás Szentjóby, *Kentaur*, 1975

the images to the concrete activities reinforces the pondering, abstract level of the texts put in the protagonists' mouths. Instead of propagandistically praising the achievements of socialism, the people speak of the possibility of freedom. The staged conversations, which in some cases have a surreal effect and mirror an anarchical view of the world, question the truth of the customary theses of usefulness, the relation of money and labor, and the dictated system of values. The unexpected combination of text and

die Montage von Bild und Ton hin, die Dialoge wurden vom Künstler nachträglich zu den Bildern hinzugefügt, und erscheinen als eine mit Absicht störend verschobene Synchronaufnahme. Diese audiovisuelle Montage ist keine unbekannte Methode des Propaganda- und Nachrichtenfilmgenres, wo die Bilder deutende Kommentare illustrieren. In *Kentaur* unterstützen Bild und Ton einander aber nicht, es wird vielmehr eine Spannung zwischen beiden Ebenen geschaffen. Die dokumentarisch angelegten Aufnahmen zeigen Schauplätze des sozialistischen Alltags zwischen Fabrik und Planungsbüro, von der Kantine bis zum Warteraum eines Bahnhofs. Szentjóby bedient sich einer distanzierten, objektivierenden Methode. Die Kamera nähert sich bei jeder Szene in einer Totale den SprecherInnen, um nach dem Abschluss des Dialogs wieder aus der Ferne auf den Ort zurückzuschauen. Diese Distanz der Bilder zu der konkreten Tätigkeit verstärkt die philosophierende, abstrakte Ebene der Texte, die den ProtagonistInnen in den Mund gelegt werden. Statt propagandistisch die Leistungen des Sozialismus zu loben, spricht das Volk über die Möglichkeit der Freiheit. Die stellenweise surrealistisch wirkenden und eine anarchistische Weltsicht spiegelnden inszenierten Gespräche hinterfragen die Wahrheit der gewohnten Thesen von Nützlichkeit, der Relation von Geld und Arbeit, das vorgeschriebene Wertesystem. Die unerwartete Kombination von Text und Bild kehrt das Genre des sozio-dokumentarischen Films ins Ironische. *Kentaur* zeigt die zweigeteilte Wirklichkeit auf, die im Sozialismus vom Individuum gelebt wurde: ein öffentliches/offizielles Leben nach Außen, und eines unter der Oberfläche, die in den Köpfen gelebte private Realität.

Die Aktualität des Films von Szentjóby ergibt sich daraus, dass auch da, wo die vorgeschriebene Zwangsgemeinschaft des Sozialismus vom individuellen Durchsetzungszwang des globalen Kapitalismus abgelöst wurde, die problematische Relation von Arbeit und Freiheit bzw. freiem Handeln weiterhin relevant bleibt.

image gives the genre of the socio-documentary film an ironic twist. *Kentaur* reveals a reality divided in two, which the individual lived in socialism: a public/official life toward the outside and a life beneath the surface, the private life lived in people's minds.

The topicality of Szentjóby's film lies in the fact that where the prescribed forced community of socialism was replaced by the individual compulsion to achieve in global capitalism, the problematic relation between labor and freedom respectively, free action remains relevant.

---

1 Quote from the script of *Kentaur*, published in Hungarian in *Szógettó. Válogatás az új magyar avantgarde dokumentumaiból Jelenlét*, Tamás Papp, (ed.), Budapest 1989, p. 271–275.
2 See Knoll, Hans, ed. *Die Zweite Öffentlichkeit: Kunst in Ungarn im 20. Jahrhundert*, Vienna 1999.
3 Quote from the credits of the film *Tequila Gang*, 1998.
4 In considerations stemming from that period, this lack is explained by the skepticism toward any kind of public. András Szántó, ed. "From Silence to Polyphony." *Polyphony. Social Commentary in Contemporary Hugarian Art*, Budapest 1993, p. 31–38.
5 For details, see: http://www.bighope.hu/insideout/index.html 1998 [04/10/05].
6 Directors: László Hudák, Imre Lénárt, camera: Imre Lénárt, Patricia Pászti, editor and advisor: Miklós Erhardt.
7 "If the economy is well, humans are well," see http://www.bighope.hu/talkingabouteconomy/index.html 2003 [04/10/05].
8 Ibid.
9 For documentation of the various installations see note 7.
10 *Kentaur*, 1975, Balázs Béla Filmstúdió (BBS), b/w, 16mm film, script and director: Tamás Szentjóby, camera: Gyula Gulyás.
11 See note 1.
12 An original version of the film no longer exists. There is only a video copy with an incomplete soundtrack.

---

1 Zitat aus dem Drehbuch zu *Kentaur*, in ungarischer Sprache erschienen in Szógettó. *Válogatás az új magyar avantgarde dokumentumaiból* [Wortghetto. Auswahl aus den Dokumenten der neuen ungarischen Avantgarde], in: Tamás Papp (Hg.): *Jelenlét*, Budapest 1989, S. 271–275. Deutsche Übersetzung: Éva Zádor.
2 Vgl. Hans Knoll (Hg.): *Die Zweite Öffentlichkeit. Kunst in Ungarn im 20. Jahrhundert*, Wien 1999.
3 Zitat aus dem Abspann des Films *Tequila Gang*, 1998.
4 Dieser Mangel wird in Überlegungen jener Zeit mit der Skepsis gegenüber jeder Art von Öffentlichkeit erklärt. András Szántó: From Silence to Polyphony, in: Ders.: *Polyphony. Social Commentary in Contemporary Hugarian Art*, Budapest 1993, S. 31–38.
5 Für Details siehe: http://www.bighope.hu/insideout/index.html [10.04.05].
6 Regie: László Hudák, Imre Lénárt, Kamera: Imre Lénárt, Patricia Pászti, Schnitt, Berater: Miklós Erhardt.
7 „If the economy is well, humans are well." Siehe: http://www.bighope.hu/talkingabouteconomy/index.html [10.04.05].
8 ebd.
9 Dokumentation der verschiedenen Installationen siehe Anm. 7.
10 *Kentaur*, 1975, Balázs Béla Filmstúdió (BBS), s/w, 16 mm Film, Drehbuch und Regie: Tamás Szentjóby, Kamera: Gyula Gulyás.
11 Siehe Anm. 1.
12 Es existiert keine Originalversion des Films, sondern nur noch eine im Ton unvollständige Videokopie.

Claudia Spinelli

What are Documentary Films Doing in Museums!?

One of the most outstanding qualities of art is its constant ability to redefine itself. Against this background, there is no possibility of separating the genres from one another. When documentary films enter the museum – as they have been doing for some years now – they become elements influencing a conception that is in a constant state of change. And this, regardless of whether the appearance of a work in an art context is due to the decision of a curator or to the training and socialization of its author.[1]

What needs to be asked, however, is how much the status of documentary material changes when it is transferred into the art context, a context with a very specific discourse and history. Of course, the question of representation, and, subsequently, the question of what constitutes reality, has a long tradition in art. Their roots extend back to well before the so-called "Documentary Turn", to which Okwui Enwezor and Mark Nash made such a fundamental contribution with Documenta11.[2]

Since the 1960s, the question of representation has been closely connected with that of the role of the observer and the intentional interaction set up between work and space. Artists like Bruce Nauman and Richard Serra brought the artwork down from its pedestal. Illusionary corporeality was replaced by human flesh and blood, temporality and a processual materiality. The fact is that the limp rubber parts that Richard Serra attached to walls do not merely purport to hang, they really do hang. Today such things are taken for granted – at the time it was a small revolution.

This step in the direction of a reality which functions according to the same physical laws as the real world had considerable consequences for the reception of art: the artwork had forfeited its totalizing status. The authentic experience of the

viewer, senses other than sight, and also inner associations became central and decisive components of the artwork.

This period also saw the birth of video art. Using today's criteria, the works made at that time can appear somewhat long-winded and technically deficient. They are the exact opposite of what we recognize as film which, right up to the present day, functions as a window on another world and yet cannot divest itself of its illusionary status even when it documents the real. It was precisely this gap between the recording and its subsequent presentation that Bruce Nauman thematized in his early video works. When he filmed his mouth speaking but then exhibited the film upside down, he was playing with the status of an image which no longer merely explained itself with respect to the action being shown, but generated its meaning only through the additional level of associations that were provoked during the playback, during the presentation. Although art has in the meantime become more narrative again, with its self-reflexivity retreating somewhat into the background, the achievements of the pioneer generation must be acknowledged. They also account for how the museum and the cinema differ.

Unfinished, inadequate: art that works with documentary elements will always have to put up with these accusations. The comparisons are always there to be made with the products of journalism, with news reports, with cinema films. In fact, one characteristic of many documentary pieces that are created and encountered in an art context is their withholding of information. However, what might be considered a deficiency from a journalistic perspective, is a plenitude in art. In the museum, a demand is placed on the visitor. It is not simply a question here of informing oneself about facts, or a story or the past. What is foregrounded are the ways and means by which something is portrayed, how something is communicated, or perhaps omitted. The museum is not the place where we weep about the sad fate of unlucky people, but a context in which we can reflect on why some-

In diesen Zeitraum fällt auch die Geburtsstunde der Videokunst. Nach heutigen Kriterien sind die Arbeiten jener Zeit langatmig und technisch unzulänglich. Und sie sind das exakte Gegenteil dessen, was wir vom Film kennen, der bis zum heutigen Tag wie ein Fenster in eine andere Welt funktioniert und selbst dann seinen Status des Illusionären nicht loswird, wenn er Reales dokumentiert. Genau diese Kluft zwischen Aufzeichnung und nachträglicher Präsentation wurde in den frühen Videoarbeiten Bruce Naumans zum Thema. Als er seinen Mund beim Sprechen filmte und die Aufnahme anschließend auf den Kopf stellte, spielte er mit dem Status eines Bildes, das sich nicht mehr allein im Rückbezug auf die aufgezeichnete Handlung erklärt, sondern seinen Sinn erst aus den zusätzlichen Assoziationsebenen bezieht, die sich beim Abspielen, bei der Präsentation einstellen. Obwohl die Kunst in der Zwischenzeit wieder erzählerischer geworden ist und die Reflexion der eigenen medialen Bedingungen etwas in den Hintergrund gerückt wurde, ist es wichtig, die Errungenschaften der Pioniergeneration zu kennen. Denn sie erklären deutlich, worin sich der Museumsraum vom Kino unterscheidet.

Unvollständig, unzulänglich: Diesen Vorwurf muss sich Kunst, die mit dokumentarischen Elementen arbeitet, immer wieder gefallen lassen. Und sie wird natürlich verglichen. Mit journalistischen Erzeugnissen, mit Nachrichtenbeiträgen, mit Kinofilmen. Tatsächlich ist es bezeichnend, dass einem Großteil dokumentarischer Arbeiten, die im Kunstkontext entstehen und rezipiert werden, Informationselemente entzogen wurden. Was indes aus einer journalistischen Perspektive ein Mangel ist, erzeugt das Mehr in der Kunst. Denn im Museumsraum ist das Publikum gefordert. Hier geht es nicht nur darum, sich über ein Ereignis zu informieren, vielmehr tritt die Art und Weise, wie etwas gezeigt, wie etwas vermittelt wird, in den Vordergrund. Wir gehen nicht ins Museum, um über das traurige Schicksal unglücklicher Menschen zu weinen, sondern das Museum ist der Ort, wo wir darüber nachdenken, weshalb uns etwas bewegt, weshalb uns etwas verunsichert oder gar kalt lässt.[3]

thing moves us, why something unnerves us, or why it leaves us quite cold.³

What can be said about photography and death applies also to film works in the documentary field. They are turned toward the past, testify to something that has already happened. In a museum space, however, the focus is shifted. Away from the presented object to the here and now of reception. Documentary works do not only allow people to speak, do not only report on facts and events, do not only infuse stories with a new life: they also develop their own independent lives – as images. Images that move and touch us, images that intermingle with our own memories and infiltrate our own thoughts. What is being mediated here can no longer be evaluated according to the dichotomy of true or false. More important is the recognition that reality and the world are always negotiable in other ways, can always be highlighted from a new angle.

Was man über die Fotografie und den Tod sagt, trifft auch auf den traditionellen Dokumentarfilm zu. Er ist rückwärts gewandt, er bezeugt etwas, das sich in der Vergangenheit abgespielt hat. Im Museumsraum hingegen hat sich der Fokus verschoben: weg vom dargestellten Gegenstand, hin auf das Hier und Jetzt der Rezeption. Dokumentarische Kunstarbeiten lassen nicht nur Menschen zu Wort kommen, sie berichten nicht nur über Tatsachen und Ereignisse, sie erwecken nicht nur Geschichten zu neuem Leben, sondern sie entwickeln auch ein Eigenleben: Als Bilder, die bewegen und berühren, als Bilder, die sich mit den eigenen Erinnerungen vermischen und das Denken infiltrieren. Die Wahrheit, die sich hier vermittelt, kann nicht mehr an der Dualität von Lüge oder Wahrheit bemessen werden. Ihr Wert liegt vielmehr darin, dass Wirklichkeit und Welt auf immer wieder andere Art verhandelbar, aus immer wieder neuer Perspektive beleuchtet werden.

1 While preparing *Reprocessing Reality*, an exhibition that I organized in collaboration with the international film festival *Visions du Réel*, Nyon, I came across more than one filmmaker who had moved into an art space on the initiative of a curator. Frammenti Elettrici, the installation by Yervant Gianikian and Angela Ricci Lucchi, for example, traces back to an initiative by Mark Nash. And Mike Hoolboom had made well over 40 films before he began a late career in the context of art.
2 See Mark Nash, ed. *Experiments with Truth*, exh. cat., Fabric Workshop and Museum, Philadelphia 2005. In particular the articles by Okwui Enwezor and the editor.
3 See Susan Sontag, *Regarding the Pain of Others*, New York 2003.

1 Während meinen Recherchen zu *Reprocessing Reality*, der Ausstellung, die ich in Zusammenarbeit mit dem internationalen Filmfestival *Visions du Réel*, Nyon, entwickelte, bin ich mehr als einmal auf Filmemacher gestoßen, die sich aufgrund der Initiative von Kuratoren zum Auftritt im Kunstraum bewegen ließen: *Frammenti Elettrici*, die Installation von Yervant Gianikian und Angela Ricci Lucchi z.B. geht auf eine Initiative von Mark Nash zurück. Auch Mike Hoolboom, der weit über 40 Filme gedreht hat, hat erst kürzlich eine späte Karriere im Kunstkontext gestartet.
2 Vgl. Mark Nash (Hg): *Experiments with Truth*. (Katalog) Fabric Workshop and Museum, Philadelphia 2005, insbesondere die Aufsätze von Okwui Enwezor und des Herausgebers.
3 Vgl. Susan Sonntag: *Das Leiden anderer betrachten*, München 2003.

invent [in'vent] **v.t. 1.** create or design (sth. not existing before): *When was the steam engine ~ed?* (Cf. discover, find sth. existing before, but unknown)
2. make up, think of: *~ a story (an excuse)*.
inventor *n.* person who ~s things.
inventive [in'ventiv] *adj.* able to ~: *an ~ive mind; ~ive powers*.
invention [in'venʃən] *n.* **1.** [U] inventing: *the ~ of the telephone*; capacity for inventing: *Necessity is the mother of ~*. **2.** [C] sth. invented: *the numerous ~s of Edison; newspapers that are full of ~s (invented, untrue stories)*.

(From *The Advanced Learner's Dictionary of Current English*)

Edison's Workbench, 2003
Wooden table, vises, b/w photograph
Table: 82,5 x 205 x 200 cm
Photograph: 33 x 48,5 cm

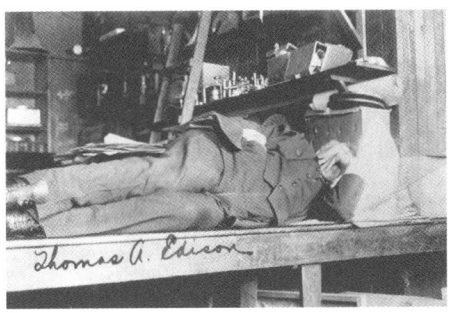

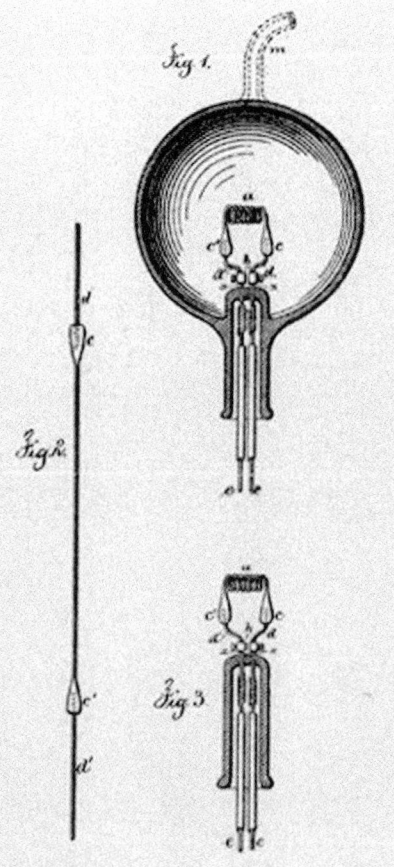

Pascale Cassagnau

"The documentary film is what happens to others, fiction is what happens to me." (Jean-Luc Godard)

"A film is good only when it achieves it best documentary performance." (Jean-Pierre Gorin citing Fritz Lang at the film festival Entrevues in Belfort, December 2004)

Future Amnesia* (The Need for Documents)

(* The title of this essay is taken from Pierre Huyghe; it is the first version of a chapter of an upcoming essay entitled "Intermezzo (Un troisième cinéma)")

Overture

Werner Herzog, *Auch Zwerge haben klein angefangen* (Even Dwarves Started Small) (1970)

In *Auch Zwerge haben klein angefangen*, Werner Herzog shows a strange human archipelago, an immoral society, and a lawless time shot the day after the end of the world. The film retraces the story of a rebellion the motives of which the filmmaker leaves aside from the very start. The rebellion stages figures who are the brothers of freaks – of Todd Browning, Kaspar Hauser, all figures of Harmory Korine's *Gummo* or Cameron Jamie.

The shape of the landscape, the desert as a main motif, the circle, and the spiral are recurring forms. As is the case with Lars von Trier, there is also an economy of exaggeration and repetition in Werner Herzog. These two modalities bear a profound reflection; referring to perception, the filmmaker formulates it as follows: "View the pictures we perceive poorly until we go into ecstasies." The lexicalization of the elements of the real, the series of figures and objects – the hens, the blind people, the witnesses, the dwarves, the limping dromedary – create a play of distorted scales in connection with the space, effectuated by reduction, condensation, and magnifying effects: "What is essential lies in the objects and in the created environment: that is, in the relation of proportions between objects and humans. Everything will be on a true-to-life scale: a doorknob in natural size, a motorcycle is a motorcycle, a chair a chair. Yet, at the end of the film, the objects will appear monstrous, cruel, and distorted, since the spectator will have

„Es ist der Dokumentarfilm, der den Anderen passiert, was mir passiert, ist die Fiktion." (Jean-Luc Godard)

„Ein Film wird erst dann gut, wenn er seine dokumentarische Höchstleistung erreicht." (Jean-Pierre Gorin, Fritz Lang zitierend, beim Filmfestival Entrevues in Belfort, Dezember 2004)

Future Amnesia* (The Need for Documents)

(* Der Titel des vorliegenden Textes ist Pierre Huyghe entliehen. Dieser Text ist die erste Version eines Kapitels des zukünftigen Essays: Intermezzo (Un troisième cinéma))

Ouvertüre

Werner Herzog, *Auch Zwerge haben klein angefangen* (1970)

In *Auch Zwerge haben klein angefangen* zeigt Werner Herzog ein seltsames menschliches Archipel, eine unmoralische Gesellschaft und eine gesetzlose Zeit – gefilmt am Tag nach dem Ende der Welt. Der Film zeichnet die Geschichte eines Aufstandes nach, dessen Motive durch den Filmemacher von Anfang an ausgeklammert werden. Die Revolte setzt Figuren in Szene, die die Brüder von Freaks sind – von Todd Browning, von Kaspar Hauser, von allen Figuren Harmory Korines *Gummo* oder Cameron Jamie.

Die Gestalt der Landschaft, die Wüste als betontes Motiv, der Kreis und die Spirale sind Gestaltungen, die wiederkehren. Wie bei Lars von Trier gibt es auch bei Werner Herzog eine Ökonomie der Übertreibung und der Wiederholung. Diese zwei Modalitäten tragen eine tiefe Reflexion in sich, zu der der Filmemacher in Bezug auf die Wahrnehmung formuliert: „Die Bilder, die wir schlecht wahrnehmen, bis zur Extase betrachten." Die Lexikalisierung der Elemente des Realen, der Serie der Figuren und der Objekte – die Hennen, die Blinden, die Zeugen, die Zwerge, das humpelnde Dromedar – bildet im Zusammenspiel mit dem Raum ein Spiel gestörter Maßstäbe, die durch Reduktion, durch Verdichtung, durch Vergrößerungseffekte zustande kommen. „Das Wesentliche liegt in den Objekten und in der geschaffenen Umgebung: das heißt, im Verhältnis der Proportionen zwischen den Gegenständen und den Menschen. Alles wird in originalgetreuem Maßstab sein: ein Türknauf in natürlicher Größe,

grown accustomed to the figures, and they will represent the norm for him. The provocation, then, will be that the horrible will be natural and the natural horrible." (Werner Herzog)

The camera is a patient and discreet witness of what is filmed. A "documentary film" about a community shot like a reportage multiplying the diversified registers of styles: documentary moments alternate with choreographed and purely descriptive moments. The script itself highlights the importance of moments without action, leaving aside any kind of narration in long, descriptive sequences that interrupt the narrative continuity.

Auch Zwerge haben klein angefangen is a Dogma film, close to what Lars von Trier attempted in *The Idiots*: to find the incredible point of transition between a system of symbolization and the limits of representation. Toward the real. From fiction to non-fiction, to its abandonment.

Pierre Huyghe, *Block Party – Future Amnesia*, 2002, 10 min.

Pierre Huyghe's cinematic work is documentary, starting with *L'Ellipse*, his film based on Wim Wender's *Der amerikanische Freund* (The American Friend), up to the temporal ellipse of *Block Party*, a ten-minute loop conveying in a very short span of time what took place between the invention of hip hop and its adoption by the record industry. The very subtle manner in which music is added to the images alludes in an elliptical way to what has changed in the history of hip hop: the experience.

ein Motorrad ist ein Motorrad, ein Stuhl ein Stuhl. Dennoch werden die Gegenstände am Ende des Films monströs, grausam und verzerrt wirken, da der Betrachter sich an die Figuren gewöhnt haben wird, und eben diese für ihn die Norm darstellen werden. Die Provokation wird also sein, dass das Schreckliche natürlich und das Natürliche schrecklich ist." (Werner Herzog)

Die Kamera ist geduldiger und diskreter Zeuge des Gefilmten. Ein „Dokumentarfilm" über eine Gemeinschaft – gedreht wie eine Reportage, welche die diversifizierten Register des Stils vervielfacht: Die dokumentarischen Momente wechseln sich mit choreografierten und ausschließlich deskriptiven Momenten ab. Das Drehbuch selbst verdeutlicht die Wichtigkeit der aktionslosen Momente, das Ausklammern jeglicher Erzählung durch lange deskriptive Absätze, welche die narrative Kontinuität unterbrechen.

Auch Zwerge haben klein angefangen ist ein Dogma-Film, nahe an dem, was Lars von Trier in *Idioten* versuchte: den unglaublichen Punkt des Kippens zwischen einem System der Symbolisation und den Grenzen der Darstellung zu finden. Hin zum Realen. Von der Fiktion zur Non-Fiktion, ihrem Verzicht.

Pierre Huyghe, *Block Party – Future Amnesia*, 2002, 10 min.

Angefangen von *L'Ellipse*, seinem Film nach Wim Wenders *Der amerikanische Freund*, bis hin zur zeitlichen Ellipse, welche *Block Party* darstellt, ist das Kino Pierre Huyghes dokumentarisch. *Block Party* ist ein zehnminütiger Loop, welcher in sehr kurzer Zeit vermittelt, was sich zwischen der Erfindung des HipHop und seiner Aufnahme durch die Plattenindustrie abgespielt hat. Die sehr subtile Art, in der die Bilder mit Klängen hinterlegt werden, deutet in elliptischer Weise an, was in der Geschichte des HipHop verändert wurde: die Erfahrung.

Pierre Huyghe, *Block Party, Africa Bambaataa*, 2002

The Third Cinema

Among the parallel histories that today mobilize contemporary art, video, photography, and the new media in terms of the question of the image, a single script establishes the aesthetic and economic relations between contemporary art and cinema.

Even if contemporary creativity is a field of economy, as Stanley Cavell writes in his autobiography, *A pitch of philosophy*[1], cinema and contemporary art continue to stand in a dialogue through a number of works that refer to cinema or to correspondences with the cinematographic imaginary. This is where cinema fits into the definition of contemporary art. The aesthetic world of a number of artists, like that of Doug Aitken, Dominique Gonzales Foerster, Douglas Gordon, Steve Mac Queen, and Rainer Oldendorf, shares with cinema the dialogical function of the filmed report, the future of any cinematographic view, an art of montage, and the articulation of the narrative sequences. In this respect, the economy of the "remake" plays a useful role for analyzing the narrative structures and for locating the viewer.

The significance of the reference to cinema in the diversified field of contemporary art designates it as the "real" of art, as if cinema had become a naturalized reference: no longer merely a medium but a culture. Some works, e.g., those of Graham Gussin or Darren Almond, discreetly mirror the entire imagery constituting cinema, which is considered fundamental for a cinema regarded as a dispositive (apparatus, screen, frame, mask, silver surface, image repository). For many artists such as Pierre Bismuth and Pierre Huyghe, cinema is a model allowing the production of hypotheses and processes shifting sense emanating from its periphery and fringes. These hypotheses have to do with the relationship to history, via the deviation from personal histories, and with its possible re-appropriation in the sense of becoming.

Intervista (1998) by Anri Sala is a cinematographic essay with which the artist attempts to re-appropriate the restless history of

Das Dritte Kino

Unter den parallelen Geschichten, die heute die zeitgenössische Kunst, das Video, die Fotografie und die neuen Medien rund um die Bildfrage mobilisieren, vollzieht ein einzelnes Drehbuch die ästhetischen und ökonomischen Zusammenhänge zwischen der zeitgenössischen Kunst und dem Kino.

Wenn auch – wie Stanley Cavell in seiner Autobiographie *Die andere Stimme*[1] schreibt – das zeitgenössische Schaffen ein Feld der Ökonomie ist, so stehen das Kino und die zeitgenössische Kunst weiterhin im Dialog durch eine Reihe von Werken, die auf das Kino verweisen oder Übereinstimmungen mit dem cinematografischen Imaginären herstellen. Hier reiht sich das Kino von jetzt an in die Definition der zeitgenössischen Kunst ein. Die ästhetische Welt einiger KünstlerInnen, wie die von Doug Aitken, Dominique Gonzales Foerster, Douglas Gordon, Steve Mac Queen, Rainer Oldendorf, teilt mit dem Kino die dialogische Funktion des gefilmten Berichts, die Zukunft jeder cinematografischen Ansicht, eine Kunst der Montage und die Artikulation der narrativen Segmente. In dieser Hinsicht spielt die Ökonomie des „Remake" eine nützliche Rolle für die Analyse der narrativen Strukturen wie auch für die Verortung des Betrachters.

Die Bedeutung des Verweises auf das Kino innerhalb des diversifizierten Feldes der zeitgenössischen Kunst kennzeichnet es als das Reale der Kunst, als sei das Kino eine naturalisierte Referenz geworden: nicht mehr nur ein Medium, sondern eine Kultur. Einige Werke – zum Beispiel die von Graham Gussin oder von Darren Almond – spiegeln auf eine diskrete Weise die Gesamtheit des Imaginären des Kinos wider, was als grundlegend für das als Dispositiv verstandene Kino gilt (Apparatur, Leinwand, Rahmen, Maske, silberne Oberfläche, Bildmagazin). Außerdem stellt das Kino für viele Künstler, so unter anderen Pierre Bismuth und Pierre Huyghe, ein Modell dar, welches es ermöglicht, Hypothesen und Sinnverschiebungsprozesse zu produzieren, die von seiner Peripherie und von seinen Rändern ausgehen. Diese Hypothesen betreffen den Bezug zur

his homeland, Albania, via the personal history of his own mother. The film is structured like an investigation, like the deciphering of a speech (stemming from the archives of the artist's mother), questioning intimacy, politics, memory and fiction, history and reality.

For several years now, the Mexican artist Francis Alÿs has been working on an oeuvre that uses the domain of the city as an experience and observation field. His performances in public space and his films document modes of social resistance and fragile, shared experiences on which the fragile social coherence within the chaotic spaces of large Latin American cities are based.

In her photographic series as well as in her films, Rineke Dijkstra creates portraits of youths that underline the questioning of identity by emphasizing the differences between the depicted persons. In her film *Buzzclub/Liverpool* (1996–1997), the artist films youths dancing before the camera. Here, the dance unites the extreme concern with self-representation and the expression of boredom, abandonment and reserve. The filmed portraits become self-portraits – documents summing up the feeling of anonymity and extreme solitude. This portrait series of youths realized in the Baltic countries, Berlin, and the United States bear witness to that precise moment in life when the feeling of being different gains the upper hand over self-affirmation.

Here, the reference to cinema relates, briefly put, to a specific economy of the works: the way they are produced, the performance, the distribution, the edition, that all deviate from the traditional economy of contemporary works.

In its broader context, the dialogue into which cinema and contemporary art enter also marks an expansion of both the sphere of art and the sphere of cinema. This expansion of the spaces and means of expression produces new styles; the notion of style itself has become an enlarged field for several decades, a platform uniting elements adopted from cinema (montage, remake, shot) and music (sample, mix, cut-up).

The work of Jean-Luc Godard bears witness to this transversality, to a cinema which is

Geschichte, über die Abweichung von persönlichen Geschichten, und ihre mögliche Wiederaneignung im Sinn von Werden.

So ist *Intervista* (1998) von Anri Sala ein kinematografischer Essay, durch den der Künstler versucht, sich die unruhige Geschichte seines Heimatlandes Albanien anhand der Geschichte seiner eigenen Mutter wieder anzueignen. Der Film ist wie eine Untersuchung gestaltet, wie das Dechiffrieren eines Textes (der aus den eigenen Archiven der Mutter des Künstlers stammt), eine Untersuchung, die das Intime, die Politik, die Erinnerung und die Fiktion, die Geschichte sowie die Realität hinterfragt.

Schon seit einigen Jahren arbeitet der mexikanische Künstler Francis Alÿs an einem Werk, welches das Stadtgebiet als Versuchs- und Observationsfeld nutzt. Seine Performances im öffentlichen Raum und seine Filme dokumentieren Formen sozialen Widerstands und fragiler, geteilter Erfahrungen, welche die zerbrechliche soziale Bindung inmitten der chaotischen Räume der großen Städte Lateinamerikas begründen.

In ihren fotografischen Serien, wie auch in ihren Filmen realisiert Rineke Dijkstra Porträts Jugendlicher, die eine Infragestellung der Identität unterstreichen, indem die Unterschiede zwischen den dargestellten Personen herausgestellt werden.

In ihrem Film *Buzzclub/Liverpool* (1996–1997) filmt die Künstlerin Jugendliche, die vor der Kamera tanzen. Der Tanz vereint hier die extreme Sorge der Selbstdarstellung und den Ausdruck der Langeweile, des Verlassenseins und der Zurückhaltung. Die gefilmten Porträts werden zu Selbstporträts – Dokumente, die das Gefühl von Anonymität und extremer Einsamkeit zusammenfassen. Diese Porträtserien Jugendlicher, realisiert in den baltischen Ländern, in Berlin und in den USA, zeugen von jenem präzisen Moment im Leben, in dem das Gefühl, anders zu sein, Oberhand gewinnt über die Selbstbestätigung.

Der Verweis auf die Welt des Kinos bezieht sich, kurz gesagt, auf eine spezifische Ökonomie der Werke: die Art ihrer Produktion, der Aufführung, der Verbreitung, der Auflage, welche von der traditionellen Ökonomie zeitgenössischer Werke abweicht.

itself traversed by video experiments and experimental cinema. The questioning of the cinematographic style corresponds to the questioning of art through cinema, of cinema through video, and of literature through cinema. *Scénario du film Passion, France/Tour/Détour/Two/Children, Histoire(s) du cinéma* and *Morceaux choisis des histoire(s) du cinéma* present themselves accordingly: Jean-Luc Godard intertwines heterogeneous elements that always however lead cinema back to the real and to history.

If it is "fiction that always leads to the real", as Anna Karina states at the end of Godard's film, *La Chinoise*, then contemporary art itself has been the scene of a "return of the real" for a few years, with its preference for the archive, the document, and the documentary view. Many recent exhibitions and events have testified to the important standing of the document within contemporary artworks and films. Documenta X and Documenta11, the last two biennials in Venice, Manifesta 5 and the entire project series, *Contemporary Arab Representations*, directed by Catherine David have highlighted this return to the real by presenting a large number of "documentary works" that manifest the triumph of a truly political art calling into question the political and the politics of representation.

Many works between fiction and documentary film indeed deal in a critical way with the different versions of a reality that is neither unambiguous nor transparent, as well as with diversified systems of truth. With works by Kutlug Ataman, Florence Lazar, Alejandra Riera, Harun Farocki, and Santiago Reyes, the exhibition *Ficciones documentales*[2] organized at the Caixa Forum in Barcelona in 2003 questioned the works' own capacity to visualize invisible or unknown dimensions or dimensions concealed from reality, their ability to invent forms in order to give an account of the ambiguity of the world. The exhibition *Fiction ou Réalité* 2003 organized at the art space FRI-ART in Fribourg (CH) focused on works that shift the relation between fiction and reality in a complex way.

Der Dialog, den Kino und zeitgenössische Kunst miteinander eingehen, bezeichnet außerdem in seinem weiter gefassten Kontext eine Erweiterung der jeweiligen Gebiete der Kunst und des Kinos. Diese Ausweitung der Ausdrucksräume und der Mittel bringt neue Stile hervor: Der Begriff des Stils selbst ist seit mehreren Jahrzehnten ein weit verbreitetes Feld geworden, eine Plattform, die dem Kino (Montage, Remake, Einstellung) und der Musik (Sample, Mixen, Cut-Up) entliehene Elemente vereint.

Das Werk Jean-Luc Godards zeugt von dieser Transversalität, von einem Kino, welches seinerseits bearbeitet und durchzogen ist von Video-Versuchen und dem experimentellen Kino. Der Infragestellung des kinematografischen Stils entspricht die Infragestellung der Kunst durch das Kino, des Kinos durch das Video und der Literatur durch das Kino. Entsprechend präsentieren sich *Scénario du film Passion, France/tour/détour/deux/enfants, Histoire(s) du cinéma* und *Morceaux choisis des histoire(s) du cinéma*: Mit ihnen verfolgt Jean-Luc Godard eine Verflechtung heterogener Elemente, die jedoch das Kino immer wieder zum Realen und zur Geschichte hinführen.

Wenn es „die Fiktion ist, die immer wieder zum Realen führt", wie es Anna Karina am Ende des Films *La Chinoise* von Godard sagt, so ist die zeitgenössische Kunst ihrerseits seit einigen Jahren der Schauplatz einer „Rückkehr des Realen", mit einer Vorliebe für das Archiv, für das Dokument und den dokumentarischen Blick. Viele Ausstellungen und Veranstaltungen haben in der letzten Zeit von der wichtigen Stellung des Dokuments innerhalb zeitgenössischer Kunstwerke, sowie innerhalb des Films gezeugt. Die documenta X und Documenta11, die letzten beiden Biennalen von Venedig, die Manifesta 5 und die gesamte von Catherine David geleitete Projektreihe *Contemporary Arab Representations* haben diese Rückkehr des Realen hervorgehoben, indem sie eine große Anzahl „dokumentarischer Werke" präsentiert haben, den Siegeszug einer wahrhaft politischen Kunst manifestierend, welche das Politische und die Politik der Repräsentation hinterfragt.

Zwischen Fiktion und Dokumentarfilm beschäftigen sich in der Tat viele Werke in kritischer Weise mit den unterschiedlichen Versionen

The film festivals in Rotterdam, Locarno, Cannes, Berlin accompany this movement of the documentary by presenting a large number of works stemming from the "third cinema". The work of Danielle Arbids turns a Lebanese family saga into the actual space of the film, a terrain of adventures, a motif to be explored, an area of language. The multiple micro-narratives that traverse all her films also address the history of Lebanon. In *Conversations de salon, Seule avec la guerre* or *Dans les chantiers de la guerre*, the family saga is revealed through the crossover between fiction and the documentary in the perspective of a transitive camera.

Apichatpong Weerasethakul has produced several short films in Thailand that question the porous borders between fiction and documentary film in a poetic way. Grasped as a series of personal portraits and geographical elevations, Apichatpong Weerasethakul's films show shots of a group of uprooted people living on the outer fringes of the country and having to cope with the difficulty of belonging to nowhere. His first feature film, *Mysterious object at noon* (2000), which became known when it was screened at the Forum des Images within the frame of the International Film Festival in Paris in 2001, made the aesthetic orientation of the filmmaker more precise in terms of a naturalistic bias and it revealed his will to keep the camera at a distance from the anonymous figures, thus allowing what he calls a temporarily enigmatic subject matter. In *Blissfully yours* and *Tropical malady,* which won awards in Cannes in 2003 and 2004, the dimension of cinematographic experimentation becomes more precise. The filmmaker depicts an episode in the life of his figures in real time. In both films, which were shot with amateur actors, the drifting off of the figures in the jungle is retraced through a sequence of revelations of clues, of tracks that indicate the course of time. *Blissfully yours* and *Tropical malady* show a moment of happiness elicited from the jungle, carried by a clear view that shows a moment of the world in a clearly defined political geography. "One must speak of the situation in Burma and Thailand, about repression on the one hand and about artificial

einer weder eindeutigen noch transparenten Realität, sowie mit diversifizierten Wahrheitssystemen. Die 2003 im Caixa Forum in Barcelona organisierte Ausstellung *Ficciones documentales*[2] hinterfragte anhand der Werke von Kutlug Ataman, Florence Lazar, Alejandra Riera, Harun Farocki und Santiago Reyes die den Werken eigene Fähigkeit, unsichtbare, unbekannte oder vor der Realität versteckte Dimensionen sichtbar zu machen, die Fähigkeit, Formen zu erfinden, um von der Zweideutigkeit der Welt zu berichten. Was die ebenfalls 2003 in der Kunsthalle FRI-ART in Freiburg (CH) organisierte Ausstellung *Fiction ou Réalité* betrifft, legte diese ihren Schwerpunkt auf Werke, welche in komplexer Weise das Verhältnis zwischen Fiktion und Realität verschieben.

Die Kino-Festivals in Rotterdam, Locarno, Cannes, Berlin begleiten diese Bewegung des Dokumentarischen, indem sie eine Vielzahl von Werken präsentieren, die einem „Dritten Kino" entstammen. Das Werk Danielle Arbids macht aus dem libanesischen Familienroman den eigentlichen Raum des Films, ein Reservoir von Abenteuern, ein zu erforschendes Motiv, ein Gebiet der Sprache. Die multiplen Mikro-Erzählungen, die alle ihre Filme durchziehen, greifen auch die Geschichte des Libanon auf. In *Conversations de salon, Seule avec la guerre* oder *Dans les chantiers de la guerre* wird der Familienroman über die spielerische Kreuzung von Fiktion und Dokumentarischem unter dem Blickwinkel einer transitiven Kamera dekliniert.

Apichatpong Weerasethakul hat in Thailand einige Kurzfilme realisiert, welche die porösen Grenzen zwischen der Fiktion und dem Dokumentarfilm auf lyrische Weise hinterfragen. Verstanden als Serien persönlicher Porträts und geografischer Erhebungen, zeigen die Filme Apichatpong Weerasethakuls Aufnahmen einer Gruppe entwurzelter Personen, die an der äußersten Grenze des Landes leben, und sich mit der Schwierigkeit auseinandersetzen müssen, keinem Ort zugehörig zu sein. Sein erster Spielfilm, *Mysterious object at noon* (2000), im Rahmen des Internationalen Filmfestivals von Paris 2001 im *Forum des Images* bekannt geworden, präzisierte die ästhetische Orientierung des Filmemachers

happiness, another form of repression, on the other." (A. Weerasethakul)

The films of Olivier Zabat also belong to this "third cinema" between fiction and documentary film. His work demands the in-between of a documentary and a sculptural approach, his examination is thus to be situated between information and visual experiences, e.g., his film, *Zona Oeste* (1990), shot in the *favelas* of Brazil. *Miguel et les mines* (2002) is a film about antipersonnel mines and the techniques of minesweeping, shot in the form of a rhapsodic, fragmentary, six-part essay evoking situations of violence via the accounts of witnesses who are kept at a distance by the artist. It is this dimension of "reserve or imminence in which the relation to chance, to virtuality and its actualization remains open", as Emmanuel Burdeau[3] reminds us, that Olivier Zabat wants to expand for the four modules of which *1/3 des yeux* (2004) consists. The narrative modules retrace four real events, situational portraits, and individual stories. They constitute a tableau of situations transporting the notions of danger, injury, transition, and perception transformed from the perspective of fear. Olivier Zabat's entire cinema consists of figures that are represented indirectly; he additionally documents different modes of representation. He concentrates on the many possibilities of blurring meaning, on the effects of translation, and on the strangeness of situations. The entirety of the modules is based on a period of time, a temporality linking all these poles with each other. Olivier Zabat's cinema invents a place for the spectator, something to which his installations (Musée d'Art Moderne de la Ville de Paris, Manifesta 5, San Sebastian) testify: a place of reading, waiting, and concern, laid out in the patient work of deciphering performed by the artist in his films; in the process, he simultaneously uncovers unknown levels of the real. Olivier Zabat's films allow us to discover sequential realities: each shown reality always entails a next one, leading to a pithy time, a tension.

zugunsten einer naturalistischen Voreingenommenheit, und seinen Willen, die Kamera auf Distanz zu den anonymen Figuren zu halten, um das zuzulassen, was er einen temporär rätselhaften Gegenstand nennt. Mit *Blissfully yours* und *Tropical malady*, 2003 und 2004 in Cannes ausgezeichnet, präzisiert sich die Dimension des cinematografischen Experimentierens: Der Filmemacher stellt eine Episode des Lebens seiner Figuren in Echtzeit dar. In beiden Filmen mit Laiendarstellern gedreht, wird das Abdriften der Figuren im Dschungel durch eine Abfolge von Enthüllungen von Hinweisen nachgezeichnet; Enthüllungen von Spuren, die den Lauf der Zeit angeben. *Blissfully yours* und *Tropical malady* zeigen einen dem Urwald entlockten Augenblick des Glücks, getragen von einem klaren Blick, der einen Moment der Welt in einer klar definierten politischen Geografie zeigt. „Es gilt, von der Situation Birmas und Thailands zu sprechen, einerseits von der Repression und anderseits vom etwas künstlichen Glück, einer anderen Form der Repression." (A. Weerasethakul)

Auch die Filme Olivier Zabats zählen zu diesem „Dritten Kino", zwischen Fiktion und Dokumentarfilm. Sein Werk beansprucht das Dazwischen einer dokumentarischen und einer skulpturalen Annäherung, womit seine Untersuchung zwischen Information und visuellen Versuchen zu platzieren ist. So z.B. in seinem Film *Zona Oeste* (1990), der in den Favelas in Brasilien gedreht wurde. Mit *Miguel et les mines* (2002) liefert uns Olivier Zabat einen Film über Tretminen und die Techniken der Minenräumung, in Form eines rhapsodischen, fragmentarischen, sechsteiligen Essays, der über Zeugenaussagen, die vom Künstler auf Distanz gehalten werden, an Szenen der Gewalt erinnert. Es ist diese Dimension „der Zurückhaltung oder des Bevorstehens, in der der Bezug einer Chance, einer Virtualität zu ihrer Aktualisierung offen bleibt", wie Emmanuel Burdeau[3] erinnert, die Olivier Zabat für die vier Module, aus denen *1/3 des yeux* (2004) besteht, erweitern möchte. Diese narrativen Module zeichnen vier wahre Begebenheiten nach, Situationsporträts und einzelne Geschichten. Sie zeigen Momente, welche die Begriffe der Gefahr, der Verletzung, des Übergangs und der Wahrnehmung

Document / Documentary Film / Documentation

If it is the case that for several years the encounter of contemporary art and documentary film has proved to be fruitful, then this has to do with the fact that the document and the archive, as the formulation of a question and a method, are a real horizon of thought, an heuristic actuality and a sign of historicity for both art and cinema.

Documentary film describes a structure of filming that artists and filmmakers have in common: The filmic elements are not arranged in a linear way, but apart from strictly narrative structures. In this respect, the relationship of the documents to reality are necessarily critical and ambiguous.

The perspective of including in a narrower or broader sense contemporary artworks and cinema takes place in a specific meta-aesthetic frame. The entity of universality and totality is no longer efficient; it has long since been replaced by the entity of intersubjectivity and personal re-appropriation of history and individual stories. The nature of the document can be described as follows: it derives its value from making use of the re-appropriation of subjectivities and from its form of historicity. In this moment of re-appropriation of oneself and others, for a biography of everyone, cinema now enters into the definition of new conditions of subjectivity.

Liisa Roberts conducts cinematographic research that questions both the structure of the images and their reception. Carlos Basualdo says that the work of Liisa Roberts on the one hand has to do with how images touch us and shape our representation of the world; on the other, it is research on the material of the images themselves.[4] This intermediate position of the image results from the juxtaposition of the film levels and its archive according to the process of decomposition and repetition. *What's the Time in Vyborg?* (2001–2004) is a film which Liisa Roberts realized with a group of youths within the frame of a project in Vyborg, a city on the border of Finland and Russia. Always subject to unter dem Blickwinkel der Angst vermitteln. Das gesamte Kino Olivier Zabats besteht aus Figuren, die indirekt repräsentiert werden; er dokumentiert außerdem unterschiedliche Module der Repräsentation. Seine Aufmerksamkeit bezieht sich auf die vielen Möglichkeiten der Sinnverwischungen, auf die Effekte der Übersetzung und auf die Fremdartigkeit der Situationen. Die Gesamtheit der Module setzt einen Zeitraum voraus, eine Zeitlichkeit, die alle diese Pole miteinander verknüpft. Das Kino Olivier Zabats erfindet einen Platz für den Zuschauer, wovon seine Installationen (Musée d'Art Moderne de la Ville de Paris, *Manifesta 5*, San Sebastian) zeugen: ein Raum des Lesens, des Wartens, der Sorge, angelegt in der geduldigen Arbeit des Entschlüsselns, die der Künstler in seinen Filmen leistet, wobei er zugleich die noch nicht bekannten Ebenen des Realen enthüllt. Die Filme Olivier Zabats ermöglichen es uns, aufeinander folgende Realitäten zu entdecken: Jede gezeigte Realität zieht immer eine neue nach sich, eine pointierte Zeit, die Spannung herbeiführt.

Dokument / Dokumentarfilm / Dokumentieren

Wenn sich in der Tat schon seit einigen Jahren das Zusammenkommen der zeitgenössischen Kunst mit dem Dokumentarfilm als besonders fruchtbar herausgestellt hat, so ist dies auf die Tatsache zurückzuführen, dass das Dokument und das Archiv als Fragestellung und Methode einen wirklichen Gedankenhorizont darstellen, als heuristische Gegebenheit und als Zeichen der Historizität, sowohl für die Kunst als auch für das Kino.

Der Dokumentarfilm bezeichnet eine Struktur des Filmens, die KünstlerInnen wie FilmemacherInnen eigen ist: Die filmischen Elemente werden nicht in linearer Weise, sondern außerhalb der strikt narrativen Strukturen angeordnet. In dieser Hinsicht sind die Beziehungen der Dokumente zur Realität gezwungenermaßen kritisch und zweideutig.

Die Perspektive des dichten oder eher weiteren Einbezugs der Kunstwerke und des zeitgenössischen Kinos vollzieht sich in einem spezifischen meta-ästhetischen Rahmen: Das Wesen von

the coincidences of history, Vyborg was initially a significant Finnish cultural center, then it became a Soviet city and today it is finally a Russian one, an area remote from time. With an architecture strongly influenced by Alvar Aalto, the city today still has a library built by him. Liisa Robert's project aims at transferring the context of the origin of Alvar Aalto's structures to the present. The current context, with a view to selected data, refers to the complexity of the historical relations: 1927-1935 (the time in which the library was built), 1944 (the city becomes Soviet), 1955 (restoration of the library begins), 1989 (the city becomes Russian), 2001 (the library is again restored). Starting from this symbolic place of a link between the past and the present, the director decided to organize a writing seminar with Russian youths in preparation for working out a film about the city that will mark the historical aporia regarding the relationships between memory work, the ideological discourse, the work of historians, and the political and social present of Vyborg's inhabitants.

The writing seminar is the fictional part, questioning in the process of writing the position of subjectivity, which plays a part in any formation of a world-view, by critically examining accounts of experiences and conventionalities. The camera films the city starting from the library and the library starting from the street, in a series of alternating levels, from the open windows pointing to the city in the library's auditorium. The library is both a mirror and a frame limiting a field of perception – the way the city sees the library today – and segments of space. The film marks the role and the position of the architecture in constituting ideological representations. The film seems less to question memory and its archives than to develop hypotheses for the present. In this respect, *What's the Time in Vyborg?* is not a documentary film, in the narrow sense of the term, about an historical reality. It documents the way in which representations are constructed in future. The film lends this "mise en abyme" a form and integrates its own moment of style.

Universalität und Totalität ist seit langem nicht mehr effizient; es hat seinen Platz längst an das Wesen der Intersubjektivität und der persönlichen Wiederaneignung der Historie und individueller Geschichten abgetreten. Die dem Dokument eigene Natur wäre also folgendermaßen zu beschreiben: Sie bezieht ihren Wert aus der Nutzung, der Wiederaneignung von Subjektivitäten und aus ihrer Form der Historizität. In diesem Moment der Wiederaneignung von sich selbst und von anderen, für eine Biografie aller, tritt das Kino nun in die Definition der neuen Konditionen von Subjektivität ein.

Liisa Roberts führt eine kinematografische Recherche durch, welche sowohl die Struktur der Bilder als auch deren Rezeption hinterfragt. Wie Carlos Basualdo schreibt, handelt die Arbeit Liisa Roberts einerseits von der Art und Weise, wie die Bilder uns berühren und unsere Darstellung der Welt formen, andererseits stellt sie eine Recherche über die Materie der Bilder selbst dar.[4] Das Dazwischen des Bildes rührt von der Gegenüberstellung der Filmebenen und seines Archivs her, gemäß des Prozesses der Aufgliederung oder der Wiederholung. *What's the Time in Vyborg?* (April 2001-2004) ist ein Film, den Liisa Roberts im Rahmen eines Projektes in Vyborg, einer Stadt an der Grenze zwischen Finnland und Russland, zusammen mit einer Gruppe Jugendlicher realisiert hat. Immer den Zufällen der Geschichte unterworfen, war Vyborg erst ein bedeutendes finnisches kulturelles Zentrum, dann sowjetische und heute schließlich russische Stadt, ein Gebiet fernab der Zeit. In ihrer Architektur stark durch Alvar Aalto geprägt, besitzt die Stadt heute noch eine Bibliothek, die von Alvar Aalto gebaut wurde. Liisa Roberts Projekt zielt darauf ab, Alvar Aaltos Bauten unter Berücksichtigung ihrer jeweiligen Kontexte bei der Entstehung in die Gegenwart zu übertragen. Der aktuelle Kontext verweist mit Blick auf ausgewählte Daten auf die Komplexität der historischen Zusammenhänge: 1927-1935 (Erbauungsdatum der Bibliothek), 1944 (die Stadt wird sowjetisch), 1955 (Beginn der Restaurierung der Bibliothek), 1989 (die Stadt wird russisch), 2001 (erneute Restaurierung der Bibliothek). Ausgehend von diesem sinnbildlichen Ort der Verbin-

The documentary film, then, can be understood as a generic concept, yet is must be put in the plural. There are no documentary films like there are cinemas. "Documentary film" is the concept of such heterogeneity, as the concept of "cinema" is a fundamental and constitute impurity of this system of symbolization. In his numerous writings on cinema, from *La Fable cinématographique* (2001)[5] to *Malaise dans l'Esthétique* (2004)[6], Jacques Rancière emphasizes the paradox raised by this theoretical object called cinema: it tends to devote itself to a theory of homonyms, an exacerbation of the distances and the differences in the field. "For me, philosophy is work on homonymy. There is, then, no philosophy of the cinema. There can be no philosophical work on cinema. But there can be work on the homonymy of the concept of 'cinema', a work that attempts to dissolve this homonymy and comprehend the paths between the different kinds of cinema. Cinema is indeed multiple: one can grasp it as a technical dispositive, namely that of the cinematographer, but it is also popular entertainment, and it is still the name of an art, this 'seventh art' and 'art'. In the end, cinema is the name of an ambiguity of art. [...] Reflecting on cinema is a journey between extremely distant points."[7]

One of the questions that contemporary art, in turn, could pose to cinema and documentary film with regard to modes of representation, though, is: how does art view cinema and what can contemporary art teach cinema and documentary film in regard to the categories of art, which art has reconsidered during the entire 20th century in terms of biography, memory, archive, and representation?

In an attempt to designate the role and the position of documentary film in contemporary art, and in art in general, contemporary art should be placed in an expanded context along the lines of what Rosalind Krauss wrote on the *photographic*[8], in order to elaborate a *theory of distance*. Documentary film plays an important role in contemporary creativity, comparable to the role of photography in modern art. Forced into retrenchment, representation acquires a reflec-

dung von Vergangenheit und Gegenwart hat die Regisseurin beschlossen, ein Schreibseminar mit russischen Jugendlichen zu organisieren, um die Ausarbeitung eines Films über die Stadt vorzubereiten, welcher die geschichtliche Ausweglosigkeit hinsichtlich der Zusammenhänge zwischen der Erinnerungsarbeit, dem ideologischen Diskurs, der Arbeit der HistorikerInnen und der politischen und sozialen Gegenwart der BewohnerInnen Vyborgs kennzeichnen wird.

Das Schreibseminar übernimmt den fiktionalen Teil und hinterfragt im Schreibprozess die Stellung der Subjektivität, die ihren Anteil an jeglicher Bildung einer Weltansicht hat, indem sie Berichte von Erfahrungen und Gebräuchlichkeiten kritisch betrachtet. Die Kamera nimmt die Stadt von der Bibliothek ausgehend und die Bibliothek von der Straße ausgehend auf; in einer Serie wechselnder Ebenen, von den offenen auf die Stadt weisenden Fenstern aus, mit welchen das Auditorium der Bibliothek ausgestattet ist. Die Bibliothek stellt sowohl einen Spiegel als auch zugleich einen Rahmen dar, der ein Wahrnehmungsfeld – wie die Stadt die Bibliothek heute sieht – und Segmente des Raums begrenzt. Der Film kennzeichnet die Rolle und Stellung der Architektur in der Konstituierung ideologischer Darstellungen. Außerdem scheint der Film weniger die Erinnerung und ihre Archive zu hinterfragen, als Hypothesen für die Gegenwart zu entwickeln. So gesehen ist *What's the Time in Vyborg?* im engeren Sinne des Begriffs kein Dokumentarfilm über eine historische Realität. Er dokumentiert die Art und Weise, in der Darstellungen zukünftig geschaffen werden. Der Film gibt dieser „Mise en abyme" eine Form und integriert sein eigenes stilistisches Moment.

Der Dokumentarfilm kann also als Gattungsbegriff verstanden werden und ist dennoch in den Plural zu setzen. Es gibt Dokumentarfilme, so wie es Kinos gibt. „Dokumentarfilm" ist der Begriff einer solchen Heterogenität, wie der Begriff „Kino" eine fundamentale und konstituierende Verunreinigung dieses Systems der Symbolisierung bezeichnet.

In seinen zahlreichen Schriften über das Kino, von *La Fable cinématographique*[5] (aus dem

tive, additional immaterial dimension: the representation of a representation. Just as photography revealed to modern art the "absence of art as one of the essential components of art", to cite Jacques Rancière[9], the characteristic of cinema also consists in revealing to art its "becoming non-art". "Photography and cinema are going through a process that the other arts have undergone in a much quicker way; to discover that what qualifies art has nothing to do with valuable objects, but, quite to the contrary, with dealing with everyday things and that which is impure. Here, I would also say that cinema is an extraordinary shortening of the path, the negotiation of the relation between art and its 'subjects' which the older arts carried out over a considerably longer period of time. This leads to a visibility, but also to a banality that attempts to conceal the general character of this negotiation of art with a reality understood as the opposite of art."[10]

The intense debates on the concept of the document and the documentary, which in the past years were held in the field of historical research, art, and the humanities[11], must be viewed in this aesthetic and theoretical perspective. The preference of the document and the archive has gained a stronger foothold in the context of the "post-postmodern" or poststructuralist criticism of the broken promises of modernism, in the context of the critical writings of Hal Foster, Douglas Crimp and, in particular, Craig Owens.[12] While for Craig Owens the archive is a fragment, an allegory opposing any kind of uniform, self-contained, and formalistic art position, for Hal Foster it develops from an economy of post-production until it constitutes a true architecture. Based on repeated readings of Michel Foucault's texts on archive as production, Hal Foster, in *An archival impulse*[13], describes the three methods of archival production work as they are applied in the work of the artists Sam Durant, Thomas Hirschhorn, and Tacita Dean: as combination, as ramification, as collection. His analysis of the works leads to the distinction between pre-production – or the phase of discovering the trace – and post-production – or the subsequently produced inscription of the "origin".

Jahr 2001) bis zu *Malaise dans l'Esthétique*[6] (2004), unterstreicht Jacques Rancière das Paradox, welches dieses theoretische Objekt – das Kino – aufwirft: Es neigt dazu, sich einer Theorie der Homonyme zu verschreiben, einer Übersteigerung der Abstände und der Unterschiede der Felder.

„Die Philosophie ist für mich eine Arbeit über die Homonymie. Es gibt also keine Philosophie des Kinos. Es kann keine philosophische Arbeit über das Kino geben. Es kann jedoch eine Arbeit über die Homonymie des Begriffs ‚Kino' geben, eine Arbeit, die diese Homonymie aufzulösen und die Wege nachzuvollziehen versucht, welche sich zwischen den unterschiedlichen Kinos abzeichnen. In der Tat ist das Kino vielfältig: Man kann es als eine technische Vorrichtung, nämlich der des Kinematografen, verstehen, aber es ist auch populäre Unterhaltung, und es ist immer noch der Name einer Kunst, diese ‚siebte Kunst' und ‚Kunst'. Schlussendlich ist das Kino der Name einer Zweideutigkeit der Kunst. [...] Das Nachdenken über das Kino ist eine Reise zwischen extrem weit entfernten Punkten."[7]

Hingegen könnte eine der Fragen, die die zeitgenössische Kunst gegenüber dem Kino und dem Dokumentarfilm hinsichtlich der Darstellungsarten hat, folgende sein: Wie sieht die Kunst das Kino und was kann die zeitgenössische Kunst dem Kino und dem Dokumentarfilm in Bezug auf die Kategorien der Kunst beibringen, welche die Kunst das gesamte 20. Jahrhundert. in Hinsicht auf die Biografie, die Erinnerung, das Archiv und die Darstellung nachvollzogen hat?

In dem Versuch, die Rolle und den Platz des Dokumentarfilms in der zeitgenössischen Kunst, und weitergefasst innerhalb der bildenden Kunst, zu benennen, sollte nach den Aussagen Rosalind Krauss' über *Das Photographische*[8] die zeitgenössische Kunst in ihren weiteren Kontext gesetzt werden, um eine *Theorie der Abstände* auszuarbeiten. Der Dokumentarfilm spielt für das zeitgenössische Schaffen eine wichtige Rolle, vergleichbar damit, was die Fotografie für die Moderne Kunst bedeutet hat: In die Defensive gedrängt, erreicht die Darstellung hier eine reflexive sowie eine zusätzliche immaterielle Dimension: die Darstel-

In his text, *Du document au monument. Quelques jalons pour une légende de l'architecture*[14], Luc Badoulet retraces the genealogy of the notion of archive, its representations and use from the 18th to the 20th century. The archive is invented, produced and fabricated in the 18th century, and exhibited and recontextualized in the 19th century. In the 20th century it attains an indexical function; it counts as evidence and must prove things. From this perspective, image and sign become the place and the stake of interpretation more than ever before. The specific use marked in such a way refers to a fundamental cinematographic question: that of montage. The archive of the 21st century is an unstable and temporary entity. An index to be established without the regime of authenticity.

In *Cinéma, Histoire: la réappropriation des récits*, Christian Delage turns cinema into a very special space of the archive when he writes: "In the interiority of its imprint as well as in the exteriority of its material supports, this archive commands us to show epistemological willingness: applied to an object of study like film, this allows us to contribute to the elucidation of an historical truth that contains documentary evidence. It is not the discovery of a new source, but the way in which reflecting upon the cinematographic style in its proximity to history leads us to return to the conditions of the work of the historian again."[15] The historian defines the work of the archive as homologous to that of film: as a reflective style constructing its own sources.

The document as such fits itself into a dialectical logic between transparency and opacity. Jean-Francois Chevrier and Philippe Roussin examine the operative value of the document in the issue of *Communication* n°71 which they conceived. The document is not the cipher of a transparency, a relation to an assumed truth, but the sign of a profound social alterity, a change of positivistic norms. Interrupted and incomplete, the document is by definition unstable and metonymic: a structure of reference.

It is the operative function and characteristic of the document that engenders a conflict-

lung einer Darstellung. So wie die Fotografie der Modernen Kunst ihre „Abwesenheit der Kunst als eine der essentiellen Komponenten der Kunst" offenbart, um hier ein Zitat Jacques Rancières' aufzugreifen, so besteht auch die Eigenschaft des Kinos darin, der Kunst ihr „Nicht-Kunst-Werden" zu offenbaren. „Das Foto und das Kino durchlaufen den Prozess, den auch die anderen Künste genommen haben, schneller; zu entdecken, dass das, was die Kunst qualifiziert, nicht mit edlen Gegenständen zu tun hat, sondern im Gegenteil, bedeutet, sich mit dem Alltäglichen und dem Unreinen auseinanderzusetzen. Auch hier würde ich sagen, dass das Kino eine außerordentliche Verkürzung des Weges ist, eines Aushandelns der Beziehung zwischen der Kunst und ihren ‚Subjekten', welches von den älteren Künsten über einen wesentlich längeren Zeitraum durchgeführt wurde. Dies ergibt eine Visibilität, aber auch eine Banalität, welche den allgemeinen Charakter dieses Aushandelns der Kunst mit der als Gegenteil der Kunst verstandenen Realität zu verstecken versucht."[10]

Die intensiven Debatten um den Begriff des Dokuments und des Dokumentarischen müssen in dieser ästhetischen und theoretischen Perspektive gesehen werden, die in den letzten Jahren im Feld der historischen Recherche, im Feld der Kunst und in den Humanwissenschaften geführt wurden.[11] Die Vorliebe für das Dokument und das Archiv fasst stärker Fuß im Kontext einer „post-postmodernen" oder post-strukturalistischen Kritik der nicht gehaltenen Versprechen der Moderne, im Kontext der kritischen Schriften Hal Fosters, Douglas Crimps oder besonders Craig Owens.[12] Während das Archiv für Craig Owens ein Fragment ist, eine Allegorie, die sich jeder einheitlichen, geschlossenen und formalistischen Kunstposition entgegenstellt, so entwickelt es sich für Hal Foster aus einer Ökonomie der Post-Produktion, bis es eine wahre Architektur darstellt. Ausgehend von der wiederholten Lektüre der Schriften Michel Foucaults über das Archiv als Produktion beschreibt Hal Foster in *An archival impulse*[13] die drei Methoden der Produktionsarbeit des Archivs, wie sie in der Arbeit der Künstler Sam Durant, Thomas Hirschhorn und Tacita Dean umgesetzt werden: als Zusammen-

ual, complex, and ambiguous relation to the real by interrogating it. While the real in the Lacanian sense is the impossible, the operativeness of the document lies in uncovering that which is not a matter of course. Instead of reproducing reality, the document furnishes reality with elements of intelligibility. In addition, the notions of the "document" and the "documentary", that leave their mark on the style and representation of reality, of history, signify two levels of signification: the use of the document and a documentary practice.

If a document, in the definition of the term, is "an object serving to identify a reality", it stands in a relation to a truth, the truth of representation.

The concept of the documentary, on the other hand, stands in a relation to a point of view, an attitude. Many works, especially all the cinematic works of Peter Watkins, testify to the alternating arrangement of documentary and documenting moments, to the inscription of the document into the center of one and the same film.

A large number of contemporary artists retrace, step by step, the contours of a pragmatics of documentary film, in particular Fikret Atay, Hassan Khan, Omer Fast, and Harun Farocki. In his hometown near the Turkish-Iraq border, the Kurdish artist Fikret Atay shoots short films with which he tries to capture moments detached from the course of everyday life; far from focusing on the striking features of a culture or the characteristics of traditions or customs, he instead films "ready-made" moments in time with a small camera. Fikret Atay's documentary cinema corresponds to a purloined logic. The video artist pursues the goal of extracting the observed realities from their context so as to reveal laws that the Occident and Orient have in common, thus also giving an account of the complexities that occur between the levels of realities tied into global/local equations. *Rebels of the dance* (2002) or *Fast and best* (2002) establish connections that arise between tradition and modernity in any cultural formation and, in the same manner, in any banal moment of everyday life.

stellung, als Verzweigung, als Sammlung. Seine Analyse der Werke führt dazu, die Prä-Produktion – oder die Phase des Aufspürens – von der Post-Produktion – oder die nachträglich produzierte Einschreibung des „Ursprungs" – zu unterscheiden.

In seinem Text *Du document au monument. Quelques jalons pour une légende de l'architecture*[14], zeichnet Luc Badoulet die Genealogie des Begriffs des Archivs nach, seiner Darstellungen und seines Gebrauchs vom 18. bis zum 20. Jahrhundert: Im 18. Jahrhundert wird das Archiv erfunden, produziert und fabriziert, im 19. Jahrhundert wird es ausgestellt und rekontextualisiert. Im 20. Jahrhundert erhält es eine Indexfunktion, gilt als Beweis und muss belegen. In dieser Perspektive werden Bild und Zeichen mehr als je zuvor Ort und Einsatz der Interpretation. Dieser so gekennzeichnete spezifische Gebrauch verweist auf eine fundamentale kinematografische Frage: die Frage nach der Montage. Das Archiv des 21. Jahrhunderts ist ein labiles und zeitliches Wesen. Ein aufzubauender Index, ohne das Regime fester Authentizität.

In seinem Text *Cinéma, Histoire: la réappropriation des récits* macht Christian Delage aus dem Kino einen ganz besonderen Raum des Archivs, wenn er schreibt: „In der Innerlichkeit seiner Prägung, wie auch in der Äußerlichkeit seiner materiellen Auflagen befiehlt uns dieses Archiv, eine epistemologische Bereitschaft zu zeigen: auf ein Untersuchungsobjekt wie den Film angewendet, bietet diese uns die Möglichkeit, zur Klärung einer historischen Wahrheit beizutragen, die eine dokumentarische Gewissheit beinhaltet. Es handelt sich hierbei nicht um die Entdeckung einer neuen Quelle, sondern um die Art und Weise, in der die Reflexion über die kinematografische Schreibweise, in ihrer Nähe zu der der Geschichte, uns dazu führt, wieder auf die Bedingungen der Arbeit des Historikers zurückzugreifen."[15] Der Historiker definiert die Arbeit des Archivs als homolog zu der des Films: als einen reflexiven Stil, der seine Quellen konstruiert.

Das Dokument als solches reiht sich in eine dialektische Logik zwischen Transparenz und Undurchsichtigkeit ein.

In *Rebels of the dance*, Fikret Atay films a group of idle youths miming a music clip in the evening in an empty ATM cubicle. This cheerful but at the same time desperate scene is a condensed cinematographic version of a complex human and geopolitical situation: a "plan-sequence" that in a very direct way characterizes the state of the world and the way things stand.

The Egyptian artist Hassan Khan belongs to the young generation of artists from the Middle East whose work is concerned with "contemporary Arabian representations", to use a term coined by Catherine David. Using specific dispositives of images, texts, films, and sounds, which are equally dispositives of enunciation, these artists question the production of self-images and collective identities from the perspective of urban public space, where cultural identities are constituted. Viewed in retrospect, the work on the metaphor of a social and cultural body in times of crises and war at the beginning of the globalization of cultures runs like a thread through a large number of works especially by Turkish, Egyptian, and Lebanese artists. Hassan Khan addresses this metaphoric space in the form of audiovisual and sonar dispositives arising equally from the collection of patterns, the new use and mixture of elements: images, sounds, and texts thus turn into truly documentary material, worked on from a perspective that stems more from music than from cinematographic montage. *Tabla dub* and *Relapse* (2004) are video performance installations that attempt to give an account, without reducing the heterogeneity of the sources. The economy of sampling and sound mixing makes use of a specific economy of reportage; the superimposition of elements and the emphasis on interstices characterize a style of multimedia aimed at highlighting the complexity of Egyptian society. Hassan Khan's films, e.g. *Sometimes/Somewhere* or *Six questions to the Lebanese* (2001) use questions which the filmmaker asks people he encounters by chance to examine what takes place at the intersection between public space and the private sphere. The films, installations, and projects carried out via the Internet

So betrachten Jean-Francois Chevrier und Philippe Roussin den operativen Wert des Dokuments in der von ihnen konzipierten Ausgabe der *Communication* n°71. Das Dokument ist nicht die Bezifferung einer Transparenz, einer Beziehung zu einer angenommenen Wahrheit, sondern das Zeichen einer tiefen sozialen Veränderung, einer Verfremdung der positivistischen Normen. Unterbrochen und unvollständig ist das Dokument in seiner Definition instabil, metonymisch: eine Struktur des Verweises.

Es ist die operative Funktion und die Eigenschaft des Dokuments, die eine streitbare, komplexe und zweideutige Beziehung zum Realen erzeugt, indem es diese verhört. Während das Reale im Lacanschen Sinn das Unmögliche ist, liegt die Operativität jedes Dokuments darin, das nicht Selbstverständliche aufzudecken: Anstatt die Realität wiederzugeben, handelt es sich für das Dokument vielmehr darum, diese mit Elementen der Klarheit auszustatten.

Außerdem bezeichnen die Begriffe des „Dokuments" und des „Dokumentarischen", die in den Stil und die Darstellung der Realität – der Historie – einfließen, zwei Ebenen der Bedeutung: den Gebrauch des Dokuments und eine dokumentarische Praxis.

Ist ein Dokument, im Sinne der Begriffsdefinition „ein Gegenstand, der dazu dient, eine Realität zu identifizieren", steht es demnach in Relation zu einer Wahrheit, der Wahrheit der Repräsentation.

Der Begriff des Dokumentarischen steht hingegen in Relation zu einer Sichtweise, zu einer Einstellung. Viele Werke, besonders das gesamte Kino Peter Watkins', zeugen von der wechselnden Anordnung dokumentarischer und dokumentierender Momente, von der Einschreibung des Dokuments in das Zentrum ein und desselben Films.

Eine große Anzahl zeitgenössischer Künstler zeichnet Schritt für Schritt die Konturen einer Pragmatik des Films nach. Im Besonderen tun dies Fikret Atay, Hassan Khan, Omer Fast und Harun Farocki. Der kurdische Künstler Fikret Atay dreht in seinem Heimatort, an der türkisch-irakischen Grenze, Kurzfilme, in denen er vom Lauf des täglichen Lebens abgelöste Momente zu

form a sort of instrument panel of images, human and territorial cartographies, as well as mixtures of spaces and synchronised times. *Relapse* is one of these instrument panels, consisting of micro-reports, dialogues, and conversations, and arranged according to the principle of a magazine. The work is a layered cross-section of the present of an extremely disparate political geography the entire complexity of which the artist reconstructs in a delicate and subtle manner.

The wide range of contemporary "documentary films" is inscribed in the even larger field of what one could call a "new economy of the symbolic". The most significant film works create a view on the reflectivity of any documentary approach and of the methods of symbolization.

In this special combination of fiction and documentary film, many works fill in the subtle contours of a documentary function. In this respect, fiction becomes an instrument to reconstruct contexts, to recontextualize works.

Joachim Koester's work is representative of the research on the concepts of narration, time, and reportage, as it is conducted by a number of artists, in particular, Eija Liisa Ahtila and Matthew Buckingham. Joachim Koester takes up historically verified events and phenomena – a scientific expedition to Greenland, the existence of a progressive region in the land of the Inuit, the lived social utopia of a community (Christiania) – in order to allude to the invisible doubling, a narrative fiction that questions history and the power of narration. His work can be located in the space between documentary film and narration, between the grey zones of facts and fiction. *Nordenskiöld and the Ice Cap* (1999) is a story in motion. This slide panorama of pictures and texts is a cinematographic montage dealing with the expedition of the scientist Nordenskiöld in the year 1870, who traveled through Greenland in the footsteps of the first Viking settlers. The artist himself followed the tracks of the explorer, repeating his journey to a blank area, to the original story. Here, Joachim Koester investigates the narrative background by juxtaposing his own experience with the report of the explorer, whose adventure failed. The work stresses the

erfassen versucht; weit davon entfernt, die hervorstechenden Merkmale einer Kultur oder die Charakteristika von Traditionen oder Bräuchen ins Zentrum rücken zu wollen, filmt er im Laufe der Zeit „Ready-made"-Momente mit Hilfe einer kleinen Kamera. Das dokumentarische Kino Fikret Atays entspricht einer entwendeten Logik: Der Videokünstler verfolgt das Ziel, die beobachteten Realitäten aus dem Kontext zu nehmen, um die dem Okzident und dem Orient gemeinsamen Gesetze zum Vorschein zu bringen, und damit auch von der Komplexität zu berichten, die sich zwischen den Ebenen der in die globalen/lokalen Gleichungen eingebundenen Realitäten abspielt. *Rebels of the dance* (2002) oder *Fast and best* (2002) stellen die Verbindungen dar, die sich zwischen Tradition und Modernität in jeder kulturellen Formation und in der gleichen Weise in jedem qualitätslosen Moment des alltäglichen Lebens ergeben.

In *Rebels of the dance* filmt Fikret Atay eine Gruppe untätiger Jugendlicher, die abends im Inneren einer leeren Kammer eines Geldautomaten einen Musik-Clip nachahmen. Diese heitere und zugleich hoffnungslose Szene ist eine kinematografische Kurzfassung einer komplexen menschlichen und geopolitischen Situation: eine Plansequenz, die in sehr direkter Art und Weise den Zustand der Welt und der Dinge kennzeichnet.

Der ägyptische Künstler Hassan Khan gehört der jungen Generation der KünstlerInnen des Mittleren Orients an, deren Arbeit sich mit den „zeitgenössischen arabischen Darstellungen" befasst, um hier den durch Catherine David geprägten Ausdruck zu verwenden. Anhand der Anordnung von Bildern, Texten, Filmen und Klängen, welche ebenso sehr Anordnungen des Ausdrucks sind, hinterfragen diese KünstlerInnen die Produktion des Selbstbildnisses, der kollektiven Identitäten in der Perspektive des urbanen öffentlichen Raums, dem Ort an dem kulturelle Identitäten gebildet werden. Die Arbeit über die Metapher einer sozialen und kulturellen Körperschaft in Krisen- und Kriegszeiten zu Beginn der Globalisierung der Kulturen, stellt, rückblickend betrachtet, den roten Faden einer großen Anzahl von Werken insbesondere türkischer, ägyptischer und libanesischer KünstlerInnen dar. Hassan Khan

paradoxical attempt to make use of a geography in order to double it through the text, although the permanent change of the landscape, of the ice and snow, renders this description impossible.

The works of Tacita Dean always take on the form of an investigation, of a journey in search of abandoned objects and missing persons. Her approach consists in documenting a real or supposed event, using a collection of clues or individual traces as a starting point for reconstructing memory during the course of her quest. Her interest in the solitary adventures of Land Art, like those of Bas Jan Ader or Robert Smithson, for example, and in the "disappearance" of the work led her to research Smithson's *Partially Buried Woodshed*: The resulting video retraces the impossibility of making use of a tangible real or to take hold of a piece of evidence.

Reports on various facts and journalistic examinations feed Tacita Dean's work, which is a mixture of fiction and documentation; she adheres to the given, related ideas of individual, anonymous destinies and to the information available on them. Within the frame of her search for the wreck of the adventurer Donald Crowhurst, who disappeared in the sea after the fabrication of his fictitious winning of the Golden Globe 1969, she traveled to one of the Caribbean islands and discovered the "Bubble House" there, built by a Frenchman who was sentenced to five years in prison after completing the construction work. The film, *Bubble House* (1999) examines modernist architecture to describe the relations between ideas of a future and of decline, of utopia and adventure. The science-fiction scenarios that Tacita Dean constantly makes use of in her work are simultaneously "autobiographic documentary films" about the love of phantoms, of that which contains imaginary things, of violence and dreams, of stories abandoned by others, stories of the world.

greift diesen metaphorischen Raum in Form von audiovisuellen und klangvollen Anordnungen wieder auf, die zu gleichen Teilen aus der Mustersammlung, dem neuen Aufgreifen der Elemente und aus der Tonmischung hervorgehen: Bilder, Töne und Texte werden so zu einer wahrhaft dokumentarischen Materie, überarbeitet in einer Perspektive, die fast noch mehr aus der Musik als aus der kinematografischen Montage hervorgeht. *Tabla dub* und *Relapse* (2004) sind Video-Peformance-Installationen, die zu berichten versuchen, ohne dabei die Heterogenität der Quellen zu schmälern. Die Ökonomie des Samplings und der Tonmischung macht Gebrauch von einer spezifischen Ökonomie des Berichts; die Überlagerung von Elementen und die Hervorhebung von Zwischenräumen charakterisieren einen Multimedia-Stil, der auf die Hervorhebung der Komplexität der ägyptischen Gesellschaft abzielt. Die Filme Hassan Khans, wie *Sometimes/Somewhere* oder *Six questions to the Lebanese* (2001) untersuchen anhand von Fragen, die der Filmemacher an Personen richtete, denen er zufällig begegnete, was sich an der Schnittstelle zwischen öffentlichem und privatem Raum abspielt. Die Filme, die Installationen wie auch die über das Internet durchgeführten Projekte stellen eine Art Armaturenbrett der Bilder dar, menschliche und territoriale Kartografien, sowie Vermischungen aus Räumen und synchronisierten Zeiten. *Relapse* ist eines dieser Armaturenbretter, hergestellt aus Mikro-Berichten, aus Dialogen und Gesprächen, angeordnet nach dem Prinzip einer Zeitschrift. Das Werk stellt einen schichtweisen Schnitt durch die Gegenwart einer extrem ungleichen politischen Geographie dar, deren gesamte Komplexität der Künstler in feiner und subtiler Art und Weise rekonstruiert.

Das breit gefächerte Gebiet des zeitgenössischen „Dokumentarfilms" fügt sich selbst in das noch weitere Feld dessen ein, was man eine „neue Ökonomie des Symbolischen" nennen könnte. Die bedeutendsten filmischen Werke stellen eine Sichtweise bezüglich der Reflexivität jeder dokumentarischen Herangehensweise und bezüglich der Methoden der Symbolisation her.

In dieser speziellen Verbindung von Fiktion und Dokumentarfilm erfüllen viele Werke die subtilen Konturen einer dokumentarischen Funk-

1 Stanley Cavell, *A Pitch of Philosophy: Autobiographical Exercises*, Cambridge, Massachusetts 1994. For a number of texts on the relationships that connect art and cinema, on the system that clarifies this collaboration and exchange between artists and filmmakers, cinema and museum. Jacques Aumont, *L'oeil interminable: Cinéma et peinture*, Paris 1989. Raymond Bellour, *L'Entre-images*, Paris, 1999. Bruce Jenkins, "The machine in the museum: On the seven art in search of authorization," *Cahiers du Witte de With* 3 (1995). Mark Lash, "Art and Cinema: Some critical reflections," *Documenta11, Platform 5—Exhibition*, Ostfildern-Ruit 2002, p. 129ff. Jim Pines and Paul Willemen, eds. *Questions of Third Cinema*, London 1989. Jessica Morgan and Gregor Muir, eds. *Time Zones: Recent Film and Video*, London 2004.
2 March 10—June 17, 2003.
3 Emmanuel Burdeau, Hélène (Feb. 2003).
4 See Carlos Basualdo, "Notes Towards the Dematerialization of the Art Exhibition," *Insertions*, Archipelago, The Nordic Museum and The Museum of Science and Technology, Stockholm 1998.
5 Jacques Rancière, *La Fable Cinématographique*, Paris 2001.
6 Jacques Rancière, *Malaise dans l'esthétique*, Paris 2004.
7 Jacques Rancière, "L'affect indécis," Critique Cinéphilosophie 692–693, (2005), p. 142f.
8 Rosalind Krauss, *Le Photographique: Pour une Théorie des Écarts*, Paris 1990.
9 Jacques Rancière, "Le destin du cinéma comme art," *Les Cahiers du Cinéma* 598 (2005), p. 64.
10 Ibid., p. 65.
11 There is quite an extensive bibliography on this topic, particularly in the Anglo-Saxon region. I do not want to provide a comprehensive list here, just a few relevant titles. Boris Groys, "Art in the age of biopolitics: from artwork to art documentation," *Documenta11, Platform5*, exhibition catalogue, Ostfildern-Ruit 2002. "Le parti pris du document: Littérature, photographie, cinéma et architecture au XX siècle," *Communications* 71 (2001). Gregor Neuerer, ed. *Untitled Experience of Place*, London, 2003. Exhibition catalogues of documenta X (1997) and Documenta11 (2002). Annette Michelson, "The Estates general of documentary films," *October* 91 (2000). Francois Niney, *L'épreuve du réel à l'écran, essai sur le principe de réalité documentaire*, Brussels 2002. Anselm Franke, ed. *Territories. Islands, Camps, and other states of utopia*, exhibition catalogue, Institute for Contemporary Art. Cologne 2003.
12 Hal Foster, "Re:post (Riposte)," *Parachute* 26; reproduced in the catalogue *L'Epoque, la mode, la morale, la passion*, Centre Georges Pompidou, Paris 1987, p. 463ff. Craig Owens, "The Allegorical Impulse: Toward a Theory of Postmodernism," *October* 13 (1980), p. 67-75.
13 Hal Foster, "An archival impulse," *October* 110 (2004), p. 3–22.
14 Luc Baboulet, *Communcations* 71 (2001), p. 435ff.
15 Christian Delage, *Vertigo* 16 (1997), p. 15.

tion. In dieser Hinsicht wird die Fiktion zu einem Instrument des Rekonstruierens von Kontexten, der Rekontextualisierung der Werke.

Die Arbeit Joachim Koesters ist repräsentativ für die Recherchen über die Begriffe der Narration, der Zeit und des Berichts, wie sie heute von einigen KünstlerInnen, im Besonderen von Eija Liisa Ahtila und Matthew Buckingham, durchgeführt werden. Joachim Koester greift historisch belegte Ereignisse und Phänomene auf — eine wissenschaftliche Expedition nach Grönland, die Existenz eines fortschrittlichen Gebiets im Land der Inuit, die gelebte soziale Utopie einer Gemeinschaft (Christiana) — um hiervon ausgehend die unsichtbare Doppelung, eine narrative Fiktion, die die Geschichte hinterfragt, und die Macht der Erzählung, zu erahnen. Es ist der Raum zwischen dem Dokumentarfilm und der Narration, zwischen den Grauzonen der Tatsachen und der Fiktion, in dem die Arbeit Joachim Koesters anzusiedeln ist. *Nordenskiöld and the Ice Cap* (1999) ist eine Geschichte in Bewegung: Das Diapanorama aus Bildern und Texten ist eine kinematografische Montage über die Expedition des Wissenschaftlers Nordenskiöld im Jahre 1870, der auf den Spuren der ersten Wikingersiedlungen in Grönland unterwegs war. Der Künstler selbst hat die Spuren des Forschungsreisenden verfolgt, indem er diese Reise zu einem weißen Fleck auf der Landkarte, hin zur ursprünglichen Geschichte wiederholt hat. Joachim Koester erkundet hier den narrativen Hintergrund, indem er seine eigene Erfahrung dem Bericht des Forschers gegenüberstellt, dessen Abenteuer fehlgeschlagen ist. Das Werk stellt den paradoxen Versuch in den Vordergrund, sich einer Geografie bedienen zu wollen, um diese durch den Text zu verdoppeln, obwohl die ständige Verwandlung der Landschaft, des Eises und des Schnees diese Beschreibung unmöglich machen.

Die Werke Tacita Deans nehmen stets die Gestalt einer Untersuchung an, einer Reise auf der Suche nach verlassenen Objekten, nach verschollenen Personen. Ihre Vorgehensweise besteht darin, ein reales oder angenommenes Ereignis zu dokumentieren, indem sie von einer Sammlung von Hinweisen oder von einzelnen Spuren ausgeht um im

Verlauf ihrer Suche die Erinnerung zu rekonstruieren. So führte sie ihr Interesse für die einsamen Abenteurer der Land Art, wie z.B. Bas Jan Ader oder Robert Smithson, und für das „Verschwinden" der Werke zu der Recherche über Smithsons *Partially buried woodshed*: Das daraus entstandene Video zeichnet die Unmöglichkeit nach, sich eines greifbaren Realen zu bedienen oder sich eines Beweisstücks zu bemächtigen.

Berichte verschiedener Fakten und journalistische Untersuchungen nähren die Arbeit Tacita Deans, welche eine Vermischung aus Fiktion und Dokumentarfilm darstellt, indem sie sich an die gegebenen verwandten Ideen von einzelnen, anonymen Schicksalen und die Informationen über sie hält.

Im Rahmen ihrer Suche nach einem Schiffswrack des Abenteurers Donald Crowhurst, der nach der Erfindung seines fiktiven Sieges beim Golden Globe 1969 auf dem Meer verschwand, reiste sie auf eine der Karibischen Inseln und entdeckte dort das „Bubble House", welches von einem Franzosen erbaut wurde, der noch vor Vollendung der Bauarbeiten zu fünf Jahren Haft verurteilt wurde. Der Film *Bubble House* (1999) beschreibt anhand einer Betrachtung der modernistischen Architektur die Zusammenhänge zwischen den Ideen für eine Zukunft und dem Verfall, zwischen der Utopie und dem Abenteuer. Die Science-Fiction-Szenarien, die Tacita Dean ständig in ihren Werken verarbeitet, sind zugleich „autobiografische Dokumentarfilme" über eine Vorliebe für Phantome; für das, was Imaginäres, Gewalt und Träume enthält, für die von anderen fallen gelassenen Geschichten, für die Geschichten der Welt.

---

1 Stanley Cavell: *Die andere Stimme. Philosophie und Autobiographie*, Berlin 2002. Hier einige Titel über die Beziehungen, die Kunst und Kino verbinden, über das System, das diese Zusammenarbeit, den Austausch zwischen KünstlerInnen und FilmemacherInnen, zwischen dem Kino und dem Museum, verdeutlichen: Jacques Aumont: *L'oeil interminable. Cinéma et peinture*, Paris 1989. Raymond Bellour: *L'Entre-images*, Paris 1999. Bruce Jenkins: The machine in the museum. On the seven art in search of authorization, in: *Cahiers du Witte de With* (Februar 1995), Nr. 3. Mark Lash: *Art and Cinema. Some critical reflexions*, in: documenta GmbH (Hg.): *Documenta11, Platform 5 — Ausstellung*, Ostfildern-Ruit 2002, S. 129ff. Jim Pines und Paul Willemen (Hg.): *Questions of third cinema*,

London 1989. Jessica Morgan und Gregor Muir (Hg.): *Time Zones. Recent film and video*, London 2004.
2 10. März–17. Juni 2003.
3 Emmanuel Burdeau, in: *Hélène* (Februar 2003), Nr. 0.
4 Vgl. Carlos Basualdo: *Notes Towards the Dematerialization of the Art Exhibition*. Insertions. Archipelago, The Nordic Museum and The Museum of Science and Technology, Stockholm 1998.
5 Jaques Rancière: *La Fable cinématographique*, Paris 2001.
6 Jacques Rancière: *Malaise dans l'esthétique*, Paris 2004.
7 Jacques Rancière: L'affect indécis, in: *Critique Cinéphilosophie* (Januar-Februar 2005), Nr. 692–693, S.142–143.
8 Rosalind Krauss: *Das Photographische. Eine Theorie der Abstände*, München 1998.
9 Jacques Rancière: Le destin du cinéma comme art, in: *Les Cahiers du Cinéma* (Februar 2005), Nr. 598, S. 64.
10 Ebd., S. 65.
11 Die Bibliografie zu diesem Thema ist sehr umfangreich, vor allem im angelsächsischen Bereich. Das Ziel ist hier nicht, eine umfassende Titelauflistung zu leisten; ich nenne vielmehr einige Titel als Maßstab. Boris Groys: Kunst im Zeitalter der Biopolitik. Vom Kunstwerk zur Kunstdokumentation, in: documenta GmbH (Hg.): *Documenta11, Platform5 — Ausstellung*, Ostfildern-Ruit 2002. *Communications* (2001), No. 71: Le parti pris du document. Littérature, photographie, cinéma et architecture au XX siècle. Gregor Neuerer (Hg.): *Untitled experience of place*, London 2003. Ausstellungskataloge der documenta X (1997) und der Documenta11 (2002), Ostfildern-Ruit. Annette Michelson: The Estates general of ducumentary films, in: *October* (2000), Nr. 91. Francois Niney: *L'épreuve du réel à l'écran, essai sur le principe de réalité documentaire*, Brüssel 2002. *Territories. Islands, Camps, and other states of utopia*. Anselm Franke (Hg.). Katalog (KW — Institut for contemporary art), Köln 2003.
12 Hal Foster: Re:post (Riposte), in: *parachute*, Nr.26. Reproduziert im Katalog *L'Epoque, la mode, la morale, la passion*. Centre Georges Pompidou, Paris 1987, S.463ff. Craig Owens: The Allegorical Impulse. Towards a Theory of Postmodernism, in: *October* (1980), Nr. 13 (2), S. 67–75.
13 Hal Foster: An archival impulse, in: *October* (2004), Nr.110, S. 3–22.
14 Luc Baboulet, in: *Communcations* (2001), Nr.71, S. 435ff.
15 Christian Delage, in: *Vertigo* (1997), Nr.16, S.15.

THE AFGHAN WHIGS: *Big Top Halloween | Up in It | Congregation | Gentlemen | Black Love | Columbia*
ALASKA!: *Emotions*
THE AMPS: *Pacer*
ANNIHILATOR: *Set the World on Fire | King of the Kill | Refresh the Demon | Criteria for a Black Widow | Carnival Diablos | Remains | King of the Kill | Alice in Live at Never Neverland | In Command | Set the World on Fire | Bag of Tricks | Waking the Fury | Double Live Annihilator | Alice in Hell | Never Neverland*
ANTHRAX: *Fistful of Metal | Armed and Dangerous | Spreading the Disease | Among the Living | State of Euphoria | Persistence of Time | Attack of the Killer B's | Sound of White Noise | Stomp 442 | Volume 8: The Threat Is Real | We've Come for You All | Sanctuary*
APHEX TWIN: *Analogue Bubblebath | Selected Ambient Works 85-92 | Selected Ambient Works, Vol. 2 | On | I Care Because You Do | Donkey Rhubarb | Richard D. James Album | Windiwlicker | Drukqs | Classics | 51/13 Aphex | Singles Collection | Singles Box | Mixes for Cash*
BABES IN TOYLAND: *Spanking Machine | The Mother | Fontanelle | Painkillers | Dystopia | Nemesisters | Lived | Minneapolism: Live - The Last Tour | Viled | Fair is Foul & Foul is Fair | The Peel Sessions | Natural Babe Killers | Devil | The Further Adventures | Intermenstral*
BAD BRAINS: *Bad Brains | Rock for Light | Live | Quickness | Youth Are Getting Restless | Spirit | Electricity | Rise | God of Love | Live in San Francisco | I & I Survived | Attitude: The ROIR Sessions | Bad Brains (Colored Vinyl) | Black Dots | Banned in DC: Bad Brains' Greatest Riffs | I Against I / Rock for Light*
JOE BAIZA: *Universal Congress Of*
BAND OF SUSANS: *Hope Against Hope | Love Agenda | The Word and the Flesh | Now | Veil | Here Comes Success | The Peel Sessions [live] | Wired for Sound*
BANYAN: *Banyan | Anytime at all*
LOU BARLOW: *... & His Sentridoh | Subsonic 6 | Winning Losers | ... & Friends*
BEASTIE BOYS: *Licensed to Ill | Paul's Boutique | Check Your Head | Ill Communication Check Your Head | Hello Nasty | Some Old Bullshit | The In Sound From Way Out! | The Sounds of Science | Anthology: Beastitude [MP3...*
BEAT HAPPENING: *Beat Happening | Jamboree | Black Candy | Dreamy | You Turn Me On | Music to Climb the Apple Tree By | 1983-85 | Crashing Through*
BETTIE SERVEERT: *Palomine | Lamprey | Dust Bunnies | Plays Venus in Furs and other Velvet... | Private Suit | Log 22*
BRANT BJORK: *Jalamanta | Brant Bjork & The Operators | Keep Your Cool | Local Angel*
BIG BLACK: *Atomizer | Songs about Fucking | Pigpile | The Hammer Party | Rich Man's 8-Track Tape*
FRANK BLACK: *Frank Black | Teenager of the Year | The Cult of Ray | The Black Sessions: Live in Paris Plus the... | Frank Black & the Catholics | Pistolero | Dog in the Sand | Devil's Workshop | Black Letter Days | Show Me Your Tears | Odd Balls*
BLACK FLAG: *Damaged | Family Man | Live 84 | My War | Slip it in | In My Head | Lose Nut | Who's got a 10" | Everything Went Black*
PETER BLEGVAD: *The Naked Shakespeare | Knights Like This | Downtime | Just Woke Up | Unearthed | Hangman's Hill | Choices Under Pressure | King Strut & Other Stories*
THE BOTTLE ROCKETS: *Bottle Rockets | The Brooklyn Side | 24 Hours A Day | Leftovers | Brand New Year | Songs of Sahm | Blue Sky*
BILLY BRAGG & WILCO: *Mermaid Avenue Vol. 1 - 2*
BLAG DAHLIA: *Let's Take a Ride | Blag Dahlia | Venus With Arms*
BREEDERS: *Pod | Last Splash | Live in Stockholm | Title TK*
JACK BREWER BAND: *Rockin' Ethereal | Harsh World*
BRUTE: *Nine-High a Pallet | Co-Balt*
BURNING BRIDES: *Fall of the Plastic Empire | Leave No Ashes*
BUTTHOLE SURFERS: *Psychic Powerless Another Man's Sac | Rembrandt Pussyhorse | Locust Abortion Technician | Hairway to Steven | Double Live | Pioughd Independent Worm Saloon | Hole Truth...And Nothing Butt | Electriclarryland | Electriclarryland [Clean] | After the Astronaut | Weird Revolution | Live | Bootleg | Humpty Dumpty L.S.D. | Live PCPPEP*
BUZZ HUNGRY: *Fried like a man | At the hands of our intercessors*
JOHN CALE: *New York in the 1960s, Vol. 1: Sun Blindness... | Vintage Violence | Church of Anthrax | The Academy in Peril | Paris 1919 | Fear | Slow Dazzle | Helen of Troy | Sabotage/Live | Honi Soit | Music for a New Society | Caribbean Sunset | Comes Alive | Artificial Intelligence | Words for the Dying | HN | Songs for Drella | Even Cowgirls Get the Blues | Fragments of a Rainy Season | Paris S'eveille | 23 Solo Pieces for La Naissance de L'Amour | Antartida | Walking on Locusts | Nico: Dance Music | Nico | Dance Music | Le Vent de la Nuit | Inside the Dream Syndicate, Vol. - 3: Day of... | HoboSapiens | Lou Reed / John Cale / Nico | The Unknown | Guts | Seducing Down the Door | The Island Years | Eat / Kiss: Music for the Films of Andy Warhol | Close Watch: An Introduction to John Cale*
CAMPER VAN BEETHOVEN: *Telephone Free Landslide Victory | II & III | Camper Van Beethoven | Our Beloved Revolutionary | Sweetheart | Key Lime Pie | Tusk | Third Album / Vampire Can Mating Oven | Camper Vantiquities | Camper Van Beethoven Is Dead: Long Live | Cigarettes & Carrot Juice: The Santa Cruz...*
CAMPER VAN CHADBOURNE: *Camper Van Chadbourne | The Eddie Chatterbox Double Trio Love Album | Eugene Von Beethoven's 69th Sin Funny | Revenge of Camper Van Chadbourne | Psychadelidoowop | Used Record Pile*
CAUSTIC WINDOW: *Compilation Caustic Window | Joyrex J9*
VIC CHESNUTT: *Little | West of Rome | Drunk | Is the Actor Happy | About to Choke | The Salesman and Bernadette | Merriment | Left to His Own Devices | Silver Lake*
CINERAMA: *Va Va Voom | Disco Volante | Torino*
COCTEAU TWINS: *Head Over Heels | The Moon & the Melodies | Blue Bell Knoll | Heaven or Las Vegas | Four-Calendar Cafe | Milk & Kisses | The Pink Opaque | Tiny Dynamine / Echoes in a Shallow Bay | Victorialand | Treasure/Aikea-Guinea | Garlands/Peel Sessions | Head Over Heels/Sunburst and Snowblind | CD Single Box Set | BBC Sessions [live] | Stars and Topsoil: A Collection 1982-90*
CONSOLIDATED: *Friendly Fascism | The Myth of Rock | Play More Music | Business of Punishment | Dropped | The End of Meaning | Tikkun*
COP SHOOT COP: *PieceMan | Consumer Revolt | White Noise | Ask Questions Later | $10 Bill | Room 429 | Release | Suck City / Nowhere / Days | Two At A Time | Any Day Now + 3*
CHRIS CORNELL: *Euphoria Morning | Can't Change Me*
CRASS: *The Feeding of the 5000 | Stations of the Crass | Penis Envy | Christ the Album | Yes Sir, I Will | 10 Notes on a Summer's Day | You'll Ruin It for Everyone | Christ: The Bootleg [live] | Best Before 1984*
CUJO: *Adventures in Foam*
DEAD CAN DANCE: *Dead Can Dance | Spleen and Ideal | Within the Realm of a Dying Sun | Serpent's Egg | Aion | Into the Labyrinth | Toward the Within [live] | Spiritchaser | A Passage in Time Dead Can Dance 1981-1998 | Wake: Best of Dead Can Dance*
DEAD KENNEDYS: *Fresh Fruit For Rotten Vegetables | In God We Trust | Plastic Surgery Disasters | Frankenchrist | Bedtime for Democracy | Give Me Convenience or Give Me Death | Mutiny on the Bay | Live at Deaf Club*
DECEMBRISTS: *Picaresque | Her Majesty | Castaways and Cutouts | Tain / 5 Songs | Billy Liar*
THE DEFTONES: *Adrenaline | Around the Fur | Live | White Pony | Back to School (Mini Maggit) | Deftones | Maximum More | Live Tracks*
DELUXX FOLK IMPLOSION: *Forgiveness Towel | Tidy Box & Crazy Bastard*
DESERT SESSIONS: *Desert Sessions Vol. 1 - 10*
DINOSAUR JR.: *Dinosaur | You are living all over me | Bug | Green Mind | Wher you been | Jayloumurth | Without a sound | Hand it over | In sessions | Fossils | Whatever's cool with me | Quest*
DIRTY ROTTEN IMBECILS (D.R.I.): *Dirty Rotten LP [1987 & 2002] / Violent Pacific | Dealing With It | 22 Songs | Crossover | 4 of a Kind | Thrash Zone | Definition | Live | Full Speed Ahead | Rotten | Dirty Rotten Imbeciles | Dirtiest...Rottenest | Live at the Ritz: N.Y.C...*
THE DISPOSABLE HEROES OF HIPHOPRISY: *Hipocrisy Is The Greatest Luxury*
DOG EYE VIEW: *Happy Nowhere | Daisy*
DOS: *Dos | Justamente Tres | Uno Con Dos*
DWARVES: *Horror Stories | Toolin' For A Warm Teabag | Blood Guts & Pussy | Thank Heaven for Little Girls | Sugarfix | Are Young And Good Looking | Free Cocaine | Come Clean | How to Win Friends and Influence People | The Dwarves Must Die*
EAGLES OF DEATH METAL: *Peace, Love, Death Metal*
EARTHLINGS?: *The Earthlings? | Human Beans | Dues Paid*
80'S MATCHBOX B-LINE DISASTER: *Mister Mental, Pt. 1*
ELEVEN: *Howling Book | Avantgardedog | Awake in a Dream | Thunk | Rainbow's End*
JAY FARRAR: *Sebastopol | ThirdShiftGrottoSlack | Terroir Blues | Stone, Steel & Bright Lights*
FATSO JETSON: *Stinky Little Gods | Power Of Three | Flames For All | Toasted*
FEELIES: *Crazy Rhytmns | The Good Earth | Only Life | Time for a Witness*
FIREHOSE: *Raggin', Full-On | If'n | Fromohio | Flyin' the Flannel | Mr. Machinery Operator*
STEVE FISK: *448 Deathless Days | Over and Thru the Night | 999 Levels of Undo*
FLAMING LIPS: *The Flaming Lips | Hear It Is | Oh My Gawd!!!...The Flaming Lips | Telepathic Surgery | In A Priest-Driven Ambulance | Hit To Death In The*

Future Head | Transmissions From The Satellite Heart | Clouds Taste Metallic | Zaireeka | The Soft Bulletin | Yoshimi Battles The Pink Robots | At War With The Mystics
FOLK IMPLOSION: Take a Look Inside | Dare to Be Suprised | One Part Lullaby | The New Folk Implosion
JOHN FOXX: Metamatic | The Garden | The Golden Section | In Mysterious Ways | Shifting City | Cathedral Oceans | The Pleasures of Electricity | The Golden Section Tour + The Omnidelic Tour [live] | Crash and Burn | Translucence/Drift Music | Assembly | Modern Art
FUGAZI: Repeater + 3 Songs | Steady Diet of Nothing | In on the Kill Taker | Red Medicine | End Hits | The Argument | 13 Songs | Instrument
FU MANCHU: (Godzilla's) Eating Dust (Elastic) | Something Beyond | Go For It! ... Live | California Crossing | King Of The Road | Start The Machine | Return To Earth 91 — 93 |
FUTURE BIBLE HEROES: Memories of Love | Eternal Youth
GANG OF FOUR: Entertainment! | Solid Gold | Songs of the Free | Hard | At the Palace | Mall | Shrinkwrapped | A Brief History of the Twentieth Century | Peel Sessions | Solid Gold/Another Day, Another Dollar | Tattoo | A 100 Flowers Bloom | Hard/Solid Gold
GARDENER: New Dawning Time | Boys of Summer
LISA GERRARD: The Mirror Pool | Duality | Whale Rider | Immortal Memory | Live at the Philadelphia Theatre of Living...
GREG GINN: Getting Even | Payday | Dick | Let It Burn (Because I don't live there...
GIRLS AGAINST BOYS: Tropic of Scorpio | Venus Luxure No. 1 Baby | Cruise Yourself | House of GVSB | Freak*on*ica | You Can't Fight What You Can't See
GOLDEN PALOMINOS: The Golden Palominos | Visions of Excess | Blast of Silence | A Dead Horse | Drunk With Passion | This Is How It Feels | Pure No Thought, No Breath, No Eyes, No Heart Heaven | Dead Inside
GONE: Let's Get Real / Real Gone For a Change | Gone II - But Never Too Gone | Criminal Mind | All The Dirt That's Fit to Print | Damage Control | Best Left Unsaid | Country Dumb Demology | Into the Bright Oxygen Of My Nod
GUIDED BY VOICES: Devil Between My Toes | Sandbox | Self-Inflicted Aerial Nostalgia | Same Place the Fly Got Smashed | Propeller | Vampire on Titus | Crying Your Knife Away | Bee Thousand | Alien Lanes | King Shit and the Golden | Boys | Jellyfish Reflector [live] | Under the Bushes Under the Stars | Benefit for Winos [live] | For All Good | Kids | Mag Earwhig! | Do the Collapse | Isolation Drills | Universal Truths and Cycles | Earthquake Glue | Fiction Man
GRANT HART: All of my senses | Intolerance | Ecce Homo | Good news for modern man
P. J. HARVEY: Dry | Rid of Me | 4-Track Demos | Bring You My Love | Is This Desire? | Stories From the City, Stories From the Sea | Uh Huh Her | The B-Sides
HATER: Hater
HELMET: Strap It On | Meantime | Betty | Aftertaste | Size Matters
KRISTIN HERSCH: Hips and Makers | Strange Angels | Murder, Misery and Then Goodnight | Sky Motel | Sunny Border Blue | The Grotto
HÜSKER DÜ: Land Speed Record | Everything Falls Apart | Zen Arcade | New Day Rising | Flip Your Wig | Candy Apple Grey Warner | Warehouse: Songs & Stories | The Living End | Amusement / Statues | In a Free Land | Eight Miles High / Masochism World | Makes No Sense at All | Love is All Around | Don't Want to Know if You are Lonely | All Work and No Play | Sorry Somehow | Could You Be the One? | Ice Cold Ice | Gotta Lotta | Eight Miles High | Makes No Sense at All | Sorry Somehow | Do You Remember? | Could You Be the One? | She's a Woman (And Now He is a Man) [Live on The Joan Rivers Show 1987] | Drug Party | Live at 1st Avenue Club, Minneapolis 1985 | Do You Remember? The Early Years 1980-1982
INDIGO GIRLS: Strange Fire | Indigo Girls | Nomads Indians Saints | Rites of Passage | Swamp Ophelia | Touch Me Fall | 1200 Curfews | Shaming of the Sun | Come on Now Social | Become You | All That We Let In | Retrospective
JANE'S ADDICTION: Jane's Addiction | Nothing's Shocking | Ritual de lo Habitual | Strays | Live and Rare | Kettle Whistle
JAYHAWKS: The Jayhawks | Blue Earth | Hollywood Town Hall | Tomorrow the Green Grass | Sound of Lies | Smile | Rainy Day Music
THE JESUS AND MARY CHAIN: Psychocandy | Darklands | Automatic | Honey's Dead | Stoned & Dethroned | Munki | Barbed Wire Kisses | The Sound of Speed | The Jesus and Mary Chain Hate Rock N' Roll | The Complete John Peel Sessions | 21 Singles | BBC Live in Concert
JOHNNY SOCIETY: It Don't Matter | Wood | Clairvoyance | Life Behind the 21st Century Wall
MIKE JOHNSON: Where Am I? | Year of Mondays | I feel allright | What would you do
JOY DIVISION: Unknown Pleasures | Closer | Preston Warehouse 28 February 1980 | Les Bains Douches 18 | December 1979 | Still | Substance | The Peel Sessions | Permanent | Heart and Soul | Complete BBC Recordings
JUNGLE FUNK: Jungle Funk | Jungle Funk Live
KILLING JOKE: Killing Joke | What's THIS For...! | Revelations MaliciousDamag | Fire Dances | Night Time | Brighter Than a Thousand Suns | Outside the Gate | The Courtald Talks | Extremities, Dirt & Various Repressed... | Pandemonium | BBC In Concert | Democracy | No Way Out But Forward Go | The Unperverted Pantomine | Killing Joke | Requiem | Laugh? I Nearly Bought One! | Wilful Days | War Dance
KUSTOMIZED: Mystery Of... | The Battle of Space | At Vanishing Point
KYUSS: Wretch | Blues for Red Sun | Welcome to Sky Valley | ...And The Circus Leaves Town | Muchas Gracias | 3 of 1
LAMBCHOP: I Hope You're Sitting Down [aka Jack's... | How I Quit Smoking | Thriller | What Another Man Spills | Nixon | Is a Woman | Aw C'mon | No, You C'mon | Tools in the Dryer: A Rarities Compilation
MARK LANEGAN (BAND): Down In The Dark | The Winding Sheet | Whiskey for the Holy Ghost | Scraps at Midnight | Stay | I'll take care of you | Field Songs | Here Comes that Weird Chill | Bubblegum | Hit the City
K. D. LANG: Friday Dance Promenade | A Truly Western Experience | Angel With a Lariat | Shadowland | Absolute Torch and Twang | Ingenue | All You Can Eat | Drag | Invincible Summer | Live by Request | 3 for 1
DANIEL LANOIS: Acadie | For the Beauty of Wynona | Cool Water | Shine
LARD: The Power of Lard | The Last Temptation Of Reid | Pure Chewing Satisfaction | 70s Rock Must Die
GARY LEE CONNER: Grasshopper's Dream/Behind The Smile
LONDON ELEKTRICITY: Billion Dollar Gravy | Pull The Plug | Rewind | Song In The Key Of Knife / The Land Sanction | P.B.E. | Sister Stalking
JASON LÖWENSTEIN: At Six and Sevens
LOW POP SUICIDE: On The Cross Of Commerce | The Death Of Excellence
JOHN LYDON: Psycho's Path
L7: L7 | Smash the magic | Bricks are heavy | Hungry for stink | The Beauty Process: Triple Platinum | Live: Omaha to Osaka | Slap Happy | Slash Years
MAD SEASON: Above
MAGNETIC FIELDS: Distant Plastic Trees | The Wayward Bus | The Charm of the Highway Strip | Holiday | Get Lost | 69 Love Songs, Pt. 1 - 3
THE MARTINIS: Smitten
MASTERS OF REALITY: Masters of Reality | Sunrise on the Sufferbus | How High the Moon: Live at the Viper Room | Welcome to the Western Lodge | Deep In The Hole | Flak N Flight | Blue Garden | Give us Barabbas
MELISSA AUF DER MAUR: Auf Der Maur
STEPHIN MERRIT: Eban & Charley
J. MASCIS: Martin + Me | More Light | Free so Free
MASSIVE ATTACK: Blue Lines | Protection | No Protection: Massive Attack Vs. Mad Professor | Mezzanine | 100th Window | Singles 90/98
HOLLY MCNARLAND: Stuff | Live Stuff | Home Is Where
MEAT PUPPETS: Meat Puppets I-II | Up on the sun | Huevos | Mirage | Monsters | Forbidden Places | Too High To Die | No Joke! | Live in Montana | Golden Lie | Live at Maxwell | No Strings Attached
MINISTRY: Work for Love | With Sympathy | Everyday Is Halloween | Twitch | The Land of Rape and Honey | The Mind Is a Terrible Thing to Taste | In Case You Didn't Feel Like Showing Up | Psalm 69: The Way to Succeed & the Way to... | Filth Pig | The Dark Side of the Spoon | Live Psalm 69 Tour | Sphincter Animositisomina | Psalm 69 Live | Twelve Inch Singles (1981-1984) | Burning Inside: Through the Years 89-92 | Houses of Mole
MINOR THREAT: Complete Discography
MINUTEFLAG: Minuteflag
MINUTEMAN: The Punch Line | Buzz and Howl under the Influence of Heat | What makes a man start fires? | Double Nickel on the Dime | 3-Wat Tie for Last | Ballot Result | The Politics of Time | My First Bells | Just a Minute, Man | 1980-83 | Post-Mersh Vol. 1-3
MISFITS: Walk Among Us | Earth A.D. / Wolfsblood | Legacy of Brutality | Die Die My Darling | Static Age | American Psycho | Famous Monsters | Cuts from the Crypt | Project 1950
MONDO GENERATOR: Cocaine Rodeo | Drug Problem That Never Existed | 3 The EP |
MOTHER LOVE BONE: Apple
MOTÖRHEAD: Motorhead | On Parole | Bomber | Overkill | Ace of Spades | No Sleep 'Til Hammersmith | Iron Fist | What's Words Worth | Another Perfect Day | Orgasmatron | Rock 'N' Roll | No Sleep At All | Blitzkrieg on Birmingham '77 | 1916 | 1916 Live...Everything Louder than... | March or Die | Bastards | Iron Fist & The Hordes from Hell | Aces High | Live 1983 | Sacrifice | Overnight Sensation | Ace of Spades | King Biscuit Flower Hour Presents Motorhead | Archive | On Parole | Snake Bite Love | Everything Louder Than Everyone Else: Live | Jailbait | Live 1977 | We Are Motörhead | Iron Fist | Bomber | Overkill | Another Perfect Day | Rock 'N' Roll | No Sleep At All | Hammered | Keep Us on the Road | Aces | Speed Not Comfort | I Got Mine | Inferno | Live at Brixton | Motörhead Plugged In!
BOB MOULD: Workbook | Black Sheets of Rain | Bob Mould | The Last Dog and Pony Show | Modulate | Live Dog 98: The Forum, London UK | Poison

Years | Mindbomb | See a little light | Wishing Well (+ 4 live tracks) | Rust Bucket Coliseum | Egoverride | Live Mould - Live In Europe | Calm before the storm | The Loner
MOVING TARGETS: Burning in Water | Brave Noise | Fall | Take This Ride
MUDHONEY: Mudhoney | Every Good Boy Deserves Fudge | Piece of Cake | My Brother the Cow | Tomorrow Hit Today | Since We've Become Translucent | Superfuzz Bigmuff (Plus Early Singles) | March to Fuzz | Here Comes Sickness: The Best of BBC...
MY BLOODY VALENTINE: This is your Bloody Valentine | It's Anything | Loveless
NAPALM DEATH: Punk Is a Rotting Corpse | Hatred Surge | From Enslavement To Obliteration | You Suffer | Scum | The Curse | From Enslavement To Obliteration | Live EP | Mentally Murdered | Live in Europe 88 | The Peel Sessions | Napalm Death/S.O.B. Split 7" Flexi | Suffer The Children | live at the ICA in London | Harmony Corruption | Live Corruption | Mass Appeal Madness | Malignant Trait | One And The Same | Utopia Banished | The World Keeps Turning | Death By Manipulation | Live Corruption | Nazi Punks Fuck Off | Fear, Emptiness, Despair | Hung | Greed Killing | Cursed to Tour | In Tongues We Speak | Diatribes | Inside The Torn Apart | Breed To Breathe | Words From The Exit Wound | Leaders Not Followers 1 - 2 | Bootlegged In Japan | The Complete BBC Sessions | Enemy Of The Music Business | The DVD | Order of the Leech | Noise For Music's Sake | Punishment In Capitals | The Code Is Red... Long Live The Code
NASHVILLE PUSSY: Let Them Eat Pussy | High as Hell | Say Something Nasty | Nashville Pussy
NEW ORDER: Movement | Power, Corruption & Lies | Low-Life | Brotherhood | Technique | The Peel Sessions | BBC Radio / Live in Concert | Republic | Get Ready | Waiting For The Sirens' Call
NICOLETTE: Now Is Early | Let No One Live Rent Free in Your Head | Dj Kicks
NOMEANSNO: Mama | Sex Mad | Small Parts Isolated and Destroyed | Wrong | 0 + 2 = 1 | Live & Cuddly | You Kill Me | Mr. Right & Mr. Wrong | Why Do They Call Me Mr. Happy? | The Worldhood of the World (As Such) | Dance of the Headless Bourgeoisie | One | Generic Shame | The Day Everything Became Isolated and... | Sex Mad / You Kill Me
NOVA MOB: Last days of Pompeii | Nova Mob
OCTOBER FACTION: October Faction | Factionalization
MARK OLSON: My Own Jo Ellen | December's Child
PAJAMA SLAVE DANCERS: Heavy Pettin' Zoo | It Came from the Barn | Blood, Sweat and Beers
PAVEMENT: Perfect Sound Forever | Watery, Domestic | Slanted & Enchanted | Stray Slack: About As Valid As a Record Contract | Westing (By Musket and Sextant) | Crooked Rain, Crooked Rain | Wowee Zowee | Brighten the Corners | Terror Twilight | Demolition Plot J-7 | Summer Babe | Trigger Cut | Cut Your Hair | Haunt You Down/Jam Kids | Gold Soundz | Range Life | Rattled by the Rush | Father To A Sister Of Thought | Give It A Day | Stereo | Carrot Rope Cd1 & Pt. 2 | Pacific Trim | Shady Lane | Spit on a Stranger | Major Leagues
PERE UBU: The Modern Dance | Dub Housing | New Picnic Time | The Art of Walking | 390° Degrees of Simulated Stereo | Song of the Bailing Man | The Tenement Year | Cloudland | One Man Drives While the Other Man Screams | Worlds in Collision | Story of My Life | Ray Gun Suitcase | Folly of Youth | B Each B Oys See Dee + | Pennsylvania Apocalypse Now | The Shape of Things | St. Arkansas | Hearpen Singles
PERFECT CIRCLE: Mer De Noms | Thirteenth Step | eMOTIVe | Judith | Hollow | 3 Libras | Weak and Powerless | Live in St. Paul 3/31/01
BRANDAN PERRY: Eye Of The Hunter
PIGFACE: Gub | Welcome to Mexico Asshole | Fook | Truth Will Out | Notes From Thee Underground | Feels Like Heaven | A New High in Low | Eat Shit, You Fucking Redneck | Easy Listening... | Head | Dubhead | Below the Belt | The Best of Pigface: Preaching to the...
PIXIES: Surfer Rosa | Doolittle | Bossanova | Trompe le Monde | Live at Brixton Academy 06.02.04 / 06.03.04 / 06.04.04 / 06.05.04 | Live in New York - 12/18/2004 (Late Show)
POLYGON WINDOW: Surfing on sine waves | Quoth
THE POLYPHONIC SPREE: Hanging Around | Light And Day | Together We Are Heavy | Hold Me Now | Soldier Girl | Adventure Of Listening
POWER PILL: Pac-Man
PUBLIC ENEMY: Yo! Bum Rush the Show | It Takes a Nation of Millions to Hold Us Back | Fear of A Black Planet | Apocalypse '91...The Enemy Strikes Black | Muse Sick-N-Hour Mess Age | He Got Game | There's A Poison Goin' On | Revolverlution
PUBLIC IMAGE LTD. (PIL): Metal Box | Paris Au Printemps | The Flowers of Romance | Live in Tokyo | This Is What You Want...This Is What You Get | Compact Disc | Happy? | 9 | That What Is Not | Plastic Box | Public Image / Second Edition
PURPLE OUTSIDE: Mystery Lane
PUSSY GALORE: Groovy Hate Fuck | Exile on Maqqin Street | 1 Yr Live | Pussy Galore: Right Now! | Dial "M" for Motherfucker | Historia dela Musica Rock | Corpse Love3: THe 1st Year | Live: In Red
QUEENS OF THE STONE AGE: Queens of the Stone Age | R | Songs for the Deaf | Lullabies to Paralyze
RAGE AGAINST THE MACHINE: Rage Against the Machine | Evil Empire | Live and Rare | The Battle Of Los Angeles | Renegades | Live at the Grand Olympic Auditorium
RAMONES: Ramones | Leave Home | Rocket To Russia | Road To Ruin | It's Alive | End of The Century | Pleasant Dreams | Subterranean Jungle | Too Tough To Die | Animal Boy | Halfway To Sanity | Brain Drain | Loco Live | Mondo Bizarro | Acid Eaters | Adios Amigos | Greatest Hits Live | We're Outta Here! | You Don't Come Close | Live, January 7, 1978 At The Palladium, NYC | NYC 1978 (King Biscuit Flower Hour Archive Series) | 4 Pinheads in Amsterdam | Unreleased Volume | Adios, Ramones
RAPEMAN: Two Nuns and Pack Mule
LOU REED: Lou Reed | Transformer | Berlin | Rock N' Roll Animal | Sally Can't Dance | Live | Metal Machine Music | Coney Island Baby | Rock And Roll Heart | Street Hassle | Take No Prisoners | The Bells | Growing Up In Public | The Blue Mask | Legendary Hearts | Live In Italy | New Sensations | Mistrial | New York | Magic & Loss | Set The Twilight Reeling | Perfect Night | Ecstasy | American Poet | The Raven | Animal Serenade
ROCKET FROM THE CRYPT: Paint as a Fragrance | Circa: Now! | Hot Charity | Scream, Dracula, Scream! | R.F.T.C. | Group Sounds | Live from Camp X-Ray | All Systems Go 1 - 2 | The State of Art Is on Fire/Plays the Music... | Hot Charity/Cut Carefully and Play Loud
(HENRI) ROLLINS BAND: Live | Big Ugly Mouth | Do It | Life Time | Hard Volume / Insert Band | Turned On | Live at McCabe's | The End of Silence | Human Butt | The Boxed Life | Weight | Get in the Van: On the Road | Everything Thirsty Ever | Come in and Burn | Black Coffee Blues | Think Tank | Hot Animal Machine / Drive By Shooting [1999... / Lifetime | Live in Australia | In Eric The Pilot | Get Some Go Again | A Rollins in the Wry | Nice | The Only Way to Know for Sure | Talk Is Cheap, Vol. 1-2 | Sweatbox | Deep Throat | Audio Airstrike Consultants Roots
THE 6TH: Wasps' Nests | Hyacinths and Thistles
SACCHARINE TRUST: Paganicons | Surviving You Always | Worldbroken | The Sacramental Element | We became Snakes | Past Lives | The Great One Is Dead
SCREAMING TREES: Clairvoyance | Even If and Especially When | Invisible Latern | Buzz Factory | Uncle Anesthesia | Sweet Oblivion | Dust | Nearly Lost You | Bed of Roses | Something About Today | Dollar Bill | Butterfly | Shadow Of The Season | All I Know | Sworn And Broken | Other Worlds | Beat Happening / Screaming Trees | Something About Today | Change Has Come | Winter Songs Tour Tracks | Winter Songs — Live | Unreleased Album 98-99
SEBADOH: The Freed Man | Weed Forestin | Freed Weed | III | Smash Your Head on the Punk Rock | Bubble and Scrape | Bakesale | In Tokyo | Harmacy | The Sebadoh
SENTRIDOH: Free Sentridoh Songs from Loobiecore | Original Losing Losers | Lou B's Wasted Pieces
SEPULTURA: Roorback | Revolusongs | Under A Pale Grey Sky (Live) | Nation | Against | Blood Rooted | B-Sides | Roots of Sepultura >> Roots | Chaos A.D. | Arise | Beneath The Remains | Schizophrenia | Morbid Visions | Bestial Devastation
SEX PISTOLS: Nevermind the Bollocks Here is the Sex Pistols | The Great Rock & Roll Swindle | Flogging a Dead Horse | Live at Chelmsford Top Security Prison | Live | Chaos | Alive | Filthy Lucre Live | Pretty Vacant Live | Live at Winterland 1978 | 76 Club | Sham Pistols Gig | Live in Chelmsford Prison | The Live Collection | Some Product
SHELLAC: At Action Park | Futurist | Terraform |1000 Hurts
SHUDDER TO THINK: Curse, Spells, Voodoo, Mooses | Ten Spot | Funeral At The Movies | Get Your Goat | Pony Express Record | Your Choice Live Series | 50,000 B.C. | High Art | First Love, Last Rites | Hit Liquor | It Was Arson | Medusa Seven |
SLAYER: Show No Mercy | Hell Awaits | Reign In Blood | South of Heaven | Seasons in the Abyss | Decade of Aggression | Divine Intervention | Undisputed Attitude | Diabolus in Musica | God Hates Us All | Angel of Death | Postmortem | Raining Blood | Criminally Insane | Mandatory Suicide | Dead Skin Mask | bDittohead | Serenity In Murder | I Hate You | Stain of Mind | Bloodline | God Send Death | Haunting the Chapel | Live Undead |
SOLOMON GRUNDY: Solomon Grundy
SONIC YOUTH: Made in USA | Evol | Sister | Daydream Nation | Touch Me I'm Sick | Halloween | Goo | Dirty | Experimental Jet Set, Trash & No Star | Washing Machine | Live in Holland | Live in Texas | A Thousand Leaves | Goodbye 20th Century | NYC Ghosts & Flower | SYR 5 - 6 | Murray Street | Live at the Royal Albert Hall | Sonic Death: Early Sonic 1981-1983 | Bad Moon Rising | Flower | Confusion Is Sex | Kill Yr. Idols | Screaming Fields of Sonic Love | Hold That Tiger | Sonic Nurse
SON VOLT: Trace | Straightways | Wide Swing Tremolo
SOUL ASYLUM: Say What You Will, Clarence...Karl Sold the Truck | Made To Be Broken | While You Were Out | Hang Time | And The Horse They Rode In On | Grave Dancer's Union | Let Your Dim Light Shine | Candy From A Stranger | After the Flood: Live at the Grand Forks Prom June 28, 1997 | Cartoon | Easy Street | Black Gold / The Break / 99% | Misery / Hope | Promises Broken / Can't Even Tell | Clam Dip & Other Delights | Runaway Train | Insomniac's Dream

SOULFLY: *Soulfly | Primitive | Back to the primitive | 3 | Prophecy | Live @ The Praca Sony - Lisbon Portugal, July 3, 2002*
SOUL SIDE: *Soul-Side | Trigger | Hot-Bodi Gram | Son Come Happy*
SOUNDTRACK OF OUR LIVES: *Welcome to the Infant Freebase | Extended Revelation for the Psychic... | Behind the Music*
SOUNDGARDEN: *Ultramega OK | Louder Than Love | Badmotorfinger | Superunknown | Down On The Upside*
STONED SHARON: *Licence to Confuse*
STORMTROOPERS OF DEATH (S.O.D.): *Speak English or Die | Live at Budokan | Bigger Than the Devil | Seasoning The Obese*
SUGAR: *Copper Blue | Beaster | File Under Easy Listening | Besides | Whatever Makes You Happy | Bleeding*
SUPERCHUNK: *Superchunk | No Pocky For Kitty | Tossing Seeds: Singles 89-91 | On The Mouth | Foolish | Incidental Music 1991-95 | Here's Where The Strings Come In | Indoor Living | Come Pick Me Up | Here's To Shutting Up | Clambake Vol. 1 — 2*
SUPREME DICKS: *Unexamined Life | Working Man's Dick | Emotional Plague | This Is Not a Dick*
SWANS: *Filth | Cop | Greed | Holy Money | Children Of God | Feel Good Now | The Burning World | White Light From The Mouth of Infinity | Love of Life | Omniscience | The Great Annihilator | Die Tür ist Zu | Soundtracks For The Blind | Swans are Dead | A Screw | Time Is Money (Bastard) | New Mind | Saved | Failure/Animus | Swans | Young God | Love Will Tear Us Apart | Body to Body Job to Job | Various Failures | Public Castration Is A Good Idea | Anonymous Bodies In An Empty Room | Kill the Child | Real Love*
TALK TALK: *The Party's Over | It's My Life | The Colour of Spring | Spirit of Eden | Laughing Stock | London 1986*
THE THE: *Spirits | Burning Blue Soul | The Pornography Of Despair | Soul Mining | Infected | Mind Bomb | Dusk | Hanky Panky | NakedSelf*
THIN LIZZY: *Thin Lizzy | Shades of a Blue Orphanage | Vagabonds of the Western World | Night Life | Fighting | Jailbreak | Johnny the Fox | Bad Reputation | Live And Dangerous | Black Rose | Chinatown | Renegade | Thunder and Lightning | Life Live | BBC Radio 1 Live In Concert | One Night Only*
THROWING MUSES: *Throwing Muses | House Tornado | Hunkpapa | The Real Ramona | Red Heaven | The Curse | University | Limbo | Throwwing Muses | In a Doghouse*
LES THUGS: *Frenetic | Radical Hysterie | Electric Troubles | Dirty White Race | Still Hungry | I.A.B.F. | As Happy As Possible | Strike | Nineteen Something*
AMON TOBIN: *Bricolage | Permutation | Supermodified | Out From Out Where | Recorded Live: Solid Steel 4 | Splinter Cell 3: Chaos Theory OST | Chomp Samba | Like Regular Chickens | Slowly | East To West | Verbal | Creatures | Mission | Piranha Breaks | 4 Ton Mantis | Verbal Remixes & Collaborations | Solid Steel Presents Amon Tobin | The Bridge*
MARTINA TOPLEY-BIRD: *Quixotic*
TRICKY: *Maxinquaye | Nearly God | Pre-Millennium Tension | Angels With Dirty Faces | Juxtapose | BlowBack | Vulnerable | Back to Mine | A Ruff Guide*
TUATARA: *Breaking The Ethers | Trading With The Enemy | Cinemathique | Loading Program*
TURBONEGRO: *Hot Cars & Spent Contraceptives | Helta Skelta | Never Is Forever | Ass Cobra | Apocalypse Dudes | Darkness Forever! Between the Lines in Hamburg and Oslo! | Scandinavian Leather*
JEFF TWEEDY / WILCO: *Chelsea Walls*
THE TWILIGHT SINGERS: *Twilight As Played By Twilight Singers | Blackberry Belle*
UNCLE TUPELO: *Still Feel Gone | No Depression | March 16-20, 1992 | Anodyne | The Long Cut: A One Hour Radio Special | 89/93: An Anthology*
UNIVERSAL CONGRESS OF: *Prosperous & Qualified | The Sad and Tragic Demise of Big Fine Salty... | The Eleventh-Hour Shine-On | Sparkling Fresh*
THE VANDALS: *Peace Thru Vandalism | When In Rome Do As The Vandals |Slippery When ILL | Play Really Bad Original Country Tunes | Fear Of a Punk Planet | Sweatin To The Oldies | Live Fast Diarrea | Oi To The World | Quickening | Hitler Bad, Vandals Good | Look What I Almost Stepped In | Internet Dating Superstuds | Hollywood Potato Chip*
VELVET UNDERGROUND: *The Velvet Underground & Nico | White Light/White Heat | The Velvet Underground | Loaded: Fully Loaded Edition | Live At Max's Kansas City | Squeeze | 1969 Velvet Underground Live Vol. 1 + 2 | 1969 Live with Lou Reed | Live MCMXCIII | La Cave | Live In Amsterdam 1971 | And So On | NYC | Velvet 1993 - Live in Milan July 7th 1993 | The Peeling Of The Velvet Underground | Head Held High - The Atlantic Sessions | Yesterday's Parties | Caught Between The Twisted Stars | EPI Live 4 Nov 1966 | Screen Test : Falling in Love with the Falling | Spikes*
TOM WAITS: *Closing Time | The Heart of Saturday Night | Nighthawks At The Diner | Small Change | Foreign Affairs | Blue Valentine | Heartattack And Vine | One From The Heart | Swordfishtrombones | Rain Dogs | Franks Wild Years | Big Time | Night On Earth | Bone Machine | The Black Rider | Mule Variations | The Dime Store Novels, Vol. 1 | Alice | Blood Money | Real Gone*
WALKABOUTS: *See Beautiful Rattlesnake Gardens | Cataract | Scavenger | Satisfied Mind | New West Motel | Setting the Woods on Fire | Devil's Road | Nighttown | Trail of Stars | Train Leaves at Eight | Ended Up a Stranger | Rag & Bone | Death Valley Days: Lost Songs and Rarities,... | Watermarks | Drunken Soundtracks*
MIKE WATT: *Ball-Hog of Tugboat? | Contemplating the Engine Room*
WE: *Wooferwheels | Livin' the Lore | Dinosauric Futurobic | Smugglers | From the Spaceways | Lightyears Ahead*
STEVE WESTFIELD: *Mangled | Reject Me... | Underwhelmet*
THE WEDDING PRESENT: *George Best | Ukrainski Vistupi V Johna Peela | Bizarro | Seamonsters | Watusi | Saturnalia | George Best Plus | Tommy (1985-1987) | The BBC Sessions | Hit Parade 1 - 2 | Peel Sessions 1987-1990 / 1992-1995*
WEEN: *Axis: Bold as Boognish | Live Brain Wedgie / Wad Excerpts | God Ween Satan: The Oneness | The Pod | Pure Guava | Chocolate and Cheese | Chocolate and Cheese Demos - Summer '92 | 12 Golden Country Greats | The Mollusk | Paintin' The Town Brown | White Pepper | Live In Toronto Canada | Live At Stubb's, 7/2000 | quebec | All Request Live | I'm Fat | Push th' Little Daisies | Sky Cruiser | Freedom of '76 | Voodoo Lady | Piss Up A Rope | Sweet Texas Fire | You Were The Fool / Piss Up A Rope / So Long Jerry | Even If You Don't | Stay Forever | Tried and True | Mountains And Buffalo | Crucial Squeegie Lip | Live in Chicago | Live at The Rathskellar | VPRO Radio | February 2nd 1990 - Trenton New Jersey | December 29th 1990 - Parkhof - Alkmaar Holland | Pod Demos aka Bilboa | Pod Outtakes 1 - 2 | March 23 1991- Court Tavern, NJ | July 15th 1991 - Court Tavern (Green Lipped Mussels) | November 1st 1991 - Eindhoven, NL | November 20th 1992 - Chicago | Peel Sessions 1992 - 1993 | May 4th, 1992 - Kennel Club | October 29th 1992 - Wetlands, NY | November 12th 1992 -Hoboken, NJ | November 28th 1992 - Emo's, Houston TX | January 27th 1993 - New York City | JJJ Radio Appearance - 1993 | February 13th 1993 - Long Beach California | May 7th 1993 - Chicago | May 9th 1993 - Minneapolis | KROQ Los Angeles - 1994 | March 4th 1994 - Asbury Park NJ | March 5th 1994 - Long Branch NJ | April 14th 1994 - WTSR Radiothon | May 7th 1994 - Morrisville PA | August 1994 - Demerest Dorm Concert - Rutgers | October 14th 1994 -Philadelphia | October 31st 1994, Minneapolis, MN | November 13th 1994 - Whiskey A Go Go, Los Angeles | 1995 - Rochester, NY | January 24, 1995 - Mercury Lounge, NYC | January 24th 1995 - WNEW Radio Appearance, NYC | February 5th 1995 - Club Detroit, St Petersburg, FL | June 16th 1995 - Skating Rink, Warrington, PA | 12 Golden Country Greats | October 12, 1996 - Fillmore | October 25th 1996 - Cambridge | October 28th 1996 - Washington DC | October 4th 1996 - Nashville TN | October 5th 1996, Atlanta | October 8th 1996 - Austin TX | July 10th 1997 - Asbury Park NJ | August 3rd 1997 - Charleston | August 8th 1997 - Great Woods | September 16th 1997 - Chicago | September 24th 1997 - Seattle | September 28th 1997 - El Ray Theatre - Los Angeles, CA | October 27th 1997 - Atlanta | October 27th 1997 - San Francisco | November 27th 1997 - Zurich | January 17th 1998 - 930 Club - Washington DC | January 18th 1998 - Ziggys, Winston Salem, NC | January 29th 1998 - AlleyKatz, Richmond, VA | January 20th 1998 - Athens, Georgia | January 30th 1998 - Philadelphia, PA - Trocadero | May 12th 1998 - J&P, New Hope, PA | May 16th 1998 - Sunflower Music Festival, Lawrence, KS | May 5th 1998 - The Brewery, Louisville, KY | Craters of the Sac | Gene Ween Solo Acoustic 07 - 27 - 02 | Rotten Cheese*
PAUL WELLER: *Paul Weller | Wild Wood | Paul Weller Live Wood | Stanley Road! | Heavy Soul | Heliocentric Days of Speed | Illumination | Maximum | Leafy Mysteries | Under the Influence | Fly on the Wall: B-Sides & Rarities 1991-2000*
WELLWATER CONSPIRACY: *Declaration of Conformity | Brotherhood of Electric: Operational Directives | The Scroll and it's Combinations | Wellwater Conspiracy*
CHRIS WHITLEY: *Living With the Law | Din of Ecstasy | Terra Incognita | Dirt Floor | Chris Whitley Live at Martyrs' | Perfect Day | Rocket House | Hotel Vast Horizon | Weed | War Crime Blues*
WILCO: *A.M. | Being There | Summer Teeth | Yankee Hotel Foxtrot | A Ghost Is Born*
LUCINDA WILLIAMS: *Ramblin' | Happy Woman Blues | Lucinda Williams | Sweet Old World | Car Wheels On A Gravel Road | Essence | World Without Tears | Live At Fillmore West | Righteously | Passionate Kisses*
WINX: *Left Above the Clouds*
WIRE: *Pink Flag | Chairs Missing | 154 | Document and Eyewitness | The Ideal Copy | A Bell Is a Cup, Until It Is Struck | It's Beginning To and Back Again | Manscape | The Drill | Turns and Strokes | Metro, Chicago, 14th September 2002 | Send | On The Box: 1979 | The Scottish Play: 2004*
WOOL: *Boxset | Budspawn*
NEIL YOUNG: *Are You Passionate | Road Rock Vol.1 | Silver And Gold | This Note's For You Too | Bridge School Concerts Vol.1 | Year Of The Horse | Broken Arrow | Dead Man | Mirror Ball | Sleeps With Angels | Unplugged | Lucky Thirteen (Excursions Into Alien Territory) | Harvest Moon | Weld | Ragged Glory | Freedom | This Note's For You | Life | Landing On Water | Old Ways | Everybody's Rockin' | Trans | Re-ac-tor | Hawks And Doves | Rust Never Sleeps | Live Rust | Comes A Time | American Stars 'N' Bars | Decade | Zuma | Tonight's The Night | On The Beach | Harvest | After The Goldrush | Everybody Knows This Is Nowhere | Neil Young | Greendale | Journey Through The Past | Time Fades Away | Getting High On Neil Young | Maximum Neil Young | Greatest Hits*
YAZOO: *Upstairs at Erics | You & Me Both*

Zbyněk Baladrán

Ruins, Archaeology, and the Gap between Images

The multitude of images which surround us, which we work with, which entertain us and of which we are a part in today's digital world is so vast that it is not at all easy to orient oneself among them. Each image has a specific context or is part of other images referring to other contexts. Modernism and the period that followed left us with a fragmented world, which is more dependent on images than ever before. Thanks to the media boom and the general subversion of the hierarchy of perception of individual images, they make up a vast, indistinguishable audiovisual field. (By "image" I mean the totality of all kinds of digitalized audiovisual components: text, static pictures, moving pictures, sound, etc.) We have become accustomed to an environment packed full of images and have learned to ignore them. Television offers us images on several dozen channels at once; we have access to other images and their links on the Internet, not to mention other possibilities. Images that are a hundred years old exist side by side with images that are ten years old and images that are a few seconds old. Today it is easy to create, modify, combine, and distribute images. Images are accumulating in this field and waiting to be used. In this text, I would like to look at the way in which we find images and how we can treat them when we want to use them as part of our testimony.

The difficulty in distinguishing between images in their great number creates the impression of a cluttered environment. The various layers overlap, disappear, reappear, participate in and use one another. Combinations create new units, which again dissolve into other images. This sort of sight evokes the ruins of a crowded city. Not an abandoned city, however, but a living one that is in constant motion. The various layers of ruins are constantly changing, collapsing even further, falling into oblivion. But not for long. They always reappear from the bottom layers to create the surface. Newly created images also become

Ruinen, Archäologie und die Lücke zwischen den Bildern

Die Vielzahl der Bilder, die uns umgeben, mit denen wir arbeiten, die uns unterhalten und zu denen wir in der heutigen digitalen Welt gehören, ist so immens, dass es sehr schwer fällt, sich darin zu orientieren. Jedes Bild hat einen spezifischen Kontext oder ist Teil anderer Bilder, die auf andere Kontexte verweisen. Die Moderne und die darauf folgende Periode hinterließen uns eine fragmentierte Welt, die mehr denn je von Bildern abhängig ist. Aufgrund des Medienbooms und der allgemeinen Subversion der hierarchischen Betrachtungsweise einzelner Bilder erzeugen sie ein riesiges, ununterscheidbares audiovisuelles Feld. (Mit „Bild" meine ich die Gesamtheit aller Arten digitalisierter audiovisueller Elemente: Texte, statische Bilder, bewegte Bilder, Töne etc.) Wir haben uns an eine mit Bildern voll gestopfte Umwelt gewöhnt und gelernt diese zu ignorieren. Das Fernsehen bietet uns Bilder auf mehreren Dutzend Kanälen gleichzeitig an; wir haben Zugriff auf Bilder und deren Links im Internet, und vieles mehr. Bilder, die 100 Jahre alt sind, existieren Seite an Seite mit Bildern, die zehn Jahre oder wenige Sekunden alt sind. Es ist heute einfach, Bilder zu erstellen, zu modifizieren, zu kombinieren und zu verteilen. In diesem Feld sammeln sich Bilder an und warten darauf benutzt zu werden. Ich möchte hier untersuchen, wie wir Bilder finden und wie wir mit ihnen umgehen können, wenn wir sie als Teil dessen, was wir aussagen wollen, benutzen möchten.

Die Schwierigkeit in der Vielfalt der Bilder Unterscheidungen zu treffen, erzeugt den Eindruck einer überladenen Umwelt. Die verschiedenen Schichten überschneiden sich, verschwinden, tauchen wieder auf, nehmen aneinander Teil und benutzen sich gegenseitig. Kombinationen erzeugen neue Einheiten, die sich dann wieder in andere Bilder auflösen. Dieser Anblick lässt einen an die Ruinen einer überfüllten Stadt denken, nicht die einer verlassenen Stadt, sondern einer lebendigen, die sich in ständiger Bewegung befindet. Die verschiedenen Schichten der Ruinen verän-

ruins. The rapidity with which this happens is proportional to the speed at which new images are created. It is the spatiotemporal field of human culture and history.

To understand how ruins can be searched and images interpreted, we can use the terminology of archaeology. The analogy with the archaeological methodology is well suited to the description of searching in an unfamiliar environment, where the only guide is the apparatus of our knowledge and the context of the site to be searched.[1] With the term "archaeological field", we designate a specific spatio-temporal area as the site of investigation of archaeological finds in the layers of earth. It is the framework for our expectation and presentiment of new contexts. In this case, one can designate the space of the ruins as the archaeological field, that is, the set of visible, suspected, or buried images. The delineation of the archaeological field occurs within the framework of the original aim of searching: what are we actually looking for. Each segment of human activity has its sum of images. From those on the surface that determine the interpretation of any kind of activity, to those that are buried, disintegrating in the lower layers, those that are forgotten. All archaeological objects, in our case images, emerge as fragments, with no clear indication of continuity. What we see and what we are able to interpret is only the broken part of some whole unit in the past. The network of contexts and connections with other objects serves as a guide to the reconstruction and interpretation of the fragments. Because, as an artist, I am interested in the search for and interpretation of images, I will give a personal example of how to delineate an archaeological field. I know that in many families there were always film amateurs, collectors, and enthusiasts who owned some kind of film material (8 mm, 16 mm, 35 mm films, VHS and old video and audio tapes). I was interested in what could be read from these fragments of personal history, located outside the main interpretive framework of the perspective on the past. For that reason, I concentrated on a reconstruction of images of the past from materials that

dern sich permanent, sie zerfallen noch weiter, geraten in Vergessenheit. Aber nicht lange, denn sie tauchen immer wieder von den untersten Schichten auf und bilden erneut die Oberfläche. Auch neu kreierte Bilder werden zu Ruinen. Die Geschwindigkeit, in der dies geschieht, verhält sich proportional zu der Geschwindigkeit, in der neue Bilder hergestellt werden. All dies bildet das raumzeitliche Feld der menschlichen Kultur und Geschichte.

Um zu verstehen, wie Ruinen durchsucht und Bilder interpretiert werden können, lässt sich die Terminologie der Archäologie anwenden. Die Analogie zur archäologischen Methodologie eignet sich hervorragend, die Suche in einer unbekannten Umgebung zu beschreiben, wo die einzigen Anhaltspunkte unser Wissensapparat und der Kontext der zu erforschenden Stelle sind.[1] Mit dem Begriff „archäologisches Feld" bezeichnen wir ein bestimmtes raumzeitliches Gebiet als Stätte, in der archäologische Funde in den Erdschichten untersucht werden. Es bildet den Rahmen unserer Erwartungen und Vorahnungen bezüglich neuer Kontexte. In diesem Fall kann man den Raum der Ruinen als das archäologische Feld bezeichnen, d.h. als eine Reihe sichtbarer, vermuteter oder begrabener Bilder. Die Einzeichnung des archäologischen Feldes findet im Rahmen des ursprünglichen Ziels der Suche statt – wonach suchen wir eigentlich? Jede Ebene menschlicher Tätigkeit besitzt eine Anzahl eigener Bilder. Von solchen an der Oberfläche, die die Interpretation jeglicher Handlung vorgeben, bis zu jenen, die in den untersten Schichten begraben sind, zerfallen und vergessen. Alle archäologischen Objekte – in unserem Fall Bilder – tauchen als Fragmente auf, ohne klare Anzeichen einer Kontinuität. Was wir sehen und was wir interpretieren können, ist nur der zerbrochene Teil irgendeines Ganzen aus der Vergangenheit. Das Netz der Kontexte und Verbindungen mit anderen Objekten dient als Richtlinie, um die Fragmente zu rekonstruieren und zu interpretieren. Denn als Künstler interessiere ich mich für die Suche nach Bildern und deren Interpretation. Ich gebe ein Beispiel aus meiner persönlichen Arbeit, um zu zeigen, wie ein archäologisches Feld eingezeichnet werden kann. In vie-

were not from the large specialized or public archives, which have their own specific focus. (Although that has changed in recent times and interest in the peripheral genres of moving images is increasing.)² The image of the past must therefore be different, splintered, less explanatory, and more subjective. In terms of time, we are talking about roughly the last 50 years, that is, a period which is still part of our memory. My archaeological field was the temporal framework of the existence of media recording moving images, and the deposit site was the individual ownership of films. The means or "archaeological equipment" that I used was an advertisement published in printed periodicals and on the Internet. In the course of half a year of collecting, I received about fourteen hours of various recordings. The film materials collected in this manner consisted of strange fragments of home movies, animation, and feature films. They included newsreels, documentary films, recordings of private events, various experiments, unsuccessful takes, and the like. On a temporal axis, these film fragments would seem unconnected, randomly grouped. They would make up a strangely incomplete network of connections spread outside the main current of history, in the period from the 1930s to the 1980s.

The term "archaeological field" is an analogy for the impossibility of seeing an image of the past or of anything else in its entirety. The archaeological field defines the spatial and temporal coordinates, defines the field of the search, and the reconstruction. Often we are unable to determine the true reason why and when a specific artifact was made (as was the case in my viewing the collected films), or we attribute to it characteristics that turn a banal phenomenon into a fundamental historical turning point. Of course, it has to be added that error of judgment, which we always have to reckon with, is also an important interpretive instrument. It is as if reality had escaped and could not be captured or interpreted in a straightforward manner. In the sense of Foucault's archaeology of knowledge, archaeology is the description of the emergence of testimonies. A testimony is an event, which cannot

len Familien gibt es Filmamateure, Sammler und Enthusiasten, die irgendwelches Filmmaterial besitzen (8mm-, 16mm-, 35mm-Filme, VHS und alte Video- und Tonbänder). Mich interessierte, was man aus diesen Fragmenten einer persönlichen Geschichte, die sich außerhalb des Hauptinterpretationsrahmens der Perspektive auf die Vergangenheit befindet, herauslesen kann. Daher konzentrierte ich mich darauf, Bilder der Vergangenheit aus Materialien zu rekonstruieren, die nicht aus den großen Spezialarchiven und öffentlichen Archiven mit ihren jeweiligen besonderen Schwerpunkten stammten. (Obwohl sich dies in letzter Zeit verändert hat und das Interesse an peripheren Genres des bewegten Bildes steigt.)² Das Bild der Vergangenheit muss daher anders sein, zersplittert, weniger selbsterklärend und subjektiver. Wir sprechen hier von den letzten ca. 50 Jahren, d.h. von einem Zeitraum, der noch Teil unseres Gedächtnisses ist. Mein archäologisches Feld war der zeitliche Rahmen, in dem es Medien zur Aufnahme bewegter Bilder gab; und die Ablagerungsstätte war der individuelle Besitz von Filmen. Die Mittel oder das „archäologische Gerät", das ich verwendete, war eine Anzeige, die in Zeitschriften und im Internet erschien. Nach einem halben Jahr des Sammelns besaß ich etwa 14 Stunden verschiedenster Aufnahmen. Das auf diese Weise zusammengekommene Filmmaterial bestand aus seltsamen Fragmenten von Amateurfilmen, Animationen und Spielfilmen. Es umfasste Reportagefilme, Dokumentarfilme, Aufnahmen privater Veranstaltungen, diverse Experimente, missglückte Aufnahmen und dergleichen. Auf einer Zeitachse platziert, würden diese Filmfragmente unzusammenhängend und beliebig gruppiert erscheinen. Sie würden ein merkwürdig unvollständiges Netz aus Verbindungen bilden, die sich abseits des Hauptstroms der Geschichte von den 30ern bis in die 80er verteilen.

Der Ausdruck „archäologisches Feld" ist eine Analogie für die Unmöglichkeit, ein Bild, sei es aus der Vergangenheit oder von irgendetwas anderem, vollständig sehen zu können. Das archäologische Feld definiert die räumlichen und zeitlichen Koordinaten, das Feld der Suche und der Rekonstruktion. Häufig sind wir nicht in der Lage, den

be exhausted by speech or sense. Something always remains, something unique or capable of being transformed into other testimonies and inserted in the dense interrelations with other testimonies.[3] Zielinski's archaeology of media makes use of Foucault's definition of archaeology and expands it, looking at the history of the audiovisual discourse over the past 150 years. He reconstructs this discourse from material objects connected with the history of audio-vision, and also seeks out phenomena that seem to have no connection with audio-vision. In cultural history, he finds figures with utopian visions, strange inventions and models of reality that seemed to be on the periphery of intellectual events. Zielinski's conception of archaeology is about the process of research, which treats itself to the gift of the true surprise.[4] By that he means searching in fields, libraries and archives, the collections which are poorly organized. The finds that one discovers in them are all the more valuable because of the surprise factor; things that a person did not expect but which can offer solutions that one wouldn't have thought of if looking for something specific. Zielinski thus offers a surprising history of audio-vision and expands its seemingly unambiguous context. In this sense, the archaeological approach is an open perspective on the world that allows us to connect phenomena, which were previously incommensurable. This recalls the well-known modernist approach of the collage. The only difference is that we do not want to shock with an unusual connection, but rather to experience, through connecting, the interpretive possibilities that arise among different units of images.[5]

Time appears strangely incomprehensible. On the one hand, it creates the illusion of linear continuity; on the other hand, one can think of it as isolated moments, which connect up, overlap, run together or exist parallel to one another. The perception of time constantly raises the question of what the present moment is and what kind of relation it has to other moments in the past, present and future.

wahren Grund, warum und wann ein bestimmtes Artefakt hergestellt wurde, zu ermitteln (wie dies beim Betrachten der gesammelten Filme bei mir der Fall war), oder wir schreiben ihm Eigenschaften zu, die ein banales Phänomen in einen historischen Wendepunkt verwandeln. Natürlich muss man hinzufügen, dass Einschätzungsfehler, mit denen man immer rechnen muss, auch wichtige Instrumente der Interpretation sind. Es ist, als wäre die Realität geflüchtet und man könnte sie nicht mehr einfangen oder auf gradlinige Art und Weise deuten. In Sinne von Foucaults Archäologie des Wissens beschreibt die Archäologie wie Zeugnisse entstehen. Ein Zeugnis ist ein Ereignis, das sich nicht in der Rede oder im Sinn erschöpft. Es bleibt immer etwas übrig, etwas Einzigartiges, oder etwas, das in andere Aussagen verwandelt und in die dichten Beziehungen zu anderen Aussagen eingefügt werden kann.[3] Zielinskis Archäologie der Medien benutzt und erweitert Foucaults Definition der Archäologie, wenn er die Geschichte des audiovisuellen Diskurses der letzten 150 Jahre untersucht. Er rekonstruiert diesen Diskurs aus materiellen Objekten, die mit der Geschichte der Audiovision verbunden sind; er sucht aber auch nach Phänomenen, die in keiner Verbindung zur Audiovision zu stehen scheinen. Er findet in der Kulturgeschichte Figuren mit utopischen Visionen, merkwürdigen Erfindungen und Realitätsmodellen, die sich am Rande geistiger Ereignisse zu befinden scheinen. Bei Zielinskis Konzept der Archäologie geht es um den Forschungsprozess, der sich das Geschenk der wahren Überraschung gönnt.[4] Damit meint er die Suche in Feldern, Bibliotheken und Archiven, deren Sammlungen schlecht organisiert sind. Die Funde, auf die man dort stößt, sind umso wertvoller aufgrund des Überraschungseffekts; Dinge, die man nicht erwartet hätte, die aber Lösungen anbieten, an die man auf der Suche nach etwas Bestimmten nie gedacht hat. So präsentiert Zielinski eine erstaunliche Geschichte der Audiovision und erweitert den angeblich eindeutigen Kontext dieser Geschichte. Der archäologische Zugang ist in diesem Sinne eine offene Perspektive auf die Welt, die es uns ermöglicht, Phänomene, die zuvor nicht vergleichbar waren, miteinander zu verbinden. Dies erinnert an die bekannte

It has to be said that the linking up of the present and images of the past creates a peculiar relationship, which could be described as a kind of contamination of the past by the present.[6] Images do not speak to us clearly with the complete context of their origin. They are necessarily distorted and supplemented by our interpretation. We impress upon them our current position, our current stance. One way or another, we enter the past and influence the outlook on the past for the present and for the future. Any kind of find is contaminated by our presence and our ability to interpret it. Thus, in a certain sense, we are a part of it.

There are too many illegible items in the nature of the "archaeological field". For this very reason, this kind of reading of the past cannot claim to be an absolute testimony. The experience of reading thus acquired compels us to move on from individual interpretations, to be constantly in motion, and to seek new connections. It is, of course, necessary to maintain a critical distance and to refrain from accepting all connections unreservedly. From what I have written above it follows that, in relation to the creation of contemporary models and descriptions of reality, the most important thing is the present moment and our position in it. Our openness to the images and their interrupted context depends on understanding that each present moment immediately moves into the past. We must not forget, therefore, that our present is also a component of any future reconstruction.

The collage, the tool introduced by modernism, became a universal and comprehensible model for creating and interpreting images. This approach has also opened up for us in time. It seems natural to us to jump from page to page on the Internet, to read books at random, to make notes, to watch video clips that are broken down into separate frames, or to switch television programs with the remote control (zapping).[7] As if our eye and our brain considered this kind of structure of perception and reception to be natural. The important thing is, as I have mentioned above, the relation between the individual

modernistische Methode der Collage. Der einzige Unterschied besteht darin, dass wir mit der ungewöhnlichen Verbindung nicht schockieren wollen, sondern die Interpretationsmöglichkeiten, die sich aus den verschiedenen Bildzusammenstellungen ergeben, erleben wollen.[5]

Die Zeit erscheint auf seltsame Weise unerklärlich. Einerseits erzeugt sie die Illusion einer linearen Kontinuität, andererseits kann man sie sich als isolierte Momente, die sich verbinden, überschneiden, zusammenlaufen oder parallel existieren, vorstellen. Die Wahrnehmung der Zeit wirft ständig die Frage auf, woraus der gegenwärtige Augenblick besteht und in welchem Verhältnis er zu anderen Augenblicken der Vergangenheit, der Gegenwart und der Zukunft steht.

Man muss sagen, dass die Verbindung der Gegenwart mit Bildern der Vergangenheit eine eigenartige Beziehung herstellt, die man als eine Art Kontaminierung der Vergangenheit durch die Gegenwart beschreiben könnte.[6] Bilder sprechen zu uns nicht mit einer Klarheit und dem gesamten Kontext ihrer Entstehungsgeschichte. Sie sind notwendig verzerrt und werden durch unsere Interpretation ergänzt. Wir drücken ihnen unsere gegenwärtige Position und Haltung wie einen Stempel auf. Auf die eine oder andere Weise treten wir in die Vergangenheit ein und beeinflussen den Blick auf die Vergangenheit bezüglich der Gegenwart und der Zukunft. Jeglicher Fund ist durch unsere Gegenwart und unsere Fähigkeit diesen Fund zu deuten, kontaminiert. Wir sind daher in einem gewissen Sinne ein Teil des Fundes.

Es gibt zu viele unleserliche Dinge in der Natur des „archäologischen Feldes". Deshalb kann diese Art, die Vergangenheit zu lesen, keinen Absolutheitsanspruch erheben. Die hierdurch gewonnene Erfahrung des Lesens zwingt uns, Abschied von individuellen Interpretationen zu nehmen. Wir müssen ständig in Bewegung bleiben und neue Verbindungen suchen. Es ist natürlich notwendig, eine kritische Distanz beizubehalten und nicht alle Verbindungen ohne Vorbehalt zu akzeptieren. Aus dem bisher gesagten folgt, dass in Bezug zur Herstellung zeitgenössischer Modelle und Be-

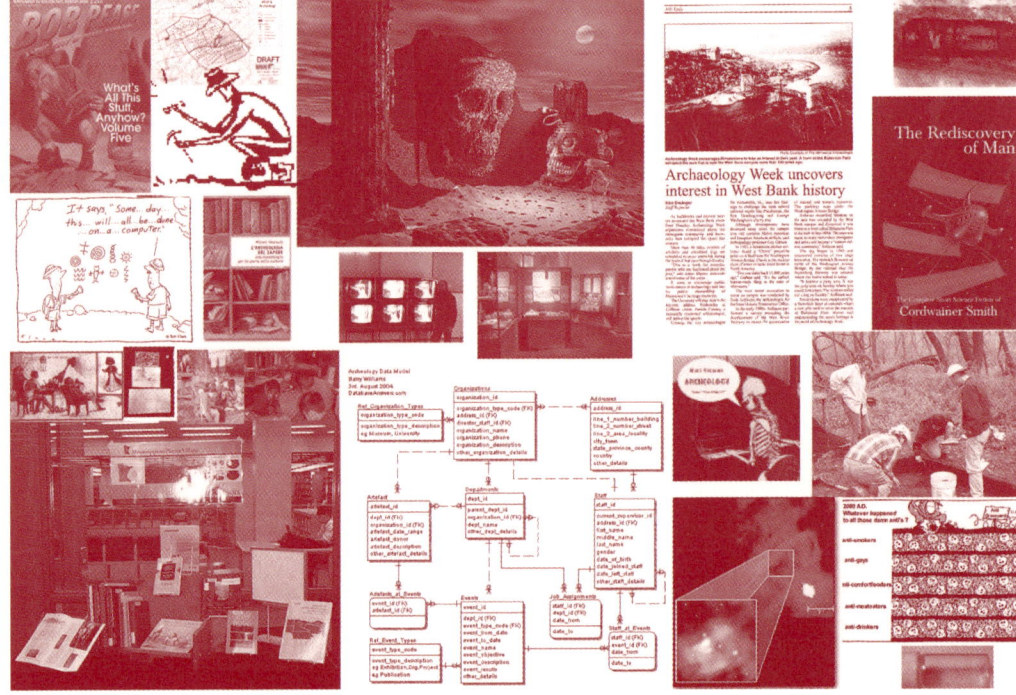

Zbyněk Baladrán, *Archaeology: Google 1*, 2005

Zbyněk Baladrán, *Archaeology: Google 2*, 2005

images in the gaps between them. Individual constructions are no longer interesting, but rather the tension, which is created by the absence of building parts in a construction. We will not manage to reconstruct reality in its original form; we have already had to reconcile ourselves to this. In the archaeological field, whether we notice it or not, we constantly assume that most of the interconnected images are hidden. With the help of sophisticated cultural technologies, such as deleting, inserting, and replacing, we have the opportunity to work in such a way that the various features can always be regrouped in a different manner. Like what Aby Warburg did in his *Mnemosyne Atlas*, in the early 20th century. Warburg grouped various images, reproductions, photographs, texts, and objects on a certain theme on a board with a black background. He altered the position and order and thus created new relations between the individual image elements. He then repeatedly photographed the panel that was the outcome of his hyper archive.[8] This is similar to the structure of switching television programs, which in itself is an excellent example of an archaeological field. We do not want to see the programs on all channels, either successively or at once. We are only interested in fragments of individual programs and the possibility of interacting in each subsequent moment. In this way, we create perspectives across the events. We know very little about the structure of switching, but it would seem inadequate to understand it as unconscious switching back and forth.

To a certain extent, the method of archaeological research is largely based on chance, which always hides in the sites of inscrutable ruins. Intuition is thus the best consultant on a journey to unexpected discoveries. It depends, of course, on the interpreter's ability to incorporate such random images into the structure of his testimony.

schreibungen der Realität der gegenwärtige Moment und unsere Position darin am wichtigsten ist. Unsere Offenheit den Bildern gegenüber und deren unterbrochener Kontext hängen von der Einsicht ab, dass jeder gegenwärtige Moment sofort zur Vergangenheit wird. Wir dürfen daher nicht vergessen, dass unsere Gegenwart auch ein Bestandteil zukünftiger Rekonstruktionen ist.

Das durch den Modernismus eingeführte Werkzeug der Collage wurde zu einem universellen und verständlichen Modell der Herstellung und Interpretation von Bildern. Dieser Ansatz hat sich uns auch in zeitlicher Hinsicht geöffnet. Es erscheint selbstverständlich, im Internet von einer Seite zur nächsten zu springen, Bücher nach dem Zufallsprinzip zu lesen, sich Notizen zu machen, Videoclips zu betrachten, die in einzelne Frames zerlegt wurden, oder beim Fernsehen mit der Fernbedienung zu zappen.[7] Als empfänden unsere Augen und unser Gehirn diese Wahrnehmungs- und Rezeptionsstruktur als etwas Natürliches. Wie bereits erwähnt: wichtig ist die Beziehung zwischen den einzelnen Bildern in den zwischen ihnen liegenden Lücken. Individuelle Konstruktionen sind nicht mehr interessant, sondern vielmehr die Spannung, die durch die Abwesenheit von Bausteinen in einer Konstruktion erzeugt wird. Wir werden es nicht schaffen, die Realität in ihrer ursprünglichen Form zu rekonstruieren. Damit mussten wir uns schon abfinden. Im archäologischen Feld nehmen wir permanent an, ob wir es merken oder nicht, dass die meisten miteinander verbundenen Bilder verborgen sind. Ausgefeilte kulturelle Techniken, wie Löschen, Einfügen und Ersetzen, ermöglichen es uns, so zu arbeiten, dass verschiedene Merkmale immer wieder auf unterschiedliche Weise gruppiert werden können. Wie das, was Aby Warburg Anfang des 20. Jahrhunderts in seinem *Mnemosyne Atlas* machte. Warburg stellte verschiedene Bilder, Drucke, Fotografien, Texte und Objekte zu einem bestimmten Thema auf einem schwarzen Brett zusammen. Er veränderte die Positionen und die Ordnung und stellte so neue Beziehungen zwischen den einzelnen Bildelementen her. Immer wieder fotografierte er das Brett. Das Resultat war sein Hyperarchiv.[8] Ähnlich verhält es sich beim

1 Evžen Neustupný, "Nástin archeologické metody [An outline of the archaeological method]," http://www.kar.zcu.cz/texty/Neustupny1986.htm 1986 [04/10/05].
2 Patricia R. Zimmermann, "Hollywood, Home Movies, and Common Sense: Amateur Film as Aesthetic Dissemination and Social Control, 1950–1962," *Cinema Journal* 27.4 (1988), p. 23–44.
3 Michel Foucault, *The Archaeology of Knowledge*, New York 1972.
4 Siegfried Zielinski, "Štastný nález místo marného hledání" (The fortunate find instead of the vain search), *Nova filmova historie* (New Film History), Petr Szczepanik (ed.), Prague 2004, p. 501–520.
5 Petr Szczepanik, "Metoda mezi" (The method between), Cinepur 30 (2003), p. 44–46.
6 Zdeněk Vašiček, *Obrazy minulosti* (Images of the past), Prague 1996.
7 Knut Hickethier, "On the History of Television as a History of Viewing in Germany: Preliminary Thoughts," *Pragmatic of Audiovisual*, D. Müller (ed.), vol. 2, Münster 1995, p. 179–194.
8 Tomáš Dvořák, "Album, atlas, archive," *Iluminace* 3 (2004), p. 121–137.

Zappen, das an sich schon ein hervorragendes Beispiel eines archäologischen Feldes ist. Wir möchten die Programme aller Sender weder nacheinander noch gleichzeitig sehen. Uns interessieren nur die Fragmente einzelner Programme und die Möglichkeit der Interaktion in jedem folgenden Moment. So stellen wir Perspektiven quer durch die Ereignisse her. Wir wissen sehr wenig über die Struktur des Zappens, aber es wäre unangebracht dieses Verhalten als ein unbewusstes Hin- und Herschalten zu verstehen.

Zu einem gewissen Grad beruht die Methode der archäologischen Forschung auf Zufall, der sich immer in den Stätten der unergründlichen Ruinen verbirgt. Die Intuition ist folglich der beste Ratgeber auf der Reise zu unerwarteten Entdeckungen. Selbstverständlich hängt es von der Fähigkeit des Interpreten ab, diese zufälligen Bilder in die Struktur seiner Aussage einzubinden.

1 Evžen Neustupný: *Nástin archeologické metody* (Entwurf der archäologischen Methode), http://www.kar.zcu.cz/texty/Neustupny1986.htm, 1986 [10.04.05].
2 Patricia R. Zimmermann: Hollywood, rodinne filmy a zdravy rozum (Hollywood, Amateurfilme und Menschenverstand), in: *Iluminace* (2004), Nr. 3, S. 53–66.
3 Michel Foucault: *Die Archäologie des Wissens*, Frankfurt a. M. 1973.
4 Siegfried Zielinski: Štastný nález místo marného hledání (Glücklicher Fund statt vergeblicher Suche), in: Petr Szczepanik (Hg.): *Nova filmova historie* (Neue Geschichte des Films), Prag 2004, S. 501–520.
5 Petr Szczepanik: Metoda mezi (Die Methode dazwischen), in: *Cinepur* (2003), Nr. 30, S. 44–46.
6 Zdeněk Vašiček: *Obrazy minulosti* (Bilder der Vergangenheit), Prag 1996.
7 Knut Hickethier: Zwischen Einschalten und Ausschalten. Fernsehgeschichte als Geschichte des Zuschauens, in: Werner Faulstich (Hg.): *Vom „Autor" zum Nutzer. Handlungsrollen im Fernsehen*, München 1995, S. 237–306.
8 Tomáš Dvořák: Album, atlas, archive, in: *Iluminace* (2004), Nr. 3, S. 121–137.

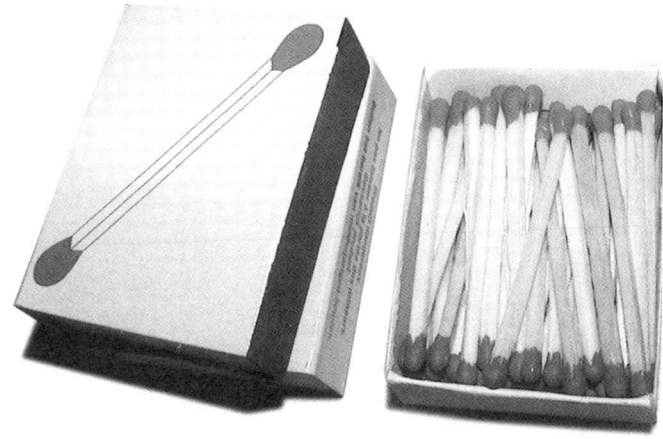

Ami Barak

Mircea Cantor and the match theory

Invited in the fall of 2002 to participate at ForwArt, an international contemporary art exhibition taking place at "Mont des Arts" Brussels every two years, a biennial after all, under the auspices of BBL banking group, Mircea Cantor decided to show, next to a 10 x 10 m panel reproducing the up-to-date vision of *My City*, another work that didn't need an institutional space to be shown in. In fact, his idea was a relational system and a multiple product to be edited in a relatively large number that instead of being shown in the everlasting white cube of a museum or art center, would be spread in the street, handed out. Given away no less. A shared object, a simple and generous gift, a false marketing product, an advertising substitute because — of course — it wasn't a sample launched by an important brand in order to make teasing. The artist has nothing to sell, and the passer-by, in spite of his fears formatted by other habits, would have in his hands an object with a meaningless status and ambiguous purpose and no practical end. Let us first describe the object, trying afterwards to analyze it in order to understand its whole conceptual span and its undeniable qualities.

    Mircea Cantor arranged so to speak, for ForwArt, the production of a matchbox. Closed, it appears as a perfectly "vulgaris" box. It is yellow and has a drawing of a two headed match as red and round as possible. This image immediately sells away the concept. The box really contains matches of a special kind and of unusual conception as they have two heads. It is not, as can be seen, an ordinary product, the vehicle of an advertising image showing off some graphics with artistic virtues. But it is really a matched match [une allumette "allumée"], if I am allowed this easy pun. It is the full ignition of both ends that becomes an issue. The interest of the object resides in this amazing novelty for anybody. And "anybody" includes, of course, the passer-by x or any consumer one can find in the urban crowd, but also the specialist in current use products. The matchbox is a matter of displacement, detour and dislocation proposed to the large public and not just to the supposed specialized one from the museums. An artistic act, at first sight playing by the rules, as in the general idea a work of art requires an appreciable amount of "fantasy" and invention. But as it is a ready-made outside the museum, our mind is easily confused. We accept today that a manufactured object be exhibited as such after being chosen by the artist and placed in the artistic institutional framework: museum

or art center, but isolated from its context, it brings confusion. The artist's condition and that of the object are thus questioned. Out of this ordinary usual product, normally away from any surprises, the artist made something resembling but not alike. The difference is that of Siamese twins. One body, two heads. The match meant to make life easier, for some time now, is one of the objects with historical longevity and anyone can say that it wouldn't be time for it to retire. But common sense has told us so far that its longevity was due to its self-sufficiency. That the match has no reason to be altered, neither in concept nor in function, in order to perform its everlasting duty: to light fire! It is known that it can have some cultural features, such as with Americans who rub it against anything and the image of the cowboy lighting his match against his jeans is surely in the everybodies memory without being radicali. The object imagined by Mircea Cantor enjoys however a different status and exists for a double stake. The famous statement "less is more" is ridiculed here as the two heads do not make the task easier nor do they increase productivity, but play a purely symbolic role. They exist only to signify, for their exclusive semiological use, for what they can and must induce in the minds and senses of all those who have it in their hands. The senses are thus involved in the destabilizing approach. It's enough to open the box completely — otherwise the other end can't be seen and the mirroring effect is not obtained—, in order to feel virtually the accidental possible burn, but evidently not wanted unless for the potential masochists. The blink of the eye is obvious and, it goes without saying, we try to read the aesthetic, and by the same time political message conveyed by the box. One remembers Raymond Hains' pop box that reproduces, on a gigantic scale, the paper matches on market in the '60s. But there, we were talking about sculpture above all and of a consumer society criticism, whereas with Mircea Cantor the other side arises the interest. We are not any longer in post pop era but in a relational aesthetic and the interest of the objects comes equally from their incongruence and from the production process that enabled its existence. The importance of this last is underlined by the leaflet accompanying the object and showing the frozen film of the fabrication in the Gherla match-factory. The political coefficient is here. In order to produce 20.000 matchboxes at a reasonable price, in a country such as Romania there was just this one factory able to

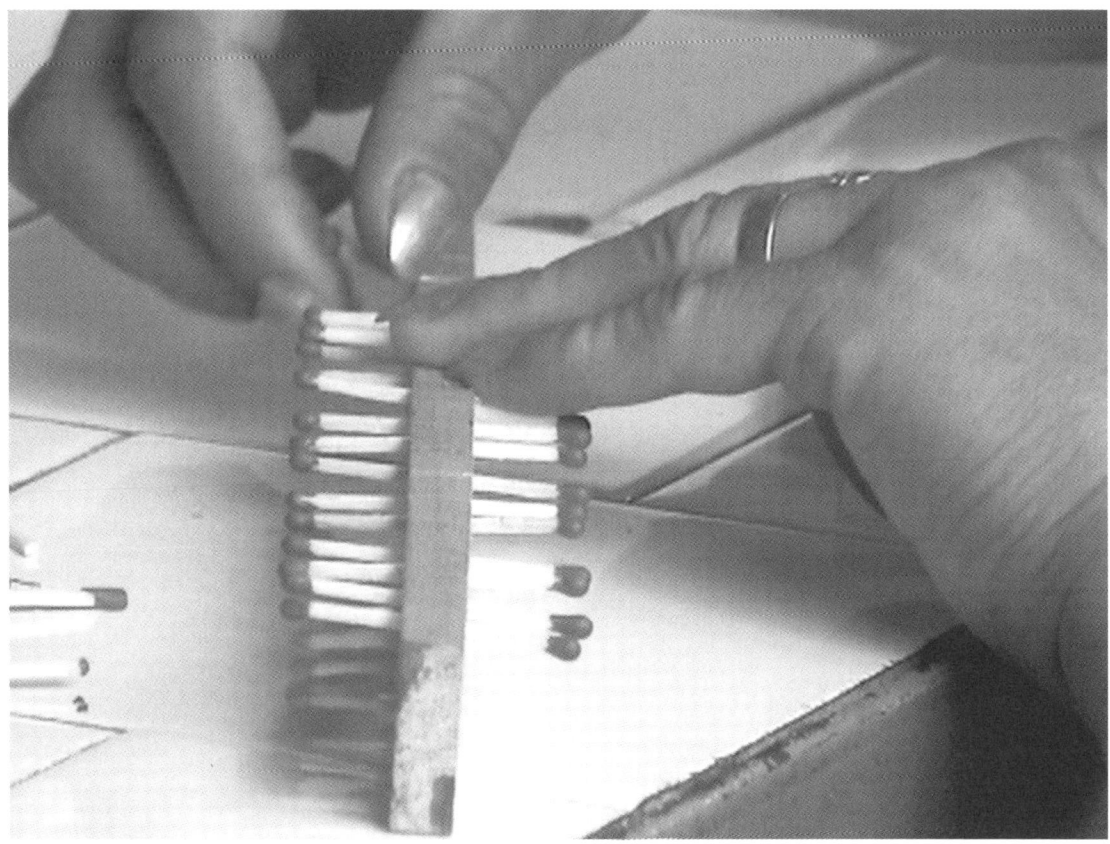

take up the challenge. The script board in images shows carefully how from the trunk of a poplar tree, in a mechanized and almost automatic process, the object wanted by the artist is born. It's just that in the task book, at the end, it says that a second head has to be added, but the machines are not designed nor programmed to do such a thing! Thus the workers, mostly women, have to finish the match by dipping it manually the other end in the red phosphor bath. At this point everything turns upside down. A box of matches is, by definition, a serial object, an almost unlimited multiple. The reproducibility idea itself is intrinsic to it. And in the end, in order to get the looks wanted by the artist we see that the hand plays its role and we are no longer, a fortiori, on the grounds of mechanical reproduction but — climax of the process — facing a unique object. One could even say that, paradoxically, each match is unique since it is handmade. And thus, through the artist's will, through his attitude and the avatars of contemporary art history a hand crafted multiple object can become a unique art object but cloned at the same time.

The coming back, the detour, the pirouette, the simulacrum and the reverse of the medal are the ingredients currently used by artists from Mircea Cantor's generation, but he, with his unmatched box of matches, achieves a nice tour de force pushing away, far away, beyond appearance and rehabilitating genuineness, this constant state of contemporary creation that requires not a renewed production but a brand new one.

Diogenes was walking on the street with his lighted candle in his hand in broad daylight. He would have been thrilled to be able to light it from a double headed match.

Double Heads Matches 20.000 double heads matches where made in the Gherla Matches factory, Romania. Stills from the film, 17 min., color, sound, 2002–2003, ©Mircea Cantor, Courtesy the artist and Yvon Lambert, Paris, New York, Text © Ami Barak, 2003

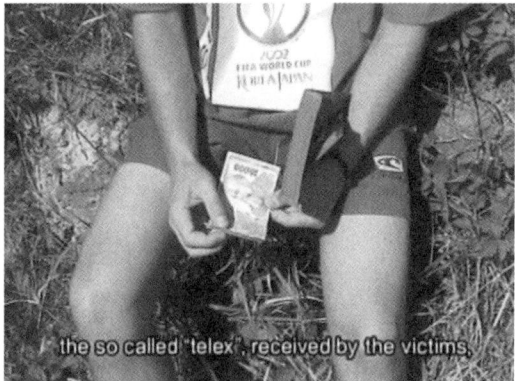

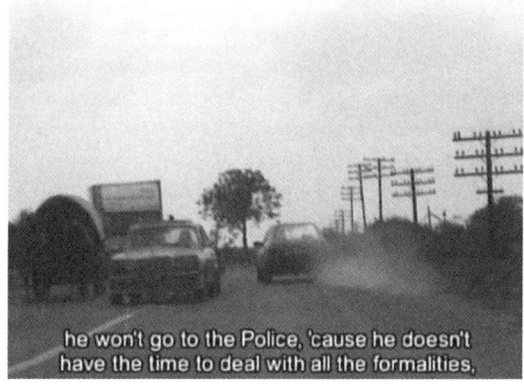

Smen
2002
stills from the film, 6:12 min., color, sound
©Mircea Cantor
Courtesy the artist and Yvon Lambert, Paris, New York

Marina Gržinić

The Photographic Documentary Effect vs. Hyper-Real Mutations

I would like to approach the topic of "documentary style" through a reflection of questions connected with social and political processes of evacuation, visibility, and the connection to documentary photography and new media technologies. I would like to propose models and paradigms of alternating identification, which question familiar forms of representation and allow the formation of new forms of articulation. There is something very definite about this condition: a specific pathology, a specific spectralization of presence that develops precisely out of absence.

I will examine the term "presence" and its counterpart "absence" from two perspectives.[1] The first is a historical perspective, as historical constructions situated within the framework of contemporary discourses, practices, and applications. My question is how this binary pair (which has played one of the key roles in post-structuralist theory) is to be conceived today, and to what extent it differs from that of the 19th century. I will approach these binary terms within the discursive contexts and representational systems of the 19th and 20th centuries in order to better grasp the roll they play, the assumptions they have fostered, and the belief systems they have confirmed. What is essential is to determine to what degree the representational politics of presence/absence were/are used in the past and present.

Secondly, I will approach the duality of presence and absence semiotically, as part of a larger system of visual and representational communication: as both a conduit and an agent of ideologies – as a sign system which contains a contingency of visual and signifying codes, which, in turn, determine reception and instrumentality. The "aesthetics and politics of presence/absence" is (if we refer to Victor Burgin) fundamentally concerned with the articulation of representational politics.[2] If we are to answer these questions, we

have to ask, what is the "real of representation?"³ We may claim that the binary terms of absence/presence function to ratify and affirm the complex ideological web that, at any moment in historical time, is perceived as reality *tout court*. It is also for this reason that there is an initial aforementioned reference to semiotics. According to Julia Kristeva, "what semiotics had discovered is the fact that there is a general social law, that this law is the symbolic dimension which is given in language and that every social practice offers a specific expression of that law."⁴ Kristeva "links semiotics to the social. She calls societal law the 'symbolic,' which is deeply embedded in language; the task of semiotics is to study the various social practices which express this social law."⁵ Thus, the function of semiotics is to "establish a heterogeneous logic of signifying practices and locate them by way of their subject in the historically determined relations of productions."⁶

To grasp the politics of representation of presence/absence, I will relocate it within the discursive contexts and representational systems of two illnesses: hysteria and AIDS, each representing the sexual illness *par excellence* of its century. Each illness functions, as I intend to show, not only in relation to the duality of presence and absence, but in addition, through specific ways of their representational politics, as a part of a larger visual-communication and social system.

Two additional important implications contribute to my decision to choose hysteria and AIDS. First, both illnesses are used to describe fantasmal and marginalized correspondences, acknowledging specific historical conditions. Hysteria embodied the mainstream discriminatory male characterization of women.⁷ AIDS, on the other hand, is overtly connected to another discriminatory mainstream image, that of homosexuals and contemporary queer practices.

The second implication concerns my interest in analyzing the binary terms of presence/absence in connection with the way these terms corre-

die wiederum die Rezeption und Vermittlung bestimmen. Die „Ästhetik und Politik von Präsenz/Absenz" ist – wenn wir uns auf Victor Burgin beziehen – grundsätzlich mit der Artikulation repräsentativer Politik befasst.² Zunächst ist herauszufinden, worin das „Reale der Repräsentation" besteht.³ Wir können behaupten, dass die binären Begriffe Präsenz/Absenz als Ratifizierung und Affirmation des komplexen ideologischen Gewebes zu jedem historischen Zeitpunkt funktionieren und schlicht als die Realität wahrgenommen werden. Nach Julia Kristeva „entdeckte die Semiotik die Tatsache, dass es ein allgemeines soziales Gesetz gibt, dass dieses Gesetz die in der Sprache gegebene symbolische Dimension ist und dass jede soziale Praxis einen spezifischen Ausdruck dieses Gesetzes bietet."⁴ Kristeva „verbindet die Semiotik mit dem Sozialen. Sie nennt das soziale Gesetz das ‚Symbolische', das tief in der Sprache eingebettet ist. Die Aufgabe der Semiotik besteht darin, die verschiedenen sozialen Praktiken, die dieses soziale Gesetz ausdrücken, zu untersuchen."⁵ Daher besteht die Funktion der Semiotik darin, „eine heterogene Logik bezeichnender Praktiken zu etablieren und diese mittels ihrer Subjekte in den historisch bedingten Produktionsverhältnissen zu verorten."⁶

Um die Politik der Repräsentation von Präsenz/Absenz zu begreifen, werde ich sie in die diskursiven Kontexte und Repräsentationssysteme zweier Krankheiten verlagern: Hysterie und AIDS, beides die dominierenden Geschlechtskrankheiten in ihrem jeweiligen Jahrhundert. Ich möchte zeigen, dass beide Krankheitsbilder nicht nur in Beziehung zu der Dualität von Präsenz und Absenz funktionieren, sondern darüber hinaus Teil eines größeren Systems visueller Kommunikation und eines Gesellschaftssystems sind.

Meine Entscheidung, Hysterie und AIDS zu wählen, beruht auf zwei weiteren wichtigen Implikationen. Zum einen werden beide Krankheiten benutzt, um fantasmatische und marginalisierte Korrelationen unter Berücksichtigung spezifischer historischer Umstände zu beschreiben. Die Hysterie verkörperte die diskriminierende männliche Charakterisierung von Frauen.⁷ AIDS hinge-

spond to a specific representational strategy, that focusing on the human body (i.e. representations of historically, gender, and class-determined bodies). Hysteria, the illness of the incongruence of image and thought, was recognized as an illness only by making visible the woman's hysterical body. On the other hand, due to specific representational techniques practiced in the mass media for the general public, AIDS coincides with new media technologies, virtual environments and/or cyberspace, which insist on and foster the erasure of the body. My thesis is that mass media representing AIDS are fostering the absence of the "real" sick body; in a similar way, the contemporary disembodiment of the subject is fostered within new media technologies.

It is very rare to see mainstream films and film documentaries that portray real people suffering from or dying of AIDS, although it is true that over the past several years, the film and video underground has developed a very important network for the presentation and distribution of such works. My interest, however, is situated in so-called mainstream and mass media images: the ones that shape and construct the view of the general public, and specific cultural forms and attitudes. Within such a context, we may say that the process has gone so far today that one of the theoretical options of the investigation of the politics of representation of our present is to find ways of putting the body, especially the (real), sick body, back into the picture.[8]

In the concluding section of this essay I will attempt to synthesize various interplays between presence/absence and Hysteria/AIDS by recycling N. Katherine Hayles' and Donna Haraway's applications of the semiotic square, which they presented in the 1990s. The semiotic square is a technique of discursive analysis that was originally developed by A. J. Greimas to disclose the implications inherent in binary relationships, thus aiding in making explicit (clarifying) the "hidden" meanings, which "stabilize" and generate significance. In this specific theoretical context, following Donna Haraway's semi-

gen ist unverhohlen mit einem anderen verbreiteten diskriminierenden Bild verbunden, dem homosexueller und, heute, queerer Praktiken.

Darüber hinaus interessiert mich die Analyse der binären Begriffe Präsenz/Absenz in Verbindung mit der Art wie diese Begriffe mit einer spezifischen, auf den menschlichen Körper bezogenen Repräsentationsstrategie korrespondieren (d.h. Repräsentationen von Körpern, die historisch, geschlechts- und klassenspezifisch bestimmt sind). Hysterie, die Krankheit als Folge der Nichtübereinstimmung von Bild und Gedanke, wurde nur durch die Sichtbarmachung des hysterischen Frauenkörpers als Krankheitsbild erkannt. AIDS dagegen fällt zeitlich, aufgrund der spezifischen Repräsentationstechniken der Massenmedien gegenüber der breiten Öffentlichkeit, mit den neuen Medientechnologien, virtuellen Umgebungen und/oder Cyberspace zusammen, die auf der Entfernung des Körpers bestehen und diese fördern. Meine These lautet, dass die massenmediale Darstellung von AIDS die Absenz des „realen" kranken Körpers auf eine ähnliche Weise begünstigt wie heute von den neuen Medientechnologien die Entkörperlichung des Subjekts begünstigt wird.

Man sieht selten Mainstream-Spielfilme oder Dokumentarfilme, in denen reale Personen, die an AIDS leiden oder daran sterben, gezeigt werden, obwohl in den letzten Jahren ein sehr wichtiges Netzwerk für die Präsentation und Verbreitung solcher Werke im Film- und Videountergrund entstanden ist. Mein Interesse gilt jedoch den Bildern des so genannten Mainstreams und der Massenmedien, die den Blick der breiten Öffentlichkeit sowie bestimmte kulturelle Formen und Haltungen bestimmen. In diesem Kontext können wir sagen, dass der Prozess so weit fortgeschritten ist, dass eine theoretische Möglichkeit zur Untersuchung der gegenwärtigen Politik der Repräsentation darin besteht, Wege zu finden, den Körper, besonders den (realen) kranken Körper, wieder ins Bild zu setzen.[8]

Zum Schluss dieses Essays werde ich versuchen, die verschiedenen Formen des Zusammenspiels von Präsenz/Absenz und Hysterie/AIDS zusam-

otic square of virtual space, and N. Katherine Hayles' semiotic square of the virtual body, I will attempt to present the semiotic square of AIDS.

Hysteria: Physical [Documentary] Presence and Juridical Absence

In *The Logic of the Gaze* Norman Bryson interprets the work of Théodore Géricault, who, in the early 19th century (1822–1823), studied the influence of mental states on the human face, and believed that the face accurately revealed the inner character, particularly in dementia and in cases of instant death. He made studies of inmates in hospitals and institutions for the criminally insane, where he himself spent time as a patient. Bryson claims that if the historic purpose of the portrait genre is to record a precise social position (a particular instance of status in the hierarchy of power), then Géricault's portraits of insane people, from the first moment, exhibit a contradiction. For Bryson, the portrait of the insane is, therefore, an impossible object and a categorical scandal, since the insane are those who have been displaced from any social hierarchy, who cannot be located on a social map, and whose portraits consequently cannot be painted. Bryson concluded that Géricault fused the categories of privilege and social void, society and asylum, and physical presence and juridical absence.[9]

Martin Charcot's documentary photographs of hysterical patients taken at Salpêtrière Hospital (1877–1880) served the same purpose.[10] Due to the invisibility of the underlying pathology of hysteria, Charcot doubted that hysteria was a disease at all. In contrast to Pierre Janet, one of the early researchers of hysteria, who believed that paralysis occurred in the hysteric because s/he was unable to form an image of his/her limbs and was therefore unable to move them, Charcot thought that hysterics were unable to obliterate pre-existing images of paralysis. For both, hysteria was a problem of representation: the incongruence of image and thought, a disease occasioned by a problem of representation. To anchor this mobile disease, Charcot enlisted

menzubringen, wobei ich auf das semiotische Quadrat von N. Katherine Hayles und Donna Haraways zurückgreife, das beide in den 90ern präsentierten. Dabei handelt es sich um eine diskursanalytische Technik, die ursprünglich von A. J. Greimas entwickelt wurde, um die inhärenten Implikationen binärer Beziehungen aufzudecken und somit die „verborgenen" Bedeutungen, die die Signifikanz „stabilisieren" und generieren, explizit (klar) zu machen. In diesem speziellen theoretischen Kontext werde ich in Anlehnung an Donna Haraways semiotisches Quadrat des virtuellen Raums und N. Kathrine Hayles semiotisches Quadrat des virtuellen Körpers versuchen, das semiotische Quadrat von AIDS zu präsentieren.

Hysterie: Körperliche [dokumentarische] Präsenz und juristische Absenz

In *The Logic of the Gaze* interpretiert Norman Bryson das Werk Théodore Géricaults, der im frühen 19. Jahrhundert (1822–23) den Einfluss psychischer Zustände auf das menschliche Gesicht untersuchte. Géricault war überzeugt, dass das Gesicht auf exakte Weise den inneren Charakter offenbart, besonders bei Demenz und in Fällen plötzlichen Tods. Er fertigte Studien von Krankenhauspatienten und Insassen von Anstalten für straffällig gewordene Geisteskranke an, wo er selbst einige Zeit als Patient verbrachte. Wenn der historische Zweck des Genres der Porträtmalerei darin bestand, eine bestimmte Soziale Position des Porträtierten aufzuzeichnen (eine bestimmte Stufe auf der Hierarchie der Macht), dann weisen, so Bryson, Géricaults Porträts von Geisteskranken von Anfang an einen Widerspruch auf. Für Bryson ist das Porträt des Geisteskranken eine Unmöglichkeit und ein kategorialer Skandal, und zwar deswegen, weil die Geisteskranken aus jeglicher sozialen Hierarchie verdrängt sind, nicht auf der sozialen Landkarte verortet werden können und deren Porträts folglich nicht gemalt werden können. Bryson kommt zu dem Schluss, dass Géricault die Kategorien von Privileg und sozialer Lücke, von Gesellschaft und Asyl, von physischer Präsenz und juristischer Absenz miteinander verbunden hat.[9]

the aid of documentary photography. With documentary photographs of the hysterics, Charcot attempted to make visible this disease that could not be acknowledged except through behavior or representations.[11] Just like Charcot's photographs, Géricault's previous studies functioned "as the institution of the subject, in the case of the insane people, within the visible."[12]

This institution of the subject within the visible was done according to a precisely chosen representational mode of the epoch: documentary photography, that is, using modes and techniques that over-determined visibility in a more general way within the period discussed. The categories of absence and presence are hence in a dual relation to the institution of the subject within the visible. Joan Copjec points out that hysteria is an illness of the imagination, and threatened knowledge. In confusing categories of real and unreal illnesses (true perception and false images), the physician was made a potential victim of trickery and deception, casting doubt on his senses that were the foundation of his knowledge.[13] The issue, therefore, was not only to discover the relation between representations and hysteria, but to use the most appropriate regime of representation for this kind of restoration.

Charcot, who was an adherent of Géricault's theories, learned from his works, such as *The Insane Women, Envy* (1822–1823), "not how malicious mischief or envy would manifest itself on the human face, but what the [documentary] photographs taken at Salpêtrière hospital 50 years after Géricault should look like."[14]

When looking at Géricault's "Envy" series, the art historian Gardner argued that Géricault's insane women had a peculiar hypnotic power, as well as an astonishing authenticity in the presentation of the psychic facts. For Gardner, *The Insane Women* series is another example of the increasingly realistic core of Romantic painting.

The closer the Romantic involved himself with nature, sane or insane, the more clarity he

Martin Charcots dokumentarische Fotos von hysterischen Patientinnen, die 1877–80 im Salpêtrière Frauenkrankenhaus entstanden, dienten demselben Zweck.[10] Wegen der Unsichtbarkeit der zugrunde liegenden Pathologie der Hysterie, bezweifelte Charcot, dass die Hysterie überhaupt eine Krankheit sei. Im Gegensatz zu Pierre Janet, einem der frühen Hysterieforscher, der glaubte Hysterikerinnen leiden an Lähmung, weil sie unfähig seien, sich ein Bild ihrer Glieder zu machen und daher bewegungsunfähig sind, war Charcot der Meinung, Hysterikerinnen seien nicht in der Lage, bereits existierende Bilder der Lähmung zu tilgen. Für beide war die Hysterie ein Problem der Darstellung: die Nicht-Übereinstimmung von Bild und Gedanke, eine Krankheit die durch ein Problem der Darstellung verursacht wurde. Um diese Krankheit der Beweglichkeit zu verankern, benutzte Charcot die dokumentarische Fotografie. Mit Hilfe dokumentarischer Abbildungen von Hysterikerinnen versuchte er diese Krankheit, die nur über das Verhalten oder mittels Repräsentationen festgestellt werden konnte, zu visualisieren.[11] Ebenso wie Charcots Fotografien funktionierten Géricaults frühere Studien „als die Einführung des Subjekts, hier des Geisteskranken, in das Sichtbare."[12]

Die Einführung des Subjekts in das Sichtbare geschah gemäß einer präzise gewählten Repräsentationsform jener Epoche: der dokumentarischen Fotografie. Es kamen also Formen und Techniken zur Anwendung, die während jener Periode Sichtbarkeit auf allgemeinere Weise überdeterminierten. Die Kategorien von Präsenz und Absenz stehen daher in einem doppelten Verhältnis zur Einführung des Subjekts in das Sichtbare. Joan Copjec weist darauf hin, dass die Hysterie eine Krankheit der Einbildungskraft und des gefährdeten Wissens sei. Indem er die Kategorien der wirklichen und unwirklichen Krankheiten (richtige Wahrnehmung und falsche Bilder) verwechselte, wurde der Arzt zu einem potenziellen Opfer von Tricks und Täuschungen, die seine Sinne, als Grundlage seines Wissens, ins Wanken brachten.[13] Es ging also nicht nur darum, das Verhältnis zwischen Darstellung und Hysterie aufzu-

gained, thus moving closer to the "truth." Increasingly, this meant painting the optical truth, as well as truth with regard to "the way things are."[15] What Charcot learned from Géricault was not the "authenticity in presentation of psychic fact," but the Renaissance notion of the artist who is instituting the visible within a rationalized system of perceptual codes.[16] Documentary photography, then theorized as both the outcome and the servant of positivism (objective, unmediated and actually imprinted by the light rays of the original form), was the ideal representational mode to utilize in order to bring the disease into a discursive construction.[17]

In summarizing Charcot's and Géricault's methodologies, I would conclude first that a physical presence was not a question of authenticity in the presentation of psychic facts, but was, in the 19th century, a process of instituting the visible within a rationalized system of perceptual codes. In the case of Charcot, this was a Renaissance notion: of the artist as a quantifier within the medium of documentary photography, the latter theorized as both the product of, and subordinate to, positivism. If the reference to hysteria is understood as a blind spot in the positivist genealogy of illnesses, then we can theorize Charcot's attempt as a method to bring something, which previously had not been subject to the rules of visibility, into the system of "presence" and representation. Jo Anna Isaak argues that Charcot did this through his reference to Renaissance paintings, utilizing Renaissance perceptual codes, such as linear perspective. Linear perspective was used to facilitate impersonal objective statements producing identical meanings within all viewers, referring to cumulative and repeatable effects.[18] It is unnecessary to go into details concerning the Renaissance perspective system. However, I would like to stress, as Isaak implies, that perspective was extremely useful to Europeans, who needed to develop a visual language of newly discovered territories (in order to possess them).

This, however, was the case in the 19th century, but how do these processes operate today? I will

decken, sondern auch das geeignetste Repräsentationsregime für diese Art der Wiederherstellung zu verwenden.

Charcot, der ein Anhänger von Géricaults Theorien war, lernte von dessen Werken, wie etwa *The Insane Woman, Envy* (1822-23), „nicht, wie sich boshafter Unfug oder Neid auf dem menschlichen Gesicht manifestierte, sondern wie die (dokumentarischen) Fotografien, die im Salpêtrière Krankenhaus aufgenommen wurden, 50 Jahre nach Géricault aussehen sollten."[14]

Beim Betrachten von Géricaults *Neid*-Serie, so der Kunsthistoriker Gardner, besitzen seine *Insane Women* eine eigenartige hypnotische Macht sowie eine erstaunliche Authentizität bei der Darstellung der psychischen Fakten. Für Gardner sind *The Insane Women* ein weiteres Beispiel für den zunehmenden realistischen Kern romantischer Malerei.

Je mehr sich der Romantiker mit der Natur, ob geistig gesund oder krank, beschäftigte, desto mehr Klarheit gewann er und desto mehr näherte er sich der „Wahrheit". In zunehmendem Maße bedeutete dies, die optische Wahrheit zu malen, sowie die Wahrheit in Bezug darauf, „wie die Dinge sind".[15] Charcot übernahm von Géricault nicht die „Authentizität bei der Darstellung psychischer Fakten", sondern die aus der Renaissance stammende Vorstellung des Künstlers als einer Person, die das Sichtbare innerhalb eines rationalen Systems von Wahrnehmungscodes einführt.[16] Dokumentarische Fotografie, theoretisch gefasst als Resultat und auch als Dienerin des Positivismus (objektiv, unmittelbar und tatsächlich geprägt von den Lichtstrahlen des Originals), war die ideale Repräsentationsform, um die Krankheit in eine diskursive Konstruktion einzubinden.[17]

In der Zusammenfassung von Charcots und Géricaults Methodologien würde ich zunächst zu dem Schluss kommen, dass eine körperliche Präsenz nichts mit der Authentizität bei der Darstellung psychischer Fakten zu tun hatte, sondern im 19. Jahrhundert ein Prozess der Einführung des Sichtbaren in ein rationales System von Wahrneh-

make a parallel between the categories of absence/presence and the different systems of representation with regard to AIDS, attempting in this way to chart the process of the institution of the subject within the visible today. AIDS also presents the problem of homogenous representation and depiction: the incongruence of the image and the gaze. In the case of AIDS, in contrast to hysteria, the underlying pathology of the disease is horribly visible, and the whole process of representation and visibility therefore operates differently, in an effort to erase and/or conceal the conspicuous nature of the disease. The "identification" of the spectator with a sick person, or with the AIDS disease, is transferred to a metonymy, whose purpose is to hide the presence of the "real" sick body. Those people who are afflicted with AIDS are, in general, listened to rather than looked at.

An artistic (creative) articulation of the above thesis is the feature film, *Blue*, directed by Derek Jarman in 1993. For 75 minutes, a blue screen is projected before the spectator. It is the sole image throughout the film, which provides a canvas for the audience, who listen to evocative words, music, and sounds. Various methods of communicating the text are used in the film: inner speech, repetitious preoccupying phrases, unconscious spoken thoughts.[19] My interest lies not in a sociological reading or reinterpretation of the text in the film, but in the representational system superimposing and depicting the text in the film on the blue-colored canvas.[20]

In Jarman's film, the institution of the subject within the visible is represented by the disembodied voice of an ill person who speaks deliriously throughout the film, anchoring the disease in the field of discourse. If we draw a parallel between this regime and the one depicting hysteria, we may posit that AIDS is represented by the physical absence of an actually sick body. Nevertheless, an urgent appeal for juridical (judicial) presence and for legal rights in the various sectors of society which cross or border the sick body pervades the text of the film. A similar example is, this time, a mainstream film

mungscodes war. Im Falle Charcots war dies eine Vorstellung der Renaissance: der Künstler als Quantifizierer innerhalb des Mediums der dokumentarischen Fotografie, die sowohl als Produkt des Positivismus als auch ihm untergeordnet theoretisch gefasst werden kann. Versteht man den Bezug zur Hysterie als blinden Fleck in der positivistischen Genealogie der Krankheiten, dann können wir Charcots Versuch als Methode verstehen, etwas, das zuvor nicht den Gesetzen der Sichtbarkeit unterworfen war, in das System von „Präsenz" und Repräsentation zu bringen. Jo Anna Isaak argumentiert, dass Charcot dies durch seinen Bezug zur Renaissancemalerei tat, durch seine Verwendung von Wahrnehmungscodes der Renaissance, z.B. die Linearperspektive. Diese wurde verwendet, um unpersönliche, objektive Aussagen zu machen, die bei allen Betrachtern unter Bezugnahme auf sich häufende und wiederholbare Effekte einen identischen Sinn herstellten sollten.[18] Es ist hier nicht notwendig, auf das System der Perspektive in der Renaissance detailliert einzugehen. Ich möchte aber Isaaks These betonen, Perspektive sei sehr brauchbar gewesen für die Europäer, die eine visuelle Sprache für die neu entdeckten Territorien entwickeln mussten (um diese zu beherrschen).

So war es im 19. Jahrhundert, doch wie funktionieren diese Prozesse heute? Ich werde eine Parallele ziehen zwischen den Kategorien von Präsenz/Absenz und den verschiedenen Repräsentationssystemen bezüglich AIDS, um so den Prozess der Einführung des Subjekts in das Sichtbare in der heutigen Zeit nachzuzeichnen. Auch AIDS wirft das Problem der homogenen Repräsentation und Abbildung auf: die Nicht-Übereinstimmung von Bild und Blick. Bei AIDS – im Gegensatz zur Hysterie – ist die zugrunde liegende Pathologie der Krankheit auf schreckliche Weise sichtbar und der ganze Prozess der Repräsentation und Sichtbarkeit funktioniert daher anders und ist von dem Bemühen geprägt, die auffällige Natur der Krankheit auszulöschen/zu verbergen. Die „Identifikation" des Betrachters mit der kranken Person, oder mit der Krankheit AIDS, wird auf eine Metonymie übertragen, deren Zweck es ist, die Präsenz des „realen" kranken

about AIDS: *Philadelphia* (directed by Jonathan Demme in 1994). In the film, the actor Tom Hanks portrays a character who is a pale image of an authentic AIDS patient. In spite the absence of an "authentically sick body" on the level of representation, we are confronted with, nevertheless, in this particular film, a clear fight for juridical presence, and for the rights pertaining to juridical proceedings of those people inflicted with AIDS, especially homosexuals.[21]

The binary terms of presence-absence in relation to the representation of the sick body and its social counterpart in the juridical system culminate in two ways simultaneously: through technological interventions and discursive practices. It is possible, however, to conceive of the relation of a social area in which the collision of bodies and reproductive technology (e.g. photography, film) takes place within the politics of power as it functions through the juridical system. Such a relation is also that between documentary photography and the logic of representation of hysteria, on the one hand, and the invention of new technologies and media and their regimes of representation of AIDS, on the other. What I am proposing here is not to recuperate some notion of pure investment of the category of absence and its counterpart – presence, but to outline the discursive-visual terrain in which such issues have functioned, both in the past and in the present. In both cases, the camera, photography, and film produce representations – iconic signs – translating the actual into the representational via the categories of absence/presence. The meanings ascribed to the categories of absence and presence, sometimes inconsistent, amorphous, and epistemologically vague, are constantly in flux, repositioned and reoriented, and involve larger discourses which engender them.

The documentary photographs of incarcerated hysterics commissioned by Dr. Charcot "prove and demonstrate the speculative nature and morphology of hysteria."[22] The success of documentary photography as a technology for and of image-making in anchoring the disease is precisely concerned with its confirmatory aspects.

Körpers zu verstecken. Im Allgemeinen wird den Personen, die an AIDS leiden, eher zugehört, als dass man sie ansieht.

Eine künstlerische (kreative) Artikulation dieser These ist der Spielfilm *Blue* des Regisseurs Derek Jarman aus dem Jahr 1993. 75 Minuten lang sehen die Zuschauer eine blaue Leinwand. Sie ist das einzige Bild des Films und dient als Projektionsfläche für das Publikum, das beschwörende Worte, Musik und Geräusche hört. Im Film kommen verschiedene Methoden der Textkommunikation zum Einsatz: innerer Monolog, sich wiederholende, gedankenverlorene Sätze, unbewusst ausgesprochene Gedanken.[19] Ich interessiere mich nicht für eine soziologische Interpretation oder eine Neuinterpretation des Filmtextes, sondern für das System der Repräsentation, das den Text im Film überlagert und ihn auf der blauen Leinwand abbildet.[20]

Die Einführung des Subjekts in das Sichtbare wird in Jarmans Film durch die körperlose Stimme einer kranken Person repräsentiert, die während des gesamten Films delirierend spricht und so die Krankheit im diskursiven Feld verankert. Wenn wir eine Parallele ziehen zwischen diesem Regime und dem, welches die Hysterie abbildet, können wir die These aufstellen, AIDS werde durch die physische Absenz des eigentlichen kranken Körpers repräsentiert. Trotzdem ist der Filmtext durchzogen von dem dringenden Appell, eine juristische Präsenz sowie gesetzlich verankerte Rechte in den verschiedenen Gesellschaftsbereichen, die den kranken Körper durchqueren oder an ihn grenzen, durchzusetzen. Ein ähnliches Beispiel ist der bekannte Mainstreamfilm über AIDS: *Philadelphia* (von Jonathan Demme, 1994). Tom Hanks verkörpert hier eine Rolle, die nur der Abklatsch eines authentischen AIDS-Patienten ist. Trotz der Absenz eines „authentischen kranken Körpers" auf der Ebene der Repräsentation, sind wir mit dem entschiedenen Kampf für juristische Präsenz und für die Rechte von AIDS-Kranken, insbesondere von Homosexuellen, bei Gerichtsverfahren konfrontiert.[21]

Die binären Begriffe Präsenz/Absenz in Bezug zur Repräsentation des kranken Körpers und sei-

The latter enabled documentary photography to succeed in rapid expansion and assimilation within the discourses of knowledge and power. This structural congruence of different viewpoints (i.e. the eye of the photographer, the eye of the camera, and the spectator's eye) in documentary photography covers the quality of pure, but delusory presence.[23] Gardner spoke of Géricault's increasingly realistic core of representation, i.e. of his obsessively intentional and representational methods of acquiring the optical truth – the truth about the way things "were." In analyzing the mechanisms internal to the media apparatus in question (i.e., documentary photography), Abigail Solomon-Godeau claims that the most important is the "reality effect," and that "a further structuring instance lies in the perspective system of representation built into camera optics in photography's infancy."[24] Modeled on the classical system of the single point monocular perspective invented in the Renaissance, camera optics were designed to yield an analogous pictorial structure. As Abigail Solomon-Godeau argues, natural vision and perception have no vanishing point, are binocular, without boundaries, in constant motion and marked by the loss of clarity in the periphery. The camera image, like many Renaissance paintings, offers a static, uniform field in which orthogonals converge at a single vanishing point.[25] "The world is no longer an 'open and unbound horizon.' Limited by the framing, lined up, put at the proper distance, the world offers itself up as an object endowed with meaning, an intentional object, implied by, and implying the action of the 'subject' which sights it."[26]

Furthermore, if we consider the act of looking at a documentary photograph with respect to gender or the operations of the psyche (e.g., the complex acts of projection, voyeurism, fantasy, and desires that inform our seeing), we cannot, as Salomon-Godeau argues, abandon the earlier, innocent belief that the camera presents us with visual facts that are simply "out there," and which we now disinterestedly observe and register. We have to accept that there are ideological effects inherent to the photographic apparatus,

and that these effects influence relations, scopic commands, and the confirmation or displacement of subject positions.

In conclusion to the first established connection between representation, documentary photography, and hysteria, we may posit that the fusion of physical presence and juridical absence in the photographs of the hysterics also offers a counter-reading. On the one hand, this specific institution of the subject within the visible was possible, or was the result of the specific ideological mechanisms of the "optical truth" intrinsic to the [documentary] photographic apparatus. On the other hand, this same apparatus reinforced the position of juridical absence of the insane person. As Pierre Bourdieu commented, discussing the social uses of photography: "In stamping photography with the patent of realism, society does nothing but confirm itself in the tautological certainty that an image of reality that conforms to its own representation of objectivity is truly objective."[27]

AIDS: Physical Absence and Juridical Presence

Thus far, I have presented (with reference to Jo Anna Isaak and Abigail Solomon-Godeau) the relationships between documentary photography, hysteria, and the notions of absence/presence, as well as those of physical presence and juridical absence. I shall proceed with the relationships between the logic of representation of the new technologies/media and the representation of AIDS.

People afflicted with AIDS show dramatic visual signs of bodily deterioration (in the advanced stages of the disease): the disintegration of the skin, sarcomas, blindness, and the degeneration of the body as a whole. Jarman has incorporated into the film *Blue* his personal blindness, a consequence of AIDS. Jarman chooses to depict this with a blue canvas: the zero degree of representation. Jarman moved from the disintegration of film structure to that of the viewer's sight. The institution of the subject suffering with AIDS

sprach von Géricaults zunehmenden realistischen Kern der Repräsentation, d.h. von seinen obsessiven intentionalen und repräsentativen Methoden, der optischen Wahrheit habhaft zu werden — der Wahrheit der Dinge, wie sie „waren". In ihrer Analyse der internen Mechanismen des fraglichen Medienapparats (d.h. der dokumentarischen Fotografie), behauptet Abigail Solomon-Godeau, dass der „Realitätseffekt" der wichtigste sei und dass „das perspektivische Repräsentationssystem, das bei der Geburt der Fotografie in die Kameraoptik eingebaut wurde, eine weitere strukturierende Instanz sei."[24] Nach dem Vorbild des klassischen Systems der monokularen Fluchtpunktperspektive, die aus der Renaissance stammt, wurde die Kameraoptik so entworfen, dass sie eine analoge Bildstruktur hervorbrachte. Nach Abigail Solomon-Godeau haben das natürliche Sehvermögen und die natürliche Wahrnehmung jedoch keinen Fluchtpunkt, sie sind binokular, ohne Grenzen, in ständiger Bewegung und durch den Verlust der Klarheit an der Peripherie gekennzeichnet. Das Kamerabild bietet, wie viele Renaissancegemälde, ein statisches, einheitliches Feld, in dem Orthogone in einem einzigen Fluchtpunkt zusammenlaufen.[25] „Die Welt ist nicht länger ein ‚offener und unbegrenzter Horizont'. Begrenzt durch den Rahmen, aufgereiht, auf Abstand gehalten, bietet sich die Welt als ein bedeutungsvolles Objekt an, als ein intentionales Objekt, bedingt durch die Handlung des ‚Subjekts', das sie sieht, und die Handlung bedingend."[26]

Wenden wir uns darüber hinaus der Betrachtung des dokumentarischen Fotos in Hinblick auf Gender oder die Operationen der Psyche zu (z.B. die komplexen Handlungen der Projektion, des Voyeurismus, der Fantasie und der Wünsche, die unser Sehen beeinflussen), so können wir laut Solomon-Godeau nicht umhin den früheren unschuldigen Glauben zurückzuweisen, dass die Kamera uns die visuellen Fakten, die einfach „dort draußen" sind, liefert, Fakten, die wir nun interesselos beobachten und zur Kenntnis nehmen. Wir müssen akzeptieren, dass es dem fotografischen Apparat innewohnende ideologische Effekte gibt, die die Beziehungen, die skopischen Befehle und die Bestätigung oder Verschiebung

within the visible is carried out by the absence of a "truly sick body." Moreover, Derek Jarman not only refused to reiterate the conventional pieties surrounding the representations of individuals suffering with AIDS, but brought to light (paraphrasing Sally Stein) the hidden agendas inscribed in the particular mode of representation of our culture and times.[28] In the film *Blue*, this is carried out more with the strategically incorporated logic of the visualization of new media, and the regime of visibility carried out by new media technologies, rather than the medium itself: film.

Jarman successfully conveys the complexities underpinning information systems and various subject positions through the way in which meaning and identities are constructed and endlessly re-negotiated. Using the establishment of blindness in the film as the zero degree of representation, Jarman subverts some of the basic parameters of the new paradigm of visuality produced by new technology and the position of the eyewitness within it. Today, all methods of proving a statement depend on technological instruments and tools, and the constitution of scientific "truth" is, to a profound degree, mediated by technology.[29] Pragmatic acceptance of axioms and specific methods of proof have entered a variety of sciences. Scientific statements have to be effectuated and are thus decisively mediated by technology. Pragmatic performativity is the post-modern sense of truth.[30] Lyotard emphasizes repeatedly the increase of acquiring scientific knowledge through its mediation with technology. The whole process is thus a process of seeing through its mediation through technology.[31]

Allow me to clarify, as well, this process "of seeing through its mediation with technology" by returning for a moment to documentary photography, summarizing its inner principle by referring to Paul Virilio (despite the fact that he was not referring here to photography). "Everything I see is in principle within my reach, at least within reach of my sight, marked on the map of the 'I can.'"[32] Documentary photography enables

von Subjektpositionen beeinflussen.

Im Anschluss an die zunächst hergestellte Beziehung zwischen Repräsentation, dokumentarischer Fotografie und Hysterie können wir behaupten, dass die Zusammenführung von physischer Präsenz und juristischer Absenz in den Fotos der Hysterikerinnen auch eine Gegeninterpretation ermöglicht. Einerseits wurde diese besondere Einführung des Subjekts in das Sichtbare durch den speziellen ideologischen Mechanismus der „optischen Wahrheit", der dem (dokumentarischen) Fotoapparat innewohnt, ermöglicht. Andererseits stärkte derselbe Apparat die Position der juristischen Absenz der geisteskranken Person. Pierre Bourdieu sagte zum gesellschaftlichen Nutzen der Fotografie: „Indem sie der Photographie Realismus bescheinigt, bestärkt die Gesellschaft sich selbst in der tautologischen Gewißheit, daß ein Bild der Wirklichkeit, das der Vorstellung entspricht, die man sich von der Realität macht, tatsächlich objektiv ist."[27]

AIDS: Physische Absenz und juristische Präsenz

Bisher habe ich (mit Bezug auf Jo Anna Isaak und Abigail Solomon-Godeau) die Verhältnisse zwischen dokumentarischer Fotografie, Hysterie und den Begriffen Präsenz/Absenz, sowie die der körperlichen Präsenz und juristischen Absenz dargestellt. Ich wende mich nun den Beziehungen zwischen der Repräsentationslogik der neuen Technologien und Medien und der Repräsentation von AIDS zu.

Menschen, die an AIDS leiden, weisen (in den fortgeschrittenen Stadien der Krankheit) dramatische visuelle Zeichen körperlichen Zerfalls auf: Auflösung der Haut, Sarkome, Blindheit und Verfall des gesamten Körpers. In seinem Film *Blue* thematisierte Jarman seine eigene Blindheit als Folge von AIDS. Jarman beschloss, sie mit einer blauen Leinwand darzustellen: der Nullpunkt der Repräsentation. Er bewegte sich von der Auflösung der Filmstruktur zu der Auflösung des Betrachterblicks. Die Einführung des an AIDS leidenden Subjekts in das Sichtbare geschieht durch die Absenz eines „wahrhaft kranken Körpers".

the encoding of a topographical memory by establishing a dialectical loop between seeing and mapping. As Virilio claims, it is possible to speak of generations of vision, and even of visual heredity from one generation to the next. However, following Virilio, the perception developed by new media and technologies (called the "logistics of perception") destroyed these earlier modes of representation preserved in the "I can" of seeing. The logistics of perception inaugurates the production of a vision machine and the possibility of achieving sightless vision, whereby a video camera or virtual technology would be controlled by a computer. Today, new media apparatus (from virtual reality to cyberspace) confer upon us a whole range of visual prosthetics which confront us with an ever-changing positioning of the subject. Changes are effectuated within our bodies, as well, as we are facing a systematic "production" of blindness, and an absence of certainty within the visibility of our world. As Virilio would say, the bulk of what I see is no longer within my reach. We have to ask ourselves: What does one see when one's eyes, depending on the instruments of new technology, are reduced to a state of rigid and practically invariable structural immobility?

Nonetheless, this is only one side of the paradigm of new media technology. On the other hand, in the 20th century, science is increasingly permeated with technology. "Technological instruments and apparatuses hold a central role within scientific research processes. These technological tools cost huge amounts of money. Consequently, the state and political institutions function as important and decisive mediators in the accomplishment of scientific knowledge. The process of knowledge is increasingly judged in terms of input (quantity) and output (quality). Science is linked to the system of political power."[33]

The blindness of the naked human eye is thus paradoxically reinforced by the growing tendency to use increasingly sophisticated electronic technologies, not only in science, but also in the leading ideological and repressive state apparatus (particularly within the legal system and

Derek Jarman weigerte sich nicht nur, die konventionellen Pietäten in Zusammenhang mit Darstellungen AIDS-Kranker zu wiederholen, sondern beleuchtete (in den Worten Sally Steins) das, was sich versteckt in die besondere Repräsentationsform unserer Kultur und Zeit eingeschrieben hat.[28] In *Blue* geschieht dies eher durch die strategische Einbeziehung der Visualisierungslogik der neuen Medien und des Regimes der Sichtbarkeit, das die neuen Medientechnologien errichten, als durch das Medium Film selbst.

Es gelingt Jarman, die Komplexitäten, die den Informationssystemen und den verschiedenen Subjektpositionen zugrunde liegen, durch die Art wie Bedeutung und Identitäten konstruiert und endlos neu verhandelt werden, zu vermitteln. Indem er die Erzeugung von Blindheit im Film als Nullpunkt der Repräsentation verwendet, untergräbt Jarman einige der grundlegenden Parameter des neuen Paradigmas der Sichtbarkeit, das die neuen Technologien produzieren, sowie die sich darin befindende Position des Augenzeugen. Heute hängen alle Methoden, mit denen eine Aussage bewiesen werden kann, von technologischen Instrumenten und Werkzeugen ab, und die Herstellung von wissenschaftlicher „Wahrheit" wird zu einem wesentlichen Grad durch Technologie vermittelt.[29] In vielen Wissenschaften hat die pragmatische Akzeptanz von Axiomen und speziellen Beweismethoden Einzug gehalten. Wissenschaftliche Aussagen müssen eine Wirkung erzielen und sind daher entscheidend an Technologien gebunden. Der postmoderne Sinn von Wahrheit ist pragmatische Performativität.[30] Lyotard betont wiederholt den Zuwachs an wissenschaftlicher Erkenntnis durch ihre technologische Vermittlung. Der ganze Prozess besteht daher darin, ihre technologische Vermittlung zu durchschauen.[31]

Ich möchte diesen Prozess dadurch verdeutlichen, dass ich kurz auf die dokumentarische Fotografie zurückkomme. Ihr innerstes Prinzip kann in Anlehnung an Paul Virilio wie folgt zusammengefasst werden (obwohl er sich hier nicht auf die Fotografie bezog): „Alles, was ich sehe, ist prinzipiell in meiner Reichweite, zumindest in der Reichweite meines Blickes, es ist vermerkt auf der

among the police). Virilio speaks of hyper-realist representational models within the police and legal systems, to the extent that human witnesses are losing their credibility; the human eye no longer remains an eyewitness. On the one side of the paradigm of new media technology we are witnessing the systematic production of blindness, and on the other, the frightening hyper-realism of a system of total visibility, which is particularly reinforced in legal and police procedures.

The tendency of the leading scopic regime of new media technologies is to produce blindness, while simultaneousl, creating a whole range of techniques to produce the credibility of the presence of objects and humans, rather than trying to demonstrate their real existence. Today, this latter process may be illustrated with military and espionage strategies: "It is more vital to trick the enemy about the virtuality of the missile's passage, about the very credibility of its presence, than to confuse him about the reality of its existence."[34]

These primary features which are currently produced by new media technology (e.g., blindness of the natural human eye, hyper-realism in legal and police procedures, and a whole range of techniques for producing the credibility of the presence of objects, people, etc.) are strategically incorporated and subverted in the film *Blue*. With the establishment of blindness in the film via the blue canvas as the zero degree of representation, Jarman emphasizes this duality. The absence of the sick body and furthermore, of *any* physical body in the film, creates the illusion of total disembodiment, and is paradoxically a subversive answer to the constant production of disembodiment through new technologies.

The created illusion of disembodiment thus raises the question that I posed at the beginning of this essay: "How do we put bodies back into the picture?"[35] One possible answer is based on Jarman's film *Blue*: as juridical presence! The body of people infected with AIDS, an "object" already lost, is shaped by its very absence. On the other

Karte des ‚ich kann'."[32] Dokumentarische Fotografie ermöglicht die Codierung eines topografischen Gedächtnisses durch die Etablierung einer dialektischen Schleife zwischen Sehen und Kartografieren. Virilio behauptet, es sei möglich, von Generationen des Sehvermögens zu sprechen, sogar von visueller Vererbung, die eine Generation an die nächste weitergibt. Doch Virilio zufolge zerstörte die durch die neuen Medien und Technologien entwickelte Wahrnehmung („Logistik der Wahrnehmung" genannt) diese früheren Repräsentationsformen, die in dem „ich kann" des Sehens aufgehoben waren. Die Logistik der Wahrnehmung leitet die Produktion einer Sehmaschine und die Möglichkeit blinden Sehens ein, wobei die Videokamera oder die virtuelle Technologie durch einen Computer gesteuert wird. Heute bietet uns der neue Medienapparat (von virtueller Realität bis Cyberspace) eine ganze Palette visueller Prothesen, die uns mit einer sich permanent verändernden Positionierung des Subjekts konfrontieren. Veränderungen werden auch innerhalb unserer Körper bewirkt, während wir Zeugen einer systematischen „Produktion" von Blindheit und der Abwesenheit von Gewissheit innerhalb der Sichtbarkeit unserer Welt werden. Virilio würde sagen, der Großteil dessen, was ich sehe, ist nicht mehr in meiner Reichweite. Wir müssen uns also fragen: Was sieht man, wenn – abhängig von den neuen technologischen Instrumenten – die Augen auf einen Zustand starrer und praktisch unveränderbarer struktureller Bewegungslosigkeit reduziert werden?

Dennoch ist dies nur die eine Seite des Paradigmas der neuen Medientechnologien. Andererseits wird im 20. Jahrhundert die Wissenschaft zunehmend von Technologie durchdrungen. „Technologische Werkzeuge und Apparate spielen eine zentrale Rolle im wissenschaftlichen Forschungsprozess. Diese technologischen Werkzeuge kosten immens viel Geld. Folglich funktionieren der Staat und die politischen Institutionen als wichtige und entscheidende Vermittler bei der Produktion von wissenschaftlichem Wissen. Der Wissensprozess wird zunehmend in Hinblick auf Input (Quantität) und Output (Qualität) beurteilt. Die Wissenschaft ist eng mit dem System politischer Macht ver-

hand, with the text heard throughout the film, thoroughly detailed in the existential, medical, and legal particularities of the postmodern condition of persons suffering from AIDS, a clear demand is made for juridical presence and the rights of those afflicted with AIDS, within the structures of power in contemporary society. Through this relationship between the logic of representation of the new technologies/media and the representation of AIDS, it is therefore possible to elaborate a different logic of representation of absence/presence as was previously proposed in the case of hysteria. Instead of physical presence and juridical absence, physical absence and legal presence is produced. Physical absence and legal presence, as proposed by Jarman, subvert the logic of a mass-produced simulated presence on the one hand, and a mass blindness of the "natural" human eye on the other.

Looking to the binary pair of presence/absence in connection with the film *Blue*, and with the new media/virtual environments, one may also argue that the common characteristics of emerging technologies and virtual environments are the elimination of duration — the collapse of time into real time. In the film *Blue*, these characteristics serve as reminders of the dimension of time, which, as Paul Virilio suggests, is under siege by real time technologies. "They kill 'present' time by isolating its presence here and now for the sake of another commutative space that is no longer composed of our 'concrete presence' in the world, but of a 'discrete telepresence' whose enigma remains forever intact."[36]

The Experiential Reception of the Image

If a "bounded image is seen from a distance... it exists unto itself and offers a perceptual experience. Images that implicate the viewer in some way, however, as is the case with interactive or immersive media, are unbounded. They require experiential cognition. The latter puts the critical viewer in an untenable position: one must assimilate an image to comprehend it, yet it must also be dismantled in order to reflect upon

knüpft."[33]

Die Blindheit des bloßen menschlichen Auges wird daher auf paradoxe Weise durch die zunehmende Tendenz forciert, immer ausgefeiltere elektronische Technologien nicht nur in der Wissenschaft, sondern auch im herrschenden ideologischen und repressiven Staatsapparat zu verwenden (dies gilt besonders für das Rechtssystem und die Polizei). Virilio spricht von hyperrealistischen Repräsentationsmodellen bei der Polizei und Justiz, die so weit gehen, dass menschliche Zeugen ihre Glaubwürdigkeit verlieren – das menschliche Auge ist kein Augenzeuge mehr. Auf der einen Seite des Paradigmas der neuen Medientechnologie beobachten wir die systematische Produktion von Blindheit, auf der anderen den erschreckenden Hyperrealismus eines Systems totaler Sichtbarkeit, das besonders in juristischen und polizeilichen Verfahren verstärkt wird.

Die Tendenz des herrschenden skopischen Regimes der neuen Medientechnologien soll Blindheit produzieren, während zur gleichen Zeit eine ganze Reihe neuer Techniken hergestellt wird, um die Glaubwürdigkeit der Präsenz von Objekten und Menschen zu sichern, statt ihre reale Existenz zu demonstrieren. Dieser letztgenannte Prozess kann heute mit militärischen und geheimdienstlichen Strategien veranschaulicht werden: „Es ist wichtig, den Feind bezüglich der Virtualität einer Raketenlaufbahn, bezüglich der tatsächlichen Glaubwürdigkeit ihrer Präsenz zu täuschen, als ihn über die Realität ihrer Existenz zu verwirren."[34]

Diese primären Eigenschaften, die zurzeit durch die neue Medientechnologie produziert werden (z.B. die Blindheit des natürlichen menschlichen Auges, Hyperrealismus in juristischen und polizeilichen Verfahren und die große Palette von Techniken, welche die Glaubwürdigkeit der Präsenz von Dingen, Menschen etc. erzeugen sollen), werden im Film *Blue* auf strategische Weise integriert und untergraben. Jarman betont diese Dualität durch die Erzeugung von Blindheit mittels der blauen Leinwand als Nullpunkt der Repräsentation. Die Absenz des kranken Körpers und darüber hinaus *jeglichen* physikalischen Körpers im

it."[37] For Timothy Druckrey, the discursive operations of information systems in the late 20th century, as proffered through cyberspace, are characterized by going beyond identity and meaning formations to provide a catalyst for agency, and therefore empowerment. The creative potential of different visual systems is represented through an interface, or "connections."[38] Meaning and phenomenology, representation and perception, are merged. The moment of reading an image within such a system has the effect "not as a navigation of the image, but of a lived moment, so that the efficacy of an image is equal to the experience of it."[39] Thus, it is the lived moment of being connected which is charged with possibilities. "It is the passion of this lived moment of connection between the user, part of the real world, and the controlled system of predictable outcomes encoded into the software of the symbolic, accessed through the hardware, which offers scope for disruptive nihilistic behavior."[40] The film *Blue* introduces these questions of the re-examination of the human body experientially in an age of virtuality, which is concerned with the apparent dematerialization of experience. Scrutinizing the reception of the blue canvas in more detail, we may argue that it is framed as a film screen, but due to its insistent and suspended immateriality, which lasts for more than an hour, the blue canvas functions as an immersive spatial container, which slowly forces the viewer into a specific interactivity – an immersion of sight and body. The film confirms Druckrey's statement regarding the reception of the cinematic image by the viewer that has not only the effect of navigation by the image, but of a lived moment. The effect of the image is an experience of the encounter not simply with the blue space, but with a person who is dying of AIDS, embodied through his proper experientiality within the blue canvas before us. This question can be re-phrased to ask: How does this specific practice of text/image relate to society? The practical dimension is found in emphasizing the practical impact, which includes, first and foremost, a reinforcement of experience centered in personal subjectivity. There is a demand for a "subjectivity"

Film, erzeugt die Illusion totaler Entkörperlichung und liefert auf paradoxe Weise eine subversive Antwort auf die permanente Produktion von Entkörperlichung durch die neuen Technologien.

Die erzeugte Illusion der Entkörperlichung wirft daher die Frage auf, die ich am Anfang des Essays stellte: „Wie können wir Körper wieder ins Bild setzen?"[35] Eine mögliche Antwort auf der Grundlage von Jarmans Film *Blue* lautet: als juristische Präsenz! Der Körper des mit AIDS infizierten Menschen, ein bereits fast schon verlorenes „Objekt", ist gerade durch seine Absenz geprägt. Andererseits wird im Filmtext, der sehr in die existenziellen, medizinischen und rechtlichen Details des postmodernen Zustands von AIDS geht, die klare Forderung nach juristischer Präsenz und Durchsetzung der Rechte von AIDS-Kranken innerhalb der Machtstrukturen der heutigen Gesellschaft gestellt. Mittels dieses Verhältnisses zwischen der Repräsentationslogik der neuen Technologien/Medien und der Repräsentation von AIDS ist es daher möglich, eine andere Repräsentationslogik von Präsenz/Absenz zu entwickeln als im Falle der Hysterie. Statt physische Präsenz und juristische Absenz, wird physische Absenz und rechtliche Präsenz produziert. Physische Absenz und rechtliche Präsenz, wie dies Jarman vorschlägt, untergraben einerseits die Logik einer massenproduzierten simulierten Präsenz und andererseits die Massen-Blindheit des „natürlichen" menschlichen Auges.

Betrachtet man das binäre Paar Präsenz/Absenz in Zusammenhang mit dem Film *Blue* und den neuen Medien/virtuellen Umgebungen, könnte man behaupten, das gemeinsame Merkmal der entstehenden Technologien und der virtuellen Umgebungen bestehe in der Beseitigung der Dauer – in dem Einstürzen der Zeit in die Echtzeit. In *Blue* dienen diese Merkmale als Erinnerung an die Dimension von Zeit, die von Echtzeittechnologien umstellt ist, wie Paul Virilio behauptet: „Sie töten die ‚gegenwärtige' Zeit, indem sie ihre Präsenz im Hier und Jetzt isolieren zu Gunsten eines anderen kommutativen Raums, der nicht mehr aus unserer ‚konkreten Anwesenheit' in der Welt besteht, sondern aus einer ‚diskreten

which perceives the contradictions within the social body because this subjectivity explores its own desires and drives.[41]

The implications of this shift to the experiential from the perceptual reception of the image may be drawn from Gianni Vattimo's juxtapositioning of Walter Benjamin and Martin Heidegger. Vattimo tried to explain the essence of Benjamin's essay *The Work of Art in the Age of Mechanical Reproduction* (1936) through Heidegger's *The Origin of the Work of Art* (1936), emphasizing that both accentuate the disorientation in contemporary perceptions of art as the direct result of contemporary art works. For Heidegger, as well as for Benjamin, the essence of technology is the manipulation of all things. Technology expresses simultaneously the completion and the end of metaphysics. Benjamin as seen through Heidegger, and Heidegger interpreted via Benjamin, offer new aesthetic concepts that can and will take on the challenges of a postmodern society, which is a society of mass media conglomeration. Benjamin purportedly links the experience of art within the media society, with the experience of a "shock," while Heidegger makes use of the term "Stoß" (translated as "blow"). "Shock" and "Stoß" mirror the urbanites' nervous and intellectual fluctuations, inconstancies and hypersensitivity. Vattimo argues that in aesthetics, a shift from the focus on work to a focus on experience must occur.[42] This is just what we witness in the film *Blue*. Jarman's dismantling of the image, resulting in its zero point, causes an overlapping of the experience of a person with AIDS with the viewer's experience of immersion in the blue canvas.

The Semiotic Square and AIDS

In this final section I am using the semiotic square, as it was re-developed and re-designed by N. Katherine Hayles and Donna Haraway in the 1990s to re-examine the implications inherent in the selected binary pairs, and to make explicit the hidden terms that help to stabilize meaning and generate significance in the their backgrounds.

Telepräsenz', deren Enigma ewig intakt bleibt."[36]

Die erfahrungsbasierte Rezeption des Bildes

Wenn ein „abgegrenztes Bild aus der Entfernung betrachtet wird [...] existiert es für sich und bietet eine Wahrnehmungserfahrung. Doch Bilder, die auf irgendeine Art den Betrachter einbeziehen, wie dies bei interaktiven oder immersiven Medien der Fall ist, sind unbegrenzt. Sie benötigen erfahrungsbasierte Wahrnehmung. Dies versetzt den kritischen Betrachter in eine unhaltbare Position: Er muss das Bild assimilieren, um es zu verstehen, doch er muss es auseinander nehmen, um darüber reflektieren zu können."[37] Für Timothy Druckrey sind die diskursiven Operationen von Informationssystemen im ausgehenden 20. Jahrhundert, wie sie durch Cyberspace angeboten werden, dadurch bestimmt, dass sie über Identitäts- und Sinnformationen hinausgehen, um einen Katalysator für Vermittlung und daher für Ermächtigung zu bieten. Das kreative Potenzial der verschiedenen visuellen Systeme wird durch eine Schnittstelle oder durch „Verbindungen"[38] repräsentiert. Bedeutung und Phänomenologie, Repräsentation und Wahrnehmung fallen zusammen. Der Augenblick, in dem ein Bild innerhalb eines solchen Systems gelesen wird, wirkt „nicht wie eine Navigation des Bildes, sondern wie ein gelebter Augenblick, so dass die Wirksamkeit eines Bildes seinem Erleben gleichkommt."[39] Es ist daher der gelebte Moment des Verbundenseins, der voller Möglichkeiten steckt. „Es ist die Leidenschaft dieses gelebten Moments der Verbindung zwischen dem Benutzer, als Teil der realen Welt, und dem kontrollierten System vorhersehbarer Resultate, das in der Software des Symbolischen kodiert ist und auf das durch die Hardware zugegriffen wird, die einen Spielraum für störendes nihilistisches Verhalten bietet."[40] Im Zeitalter der Virtualität, die mit der scheinbaren Entmaterialisierung der Erfahrung zu tun hat, adressiert der Film *Blue* diese Fragen der Neuuntersuchung einer erfahrungsbasierten Gegebenheit des menschlichen Körpers auf experimentelle Weise. Wirft man einen genaueren Blick auf die Rezeption der blauen Leinwand, können wir behaupten, dass sie als Filmleinwand gerahmt ist, doch aufgrund ihrer beharrlichen und in der

The semiotic square is a technique of discursive analysis, which begins with the choice of a binary pair.[43] Presence and absence can form a pair, and the primary duality of such a square. The duality of presence and absence in the semiotic square signifies concepts in dynamic interplay with each other, rather than as independently existing terms. The purpose of choosing the second duality is to detect the implications contained in the first pair. Since my interest lies in representations of the body in relation to presence/absence within the juridical terrain, I will choose hysteria (physical presence, juridical absence) as the third term. The fourth term is generated by taking the negative of hysteria: AIDS (physical absence, juridical presence).

Since the interplay between presence and absence generates a specific material inscription in the social-political context (through the juridical system and other apparatus connected with law), the axis connecting these terms should be named as the juridical (material) inscription:

juridical (material) inscription

Presence ⟷ Absence

The interplay between hysteria and AIDS generates different representational inscriptions; the axis connecting these terms should be named as representational regimes:

representational regimes

AIDS ⟷ Hysteria

Now that both sets of duality are in place, the semiotic square can be used to investigate the implications of the shift from the real effect of documentary photography to the impact of the virtuality of new media technologies toward different systems of representation, in particular, a shift toward different ways of inscribing the body within the visible and the political context. These implications are made explicit by considering the relationships that connect different terms.

Schwebe gehaltenen Immaterialität, die über eine Stunde währt, funktioniert die blaue Leinwand als ein immersiver räumlicher Behälter, der die Betrachter allmählich in eine bestimmte Interaktivität zwingt – ein Versunkensein des Blicks und des Körpers. Der Film bestätigt Druckreys Aussage zur Rezeption des kinematischen Bildes durch den Betrachter, das nicht nur den Effekt der Navigation durch das Bild, sondern einen gelebten Augenblick erzeugt. Die Wirkung des Bildes besteht in dem Erlebnis der Begegnung, nicht nur mit dem blauen Raum, sondern mit einer Person, die an AIDS stirbt, verkörpert durch ihre eigentliche Erfahrungsbasiertheit innerhalb der blauen Leinwand vor uns. Man kann die Frage anders stellen: Wie verhält sich die spezifische Praxis des Textes/Bildes zur Gesellschaft? Die praktische Dimension besteht in der Betonung der praktischen Wirkung, die in erster Linie die Verstärkung eines auf persönliche Subjektivität zentrierten Erlebens beinhaltet. Es gibt die Forderung nach einer „Subjektivität", die die Widersprüche innerhalb des gesellschaftlichen Körpers wahrnimmt, weil diese Subjektivität ihre eigenen Wünsche und Triebe erforscht.[41]

Die Implikationen dieser Verschiebung von der wahrnehmungsorientierten hin zur erfahrungsbasierten Rezeption des Bildes können aus der Gegenüberstellung von Walter Benjamin und Martin Heidegger, wie sie Gianni Vattimo vornahm, gezogen werden. Vattimo versuchte das Wesentliche in Benjamins Essay *Das Kunstwerk im Zeitalter seiner technischen Reproduzierbarkeit* (1936) mit Hilfe von Heideggers *Der Ursprung des Kunstwerks* (1936) zu erklären. Dabei hob er hervor, dass beide die Desorientierung in der zeitgenössischen Wahrnehmung von Kunst als direktes Resultat der zeitgenössischen Kunstwerke selbst betonten. Für Heidegger wie für Benjamin besteht das Wesen der Technik in der Manipulation aller Dinge. Die Technik drückt zugleich die Vollendung und das Ende der Metaphysik aus. Benjamin durch Heidegger zu betrachten und Heidegger durch Benjamin zu interpretieren, bietet neue ästhetische Begriffe, die die Herausforderungen einer postmodernen Gesellschaft annehmen kann und wird, einer Gesellschaft massenmedialer

juridical (material) inscription

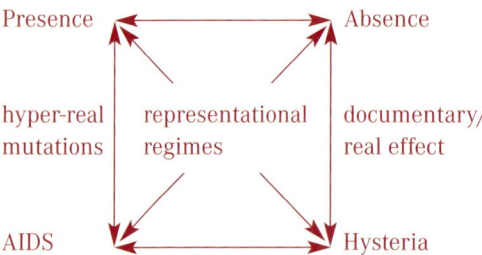

The diagonal connecting presence with hysteria can be labeled "replication."[44] Where presence and hysteria coincide, object and form are united without dissonance or separation. This is the realm of mimesis, ruled by common sense assumptions about objects that retain their form. The diagonal connecting absence and AIDS can be labelled "disruption."[45] Just as absence disrupts the abundance of presence, AIDS disrupts the mimesis effect that has, until now, been sufficient to anchor the disease within the social field, making it visible, but not going much further than that. The vertical axis connecting absence and hysteria alludes to the "real" effect of documentary photography. We can label the vertical axis connecting presence and AIDS (as a result of the interplay between the axes of juridical material inscriptions with representational regimes) hyper-real mutations. When AIDS becomes physically manifested in an image, it "disappears"; the image is disembodied. AIDS is thus capable of disrupting the established and accepted conformity of the photographic documentary effect of hysteria at any moment.

The four nodes of the semiotic square, according to Hayles, recall the four quadrants of a Cartesian graph, which helps to explain why the positive term of the second pair, hysteria, is placed on the lower right, rather than lower left.[46] In Cartesian grids, the lower right quadrant represents a positive x-value combined with the negative y-value.

We should recall that hysteria is generated by the absence of the positive first term: presence. The fourth term, AIDS, is produced by the nega-

Konglomeration. Benjamin verbindet angeblich das Kunsterlebnis in der Mediengesellschaft mit der Erfahrung des „Schocks", während Heidegger den Begriff „Stoß" verwendet. „Schock" und „Stoß" spiegeln die nervliche und geistige Mobilität, die Erregbarkeit und Hypersensibilität der Städtebewohner wider. Vattimo sagt, dass in der Ästhetik die Aufmerksamkeit vom Werk auf die Erfahrung verschoben werden muss.[42] Genau dies geschieht in *Blue*. Jarman zerlegt das Bild, führt es auf seinen Nullpunkt zurück und erzeugt die Überschneidung der Erfahrung einer AIDS-kranken Person mit der Erfahrung des Zuschauers, in die blaue Leinwand einzutauchen.

Das semiotische Quadrat und AIDS

In diesem letzten Abschnitt verwende ich das semiotische Quadrat, das in den 90ern von Katherine Hayles und Donna Haraway neu entwickelt und entworfen wurde, um die inhärenten Implikationen der gewählten Paare neu zu untersuchen und die versteckten Begriffe, die im Hintergrund dazu beitragen, Bedeutung zu stabilisieren und Signifikanz zu generieren, explizit zu machen.

Das semiotische Quadrat ist eine diskursanalytische Technik, die mit der Wahl eines binären Paares beginnt.[43] Präsenz und Absenz können das Paar und die primäre Dualität eines solchen Quadrats bilden. Die Dualität von Präsenz und Absenz im semiotischen Quadrat bezeichnet Begriffe, die in einem dynamischen Wechselspiel stehen, und nicht unabhängig voneinander existierende Ausdrücke sind. Die zweite Dualität wurde gewählt, um die Implikationen des ersten Paares festzustellen. Da mein Interesse in den Repräsentationen des Körpers im Verhältnis zu Präsenz/Absenz innerhalb des juristischen Feldes besteht, wähle ich die Hysterie (physische Präsenz, juristische Absenz) als dritten Terminus. Der vierte wird durch die Negation der Hysterie erzeugt: AIDS (physische Absenz, juristische Präsenz).

Da das Wechselspiel zwischen Präsenz und Absenz eine spezifische materielle Einschreibung in den sozialpolitischen Kontext generiert (durch das Rechtssystem und andere mit dem Gesetz

tive of the third term, hysteria, which is already marked by negativity. "Thus the fourth term represents a negation of negation. Because of this double negation, it is the least explicitly specified of all the four terms and therefore the most productive of new complications and insights."[47] It is from the double (elusive) negativity of the fourth term that the 'new' is likely to emerge. For the fourth term carries within it the most open and critical potentiality.[48]

The same semiotic square was used by Donna Haraway to travel to Virtual Space: "To get through the artifactual to elsewhere, it would help to have a little travel machine that also functions as a map." (A. J. Greimas' "infamous" [Haraway's term] semiotic square.)[49] The semiotic square, as Haraway stated, so subtle in the hands of Frederic Jameson, was used in a more rigid and literal way in her essay: to keep four spaces in differential and relational separation, while she explored how certain local/global struggles for meanings and embodiments of nature occur within them. The four regions through which Haraway moved were: Real Space or Earth; Outer Space or the Extraterrestrial; Inner Space or the Body; and finally, Virtual Space or the SF world. Virtual Space takes the same position as AIDS in my semiotic square.

Donna Haraway's semiotic square of Virtual Space from *The Promises of Monsters*:

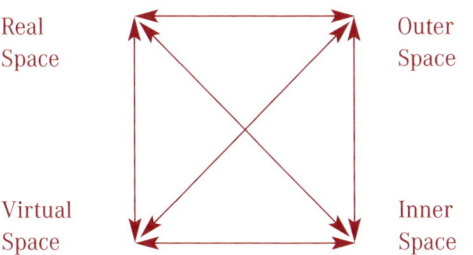

What can we learn from such an application of the semiotic square? It schematically demonstrates possible relations that can emerge when the juridical realm and representational influence each other, thus providing a theoretical framework in which such apparently diverse

verbundenen Apparate), sollte die Achse, die diese Termini verbindet, juristisch-materielle Einschreibung genannt werden:

Juristisch-materielle Einschreibung

Präsenz ←——→ Absenz

Das Wechselspiel von Hysterie und AIDS generiert unterschiedliche repräsentative Einschreibungen; die Achse, die beide Termini verbindet, soll Repräsentationsregime genannt werden:

Repräsentationsregime

AIDS ←——→ Hysterie

Nun, da beide Dualitäten gesetzt sind, kann das semiotische Quadrat verwendet werden, um die Implikationen der Verschiebung von dem realen Effekt der dokumentarischen Fotografie hin zur Auswirkung der Virtualität der neuen Medientechnologien auf die unterschiedlichen Repräsentationssysteme zu untersuchen, insbesondere die Verschiebung zu unterschiedlichen Arten, den Körper in den sichtbaren und politischen Kontext einzuschreiben.

Diese Implikationen werden durch die Berücksichtigung der Beziehungen, die die verschiedenen Termini verbinden, explizit gemacht.

Juristisch-materielle Einschreibung
Präsenz ←——————→ Absenz

| hyper– reale Mutationen | Repräsentations- regimes | dokumenta- rischer/realer Effekt |

AIDS ←——————→ Hysterie

Die Diagonale, die die Präsenz mit der Hysterie verbindet, kann als „Replikation"[44] bezeichnet werden. Dort wo Präsenz und Hysterie zusammenfallen, werden das Objekt und die Form ohne

ideas can be understood as different manifestations of the same underlying phenomena. The devastating effects that this interplay between AIDS and presence within the realm of representation can have on traditional concepts of identity appear in different modes. One mode shows that the physical durability of the body is just an illusion. On the one hand, the specific institution of the subject within the visible established in hysteria was possible (or at least was the result of a specific ideological mechanism of the optical "truth," which is intrinsic to the photographic apparatus). On the other hand, this same apparatus reinforced the position of the juridical absence of the hysterical person. The disruption of the visibility of hysteria by AIDS is therefore as inevitable as, at present, in most cases, the linkage of AIDS with death.

No person in the film *Blue*, including the narrator, is seen on screen. As viewers, we are eavesdroppers in a one-sided conversation from places and people totally outside the depicted fictitious space of the film – a space that is both familiar and alien to that occupied by the audience. The viewer's initial *jouissance*, or sense of wholeness, is disrupted when it becomes evident that the camera, not the viewer, controls the gaze. In *Blue*, this occurs from the very first moment. Throughout the film, we await the point of subversion, for the unmasking by the camera – but only the color blue remains. Thus, the highlighting of the information which the camera controls causes intense displeasure for the viewer. The narrative authority, often signified by the soundtrack of a voiceover, is displaced from its naturalized associations to the "Other" by a radical dispersion of narrative space. This radical decentralization of the narrative space is produced by the absence of a visible physical presence. In a traditional narrative form, the speaker would most likely be shown. The film forces the viewer to ask "who is speaking?" and to dismantle traditional hegemonic narrative structures. The speaker, whom the film is about, does not emerge as a subject, but is referred to indirectly, and is therefore present by his absence, existing as a void in the text. Maybe this alternating iden-

Dissonanz oder Trennung vereint. Dies ist der Bereich der Mimesis, der durch die Annahmen des gesunden Menschenverstands bezüglich der Dinge, die ihre Form behalten, beherrscht wird. Die Diagonale, die Absenz und AIDS verbindet, kann als „Entzweiung"[45] bezeichnet werden. So wie die Absenz die Fülle der Anwesenheit stört, stört AIDS den Effekt der Mimesis, der bis jetzt ausreichte, die Krankheit innerhalb des gesellschaftlichen Feldes zu verankern, sie sichtbar zu machen – mehr aber nicht. Die vertikale Achse, die Absenz und Hysterie verbindet, spielt auf die „reale" Wirkung der dokumentarischen Fotografie an. Wir können die vertikale Achse, die Präsenz und AIDS (als Resultat des Zusammenspiels der Achsen der juristischen materiellen Einschreibungen mit den Repräsentationsregimes) als hyperreale Mutationen bezeichnen. Wenn AIDS sich physisch in einem Bild manifestiert, „verschwindet" es; das Bild wird entkörperlicht. AIDS kann aus diesem Grund die etablierte und akzeptierte Konformität des dokumentarischen fotografischen Effekts der Hysterie zu jeder Zeit stören.

Die vier Knoten des semiotischen Quadrats erinnern laut Hayles an die vier Quadranten des kartesischen Diagramms, das erklärt, warum der positive Terminus des zweiten Paars, die Hysterie, unten rechts platziert ist, statt unten links.[46] In den kartesischen Rastern steht der untere rechte Quadrant für einen positiven X-Wert in Verbindung mit einem negativen Y-Wert.

Wir sollten uns daran erinnern, dass die Hysterie durch die Absenz des ersten positiven Terminus, Präsenz, hervorgerufen wird. Der vierte Terminus, AIDS, wird durch das Negativ des dritten Terminus, Hysterie, die bereits durch Negativität markiert ist, produziert. „Daher steht der vierte Terminus für eine Negation der Negation. Aufgrund dieser doppelten Negation ist er von allen vier Termini der am wenigsten spezifizierte und daher der produktivste in Hinblick auf neue Komplexitäten und Einsichten."[47] Aus der doppelten (schwer fassbaren) Negativität könnte am ehesten das „Neue" entstehen. Denn der vierte Terminus birgt die offensten und kritischsten Möglichkeiten in sich.[48]

tification is what Jarman was implying with *Blue's* extreme immersion into discursivity, which allows people afflicted with AIDS not only to be represented differently, but also to be the ones who will participate in the production and articulation of new meanings concerning their own condition.

The author would like to thank Prof. Dr. Rado Riha, Ljubljana, for his generous and dedicated work and corrections while checking the translation of this text into German.

This text originally was published in *Filozofski vestnik, Acta Philosophica*. Marina Grzinic, "Hysteria: Physical presence and juridical absence & AIDS: Physical absence and juridical presence," *Filozofski vestnik, Acta Philosophica 2* (1996), English edition, p. 44–63.

---

1 See Abigail Solomon-Godeau, "Who is Speaking Thus? Some Questions about Documentary Photography," *The Event Horizon*, Lorne Falk and Barbara Fischer (eds.), Toronto 1987, p. 195–196.
2 This term was suggested by Abigail Solomon-Godeau in reference to Victor Burgin's essays "Looking at Photographs" (1977) and "Photography, Phantasy and Function" (1980). See Solomon-Godeau, ibid., p. 197.
3 Ibid., p. 199.
4 Toril Moi, ed., *The Kristeva Reader*, Oxford 1986, p. 25. For a helpful account of Kristeva's general approach to semiotic issues, see Heinz Paetzold, *The Discourse of the Postmodern and the Discourse of the Avant-Garde*, Maastricht 1994, p. 58–70.
5 Ibid., p. 58, and Julia Kristeva, *Pouvoirs de l'horreur. Essai sur l'abjection*, Paris 1980.
6 Toril Moi, *The Kristeva Reader*, p. 32.
7 See Luce Iragaray, *This Sex Which is Not One*, Ithaca 1985.
8 See N. Katherine Hayles, "Embodied Virtuality: Or How to Put Bodies Back into the Picture," *Immersed in Technology: Art and Virtual Environments*, Mary Anne Moser and Douglas MacLeod (eds.), Cambridge, Massachusetts/London 1996, p. 4.
9 See Norman Bryson, *Vision and Painting: The Logic of the Gaze*, London/New Haven 1983, p. 145.
10 See Jo Anna Isaak, "Mapping the Imaginary," *The Event Horizon*, Lorne Falk and Barbara Fischer (eds.), Toronto 1987, p. 137. In this first section of my essay, I am following and reconsidering Isaak's thesis regarding hysteria and representation from her essay, "Mapping the Imaginary."
11 Ibid., p. 137–138.
12 Ibid., p. 139.
13 See Joan Copjec, "Flavit et Dissipati Sunt," *October* 18 (1981), p. 23.
14 See Jo Anna Isaak, "Mapping the Imaginary," p. 142.
15 See Louise Gardner, *Art Through the Ages*, New York 1980, p. 737.
16 See Jo Anna Isaak, "Mapping the Imaginary."
17 Ibid., p. 139.
18 See Samuel Edgerton, "The Renaissance Artist as Quantifier," *The Perception of Pictures*, vol. I, Margaret A. Hagen (ed.), New York 1980, p. 182.
19 The text in the film is about AIDS, about dying from AIDS, and the inner feelings of a sick person who knows exactly that his/her end is near. Jarman develops a strong critique about the hospitalization process of a person suffering from AIDS, about the quantity

---

Dasselbe semiotische Quadrat benutzte Donna Haraway, um in den virtuellen Raum zu reisen: „Um durch das Artefaktuelle zu einem Anderswo zu gelangen, wäre es hilfreich eine kleine Reisemaschine zu haben, die auch als Landkarte funktioniert." (A. J. Greimas' „berüchtigtes" (so Haraway) semiotisches Quadrat.⁴⁹) Das, laut Haraway, so feinfühlig von Frederic Jameson verwendete semiotische Quadrat benutzte sie in ihrem Essay in einer strengeren und wörtlicheren Form: um vier Räume zu unterscheiden und in Beziehung zueinander zu halten, während sie untersuchte, wie darin gewisse lokale/globale Kämpfe um die Bedeutungen und Verkörperungen von Natur stattfinden. Haraway bewegte sich durch vier Regionen: den realen Raum oder die Erde; den Weltraum oder das Außerirdische; den inneren Raum oder den Körper; und schließlich den virtuellen Raum oder die Welt der Science-Fiction. In meinem semiotischen Quadrat besetzt AIDS dieselbe Position wie der virtuelle Raum.

Donna Haraways semiotisches Quadrat des virtuellen Raums aus *The Promises of Monsters*:

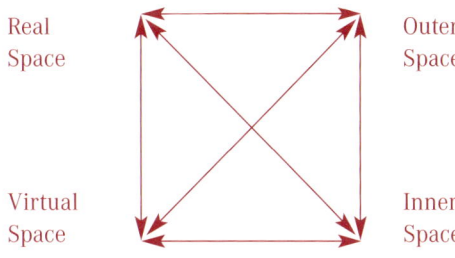

Was können wir von einer derartigen Anwendung des semiotischen Quadrats lernen? Es demonstriert auf schematische Weise mögliche Beziehungen, die entstehen können, wenn die juristische Sphäre und Repräsentation sich gegenseitig beeinflussen. Es wird so ein theoretischer Rahmen geliefert, in dem anscheinend unterschiedliche Ideen als verschiedene Erscheinungen derselben zugrunde liegenden Phänomene verstanden werden können. Die verheerenden Auswirkungen, die dieses Wechselspiel zwischen AIDS und Präsenz innerhalb der Sphäre der Repräsentation auf traditionelle Vorstellungen von Identität haben kön-

of drugs needed to slow down not the disease, but the process of dying, and, last but not least, about the whole social system (medical, social, and legal), which is unfavorable to persons affected by AIDS. Jarman meticulously describes the whole personal drama of a sick person, especially the loss of vision and of becoming blind: "My retina is a distant planet. I played this scenario for the last six years [...] My vision will never come back [...] The virus rages, I have no friends now. I lost the sight [...] I shall not win the battle with the virus [...]". Citation from the film *Blue*.

20 Jarman: "I am helpless. I can't see him. Just the sound. In the pandemonium of the image I present you the universe of blue." Citation from the film *Blue*.

21 Andrew Beckett (actor Tom Hanks) is a young lawyer with a splendid career before him, who is suddenly found incompetent by the law firm for which he works. Beckett knows that the real reason is that he is gay and has AIDS. Beckett decides to fight and defend his professional reputation, and through this act, the rights of other gay people with AIDS. Joe Miller (actor Denzel Washington), a black lawyer of high reputation, at first decides not to take the case because of his personal prejudices against people who are gay and has AIDS, but finally accepts the case. One of the most striking conclusions of the trial, resulting from Miller's way of conducting the affair in court, is that gay people and AIDS are submitted to a double process of injustice, and that the fight for juridical rights in the case of gay people with AIDS is, more generally speaking, also a fight for gay rights against society's strong prejudices. Joe Miller: "People with AIDS are submitted to social death which precedes the physical death [...] What is it all about? [...] About our fears of homosexuals." The judge: "Mr. Miller, justice is blind regarding race and sex in this courtroom!" Miller: "But your Honor, we are not living in this courtroom." Citation from the film *Philadelphia*. This specific situation recalls that modernity as a cultural and social project brought about the distinction between law and morality. It makes sense to measure the legal and political acts of the state against the criteria of morality, but it is not possible to conflate them into one sphere.

22 See Abigail Solomon-Godeau, "Who is Speaking Thus?" p. 201.
23 Ibid., p. 208–209.
24 Ibid., p. 209.
25 Ibid.
26 Jean-Louis Baudry, "Ideological Effects of the Basic Cinematographic Apparatus," *Apparatus*, Theresa Hak Kyung Cha (ed.), New York 1980, p. 26.
27 Cited in Rosalind Krauss, "A note on Photography and the Simulacra," *October* 31 (1984), p. 57.
28 See Sally Stein, "Making Connections With The Camera: Photography and Social Mobility in the Career of Jacob Riis," *Afterimage*, 10:10 (1983), p. 14.
29 See Heinz Paetzold. "Definitions of the Postmodern Status of Knowledge," *The Discourse of the Postmodern and the Discourse of the Avant-Garde*, Paetzold (ed.), Maastricht 1994, p. 14–21.
30 Ibid., p. 16.
31 See Jean-François Lyotard, *The Postmodern Condition: A Report on Knowledge*, Minneapolis 1984, p. 42–52.
32 Paul Virilio, *Vision Machine*, London/Bloomington, Indiana 1994, p. 7.
33 Heinz Paetzold, "Definitions of the Postmodern Status of Knowledge," p. 15.
34 See Paul Virilio, *Vision Machine*, p. 43–44.
35 See N. Katherine Hayles, "Embodied Virtuality," p. 4.
36 Paul Virilio, "The Third Interval: A Critical Transition," *Re-thinking Technologies*, Verena Andermatt Conley (ed.), Minneapolis 1993, p. 4.

nen, erscheinen in unterschiedlichen Formen. Eine Form zeigt, dass die bloß physische Erhaltung des Körpers in der Zeit uns eine politische Illusion ist. Einerseits war die spezifische Einführung des Subjekts in das Sichtbare, die bei der Hysterie stattfand, das Resultat eines spezifischen ideologischen Mechanismus der optischen „Wahrheit", die dem fotografischen Apparat innewohnt. Andererseits stärkte derselbe Apparat die Position der juristischen Absenz der hysterischen Person. Die Unterbrechung der Sichtbarkeit der Hysterie durch AIDS ist daher so unausweichlich wie zurzeit in den meisten Fällen die Verbindung zwischen AIDS und Tod.

In *Blue* ist keine Person, auch nicht der Erzähler, auf der Leinwand zu sehen. Als Zuschauer lauschen wir einem Monolog, der von Orten und Menschen handelt, die sich gänzlich außerhalb des abgebildeten fiktiven Raums des Films befinden – in einem Raum, der dem Publikum sowohl vertraut als auch fremd ist. Die anfängliche *jouissance* der Zuschauer, ihr Gefühl der Ganzheit, wird in dem Moment gestört, in dem klar wird, dass die Kamera – nicht der Zuschauer – den Blick kontrolliert. In *Blue* geschieht dies gleich zu Beginn. Während des gesamten Films warten wir auf den Moment der Subversion, auf die Entlarvung durch die Kamera – doch es bleibt nur die Farbe Blau. Daher verursacht die Betonung der Information, die die Kamera kontrolliert, ein intensives Unbehagen beim Zuschauer. Die narrative Autorität, die häufig durch eine Off-Stimme gekennzeichnet ist, wird von ihren naturalisierten Assoziationen hin zum „Anderen" durch eine radikale Auflösung des narrativen Raums verschoben. Diese radikale Dezentrierung des narrativen Raums wird durch die Absenz einer sichtbaren physischen Präsenz erzeugt. In einer traditionellen narrativen Form würde man den Sprecher wahrscheinlich sehen. Der Film zwingt den Zuschauer, sich zu fragen: „Wer spricht?" und die traditionellen hegemonialen narrativen Strukturen zu demontieren. Der Sprecher, von dem der Film handelt, taucht nicht als Subjekt auf. Indirekt wird ein Bezug zu ihm hergestellt, und er ist daher durch seine Absenz präsent – er existiert als eine Leerstelle im Text. Vielleicht war es diese

37 Timothy Druckrey, "The Transient Image," A Symposium on the Changing Status of the Image, Banff, Canada, November 4 and 5, 1994. Quoted in Mary Anne Moser, "Introduction," *Immersed in Technology: Art and Virtual Environments*, Cambridge and London 1996, p. XVIII.
38 I am referring here to Helen Cadwallader's report and evaluation of the presentation of Timothy Druckrey's paper "Crash, Crisis, Containment and Cyberia," given at the 5th International Conference on Cyberspace, Cyberconf, Madrid, June 1996. In Helen Cadwallader, "5th International Conference on Cyberspace," *Mute* 6 (1996), p. 4.
39 Ibid.
40 Ibid.
41 See Heinz Paetzold, "Definitions of the Postmodern Status of Knowledge," p. 63.
42 See Gianni Vattimo, *The Transparent Society*, Cambridge/Oxford 1992, p. 58. For a helpful account of this, see Paetzold, "Vattimo and the 'Weak' Being," in Paetzold, "Definitions of the Postmodern Status of Knowledge," p. 44–45.
43 I am, to a large extent, relying on the application of A. J. Greimas' semiotic square, developed by N. Katherine Hayles. See N. Katherine Hayles, "Embodied Virtuality," p. 7–10.
44 Ibid., p. 9.
45 Ibid.
46 Ibid., p. 10. Numerous commentators, including Fredric Jameson and Shoshana Felman, have pointed this out.
47 Ibid.
48 Ibid.
49 See Donna Haraway, "The Promises of Monsters: A Regenerative Politics for Inappropriate/d Others," *Cultural Studies*, Lawrence Grossberg, Cary Nelson, and Paula A. Treichler (eds.), New York and London 1992, p. 304.

alternierende Identifikation, auf die Jarman hinaus wollte durch das extreme Eintauchen in die Diskursivität in *Blue*, durch die ermöglicht wird, dass AIDS-Kranke nicht nur anders repräsentiert werden, sondern auch diejenigen sind, die an der Produktion und Artikulation neuer Bedeutungen bezüglich ihrer eigenen Lage teilnehmen.

Die Autorin dankt Prof. Dr. Rado Riha, Ljubljana, für sein großzügiges Engagement bei der Prüfung und Korrektur der deutschen Übersetzung dieses Textes.

1 Vgl. Abigail Solomon-Godeau: Who is Speaking Thus? Some Questions about Documentary Photography, in: Lorne Falk und Barbara Fischer (Hg.): *The Event Horizon*, Toronto 1987, S. 195-96.
2 Dieser Begriff wurde von Abigail Solomon-Godeau in Zusammenhang mit Victor Burgins Essays *Looking at Photographs* (1977) und *Photography, Phantasy and Function* (1980) vorgeschlagen. Vgl Abigail Solomon-Godeau, ebd., S. 197.
3 Ebd., S. 199.
4 Toril Moi (Hg.): *The Kristeva Reader*, Oxford 1986, S. 25. Übersetzung K.H. Für eine hilfreiche Darstellung von Kristevas allgemeinem Zugang zu semiotischen Themen vgl. Heinz Paetzold: *The Discourse of the Postmodern and the Discourse of the Avant-Garde*, Maastricht 1994, S. 58–70.
5 Heinz Paetzold: *The Discourse of the Postmodern and the Discourse of the Avant-Garde*, Maastricht 1994, S. 58. Übersetzung K.H. Vgl. auch Julia Kristeva: *Pouvoirs de l'horreur. Essai sur l'abjection*, Paris 1980.
6 Toril Moi, a.a.O., S. 32. Übersetzung K.H.
7 Vgl. Luce Iragaray: *This Sex Which is Not One*, Ithaca 1985.
8 Vgl. N. Katherine Hayles: Embodied Virtuality. Or How to Put Bodies Back into the Picture, in: Mary Anne Moser und Douglas MacLeod (Hg.): *Immersed in Technology. Art and Virtual Environments*, Cambridge, Mass./London 1996, S. 4.
9 Vgl. Norman Bryson: *Das Sehen und die Malerei. Die Logik des Blicks*, München 2001, S. 177.
10 Vgl. Jo Anna Isaak: Mapping the Imaginary, in: Lorne Falk und Barbara Fischer (Hg.): *The Event Horizon*, Toronto 1987, S.137. Im ersten Teil meines Essays beziehe ich mich auf Isaaks Thesen zu Hysterie und Repräsentation in ihrem Essay *Mapping the Imaginary*.
11 Ebd., S. 137–138.
12 Ebd., S.139. Übersetzung K.H.
13 Vgl. Joan Copjec: Flavit et Dissipati Sunt, in: *October* (1981), Nr. 18, S. 23.
14 Vgl. Jo Anna Isaak, a.a.O., S. 142. Übersetzung K.H.
15 Vgl. Louise Gardner: *Art Through the Ages*, New York 1980, S. 737.
16 Vgl. Jo Anna Isaak, a.a.O.
17 Ebd., S. 139.
18 Vgl. Samuel Edgerton: The Renaissance Artist as Quantifier, in: Margaret A. Hagen (Hg.): *The Perception of Pictures*, Vol. I., New York 1980, S. 182.
19 Der Text des Films handelt von AIDS, davon, an AIDS zu sterben und von den inneren Gefühlen eines kranken Menschen, der genau weiß, dass sein Ende naht. Jarman entwickelt eine starke Kritik an dem Prozess der Einlieferung von AIDS-Kranken ins Krankenhaus, der Menge an Medikamenten, die nötig ist, um nicht den Krankheitsverlauf zu verlangsamen, sondern den Prozess des Sterbens,

und schließlich des ganzen gesellschaftlichen Systems (medizinisch, sozial und rechtlich), das Menschen mit AIDS gegenüber negativ eingestellt ist. Jarman beschreibt mit größter Genauigkeit das ganze persönliche Drama eines kranken Menschen, besonders den Verlust des Sehvermögens und das Blindwerden: „Meine Retina ist ein entfernter Planet. Ich spielte dieses Szenario die letzten sechs Jahre durch. [...] Ich werde nie wieder sehen können [...] Der Virus wütet, ich habe keine Freunde mehr. Ich habe das Augenlicht verloren [...] Ich werde den Kampf gegen den Virus nicht gewinnen [...]." Zitat aus dem Film *Blue*. Übersetzung K.H.
20 Jarman: „Ich bin hilflos. Ich kann ihn nicht sehen. Nur das Geräusch. Im Pandämonium des Bildes präsentiere ich Ihnen das Universum des Blaus.". Zitat aus dem Film *Blue*. Übersetzung K.H.
21 Andrew Beckett (gespielt von Tom Hanks) ist ein junger Anwalt, der von der Anwaltskanzlei, für die er arbeitet, plötzlich für inkompetent befunden wird. Beckett weiß, der wahre Grund liegt in seiner Homosexualität und daran, dass er AIDS hat. Er beschließt, zu kämpfen und sein professionelles Ansehen zu verteidigen, und sich damit für die Rechte anderer mit AIDS infizierten Homosexuellen einzusetzen. Joe Miller (gespielt von Denzel Washington), ein hoch angesehener schwarzer Anwalt, will den Fall zunächst aufgrund seiner Vorurteile gegenüber Schwulen und AIDS-Kranken nicht annehmen, entschließt sich dann aber doch dafür. Als Resultat der Art und Weise wie Miller die Sache vor Gericht angeht, ist eine der bemerkenswertesten Schlussfolgerungen des Verfahrens, dass Schwule und AIDS einem doppelten Prozess des Unrechts unterworfen sind und dass der Kampf um juristische Rechte im Falle von Schwulen mit AIDS auch ein Kampf für die Rechte von Schwulen allgemein gegen die starken Vorurteile der Gesellschaft ist. Joe Miller: „Noch vor ihrem körperlichen Tod sind Menschen mit AIDS dem gesellschaftlichen Tod ausgesetzt [...]. Womit hat das alles zu tun? [...] Mit unseren Ängsten vor Homosexuellen." Der Richter: „Mr. Miller, die Gerechtigkeit in diesem Gerichtssaal ist blind gegenüber Rasse und Geschlecht!" Miller: „Aber Euer Ehren, wir leben nicht in diesem Gerichtssaal.". Zitat aus dem Film *Philadelphia*. Übersetzung K.H.
Diese spezifische Situation erinnert daran, dass die Moderne als kulturelles und soziales Projekt die Unterscheidung zwischen Gesetz und Moral hervorbrachte. Es ist sinnvoll, die rechtlichen und politischen Handlungen eines Staates mit moralischen Kriterien zu messen, doch es ist nicht möglich sie in einer Sphäre zusammenzufassen.
22 Vgl. Abigail Solomon-Godeau, a.a.O., S. 201.
23 Ebd., S. 208–209.
24 Ebd., S. 209. Übersetzung K.H.
25 Ebd.
26 Jean-Louis Baudry: Ideological Effects of the Basic Cinematographic Apparatus, in: Theresa Hak Kyung Cha (Hg.): *Apparatus*, New York 1980, S. 26. Übersetzung K.H.
27 Pierre Bourdieu: Die Gesellschaftliche Definition der Photographie, in: Ders., Luc Boltanski u.a. (Hg.): *Eine illegitime Kunst. Die soziale Gebrauchsweise der Photographie*, Frankfurt a. M. 1981, S. 89.
28 Vgl. Sally Stein: Making Connections With The Camera. Photography and Social Mobility in the Career of Jacob Riis, in: *Afterimage* Vol. 10 (1983), Nr. 10, S.14.
29 Vgl. Heinz Paetzold: Definitions of the Postmodern Status of Knowledge, in: Heinz Paetzold: *The Discourse of the Postmodern and the Discourse of the Avant-Garde*, Maastricht 1994, S. 14–21.
30 Ebd., S. 16.
31 Vgl. Jean-François Lyotard: *The Postmodern Condition. A Report on Knowledge*, Minneapolis 1984, S. 42–52.
32 Maurice Merleau-Ponty: *Das Auge und der Geist*, Hamburg 1984, S. 16, zitiert in: Paul Virilio: *Die Sehmaschine*, Berlin 1989, S. 26.

33 Heinz Paetzold: The Discourse of the Postmodern and the Discourse of the Avant-Garde, Maastricht 1994, S.15. Übersetzung K.H.
34 Vgl. Paul Virilio: *Die Sehmaschine*, Berlin 1989, S. 128–129.
35 Vgl. Hayles: Embodied Virtuality. Or How to Put Bodies Back into the Picture, in: Moser und MacLeod (Hg.): *Immersed in Technology: Art and Virtual Environments*, Cambridge, Mass./London 1996, S. 4.
36 Paul Virilio: The Third Interval. A Critical Transition, in: Verena Andermatt Conley (Hg.): *Re-thinking Technologies*, Minneapolis 1993, S. 4. Übersetzung K.H.
37 Timothy Druckrey: The Transient Image, in: *A Symposium on the Changing Status of the Image*, Banff, Kanada, 4. und 5. November 1994, zitiert in: Mary Anne Moser: Einleitung, in: Dies. (Hg.): *Immersed in Technology. Art and Virtual Environments*, Cambridge/London 1996, S. XVIII. Übersetzung K.H.
38 Ich beziehe mich hier auf Helen Cadwalladers Bericht über und die Bewertung von Timothy Druckreys Referat *Crash, Crisis, Containment and Cyberia*, das sie auf der *5th International Conference on Cyberspace, Cyberconf* in Madrid im Juni 1996 gehalten hat. Zitiert in: Helen Cadwallader: 5th International Conference on Cyberspace, in: *Mute* (1996), Nr. 6, S. 4.
39 Ebd. Übersetzung K.H.
40 Ebd. Übersetzung K.H.
41 Vgl. Heinz Paetzold, a.a.O., S. 63.
42 Vgl. Gianni Vattimo: *Die transparente Gesellschaft*, Wien 1992, S. 81. Für eine nützliche Darstellung siehe Paetzold: Vattimo and the ‚Weak' Being, in: Paetzold, a.a.O., S. 44–45.
43 Ich verlasse mich zu einem großen Teil auf die Anwendung des semiotischen Quadrats, wie sie von N. Katherine Hayles entwickelt wurde. Vgl. N. Katherine Hayles: Embodied Virtuality. Or How to Put Bodies Back into the Picture, in Moser und MacLeod (Hg.): *Immersed in Technology. Art and Virtual Environments*, Cambridge, Mass./ London 1996, S. 7–10.
44 Ebd., S. 9.
45 Ebd.
46 Ebd., S. 10. Zahlreiche Interpreten, darunter Fredric Jameson und Shoshana Felman, haben hierauf hingewiesen.
47 Ebd. Übersetzung K.H.
48 Ebd.
49 Vgl. Donna Haraway: The Promises of Monsters. A Regenerative Politics for Inappropriate/d Others, in: Lawrence Grossberg, Cary Nelson und Paula A. Treichler (Hg.): *Cultural Studies*, New York/London 1992, S. 304. Übersetzung K.H.

Joachim Koester
From the Travel of Jonathan Harker

10 photographs, 2003

The Bargau Valley in Northeastern Transylvania provides the setting for much of Bram Stoker's novel *Dracula* (1897). Here Stoker situated Count Dracula's Castle, Jonathan Harker's wolf-haunted journey through the Borgo Pass, and the last part of the novel concluding with the beheaded Dracula evaporating into dust.
Bram Stoker never visited Transylvania but conducted extensive research in the reading room of the British Museum. Studying travel accounts and books on Transylvanian Folklore, Stoker added excerpts from these to his story, anchoring his imaginary scenes in a geographic region which, at the time, was considered to be one of the "wildest and least known parts of Europe."
In Spring 2003 I was invited to Iasis, Romania, to participate in the exhibition *Prophetic Corners*. Intrigued by the speculative nature of the exhibition's title and

concept — that some places have the power of letting us see into the future — I went to Transylvania and traveled towards the Carpathians from Bistrita, just like Jonathan Harker in Stoker's book.

I was not sure what I was looking for. My attention being equally divided between an interest in this region that had been re-created as a 'landscape of the mind' in countless films and narratives, and the idea of 'prophetic corners' which also implied a mapping of a somewhat invisible territory.

At the outskirts of Bistrita, which Stoker described as covered with "a bewildering mass of fruit blossom," I passed a development of suburban houses. Enormous one-family houses in pastel colors, most of them newly built with the windows covered in black plastic. While the gray high-rises of Bistrita in the horizon

and the absence of people gave a slight edge to the scenery, it also seemed very familiar. The houses looked no different than what I had seen anywhere else, pointing to a future of all encompassing sameness.

The future might also be found in places that have been left alone or forgotten, where everything that lies ahead seems like the past. On the way to the Borgo Pass, I came across ruined projects from the communist era. Discarded among the trees were the concrete remains of washed away roads, light poles and even a three-story housing development looming in disrepair. Half overgrown, it looked like a set from a sci-fi movie, like the obsolete in reverse.

My trip ended at Hotel Castle Dracula, built in 1982, to accommodate a steady stream of vampire aficionados visiting the region, at approximately the place

where Dracula's Castle is located in Stoker's novel. The area was not being haunted by 'the undead' though, but by a series of scandals involving illegal logging with profits benefiting a group of corrupt government officials joining with local entrepreneurs. Everywhere I looked, even on the remotest mountaintops, the landscape showed signs of the logging industry in the form of treeless spots. Spots that did add a post-historic touch to the surroundings, but also pointed to something familiar from the (recent) past and present, the transformation of a landscape by the forces of market economy.

Joachim Koester, 2003

CAC TV — Every Program is a Pilot, Every Program is the Final Episode

Dominyka and Paulina, the hosts of the CAC TV program (the TV program of The Contemporary Art Centre, Vilnius, www.cac.lt/tv), gave an interview to Raimundas Malasauskas:

Raimundas: Do you play computer games?
Dominyka: A lot. Now there is a very popular game called *Sims*. I like games where you live with people, do everything with them, watch that they aren't late to work… Where you can have children, take care of them, etc.
R: So what is your role in these games?
Paulina: Just an author. There is a narrative, there are characters, and you show, what to do.
D: You show an example, a model.
P: No, you do not show any model.
R: But can you be just a normal character? Let's say, if I would like to be a part of *Sims*, and I show up there like a…
P: Like a human?
R: Yes.
P: You are a part of all these characters. Because you make them. Their hair, their faces.
D: You choose the clothes for them. With a computer mouse you can show that, for instance, they should go to a bathroom to wash themselves. On the side you see a diagram of their needs — if they need games, food, sleep, or just to sit down for a while.
P: Yes, I think you named everything.
R: Can the *Sims* revolt against your will?
D: They can show that they refuse to continue looking for a job. In that case, you have to do everything so that their diagram is filled up again well, and they will continue searching for a new job.
P: It does not happen so often that a computer revolts against you, because it is rather perfect — it is a machine. The characters are programmed.
R: Does this mean that they would not do something completely against your will?
P: Yes.

R: Are there many similarities between playing *Sims* and making a TV program? I would imagine, that while making a show you also invite certain characters, make up certain narratives for them, just like in computer games, right?
P: You could say so...

CAC TV: Every program is a pilot. Every program is the final episode.

Log-Line:
An amorphous group of social misfits and cultural outcasts are handed the reigns of a fledgling television program. Not having any experience in making television, they decide to re-invent the medium.

P.S. As the slogan of CAC TV suggests, it is a project based on a continuous reinvention of its format, which means that it always functions as a document of itself instead of something external to it; however, as reality shows, the logic of documentation gets twisted in a manner typical to *Junkspace*: "it cancels distinctions, undermines resolve, confuses intention with realization" (Rem Koolhaas). Stay tuned for more.

er ist eine Maschine. Die Charaktere sind programmiert.
R: Bedeutet das, sie würden nichts tun, was absolut gegen deinen Willen geht?
P: Ja.
R: Gibt es viele Überschneidungen zwischen *Sims* spielen und der Gestaltung eines Fernsehprogramms? Ich könnte mir vorstellen, dass du, wenn du eine Sendung machst, auch bestimmte Charaktere einlädst, ihnen eine gewisse Erzählung vorgibst; eben wie bei einem Computerspiel, oder?
P: Das könnte man so sagen...

CAC TV: Jede Folge ist gleichzeitig Pilotfilm und letzte Episode ein und derselben Serie.

Log-Line:
Einer amorphen Gruppe von AußenseiterInnen und gesellschaftlich Ausgestoßenen wird die Alleinherrschaft über ein Fernsehprogramm übergeben, das noch in den Kinderschuhen steckt. Ohne Erfahrung, wie man ein Fernsehprogramm macht, entscheiden sie, das Medium neu zu erfinden.

P.S. Wie der Slogan von CAC TV andeutet, basiert das Projekt auf der ständigen Neuerfindung seines Formats, was bedeutet, dass es immer als ein Dokument seiner selbst anstelle eines anderen funktioniert. Wie auch immer, die Wirklichkeit zeigt, dass die Logik der Dokumentation sich auf eine Art verdreht, die typisch ist für den *Junkspace*: „it cancels distinctions, undermines resolve, confuses intention with realization" (Rem Koolhaas). Bleiben Sie dran bis zur nächsten Folge.

DENIZ
Track suit trousers by Adidas 200 DKK. Sweat shirt by Benetton bought in Turkey for the equivalent of 80 DKK. White T-shirt 20 DKK. Shoes by Fila 600 DKK. Nylon belt purse, present. Socks by Adidas 30 DKK. Underwear 30 DKK at Føtex.

SHABEER
Track suit trousers by Adidas 200 DKK at Sport Master. Hood sweat shirt 300 DKK at H & M. Black T-shirt with Ice T Syndicate print 150 DKK. Shoes by Reebok 400 DKK. White tennis socks 25 DKK at Daells Varehus. Underwear 20 DKK at H & M. Belt purse 75 DKK at Glostrup Centeret. Golden watch by Rado and silver necklace, both presents. Mobile phone by Nokia (6110), 500 DKK.

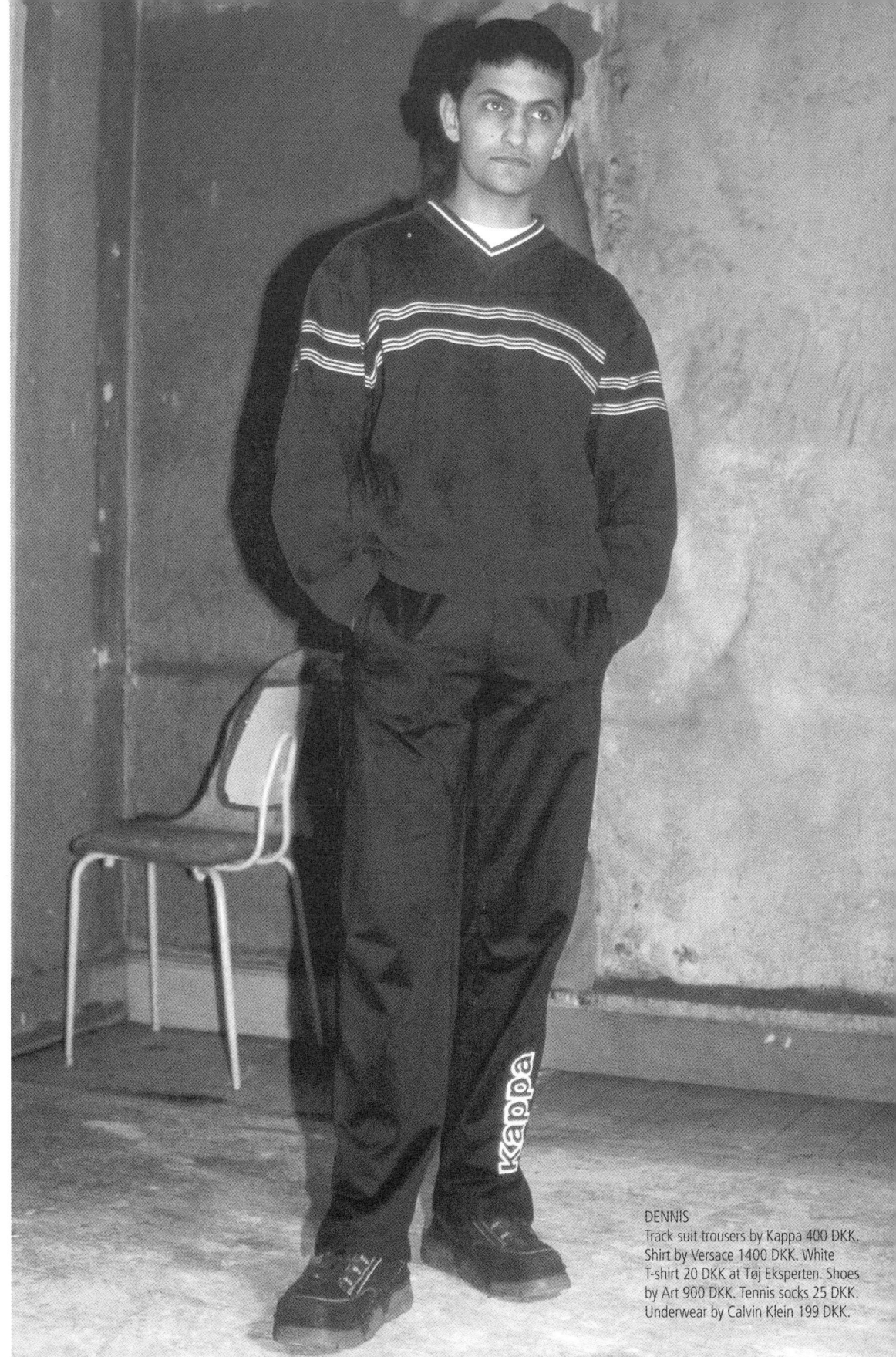

DENNIS
Track suit trousers by Kappa 400 DKK.
Shirt by Versace 1400 DKK. White
T-shirt 20 DKK at Tøj Eksperten. Shoes
by Art 900 DKK. Tennis socks 25 DKK.
Underwear by Calvin Klein 199 DKK.

ANTONIO
Second-hand work trousers by Kansas 35 DKK at Red Cross. Check patterned shirt 49 DKK at Bilka. Shoes by Vagabond 600 DKK at Birk Sko. Woollen socks 40 DKK at Føtex. Underwear by Calvin Klein 250 DKK. Mobile phone by Motorola (CD 930) 500 DKK.

Attila Tordai-S.

Issuing Publications

The fact that art institutions in Romania were reluctant to develop even during the 15 years following the political changes has certainly influenced not only the national art scene but the fate of art in the country as well. At the beginning of the 1990s, when bigger or smaller exhibitions presenting the art in post-communist countries were initiated, a few artists, such as Dan Perjovschi, the subReal group, Alexandru Patatics, and others, were offered the possibility to join these events. They have become key figures of contemporary Romanian art. For all this, no national institutions were needed, the presence of a few mediators sufficed. The Eastern European cultural politics of the Soros Foundation embraced Romania as well, and as happened elsewhere, cultural programs were initiated influencing cultural life to take a certain turn. But support funds in Romania were rather used for exhibitions than for the creation of institutional structures. Money dried up, support withdrew from the country and Romania was left behind with no real institutional network.

In the meantime a new generation grew up, young professionals that did not have the luck to be welcomed with the optimism characteristic of the 1990s, artists that had to assert themselves in a country bereft of galleries and institutions. Nonetheless, the constraint of *self-promotion* and the void created by the lack of institutions have led to the emergence of quite a remarkable artistic practice. The tasks of executing multiplications, issuing publications and documenting the products of the alternative culture that had appeared in the meantime, were parts of a practice that was meant to fill in the lack of state-supported art institutions in Romania during the 1990s.

Lia and Dan Perjovschi in Bucharest were probably the first and most determined to defy the existing institutional framework by opening their own gallery for those interested in alternative culture as well as for young artists on the hunt for information. As early as the dawn of the

Publikationen herausgeben

Die Tatsache, dass sich die Kunstinstitutionen in Rumänien auch in den 15 Jahren nach dem politischen Umbruch schwer taten sich weiterzuentwickeln, hatte sicherlich nicht nur Auswirkungen auf die nationale Kunstszene, sondern auch insgesamt auf das Schicksal der Kunst im Land. Anfang der 90er, als größere und kleinere Ausstellungen die Kunst der postkommunistischen Länder zeigten, erhielten einige Künstler wie Dan Perjovschi, die subReal group oder Alexandru Patatics die Möglichkeit daran teilzunehmen. Sie wurden zu Schlüsselfiguren der zeitgenössischen rumänischen Kunst. Hierzu bedurfte es keiner Unterstützung durch nationale Institutionen – einige wenige VermittlerInnen genügten. Die osteuropäische Kulturpolitik der Soros Foundation wandte sich auch Rumänien zu, und wie anderswo wurden Kulturprogramme ins Leben gerufen, die dazu führten, dass das Kulturleben sich in eine bestimmte Richtung entwickeln konnte. In Rumänien wurden die Fördermittel jedoch für Ausstellungen statt für die Schaffung institutioneller Strukturen verwendet. Die Geldreserven waren bald aufgebraucht, die Förderung zog sich aus dem Land zurück und Rumänien blieb ohne ein wirkliches institutionelles Netzwerk.

Inzwischen wuchs eine neue Generation heran, junge Professionelle, denen es nicht gelang, vom Optimismus der 90er Jahre mitgerissen zu werden. Sie waren KünstlerInnen, die sich in einem Land ohne Galerien und Institutionen durchsetzen mussten. Die Beschränkung auf Selbstvermarktung und die Leere, die durch das Fehlen von Institutionen erzeugt wurde, führten jedoch zur Entstehung einer bemerkenswerten künstlerischen Praxis. Die Praktiken der Vervielfältigung, der Herausgabe von Publikationen und der Dokumentation der Produkte einer alternativen Kultur sollten im Laufe der 90er Jahre das Fehlen staatlich unterstützter Kunstinstitutionen in Rumänien kompensieren.

Lia und Dan Perjovschi aus Bukarest waren vermutlich die Ersten und Entschlossen-

nineties Lia Perjovschi founded the *Contemporary Art Archive*, a collection of publications and reproductions. By the end of the 1990s the *CAA* became a valuable data-base for all alternative art initiatives, a self-supporting archive created outside the network of state funds or self-government support. Besides issuing, based on archive material, publications of cheap design meant to inform about and to classify various tendencies, and thus also managing to create sort of a virtual art scene, the *CAA* presented several exhibitions paired with open discussions or series of lectures. Besides these *CAA* publications, Lia Perjovschi has also managed to issue limited-edition samples of some of the most intriguing materials of her own documentary collection (*Sense, Angels, The Globe*). An exhibition was organized in 2003, centered around the material of *The Globe*, the result of a ten-year collection of artifact symbols of the globe, throwing some light on the genuine value of the ever-growing archive founded by Lia Perjovschi. Beginning in the year 2003, the *CAA* has modified its function and is currently operating under the title of *Center For Art Analysis*. The latest publication of the Center was issued for the sixth Periferic Biennial in Iasi, and it contains a series of interviews taken from various intellectuals on the topic of how they contrive their everyday life, how they relate to the contexts they live in, and their ideas on how the future will appear to them, the publication managing thus to reflect the current state of spiritual life in Romania.[1]

Ioan Godeanu, also of Bucharest, finds himself in a slightly different situation, insofar as he figures as a multi-member institution despite the fact that he does everything by himself. The artist has founded *The Institute of Construction and Deconstruction* in 1998 with a program of "creating corporate identities that express basic individual aspirations." The Institute reports on its own activity in the *Official Bulletin*. The language of this publication draws on illegal or partly formal institutional discourses and manages to assume the most competent variants for all matters concerned, reaching as far as appearing in the disguise of true art. At the Frankfurt Manifesta he openly treated the

issues of emigration, immigration, and social discrimination, presenting itself as an artistic entity that is nevertheless an agency actually functioning outside the la. (Manifesta 4, *The One-way Ticket Worldwide Travels*). Simulating the landing on the site with a parachute explicitly manufactured for the purpose, Godeanu had installed a container in the downtown area, explaining to the visitors in *Official Bulletin* that despite the seemingly artistic quality of the action, he was the representative of an agency designed to securely help anyone who wished to illegally immigrate to any of the German cities. This pseudo-institutional language which Godeanu uses in his publication appears in one of his latest projects too (*Temporary Autonomous Zone*) that imitates the design of the Berlin newspaper, *die tageszeitung*. He points it out at the very start that the *Temporary Autonomous Zone* is not at all what it seems to be. "It may look like the *taz* (the popular *tageszeitung* newspaper published in Germany) but it is a different *taz* from the one you know, just like many other things that are not what they appear to be at first sight." After securing reader confidence by thus effacing himself, the artist proceeds to relentlessly criticize the society, of which the very reader must necessarily be a constituent part. Godeanu's total publication material may be viewed also on the Web site operated by him.[2]

The *Version* magazine was created in 2001 at Cluj by Mircea Cantor, Vanga Gabriela, Ciprian Muresan, and Nicolae Baciu to create their own institutional platform. The first issue experimented with presenting public art, the following numbers outlined a cumulative platform for professionals, artists, curators, and theoreticians coming from various fields. The magazine functions as an institution as well with the telling difference that Cantor and his associates are the artists, curators, managers, and so on of an establishment that is not a building with a reliable budget but merely a magazine. The passion of Mircea Cantor for multiplications is manifested in other works as well. For an exhibition organized last year in Brussels he ordered several tens of thousands of boxes of *Double Heads Matches* (with a flammable head on both ends)

die aus mehreren Mitgliedern besteht, obwohl Godeanu tatsächlich alles selbst macht. Das Institut berichtet im *Official Bulletin* über seine Aktivitäten. Die Sprache dieser Publikation stützt sich auf illegale oder semi-formelle institutionelle Diskurse und bietet kompetente Lösungen für alle möglichen Angelegenheiten, bis hin zur Tarnung als wahre Kunst. Auf der Frankfurter Manifesta setzte der Künstler sich offen mit den Themen Emigration, Immigration und soziale Diskriminierung auseinander, präsentiert als ein Kunstgebilde, das nichtsdestotrotz eine Agentur ist, die außerhalb der Legalität operiert (*The One-way Ticket Worldwide Travels*, Manifesta 4). Als Simulation einer Landung vor Ort mit einem eigens dafür hergestellten Fallschirm installierte Godeanu einen Container im Stadtzentrum. Er erklärte den Besuchern im *Official Bulletin*, dass er trotz der scheinbar künstlerischen Qualität der Aktion, eine Agentur vertrete, die jedem, der illegal in eine deutsche Stadt immigrieren möchte, auf sichere Weise hilft. Diese pseudoinstitutionelle Sprache, die Godeanu in seiner Publikation benutzt, findet man auch in seinem jüngsten Projekt (*Temporary Autonomous Zone*), dessen Design vollständig der Berliner *die tageszeitung* nachempfunden ist. Er macht gleich zu Anfang klar, dass die *Temporary Autonomous Zone* überhaupt nicht das ist, was sie zu sein scheint. „Sie sieht vielleicht aus wie die *taz*, doch sie ist anders als die *taz*, die man kennt, so wie viele Dinge nicht das sind, was sie auf den ersten Blick zu sein scheinen." Nachdem er das Vertrauen der Leser durch diese Bescheidenheit gewonnen hat, kritisiert der Künstler auf unerbittliche Weise die Gesellschaft, deren Mitglied jeder Leser notwendigerweise ist. Godeanus gesamtes publiziertes Material kann auf der von ihm betriebenen Webseite eingesehen werden.[2]

Die Zeitschrift *Version* wurde 2001 in Cluj von Mircea Cantor, Vanga Gabriela, Ciprian Muresan und Nicolae Baciu als eigene institutionelle Plattform gegründet. Die erste Ausgabe experimentierte mit der Präsentation öffentlicher Kunst, die darauf folgenden Ausgaben bildeten eine wachsende Plattform für Professionelle, KünstlerInnen, KuratorInnen und TheoretikerInnen aus den verschiedensten Bereichen. Die Zeitschrift

that were then distributed among people on the streets of the city. He disclosed the procedure for manufacturing double head matches on posters revealing that due to the strange, not exactly economical manufacture process (there was no possibility for the use of prefabricated models) the matches in question were hand-made only in Romania. The same sensibility for the contextualized environment and multiplied object was revealed when Cantor proposed the magazine he had edited at the age of 12, entitled *Super Star*, as the supplement of a contemporary art and social criticism magazine.

The activity of Csaba Csíki and Péter Szabó from Cluj is also closely related to promoting Romanian alternative art. As members of the Protokoll Studio founded in 2001, they tried each month to present the works of hardly heard-of artists to the public of Cluj. Their involvement in the organizing of more than 25 exhibitions, lectures, edited publications and musical performances signals an interest taken not so much in product-oriented artistic practice but rather in social cohesion. Besides their studio work, Csíki and Szabó also exhibit their own work from time to time. Since the Protokoll Studio has lost its exhibition space, the two artists have been trying to discover solutions that would allow them to carry on their socially sensitive exhibition practice. Their latest product is a publication (*Moszkva square Plus*) issued for an exhibition organized by the Ludwig Museum in Budapest, entitled *Gravitation*. The publication contains the mental, informal, and historical picture of one of Budapest's most crowded squares that also plays an important role in the life of the homeless and the unemployed of the city. The free newspaper documents a colorful image of the place which is a mere set to people rushing to their daily work, but is something of a home to the homeless and the epitome of daily insecurity for those hoping to find casual work here. *Moszkva square Plus* emphasizes the connections between a place and the tumult of minor everyday events, the asynchronous aspects of social and urban planning as well as the contrasts in between the aesthetics of a society based on information and the isolation of social strata that question through their

funktioniert tatsächlich auch als Institution. Der Unterschied liegt darin, dass Cantor und seine MitarbeiterInnen die KünstlerInnen, KuratorInnen, ManagerInnen etc. einer Einrichtung sind, die nicht über ein Gebäude oder ein verlässliches Budget verfügt, sondern nur über eine Zeitschrift. Mircea Cantors Leidenschaft für Vervielfältigungen zeigt sich auch in anderen Arbeiten. Für eine Ausstellung, die letztes Jahr in Brüssel stattfand, bestellte er mehrere Tausend Schachteln *Double Head Matches* (Streichhölzer mit entzündbaren Köpfen an beiden Enden), die an Menschen auf der Straße verteilt wurden. Auf Postern beschrieb er das Verfahren, zweiköpfige Streichhölzer herzustellen: Auf Grund des komplizierten, nicht gerade wirtschaftlichen Fertigungsprozesses (es gab keine Möglichkeit vorgefertigte Modelle zu verwenden), wurden die fraglichen Streichhölzer ausgerechnet in Rumänien per Hand produziert. Die gleiche Sensibilität gegenüber der kontextualisierten Umgebung und dem vervielfältigten Objekt zeigte Cantor, als er die Zeitschrift *Super Star*, die er im Alter von zwölf herausgegeben hatte, als Beilage einer Zeitschrift für zeitgenössische Kunst und Gesellschaftskritik vorschlug.

Die Aktivitäten von Csaba Csíki und Péter Szabó aus Cluj haben ebenfalls mit der Förderung alternativer rumänischer Kunst zu tun. Als Mitglieder des 2001 gegründeten Protokoll Studios, versuchten sie jeden Monat Arbeiten von unbekannten Künstlern der Öffentlichkeit in Cluj vorzustellen. Sie waren an der Organisation von mehr als 25 Ausstellungen, Vorträgen, Publikationen und Musikperformances beteiligt – ein Zeichen dafür, dass sie eher an sozialem Zusammenhalt als an produktorientierten Kunstpraktiken interessiert sind. Neben ihrer Arbeit im Studio stellen Csíki und Szabó hin und wieder auch eigene Arbeiten aus. Seit das Protokoll Studio nicht mehr über einen Ausstellungsraum verfügt, versuchen die beiden Künstler Lösungen zu finden, die es ihnen ermöglichen, ihre sozial ausgerichtete Ausstellungspraxis fortzuführen. Ihr letztes Produkt ist eine Publikation (*Moszkva square Plus*), die anlässlich einer vom Museum Ludwig in Budapest organisierten Ausstellung namens *Gravitation* erschien. Sie enthält das geistige, ungezwungene und historische Bild eines der geschäf-

very existence the morally quite controversial gloss of the former.

This new phenomenon of artistic practice — collecting documents, producing books and publications, editing pages instead of simply making visual works — has created a different sensibility for receiving and participating in the artistic discourse. In addition to creating a platform for socially oriented art, this practice presents an alternative to individualistic approaches and opens new territories for collaborative work.

This text originally was published in *Flash Art International*. Attila Tordai-S., "Aperto Romania," *Flash Art International* 233 (2003), p. 57–60.

1 *Prophetic Corners. Normalcy, Meaning, Relaxation*, Periferic 6, Center For Art Analysis, Iasi 2003.
2 http://www.theinstitute.ro

tigsten Plätze in Budapest, der auch eine wichtige Rolle im Leben der Obdachlosen und Arbeitslosen der Stadt spielt. Die kostenlose Zeitung dokumentiert ein farbenfrohes Bild des Platzes, der für Menschen, die täglich zur Arbeit eilen, lediglich eine Kulisse ist, jedoch ein Zuhause für die Obdachlosen und der Inbegriff der täglichen Unsicherheit für diejenigen, die hoffen hier eine Gelegenheitsarbeit zu finden. *Moszkva square Plus* betont die Zusammenhänge zwischen einem Platz und dem Wirbel kleiner alltäglicher Ereignisse, die asynchronen Aspekte sozialer und städtischer Planung sowie die Kontraste zwischen einer informationsbasierten Gesellschaft und der Isolation sozialer Schichten, die durch ihre pure Existenz den moralisch zweifelhaften Glanz jener Gesellschaft in Frage stellen.

Dieses neue Phänomen einer künstlerischen Praxis — Dokumente zu sammeln, Bücher und Publikationen herauszugeben, Seiten zu gestalten statt einfach visuelle Werke herzustellen — hat eine andere Sensibilität für die Rezeption und die Teilnahme an künstlerischen Diskursen erzeugt. Zusätzlich zu der Bereitstellung einer Plattform für sozial ausgerichtete Kunst, bietet diese Praxis eine Alternative zu individualistischen Ansätzen und öffnet neue Felder für gemeinsames Arbeiten.

1 Center For Art Analysis (Hg.): *Periferic 6. Prophetic Corners. Normalcy, Meaning, Relaxation*, Iasi 2003.
2 http://www.theinstitute.ro

The international symposium *Droits d'images* (Image Copyright), organized by the Centre pour l'image contemporaine Geneva, Switzerland, took place on December 3 and 4, 2004.

Invited Speakers for the panel *Is Art Protected? Protection, Legitimacy and Protection Limits* were the London-based lawyer Daniel McClean, Eduard Treppoz, senior lecturer in law, University of Lyon, Canadian Dominique Noah, research fellow at the Amsterdam School for Cultural Analysis, and Nathalie Heinich, sociologist and researcher at the CNRS, Paris.

Dominique Noah

Owning culture. Artistic creation and transmission of cultural heritage

[...] My contribution wishes to focus on a shift of perspective. In order to critically investigate the common sense assumption that material — also cultural material — implies ownership, which the current legal setting identifies as given, I propose the reading of a number of chosen artistic practises in the light of a different and expanded understanding on what transmission of cultural material can mean.

Focusing on the relationship between authorship and ownership one can state, after all, that from a neoliberal perspective the signature of the author — in addition to guaranteeing symbolic value — signalizes that one is the owner of ideas, which enables him/her to sell that possession at a profit. In other words: the author is an owner. The author is the legally confirmed producer of private property.

It is exactly here that we can point out the system's own contradictions. The above perspective and prevailing authorial practice does not at all want to take the preliminary context of the authoring process into consideration, the very conditions, relations and information within which the newly created material, now attached to it's author, emerges.

Whereas a playful appropriation and transformation of the world in the *kindergarten* and further educational levels seems acceptable, copyrighting widely neglects the public nature of the specific cultural environment from which it stemmed, with its transfer of meaning for assuring continuity.

The dead-end situation for artists should become clearly visible to you now. As cultural production in general can be localized within the services-sector — wether we are talking about objects made or a cultural product conceived and directed —, artists are bound to put their assets forward in order to make a living, in other words: they need to act socially on the level of the author/owner. [...]

Nathalie Heinich, Dominique Noah, and Daniel MacLean, Geneva 2004   photo: Marc Blondeau

Pressure on the other side of the spectrum is induced by the current climate of criminalizing illegal copying of cultural material (certainly more related to music, and other digitized material, but still noticeable as the general climate), adding to the moment of creating new work a heavy burden. Backed up with massive legal support, copyright, and trademark-holders of cultural material (such as images) it is much easier start to prosecute infringements by anybody that goes public with work that builds on existing forms. Concrete numbers of daily appropriations and detournements of owned material are certainly not yet measurable, but the prevailing logic of private property allows one to envision cultural production constantly paying licence fees.

What are the possible perspectives in dealing with this currently contradictory setting? [...]

A pointed contemporary practice is the case of South African born, Berlin-based Candice Breitz. Several of her works master the creation of unexpected, even disturbing new meanings from remixing and reediting existing cultural material, and the international presence of her work proves her recognition by the market (gallery shows, museum shows, private collections), yet she is acting in a legally absolutely unprotected zone.

As an example I cite her *Soliloquy (Jack),* (1987–2000), 00:14:06:25, where the Hollywood movie *The Witches of Eastwick* with Jack Nicholson in the leading role is condensed into a 14 min. monologue of Nicholson's vocal presence, accelerating the acted and enacted into a violent stream of the narrative as well as its opposite, the usually invisible dead space of directing and editing: the montage of the social. But please, do not publicly mention to those collecting Breitz's works, that the appropriated material is legally protected... The artist says that she uses material easily accessible in every video rental around the corner...

Comparable to Breitz, the German-born and Basel-based artist Hinrich Sachs works with iconographic material considered to be "part of the collective cultural memory". In this context I would like to mention his recently produced *Kami, Cookiemonster, Bert and Ernie (all together now)*. Basically the project makes a group of nine characters public that are derived from the American children's TV program *Sesame Street*, which has started a wide number of franchised co-productions over the last 30 years in countries so diverse as Mexico, South Africa, Egypt, and Russia. This making public is orchestrated: from an exhibition with the life-size costumes of the puppets, via a theatre play invented and performed by pupils of a neighboring school and a concert of the Parisian electronic music dj's teamtendo to a press-conference in the presence of a lawyer, where we are informed about the legal conditions of using the copyrighted and trademarked material of the *Sesame Street*.

In the "Terms and Conditions of Use" we read: "You may NOT modify, copy, distribute, transmit, display, perform, reproduce, publish, license, create derivative works from, transfer, sell, or make other use of any of the materials obtained from the site."

And a bit further: "By communicating with Sesame Workshop, you grant to Sesame Workshop an irrevocable, transferable, and worldwide right to use, reproduce, publicly perform and display, distribute, sublicence, and sell any suggestions, ideas, concepts or other information communicated to Sesame Workshop for any purpose Sesame Workshop chooses, commercial or otherwise, without any compensation to you."
Placing us and himself in the suspense of whether the copyright-owners

will manifest themselves, the artist consciously works with meanings in more then one context, and has created a risky and open-ended timing of transaction, a possible beginning of a discussion with — amongst other — lawyers about concepts of cultural transmission. [...]

The Hamburg-based artist Cornelia Sollfrank has recently proposed to the Swiss new media oriented institute plug-in to open a Sollfrank-show with a series of large prints with flowers derived from a software called Net.Art.Generator, co-authored by herself and several programmers. This piece of software functions on the base of keywords that the user — me for example — wishes to type, browses the web and after some seconds comes up with a multilayered stylish image. The exhibition proposal included using the terms "Warhol" and "flowers". Assuming a precarious legal situation, the board of the institution preferred not to permit the project going public, maybe because it is known that the Warhol-Foundation actively prosecutes infringements of their copyrighted Warhol Estate.

The central questions are certainly revolving around the fact that the aesthetic results generated by the Net.Art.Generator software dissolve all classical aspects of authorship and at the same time build on the gray zone of image material drifting through the net, which in itself has loosened the boundaries of ownership. On the one hand, a German Insurance company has acquired the Net.Art.Generator for their art-collection, on the other one can listen to lawyers in a series of video-interviews that Cornelia Sollfrank has produced as an artistic reply to the board and to us, the public.

With this example the brief *tour d'horizon* of challenging artistic practices has come to an end for today. Instead of a conclusion, I would like to formulate a hypothesis.

The current legal setting tying authorship and copyrights to the concept of private property can be identified as a historically specific cultural framework. Cultural settings are themselves immaterial constellations due to change in the same way as the material-world changes. From this anthropological point of view the current legal setting is loosing its societal credibility in the many occurring cases where law places the logic of private property as the *ultima ratio,* and overrules the public domain property (e.g. with copyright infringement and piracy terminology). The accumulation of private property in societies building their value system upon capitalizing on *everything* material *and* immaterial neglects the gratuitious, given presence from which everything was originally claimed.

Succesfully tranferring cultural material to the next generations for guaranteeing continuity has in all societies been built on making available, sharing and distributing within a collective. Therefore one can easily show that current intellectual property and copyright law broadly fails to recognize the modes of transfer and renewal of the cultural process in its collective and public nature. [...]

The character and the script for *Dominique Noah (as speaker)* was developed and realized in collaboration with Solveig Dufour, Peter Stoffel, Barnaby Drabble, and Albert Liebl.

Make Film Political

**Interview
with Dorit Margreiter by Vít Havránek**

The hypothesis of my article in "The Need to Document" is based on the political and cultural experience we have gained in the countries of the East undergoing a transformation. The so called "Need to Document" is something different than just a conceptual method of working. It is a base of such a concept, an ontology, we could say. This ontology creates a relation of responsibility in between the documented and documenting.

Would you agree that there is an ontological basis of your work connecting the social facts and movements with your method of work?

Although I agree that there is a "need to document" which comes with a social responsibility, I think that the document itself cannot be detached from a conceptual method, also because there is a history of documentary and a history of documenting methods that always play a role in every "document" whether one is aware of it or not.

Within my work I am using different methods of documentary related to the content. For instance my last piece where I used film, the specific history of film in early documentary played an important part.

In another piece, which I co-produced with the filmmaker Martina Aichhorn, we taped every demonstration against the new government in Austria in 2000 in order to produce an alternative archive, since the official media almost did not cover the demonstrations at all. Luckily we were not the only ones who tried to do that, quite to the contrary, there were so many handheld cameras in all the demonstrations that our project became a documentary about documenting the absence of the official media.

How was it in terms of technical treatment and postproduction of such a film archive, was it a creative work for you or more of a technical process?

Both actually. We did not leave the material to itself, which would have been an option. Instead, we placed the material within a dialogue between Martina and me, as the filmmakers but also as participants of the demonstration. In addition, we started a parallel archive which was to interview the individuals behind the mass of people. Of course, that was a process that could never reach an end, which was also the idea behind it.

So was it for you the work that was most related to documentary?

No, I would not put it that way. I think it would be a mistake to look at one piece as "more direct" just because it has not been edited or because no tripod was used.

In your works, you deal with different topics in relation with concrete places; how do you choose these topics, is there always a personal connection to the contexts and places?

It starts with a certain question. When I worked on a project about the Case Study House #22 in Los Angeles, the starting point was a very well-known photograph by Julius Schulman which led me to the site of the house. The Sheats Goldstein House which is the base for the piece *10104 Angelo View Drive*, for instance, is a location for numerous Hollywood and independent film productions, so it got my attention through films, TV shows, and music videos.

In both cases, I was interested in the documentation of the space and that led me to other discussions about the relation between the location and its document and the question of an "ideal" media to document a three dimensional space.

It is quite significant that we are today talking more about Godard than about some pioneers of documentary photography and film.

I think what I am trying to say, in general, is that there is no graduation between a "more political" and a "less political" in documentary.

Mit Blick auf die technische Bearbeitung und Postproduktion eines solchen Filmarchivs, war das für dich eine kreative Arbeit oder eher ein technischer Prozess?

Beides eigentlich. Wir haben das Material nicht sich selbst überlassen, obwohl das eine Option gewesen wäre. Stattdessen platzierten wir es in einen Dialog zwischen Martina und mir, als Filmemacherinnen aber auch als Demonstrantinnen. Zudem starteten wir ein paralleles Archiv, in dem wir Individuen hinter den Menschenmassen interviewten. Natürlich war das ein Prozess der ins Endlose lief, was auch die Idee war.

Also kam diese Arbeit für dich einer Dokumentation am nächsten?

Nein, so würde ich das nicht sagen. Ich denke, es wäre falsch, ein Stück als „direkter" zu betrachten, nur weil es nicht bearbeitet und ohne Stativ aufgenommen wurde.

In deinen Werken arbeitest du mit verschiedenen Themen in Bezug auf konkrete Orte. Wie suchst du diese Themen aus, besteht da immer eine persönliche Verbindung zu den Inhalten und Orten?

Es beginnt mit einer bestimmten Frage. Als ich an einem Projekt über das Case Study House #22 in Los Angeles arbeitete, war mein Ausgangspunkt eine sehr bekannte Fotografie von Julius Schulman, die mich zu dem Haus führte. Das Sheats Goldstein House, die Basis für die Arbeit *10104 Angelo View Drive*, ist zum Beispiel eine Lokalität für viele Hollywood- und Independent-Filmproduktionen. Daher wurde ich durch Filme, Fernsehserien und Musikvideos darauf aufmerksam.

In beiden Fällen galt mein Interesse der Dokumentation von Raum, und das führte mich zu anderen Diskussionen über die Relation zwischen der Lokalität und ihrem Dokument. Außerdem beschäftigte mich die Frage nach dem „idealen" Medium, um einen dreidimensionalen Raum zu dokumentieren.

Godard said that it is more important to make film political and not to make political films. This is a very useful thought. Also, there is a tendency in thinking about documentary to make a statement about reality, to think that there is a graduation between what is more and what is less real. The question is, what do you want to document, and then how you want to document it, the question is not whether it is reality or not.

Es ist recht deutlich, dass wir heute mehr über Godard sprechen als über einige Pioniere der dokumentarischen Fotografie und des Dokumentarfilms.

Ich glaube, was ich generell zu sagen versuche ist, dass es keine Einteilung zwischen „mehr politisch" oder „weniger politisch" in der Dokumentation gibt. Godard sagt, dass es wichtiger ist einen Film politisch zu machen als politische Filme zu drehen. Das ist ein sehr nützlicher Gedanke. Außerdem gibt es eine Tendenz, in der Dokumentation eine Aussage über die Realität zu machen, also darüber zu entscheiden, was mehr oder weniger real ist. Die Frage ist, was du dokumentieren willst, und dann, wie du es dokumentieren willst. Die Frage ist nicht, ob es die Realität ist oder nicht.

Venezuela from Below

A film by Dario Azzellini and Oliver Ressler
67 min., 2004

In Venezuela, a profound social transformation identified as the Bolivarian process has been underway since Hugo Chávez's governmental takeover in 1998. It concerns a broad process of self organization, from which has developed a progressive constitution, a labor law, new educational possibilities, and a number of further reforms for the impoverished majority of the population of what is potentially a wealthy state. The government's politics, which take an open stance against neo-liberalism, have experienced vehement rejection from Venezuela's major private industries and from the US, expressed in two attempted coups and boycotts. Nonetheless, Chávez and his government enjoy the trust of the majority of the population. The society is heavily politicized; many people who had never before thought of what they wanted to change are now a part of a profound transformation taking place in the country.

In the film *Venezuela from Below*, the true actors in the social process are able to speak: the grassroots. After an introduction by philosopher Carlos Lazo, workers from the oil company PDVSA in Puerto La Cruz report how in 2002/2003 they protected the refinery from breaking down during the oil sabotage, which was pawned off as a strike, and how they were able to reinstate oil production. Several farmers from a newly founded cooperative in Aragua report on their process of self organization, on the literacy campaign, and how things should continue. A women's bank project in Miranda and several loan recipients from Caracas' disadvantaged district, 23 de Enero, present their projects. Indígena community members near the Orinoco river in Bolívar speak about how their demands and struggles are reflected in the constitution and what has changed for them. Workers from the occupied National Valve Company in Los Teques and the paper production company Venepal in Carabobo — which was occupied by 350 workers after the owners drove it to bankruptcy, and which now, after a partial agreement, is running production again — speak about corrupt unions, labor control, and their struggles. Protagonists in the revolutionary movement Tupamaro, the cultural foundation Simón Bolívar, the leftist website www.23.net, and the Bolivarian Circle Abrebrecha from 23 de Enero report on their work and what has changed for them through the social revolutions.
They are the people of the grassroots and they speak about what they did and what they are doing, how they feel about the Bolivarian process, about their expectations and ideas. They see themselves as part of the process that is underway, but also problematize numerous points. The search for a social and economic model beyond neo-liberalism is no easy terrain; there are currently no successful, tested alternatives. The protagonists in the Bolivarian process have, however, started upon a path from which there is no return.

Concept, interviews, film editing, production: Dario Azzellini and Oliver Ressler
Camera: Volkmar Geiblinger
Image editing and titles: Markus Koessl
Interviewees: Titina Azuaje, Gustavo Borges, Stalin Pérez Borges, Juan Brizuela, Bertha de Castillo, José Ramón Castillo, Eduardo Daza, Arlenis Espinal, Freddy Farias, Juán Fermín, José Flores, Randy García, Círe y Guarán, Sandra Heredia de Goncalves, Juana Catalina Guzman, María Elisa Irazabal de Píneda, Natalí Jaimes, Carlos Lazo, Henry Mariño, Maritza Marquez, Esther de Mena, Esteban Michelena, Argelia Naguanagua de Ramos, Emma Ortega, Edgar Peña, Judith Sánchez, José Mercedes Sifontes, Alfonso Tovar, Antolino Vasquez, Eduardo Yaguaracuto
Grants: Kunstsektion des BKA, Stiftung Umverteilen

The film is available in Spanish, with English or with German subtitles.

www.ressler.at

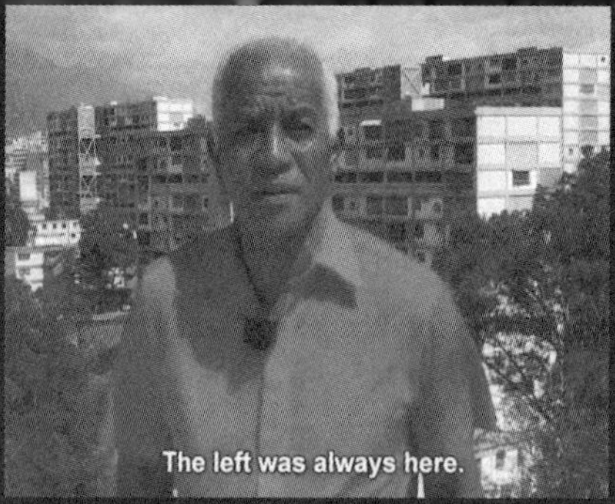
The left was always here.

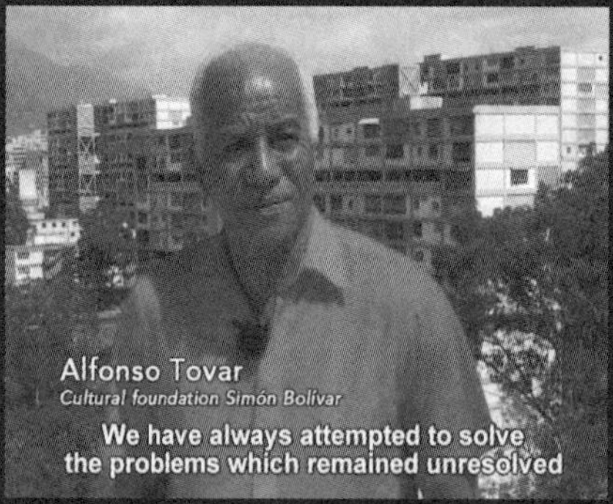
Alfonso Tovar
Cultural foundation Simón Bolívar
We have always attempted to solve
the problems which remained unresolved

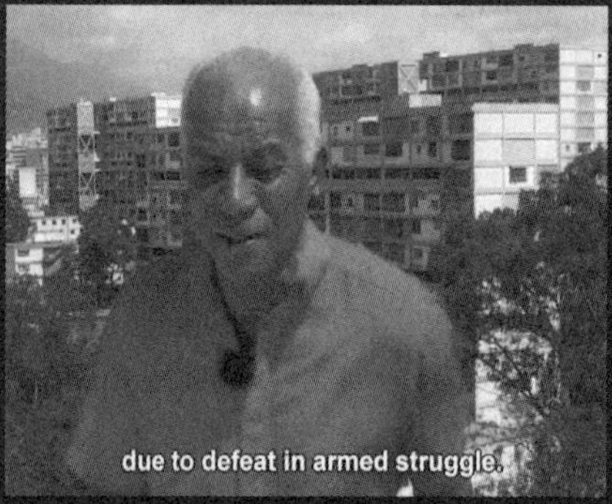
due to defeat in armed struggle.

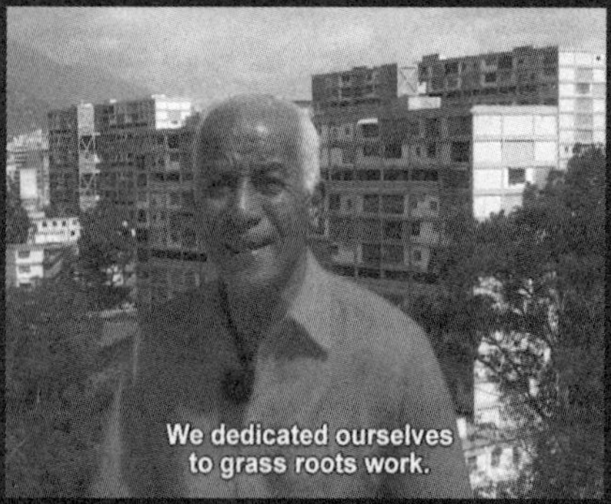
We dedicated ourselves
to grass roots work.

The left was very divided back then,
and we were searching for the great unity

that never came about.

All of our attempts were futile.
Then Chávez entered the scene.

He is the great integrating
figure in this entire process.

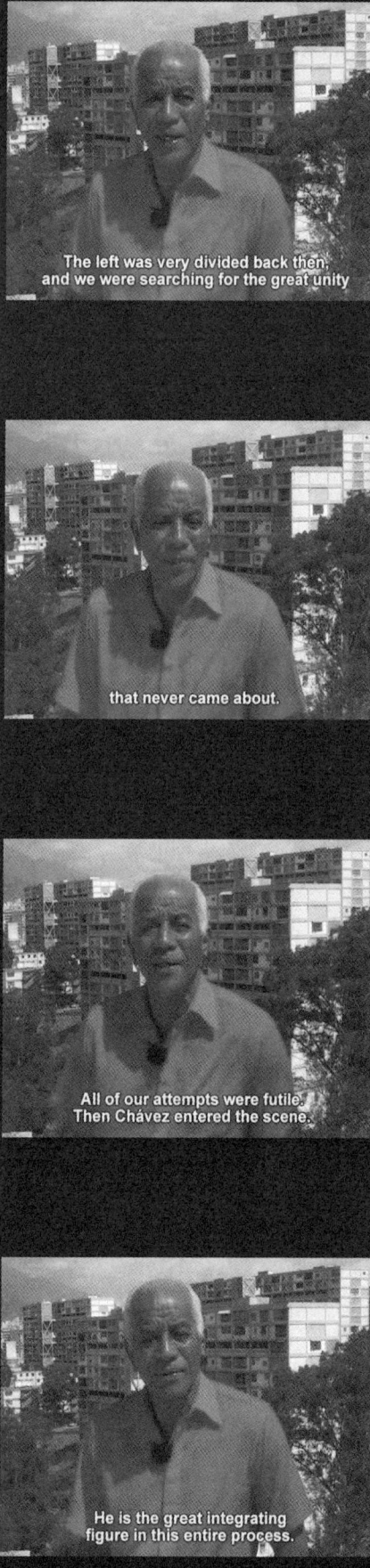

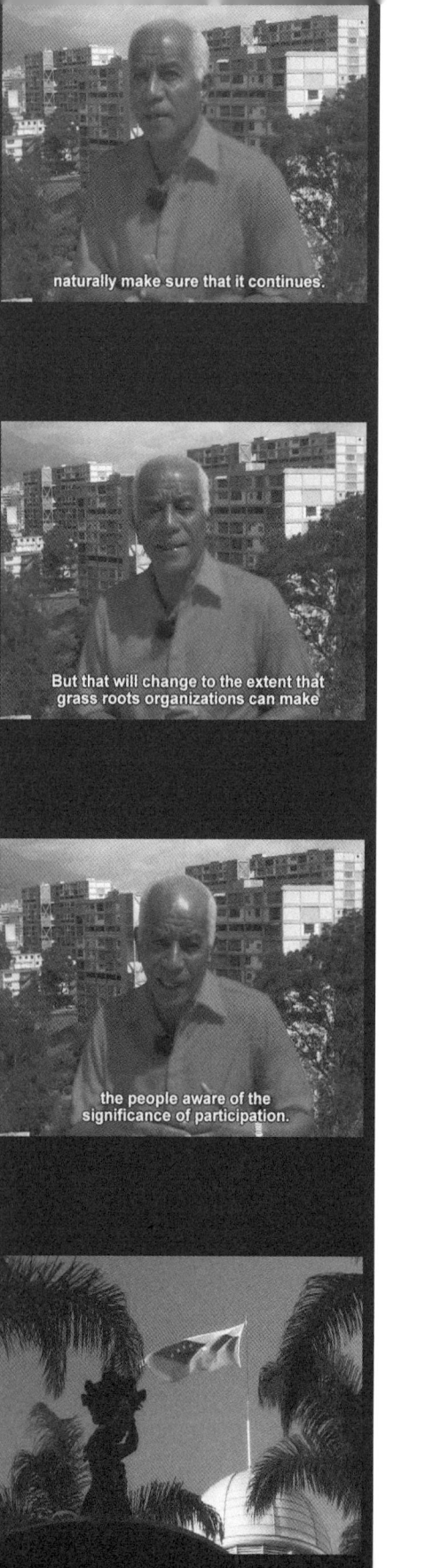

Bibliography

Aitken, Ian, ed., *The Documentary Film Movement: An Anthology*, Edinburgh 1998.
Albersmeier, Franz-Josef, ed., *Texte zur Theorie des Films*, Stuttgart 1995.
Arbeitsgemeinschaft Dokumentarfilm, *Dokumentarfilmschaffen in Österreich*, Vienna 1986.
Arriens, Klaus, *Wahrheit und Wirklichkeit im Film: Philosophie des Dokumentarfilms*, Würzburg 1999.
Arendt, Hannah. *Wahrheit und Politik: Wahrheit und Lüge in der Politik*, München 1967.
Arthur, Paul, "Jargons of Authenticity (Three American Moments)," *Theorizing Documentary*, Michael Renov (ed.), New York/London 1993, p. 108–134.
Aumont, Jacques, *L'oeil interminable: Cinéma et peinture*, Paris 1989.
Aurich, Rolf, ed., *Der Ärger mit den Bildern: Die Filme von Harun Farocki*, Konstanz 1998.
Badiou, Alain, *Theoretical Writings*, London 2004.
Baldwin, Sidney, *Poverty and Politics: The Rise and Decline of the Farm Security Administration*, Chapel Hill 1968.
Balkenhol, Bernhard, Heiner Georgsdorf and Pierangelo Maset, eds., *XXD11: Über Kunst und Künstler der Gegenwart. Ein Nachlesebuch zur Documenta11*, Kassel 2002.
Ballhaus, Edmund and Beate Engelbrecht, eds., *Der ethnographische Film: Eine Einführung in Methoden und Praxis*, Berlin 1995.
Baltzer, U., *Erkenntnis als Relationengeflecht: Kategorien bei Charles S. Peirce*, Paderborn 1994.
Barbash, Ilisa, *Cross-cultural Filmmaking. A Handbook for Making Documentary and Ethnographic Films and Videos*, Berkeley 1997.
Barnouw, Eric, *Documentary: A History of the Non-Fiction Film*, New York/Oxford 1993.
Basualdo, Carlos, "Notes Toward the Dematerialization of the Art Exhibition," *Insertions, Archipelago*, The Nordic Museum and The Museum of Science and Technology, Stockholm 1998.
Baudry, Jean-Louis. "Ideological Effects of the Basic Cinematographic Apparatus," *Apparatus*, Theresa Hak Kyung Cha (ed.), New York 1980.
Baudrillard, Jean, "Die Gewalt am Bild," *Die Abwesenheit der Welt*, exhibition catalogue, Kunsthalle Fridericianum, Kassel 2003, p. 4–9.
Bechtold, Gerhard, *Sinnliche Wahrnehmung von sozialer Wirklichkeit: Die multimedialen Montage – Texte Alexander Kluges*, Tübingen 1983.
Belloi, Livio, "Lumière und der Augen-Blick," *Anfänge des dokumentarischen Films*, Frank Kessler (ed.), Basel 1995, p. 27–49.
Bellour, Raymond, *L'Entre-images*, Paris 1999.
Benjamin, Walter, *Das Kunstwerk im Zeitalter seiner technischen Reproduzierbarkeit*, Frankfurt a. M. 1978.
Berg, Jan, "Techniken der medialen Authentifizierung Jahrhunderte vor der Erfindung des ‚Dokumentarischen'," *Die Einübung des dokumentarischen Blicks*, Ursula von Keitz and Kay Hoffmann (eds.), Marburg 2001, p. 51–70.
Berg, Ronald, *Die Ikone des Realen: Zur Bestimmung der Photographie im Werk von Talbot, Benjamin und Barthes*, München 2001.
Berger, Peter L. and Thomas Luckmann, *Die gesellschaftliche Konstruktion der Wirklichkeit*, Frankfurt a. M. 2000.
Beyerle, Mo, ed., *Der amerikanische Dokumentarfilm der 60er Jahre: Direct cinema and radical cinema*, Frankfurt a. M. 1991.

Beyerle, Mo, ed., *Authentisierungsstrategien im Dokumentarfilm: Das amerikanische direct cinema der 60er Jahre*, Trier 1997.
Bhaskar, Roy, *A Realist Theory of Science*, 2nd edition, New York 1979.
Bitomsky, Hartmut, *Kinowahrheit*, Berlin 2002.
Blümlinger, Christa, ed., *Sprung im Spiegel: Filmisches Wahrnehmen zwischen Fiktion und Wirklichkeit*, Vienna 1990.
Blümlinger, Christa, ed., *Von der Welt ins Bild: Augenzeugenberichte eines Cinephilen*, Berlin 2000.
Blumenberg, H., *Die Lesbarkeit der Welt*, Frankfurt a. M. 1981.
Bolesch, Cornelia, ed., *Dokumentarisch Arbeiten: Ein Werkstattbericht in 48 Portraits*, München 1990.
Bordwell, David and Noël Carroll, eds., *Post-Theory: Reconstructing Film Studies*, Madison, Wisconsin, 1996.
Bourdieu, Pierre, et al., *Eine illegitime Kunst: Die sozialen Gebrauchsweisen der Photographie*, Frankfurt a. M. 1981.
Bruzzi, Stella, *New Documentary: A Critical Introduction*, London/New York 2004.
Bryson, Norman, *Vision and Painting: The Logic of the Gaze*, London and New Haven 1983.
Bullert, B. J., *Public Television: Politics and the Battle Over Documentary Film*, New Brunswick 1997.
Cavell, Stanley, *A Pitch of Philosophy: Autobiographical Exercises*, Cambridge, Massachusetts, 1994.
Coles, Robert, *Doing Documentary Work*, Oxford 1998.
Corner, John, *Documentary and the Mass Media*, London 1986.
Corner, John, *The Art of the Record: A Critical Introduction to Documentary*, Manchester 1996.
Cowie, Elizabeth, "Identifizierung mit dem Realen – Spektakel der Realität," *Der andere Schauplatz: Psychoanalyse – Kultur – Medien*, Marie-Luise Angerer and Henry P. Krips (eds.), Vienna 2001, p. 151–180.
Davidson, D., *Wahrheit und Interpretation*, Frankfurt a. M. 1986.
De Bromhead, Toni, *Looking Two Ways: Documentary Film's Relationship with Cinema and Reality*, Hojbjerg 1996.
Dehnert, Walter, ed., *Aspekte eigener und fremder Kulturen im Film*, Marburg 1999.
Deleuze, Gilles, *Unterhandlungen*, Frankfurt a. M. 1993.
documenta GmbH, ed., *Das Buch zur documenta X: Politics-Poetics*, Ostfildern-Ruit 1997.
Emmison, Michael and Philip Smith, *Researching the Visual: Images, Objects, Contexts and Interactions in Social and Cultural Inquiry*, London/New Delhi 2000.
Enwezor, Okwui, et al., eds., *Democracy Unrealized: Documenta11_Platform1*, Ostfildern-Ruit 2002.
Ertel, Dieter, ed., *Strategie der Blicke: zur Modellierung von Wirklichkeit in Dokumentarfilm und Reportage*, Konstanz 1996.
"Ficcions" documentales, Fundació "la Caixa" (ed.), exhibition catalogue, CaixaForum, Barcelona 2004.
Fiske, John, "Videotech," *The Visual Culture Reader*, Nicholas Mirzoeff (ed.), London/New York 1998.
Foster, Hal, *The Return of the Real*, Cambridge/London 1996.
Foucault, Michel, *The Archaeology of Knowledge*, New York 1972.
Foucault, Michel, "Technologien der Wahrheit," *Foucault – Botschaften der Macht: Reader Diskurs und Medien*, Jan Engelmann (ed.), Stuttgart 1999, p. 133–144.
Franke, Anselm, ed., *Territories. Islands, Camps, and Other States of Utopia*, exhibition catalog, KW – Institute for Contemporary Art, Cologne 2003.
Frisinghelli, Christine and Franz Schultheis, *Pierre Bourdieu in Algerien: Zeugnisse der Entwurzelung*, Graz 2003.
Gaines, Jane M. and Michael Renov, *Collecting Visible Evidence*, Minneapolis 1999.

Gardner, Louise, *Art Through the Ages*, New York 1980.
Gauthier, Guy, *Le documentaire: Un autre cinema*, Paris 1995.
Gludovatz, Karin, ed., *Auf den Spuren des Realen: Kunst und Dokumentarismus*, exhibition catalog, Museum Moderner Kunst Stiftung Ludwig, Vienna 2003.
Gludovatz, Karin and Clemens Krümmel, "Nichts als die Wahrheit," *Texte zur Kunst* 51, 2003, p. 4–5.
Gludovatz, Karin, "Grauwerte: Ein Projekt von Klub Zwei zum Gebrauch historischer Dokumentarfotografie," *Texte zur Kunst* 51, 2003, p. 58–67.
Godard, Jean-Luc, *Einführung in eine wahre Geschichte des Kinos*, Frankfurt a. M. 1984.
Grammel, Søren, "The Reader is the Extended Author. Or: Does putting a water-cooker and some teabags into an exhibition space really cause a change in the hierarchy between artist and audience?" *Revisiting the Show*, Vector Association, Matei Bejenaru (ed.), Iasi 2003.
Grant, Barry Keith, ed., *Documenting the Documentary. Close Readings of Documentary Film and Video*, Detroit 1998.
Grammel, Søren, "Es ist schwer das Reale zu beruehren," *Drucksache*, Kunstverein München, spring 2002, p. 44–45.
Grimshaw, Anna, *The Ethnographer's Eye: Ways of Seeing in Anthropology*, Cambridge 2001.
Groys, Boris, "Kunst im Zeitalter der Biopolitik: Vom Kunstwerk zur Kunstdokumentation," *Documenta11_Plattform 5: Ausstellung*, exhibition catalogue, documenta GmbH. Ostfildern-Ruit 2002.
Hattendorf, Manfred, *Dokumentarfilm und Authentizität: Ästhetik und Pragmatik einer Gattung*, Konstanz 1994.
Hattendorf, Manfred, ed., *Perspektiven des Dokumentarfilms*, Munich 1995.
Haraway, Donna, "The Promises of Monsters: A Regenerative Politics for Inappropriate/d Others," *Cultural Studies*, Lawrence Grossberg, Cary Nelson and Paula A. Treichler (eds.), New York/London 1992.
Hayles, N. Katherine, "Embodied Virtuality: Or How to Put Bodies Back into the Picture," *Immersed in Technology: Art and Virtual Environments*, Mary Anne Moser and Douglas MacLeod (eds.), Cambridge, Massachusetts/London 1996.
Hedgpeth, T., "Expanding the Documentary: Jim Smith, Sid Kaplan, Jim Goldberg, Susan Felter (Mary Porter Sesnon Art Gallery, Santa Cruz, California: Exhibition Review)," *Artweek* 40, 1979, p. 17.
Heiser, Jörg and Jan Verwoert. "What's the Difference? Interview with Yael Bartana, Annika Eriksson, Anri Sala, and Gitte Villesen," *Frieze* 84, 2004, p. 72–77.
Hickethier, Knut, "On the History of Television as a History of Viewing in Germany: Preliminary Thoughts," *Pragmatic of Audiovisual*, D. Müller (ed.), vol. 2., Münster 1995.
Hohenberger, Eva, *Die Wirklichkeit des Films: Dokumentarfilm, ethnographischer Film, Jean Rouch*, Hildesheim 1988.
Hohenberger, Eva, *Bilder des Wirklichen: Texte zur Theorie des Dokumentarfilms*, Berlin 1998.
Hohenberger, Eva, and Judith Keilbach, *Die Gegenwart der Vergangenheit: Dokumentarfilm, Fernsehen und Geschichte*, Berlin 2003.
Hoffmann, Kay, ed., *Die Einübung des dokumentarischen Blicks: "Fiction Film" und "Non Fiction Film" zwischen Wahrheitsanspruch und expressiver Sachlichkeit*, Marburg 2001.
Hoffman, Michael J., *Essentials of the Theory of Fiction*, Durham 1996.
Holmlund, Chris and Cynthia Fuchs, eds., *Between the Sheets, In the Streets: Queer, Lesbian, Gay documentary*, Minneapolis 1997.

Honnef, Klaus, "Das subjektive Moment in der Dokumentar-Fotografie: Materialien und Gedanken zu einer neuen Ansicht über Fotografie," *Kunstforum International* 41, 1980, p. 210–229.

Hügler, Elmar, *Anstiftung zur Vorspiegelung wahrer Tatsachen*, Osnabrück/Zurich 1994.

Iragaray, Luce, *This Sex Which is Not One*, Ithaca 1985.

Isaak, Jo Anna, "Mapping the Imaginary," *The Event Horizon*, Lorne Falk and Barbara Fischer (eds.), Toronto 1987.

Jansson, Peder, "Photography's Dissidents: Documentarism vs. Visual Art? The aesthetic transformation of the documentary photograph," *Katalog: Journal of Photography and Video* 1, 2001, p. 42–46.

Kaimer Anita, *Die Problematik des Dokumentar(film)journalismus unter Einbeziehung des Projektes 'Planquadra'*, Vienna 1998.

Kaplan, E. Ann, "Looking for the Other," *Feminism, Film, and the Imperial Gaze*, Routledge 1997.

Kiener, Wilma, *Die Kunst des Erzählens: Narrativität in dokumentarischen und ethnographischen Filmen*, Konstanz 1999.

Krakauer, Siegfried, *Theorie des Films: Die Errettung der äußeren Wirklichkeit*, Frankfurt a. M. 1993.

Krakolinig, Gerald, *Medienethik im Dokumentarfilm*, Klagenfurt 1997.

Krauss, Rosalind, *Le Photographique: Pour une Théorie des Écarts*, Paris 1990.

Kreimeier, Klaus, "Dokumentarfilm. Ein doppeltes Dilemma," *Geschichte des Deutschen Films*, W. Jacobson et al (eds.), Stuttgart 1993.

Kreimeier, Klaus, "Fingierter Dokumentarfilm und Strategien des Authentischen," *Trau-schau-wem: Digitalisierung und dokumentarische Form*, Kay Hoffmann (ed.), Konstanz 1997.

Krieger, David J., *Kommunikationssystem Kunst*, Vienna 1997.

Lammer, Christina, *doKU: Wirklichkeit inszenieren im Dokumentarfilm*, Vienna 2002.

Lasselsberger, Dietlinde, *The Flaherty way: Dokumentarismus in den Filmen Robert J. Flahertys*, Vienna 1997.

Levi-Strauss, David, "The documentary debate," *Camerawork* 1, 1992, p. 4ff.

Levine, George, ed., *Realism and Representation. Essays on the Problem of Realism in Relation to Science, Literature and Culture*, London 1993.

Lundström, Jan-Erik, "Real Stories," *Revisions in Documentary and Narrative Photography*, exhibition catalogue, Museet for Fotokunst, Odense (no year of publication), p. 3–10.

Lyotard, Jean-François, *The Postmodern Condition: A Report on Knowledge*, Minneapolis 1984.

Macdonald, Kevin and Mark Cousins, eds., *Imagining Reality: the Faber Book of the Documentary*, London 1996.

Marcus, George E., *Cultural Producers in Perilous States: Editing Events Documenting Change*, Chicago 1997.

Marschall, Susanne, ed., *"Wir sind alle Menschenfresser". Georg Stefan Troller und die Liebe zum Dokumentarischen*, St. Augustin 1999.

Messerli, Alfred and Janis Osolin, eds., "Non-Fiction. Über Dokumentarfilme," *Cinema* no. 39, Basel 1993.

Michelson, Annette, ed., *Kino-eye. The Writings of Dziga Vertov*, Berkeley 1984.

Möller-Nass, Karl-Dietmar, *Filmsprache: Eine kritische Theoriegeschichte*, Münster 1988.

Mohn, Elisabeth, *Filming Culture: Spielarten des Dokumentierens nach der Repräsentationskrise*, Stuttgart 2002.

Moi, Toril, ed., *The Kristeva Reader*, Oxford 1986.

Monaco, James, *Film verstehen: Kunst, Technik, Sprache. Geschichte und Theorie des Films und der Medien*, Reinbek 1996.

Morgan, R. C., *The Role of Documentation in Conceptual Art: An Aesthetic Inquiry*, Ph. D. NYU 1978.

Morgan, Jessica, and Gregor Muir, eds., *Time Zones. Recent Film and Video*, London 2004.
Moser, Mary Anne, *Immersed in Technology: Art and Virtual Environments*, Cambridge/London 1996.
Mulvey, Laura, *Visual and Other Pleasures*, Bloomington 1989.
Nash, Marc, "Bildende Kunst und Kino: Einige kritische Betrachtungen," *Documenta11_Plattform 5: Ausstellung*, exhibition catalog, documenta GmbH, Ostfildern-Ruit 2002.
Nelmes, Jill, *An Introduction to Film Studies*, London 1996.
Neumann, Pia, *Metaphern des Misslingens: Amerikanische Dokumentarfotografie der 60er und 70er Jahre zwischen Konzeptkunst und Gesellschaftskritik*, Frankfurt a. M. 1996.
Neubauer, Susanne, ed., *Documentary Creations*, exhibition catalog, Kunstmuseum Luzern, Frankfurt a. M. 2005.
Neuerer, Gregor, ed., *Untitled Experience of Place*, London 2003.
Nichols, Bill, "The Voice of Documentary," *Movies and Methods*, Bill Nicols (ed.), vol. II, Berkeley/Los Angeles 1985, p. 258-273.
Nichols, Bill, *Representing Reality. Issues and Concepts in Documentary*, Bloomington/Indianapolis 1997.
Niney, François, *L'épreuve du réel à l'écran, essai sur le principe de réalité documentaire*, Brussels 2002.
Obrist, Hans Ulrich, and Barbara Vanderlinden, eds., *Laboratorium*, Cologne 2001.
Orvel, Miles, *After the Machine: Visual Arts and the Erasing of Cultural Boundaries*, Jackson 1995.
Paetzold, Heinz, *The Discourse of the Postmodern and the Discourse of the Avant-Garde*, Maastricht 1994.
Pasquino, Pasquale and Allessandro Fontana, "Wahrheit und Macht. Gespräch mit Michel Foucault vom Juni 1976," *Dispositive der Macht*, Berlin 1978.
Pines, Jim, and Paul Willemen, eds., *Questions of Third Cinema*, London 1989.
Plantinga, Carl R., *Rhetoric and Representation in Nonfiction Film*, Cambridge 1997.
Pohn, Ernst, "Eine Frage der Perspektive," *Dokumentarfilm im Spannungsfeld zwischen subjektiver und objektiver Realitätsvermittlung*, diploma, 2001.
Putnam, Hilary, *Representation and Reality*, Cambridge/London 1988.
Rabinowitz, Paula, *They Must Be Represented: The Politics of Documentary*, London 1994.
Rancière, Jacques, *La Fable cinématographique*, Paris 2001.
Rancière, Jacques, *Malaise dans l'esthétique*, Paris 2004.
Raunig, Gerald, ed., *Bildräume und Raumbilder: Repräsentationskritik in Film und Aktivismus*, Vienna 2004.
Raunig, Gerald, ed., *Kunst und Revolution: Künstlerischer Aktivismus im langen 20. Jahrhundert*, Vienna 2005.
Renov, Michael, ed., *Theorizing Documentary*, New York/London 1993.
Renov, Michael, "Animation: Der imaginäre Signifikant des Dokumentarischen," *Texte zur Kunst* 51, 2003, p. 36-45.
Renov, Michael, *The Subject of Documentary*, Minneapolis 2004.
Ressler, Oliver, "Proteste gegen die kapitalistische Globalisierung auf Video," *Raumbilder und Bildräume*, Gerald Raunig (ed.), Vienna 2004, p. 140-144.
Roscoe, Jane, and Craig Hight, *Faking it: Mock-documentary and the Subversion of Factuality*, Manchester 2001.
Rosenthal, Alan, and John Corner, eds., *New Challenges for Documentary*, Berkeley 1988.
Rosler, Martha, *Three works*, Halifax 1981.

Rosler, Martha, "Drinnen, Drumherum und nachträgliche Gedanken (zur Dokumentarfotografie)," *Positionen in der Lebenswelt*, Sabine Breitwieser (ed.), Cologne 1999.

Rosler, Martha, RAQS Media Collective, Karin Rebbert, Holger Kube Ventura, and Stefanie Schulte Strathaus, "Dokumente sprechen nicht: Stimmen zu alten und aktuellen Dokumentarismen in der Kunst," *Texte zur Kunst* 51, 2003, p. 90–103.

Rubelt, Ortrud, *Soziologie des Dokumentarfilms: Gesellschaftsverständnis, Technikentwicklung und Filmkunst als konstitutive Dimensionen filmischer Wirklichkeit*, Frankfurt a. M. 1994.

Sandkühler, Hans Jörg, ed. *Wirklichkeit und Wissen: Realismus, Antirealismus und Wirklichkeits-Konzeptionen in Philosophie und Wissenschaft*, Frankfurt a. M./Bern/New York 1992.

Sandkühler, Hans Jörg, ed., *Repräsentation und Modell: Formen der Welterkenntnis*, Bremen 1993.

Sandkühler, Hans Jörg, ed., *Repräsentation, Denken und Selbstbewußtsein*, Bremen 1998.

Sandkühler, Hans Jörg, ed., *Selbstrepräsentation in Natur und Kultur*, Frankfurt a. M. 2000.

Schadt, Thomas, *Das Gefühl des Augenblicks. Dramaturgie des Dokumentarfilms*, Bergisch Gladbach 2002.

Schmoll, J. A., "Fotografie als Dokumentation und als Gestaltung: Gegen die Gefahr ihrer ideologischen Einengung," *Kunstforum International* 26, 1978, p. 243–247.

Schulte, Christian, ed. Alexander Kluge, *In Gefahr und größter Not bringt der Mittelweg den Tod: Texte zu Kino, Film, Politik*, Berlin 1999.

Sherman, Sharon R., *Documenting Ourselves: Film, Video, and Culture*, Lexington, Kentucky, 1998.

Shivly, Efrat, *Palestinian Cabinet Ministers 2000*, exhibition catalogue, Witte de With, Rotterdam 2003.

Shvily, Efrat, *New Homes In Israel And The Occupied Territories*, exhibition catalogue, Witte de With, Rotterdam 2003.

Silverman, Kaja, *The Subject of Semiotics*, Oxford 1983.

Silverman, Kaja, and Harun Farocki, *Speaking about Godard*, New York 1998.

Solomon-Godeau, Abigail, "Who is Speaking Thus? Some Questions about Documentary Photography," *The Event Horizon*, Lorne Falk and Barbara Fischer (eds.), Toronto 1987.

Solomon-Godeau, Abigail, *Photography at the Dock*, Minnesota 1991.

Sontag, Susan, *Über Fotografie*, Frankfurt a. M. 1992.

Spinelli, Claudia, ed., *Reprocessing Reality*, Zurich 2005.

Springerin 2, 1999, Wahl der Waffen (Arbeitsfelder und Methoden).

Springerin 3, 2003, Reality Art: Dokumentarisches Arbeiten in Kunst, Film, Video, Fotografie.

Steyerl, Hito, "Politik der Wahrheit: Dokumentarismen im Kunstfeld," *Springerin* 9:3, 2003, p. 18–21.

Steinmetz, Rüdiger and Helfried Spitra, eds., *Dokumentarfilm als „Zeichen der Zeit": Vom Ansehen der Wirklichkeit im Fernsehen*, München 1992.

Steyerl, Hito, "Framing Globalities," *Gouvernementalität: Ein sozialwissenschaftliches Konzept in Anschluss an Foucault*, Encarnación Gutiérrez-Rodriguez and Marianne Pieper (eds.), Frankfurt a. M. 2003.

Steyerl, Hito, "Dokumentarismus als Politik der Wahrheit," *Raumbilder und Bildräume*, Gerald Raunig (ed.), Vienna 2004, p. 165–174.

Steyerl, Hito, "Dokumentarismus und Dokumentalität," *Theorie der Visualität, Visualität der Theorie: eine Anthologie zur Funktion von Text und Bild in der zeitgenössischen Kultur*, Nina Möntmann and Dorothee Richter (eds.), Frankfurt a. M. 2004, p. 140–160.

Steyerl, Hito, *Die Farbe der Wahrheit: Dokumentarismus im Kunstfeld*, Vienna 2005.

Texte zur Kunst, 51, 2003, Nichts als die Wahrheit.

Tholen, Georg Christoph, *Die Zäsur der Medien, Kulturphilosophische Konturen*, Frankfurt a. M. 2002.

Tobias, Michael, ed., *The Search for Reality: The Art of Documentary Filmmaking*, Studio City, California, 1998.
Vattimo, Gianni, *The Transparent Society*, Cambridge/Oxford 1992.
Ventura, Holger Kube, *Politische Kunst Begriffe in den 1990er Jahren im deutschsprachigen Raum*, Vienna 2002.
Ventura, Holger Kube, "Shortcut," *Texte zur Kunst*, 51, 2003, p. 98-100.
Verwoert, Jan, "Research and Display. Of Transformations of Documentary Practice in Recent Art," *Untitled (Experience of Place)*, Gregor Neuerer (ed.), London 2003.
Verwoert, Jan, "Dokumentation als künstlerische Praxis: Über journalistisches und ethnografisches Arbeiten im Kunstbereich," *Springerin* 9:3, 2003, p. 26-29.
Verwoert, Jan, *Es könnte genauso gut wahr sein: Fiktion, Narration und offene Bilder in der künstlerischen Arbeit mit Mitteln des nonfiktionalen Films*, unpublished manuscript, 2005.
Virilio, Paul, "The Third Interval: A Critical Transition," *Re-thinking Technologies*, Verena Andermatt (ed.), Minneapolis 1993.
Virilio, Paul, *Vision Machine*, London/Bloomington, Indiana 1994.
Vor der Information 1-2, 1994, Dokumentarische Arbeitsweisen.
Voss, Gabriele, ed., *Dokumentarisch arbeiten*, Berlin 1998.
Waldman, Diane, ed., *Feminism and Documentary*, Minneapolis 1999.
Warren, Charles, *Beyond Document: Essays on Nonfiction Film*, Hanover, New Hampshire 1996.
Wells, Paul, *The documentary form: personal and social 'realities'. An introduction to Film Studies*, Jill Nelmes (ed.), London/New York 1996.
Williams, Raymond, "A Lecture on Realism," *Afterall* 5, 2002, p. 107-114.
Winston, Brian, *Claiming the Real*, London 1995.
Wippersberg, Julia, *Was dokumentiert der Dokumentarfilm? Über die Wirklichkeit und ihre Konstruktion im Dokumentarfilm*, Vienna 1998.
Woolgar, Steven, "The Ideology of Representation and the Role of the Agent," *Dismantling Truth. Reality in the Post-Modern World*,. H. Lawson and L. Appignanesi (eds.), London 1989, p. 131-144.

Gunilla/Sofia

L. *Do you get nervous when you have to talk in public?*
S. I get nervous, but I like the attention and the spotlight.
G: I don't.
S. You do.
G. I don't, but you need the experience. I am always nervous, but I do it, because I think it is important.

L. *Can you tell me a little bit about your study?*
S. We did a study on recruitment managers and the recruitment process in both the public and the private sector. [...]

L. *In what kind of situations did you conduct the interviews?*
G. We met them at their offices. We were three people writing the paper, and two of us always did the interviews together.
S. We took turns, so it was not one person doing all the interviews. If there was something to add, the other person could also ask questions. And take notes as well.
G. We wanted to have two people present, because you always make different interpretations. The interviews lasted an hour, and we had a guideline to follow …
S. We had divided the questions in three sections.
G. First, lighten up the atmosphere. We asked about the company and how long they have been working there.
S. And how they got recruited themselves. Then we asked them to describe the process of hiring people.
G. Later we asked, how do you actually make the decision to recruit a person. Finally we asked about who they last recruited.
S. We asked about three aspects; gender, age and cultural/ethnic background. We also asked if it was important to know Swedish. [...]
G. When we processed the interviews, we realized that we need to include more text than we thought.
S. We could not just take a sentence out, we needed the context. Maybe someone was saying something that could sound discriminating, but in the context it was no longer that way.

L. *You say that a lot of emphasis is put on studying the immigrants, so do you want to say something more about that?*
G. When you are in an environment like this, some want to do research in Africa or Asia, or maybe Europe, but not in Sweden.

S. We believe that you have to look at yourself, and if we live in Sweden, we have to look at what it is in Swedish society that is difficult for some people and easier for some … since everyone should have the same opportunities. There are many diversity projects, but they focus on the people, who do not get a job. But we believe you must look at the norms, values and structures that exclude people.

Araz

Has the city been important to you, have you done some field research here?
Yes, we did a paper on segregation and criminality; we tried to find links between them. I did interviews with friends and some people I know from Rosengård, who had some relation to criminality. In Malmö, seeing immigrants all the time, hearing debates all the time, it makes you want to, not naively make it better, but to understand it. Yes, Malmö has helped me a whole lot.

Can you talk a bit about your research process?
First we thought of looking at the media and how they represent immigrants and all that, but then we thought, come on, everyone is doing that, let's do something that's really taboo. Linking segregation and criminality, what some people might feel is racism.

When I go to my friends in Rosengård, not just Swedes, but also immigrants, they ask aren't you afraid about being robbed, aren't you afraid of being stabbed? I say come on; these are people, not animals. Instead of trying to make it worse, try to do something about it.

We chose four places, segregated areas. Three girls and three guys to keep the gender perspective. We wanted to get to know their experiences, how the state has been trying to do things about segregation and if there are factors making them turn to criminality.

All of them were second generation immigrants. They are supposed to know the Swedish culture, but you'd be surprised to know, that they don't. [...]

One could argue that you students are used to objectify the discourse of integration and immigrants.
Of course they are using us; almost all of the pictures are of immigrants. Come on, more than 50% of us in the school are Swedish. We are being the face of the university. If you had pictures of immigrants and Swedes and trying to mix them somehow – that would be something good. The whole idea of integration is to mix, isn't it?

 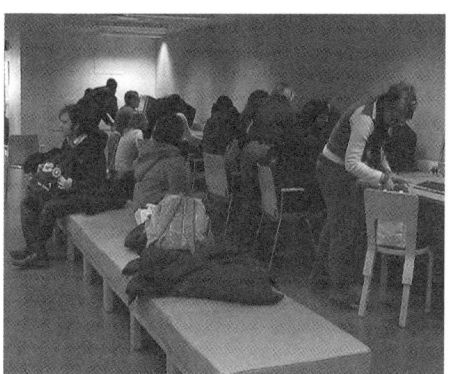

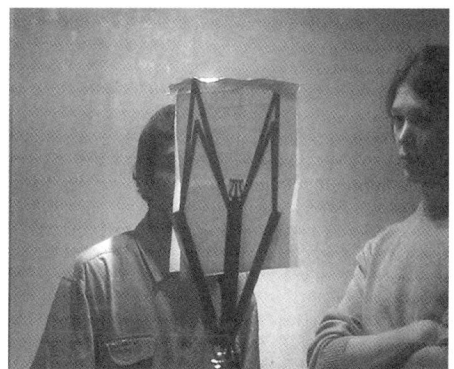 

712 Interviews?, two-channel video, 16 min., 2005
With Ramin Baghir-Zada, Gunilla Holmlin / Sofia Karlsson / Linda Harju, and Araz Zeighami

You still talk about such divisions as the Swedes and the immigrants.
Exactly. I am sorry to say that, but it is true. Swedes don't see themselves as immigrants, and immigrants do not see themselves as Swedes either. And this hybrid culture of every immigrant from every country in the world coming together, building a new culture that is very anti-Swede. So you laugh about it, to show your solidarity to the group. But I do not think that is correct. Because I do not think Swedish women are this or Swedish guys are this and that. I believe in giving everybody a chance, but of course you can't give everybody a chance, you don't know everybody.

If you are from England, everyone wants to be your friend. If you're from US, oh man, you're the best. If you come from the Middle East, then everyone is sceptic; Muslim, guy, wife beater. I've heard them all. [...]

So what could you do ... you have to go to the extremes, right. That's the same thing liberals did when they came out, what the feminists did when they came out. Sometimes it is so clear in front of your eyes, but you do not see it because it has not become part of you.

Ramin

Last year I finished my Masters thesis. I wrote it about labor market integration of immigrants in Sweden, and I chose Malmö as a case study. My research was based on 1200 questionnaires, which were distributed throughout the city.

You talked to 1200 people in Malmö?
Yes, actually I talked to a lot more, but many of them were not relevant to my research.

I was the one who was basically walking around and people were filling them in at cultural associations, religious institutions, or just randomly on the street. My general aim was to study possible relation between multicultural policy and the problems with labour market integration of immigrants in Sweden. [...]

The easiest would be to find people in the center and the most difficult would be in suburban areas.

So how would you find people in those areas?
Just basically waiting on the bus stops and walking on the streets.

Were people sometimes rude, like if you asked a total stranger?
Well, not rude, but sometimes they just said, we do not have time. [...]

Lets say if you and me were approaching a group of people for information, our findings might be quite different just according to the different persons we are. You recently moved to Malmö, so was that useful?
When I was distributing these questionnaires in Malmö, many people probably considered me to be an immigrant.

And are you an immigrant?
Well, if we follow the definition of the word immigrant, well then, yes, I am an immigrant. But I don't consider myself to be an immigrant, I am more of a free mover and feel myself to be a global citizen. But I guess because I don't have stereotypical Swedish features, many people considered me to be an immigrant. Some immigrants I think treated me as an insider, as a part of their group, so from this perspective it had a positive impact and helped me to gain some material.

Can you say something about the impact this education has had on you?
Even if we receive the same education, it doesn't necessarily mean that everyone interprets it in the same way. The discourse on racism and races is racist in itself. For example when I lived in Azerbaijan I never thought about non-ethnic Azerbaijanis as of foreigners or immigrants, they were just classmates and friends. But when I went back last summer, I started thinking, God, we have some Russians in class! Or this person is of Russian origin and this person is of Azerbaijan origin. Nowadays when I walk on the street or interact with people, certain things immediately come to my mind, like did this person come as a refugee or did this person come as a labour migrant? Does this person live from social welfare benefits? It's quite scary if you think about it, but the more you talk about racism, the more racist you become, but at the same time I think you have to talk about it, otherwise there would be no changes made in society.

Biographies

Edgar Arceneaux
Born in 1972. Lives and works in Los Angeles (USA). Studied at the California Institute of the Arts in Valencia (USA) and at the Art Center of Design Pasadena (USA). His work has been shown in solo exhibitions among others at the project space of UCLA Hammer Museum, the Kunstverein Ulm, the Studio Museum Harlem (New York), Galerie Kamm (Berlin) and at the Pomona College Museum (Claremont). His work was most recently featured in group exhibitions at de Appel (Amsterdam), at the Luckman Gallery (Cal State Los Angeles), at Witte de With Museum (Rotterdam), at the University Art Museum Santa Barbara, at the Atlanta College of Art, at the New Museum (New York), at Kunsthalle Basel, at Kunsthalle Baden Baden, and at the Bronx Museum (New York).

Azorro
is Oskar Dawicki, Igor Krenz, Wojciech Niedzielko, and Lukasz Skapski. In their installations, objects, performances, photographs, paintings, and videos they bring together their diverse skills. The members of Azorro first collaborated in 2001 producing the short film *We Like it a lot*. Since then they took part in shows at Modern Art Museum (Moscow), Tate Gallery (London), The Renaissance Society (Chicago), Museum of Contemporary Art (St. Louis), Passage de Retz (Paris), Musée d'Art Moderne de Saint-Étienne, Kiasma Museum (Helsinki), Museum Ludwig (Vienna), Kunsthalle Wien, Galeria Zacheta (Warszawa), *Videozone* (Tel Aviv), Lodz Biennial, Prague Biennial 1, Radiator (Nottingham), WRO 03 (Wroclaw), 8th Baltic Triennial of International Art (Vilnius).

Dario Azzellini
Born in 1967. MA in political sciences. Social investigator, author, and translator. Member of the council and collaborator of the foundation "Bildungswerk Berlin der Heinrich-Böll-Stiftung", collaborator of the Research and Documentation Centre Chile and Latin America (FDCL), collaborator of the Migration Research-Centre (FFM), and of the Latin America Commission of the foundation "Umverteilen".

Zbyněk Baladrán
Artist. He studied history of art at the Philosophical Faculty of Charles University in Prague from 1992 to 1996 and painting and video at the Academy of Fine Arts in Prague from 1997 to 2003. In 2001 he co-founded the gallery Display, space for contemporary art (Prague). Display is a non-profit organization representing current tendencies of European contemporary art (exhibitions, lectures, film projections). For the moment, in editing old 8mm and 16mm films, he is creating alternative pictures of the continuity of history.

Christoph Behnke
PhD. Academic lecturer in the Department of Cultural Sciences at Lüneburg University. Lives in Hamburg. He has published extensively in the fields of art sociology and cultural economy. As well, he works on a project basis at the Kunstraum of Lüneburg University.

Ursula Biemann
Studied art and cultural theory in Mexico and New York. Her art, curatorial, and video practice focuses on gender relations in economy, media, and geography. Her video essays and installations have been shown at exhibitions and institutions such as Manifesta 3 (Ljubljana), Insite (Los Angeles), MOMA (New York), MACBA (Barcelona), Centre George Pompidou (Paris), and Tate Modern (London). Biemann has published books on video essays, geography, and the politics of mobility. Current projects include *The Black Sea Files*, a video on the Caspian oil politics. Biemann researches at the Institute for Theory of Art and Design at HGK Zurich, lect-

ures at the CCC program of the Arts Academy in Geneva, and teaches seminars and workshops internationally. www.geobodies.org

Big Hope
Miklós Erhardt studied art in Budapest (H) and Dominic Hislop studied art in Edinburgh and Glasgow (UK). In 1998, they formed the project group Big Hope based on a mutual interest in discussing strategies of engaging with social issues and communicating with a broader public in art. Together, they have worked on a number of internationally exhibited, collaborative photographic, video, and mapping projects – often involving certain marginalized social groups, as both project participants and audience. Elske Rosenfeld – artist/anthropologist from Halle (D) – has joined Big Hope for their recent series of exhibitions *Talking about Economy/ies* that have been exhibited in Berlin, Linz, Madrid, Milan, Taipei, and Vienna. www.bighope.hu

Kaucyila Brooke
Artist. Based in Los Angeles and Vienna. Produces photo and text narratives for installation and publication, photographs, critical texts, and works in video art. Current projects include *Vitrinen in Arbeit* (2002-2005), *Kathy Acker's Clothes* (1998-2004), the photomontage novella installation *Tit for Twat* (1993 ongoing), the photography and video project *The Boy Mechanic* (1996 ongoing) and she edited the book *Gendered Geographies*, published by Hochschule für Gestaltung und Kunst Zurich (2002). Her text *Beaded Curtains: The Veiled Influences of Verboten Entrances* is published with Dorit Margreiter's photographic series *Two or Three Things You Know About Me*, edited by Hans Ulrich Obrist, Mexico City/Vienna (2003). She produced the artist's book *Vitrinen in Arbeit*, published by Michael Dawson Gallery, Los Angeles (2004). She is a member of the faculty and the former Director of the Program in Photography and Media at CalArts.

Duncan Campbell
Born in 1972 in Dublin. Lives and works in Glasgow. Studied Fine Arts at the University of Ulster (Belfast) and Glasgow School of Art. He had recent solo exhibitions at Galerie Luis Campaña (Cologne) and at Transmission Gallery (Glasgow). He also took part in Manifesta 5 (San Sebastian), and in Emotion Eins at Frankfurter Kunstverein. "Quixotically he profanes that documentary as a form is embedded with fundamental errors of reason while maintaining a belief in its latent potential if only these contradictions could be worked through (by him presumably!)"

Mircea Cantor
Born in 1977 in Oradea (RO). Works in Paris and Cluj Napoca. In 1989, he published his first magazine. In 1999, he moved to France. In 2001, he founded the magazine *Version* together with Gabriela Vanga and Ciprian Muresan. In 2002-2003, the project *Double Heads Matches* was realized in the Gherla Matches Factory (RO). In 2003, he made the film *The Landscape is Changing*, in which a group of demonstrators walk across Tirana with mirrors. In 2005, *Version* is published as a coloring book for children, including more than 69 artists.
www.versionmagazine.com

Pascale Cassagnau
Art historian, art critic (e.g. *Art Press*), and curator. She is inspector for contemporary creation at the Ministry of Culture in Paris. She is in charge of the new media and video department and of the video collections from the National Fund for Contemporary Art (FNAC). Her essay *A Third Cinema* on the relationship between contemporary art and cinema is soon to be published.

Søren Grammel
Born in 1971. Curator of numerous exhibitions at e.g. Kunstverein Munich, Videonale Bonn, Germ-

inations Europe/Galeria Arsenal Bialystock, Rooseum (Malmø) and Frankfurter Kunstverein. Academic lecturer at the Academy of Fine Arts in Kassel. Guest lecturer at the Academy of Fine Arts Umeå (S). In 2005, he published *Ausstellungsautorschaft* with Revolver Books (Frankfurt a. M.). He is director of the Kunstverein Graz since June 2005.

Marina Gržinić

Researcher at the Institute of Philosophy at the Scientific and Research Center of the Slovenian Academy of Science and Art (ZRC SAZU) in Ljubljana. Professor at the Academy of Fine Arts (Vienna). Working as a freelance media theorist, art critic and curator. She has been involved with video art since 1982. Her field of interest covers globalization, post-socialism and transition, democracy and the institution of contemporary art in relation to capital and the art market. Marina Gržinić has published hundreds of articles and essays and she has (co)edited 13 books. www.videoart.furinkazan.biz

Jens Haaning

Born in 1965 in Hoersholm (DK). Lives and works in Berlin (D) and in Vordingborg (DK). His works have been exhibited in solo shows among others at Galleri Nicolai Wallner (Copenhagen), Goodwater Gallery (Toronto), Kunstverein Springhornhof (Neuenkirchen), Fundació Joan Miró (Barcelona), and Johann König (Berlin). His work was most recently featured in group exhibitions at the Hamburger Bahnhof (Berlin), at the Sydney Biennial, at the ICA (London), at a public art project in Utrecht, and at Documenta11 (Kassel).

Vít Havránek

Art theoretician and curator. Lives and works in Prague (CZ). He is currently working as project leader for tranzit. He has worked as a curator at the National Gallery Prague and the Municipal Gallery Prague. He has organized exhibitions and he is editor of numerous catalogues. Together with T. Vanek and J. Skála he is founding member of the group pas (production of contemporary activities). He lectures on contemporary art at the Academy of Applied Arts (Prague). www.tranzit.org

Dóra Hegyi

Art historian and curator. Curator at the Ludwig Museum Budapest since 1996. In 1999 she initiated the project room of the museum. In 2001 she co-formed the independent initiative KMKK (Two artists – two curators)-"attention recycling". In 2004, she was founding member of CAB (Curators' Association Budapest). Recent projects include Budapest Box. The hidden scene of the 1990s, 2002; Moszkva ter (Gravitation), 2003.

Laura Horelli

Born in 1976 in Helsinki (FIN). Lives and works in Berlin. Her work has been shown in exhibitions among others at the Rooseum (Malmö), the Galerie im Taxispalais (Innsbruck), at Manifesta 5 (San Sebastian), and at Galerie Barbara Weiss (Berlin).

Johanna Kandl

Born in Vienna. Lives in Berlin. Studied painting at the Academy of Fine Arts in Vienna and at the Academy of Fine Arts in Belgrade. Her work has been shown in solo exhibitions among others at Galerie für Zeitgenössische Kunst (Leipzig, 2002), in various international exhibitions in Europe (Werkleitz Biennial, 2002, museum in progress, Vienna 2001), USA, and Africa (Cairo Biennial, 2003).

Klub Zwei (Simone Bader and Jo Schmeiser)

Klub Zwei was founded in 1992. Their work is focused on the politics of representation. That implies the question of whose voices are heard in European democracies and the analysis of how political issues are represented in the mass

media. Their works on video and in public space have focused recently on the experience and the perception of migration, of women, and the legacy of the Holocaust. www.t0.or.at/~klubzwei

Joachim Koester
Artist. Lives in New York and Copenhagen. His works have been shown at documenta X (Kassel), Johannesburg Biennial, Gwangju Biennial (ROK), Venice Biennial; Van Abbe Museum (Eindhoven), Museum of Contemporary Art (Chicago), Musée d'Art Moderne de la Ville de Paris, Kiasma Museum of Contemporary Art (Helsinki), Statens Museum for Kunst (Copenhagen), Malmö Konst Museum, as well as in solo shows at Kunsthalle Nuremberg; Centre National de la Photographie (Paris), Galleri Nicolai Wallner (Copenhagen), Galerie Jan Mot (Brussels), and Gallery Greene/Naftali (New York).

Dorit Margreiter
Works as an artist on projects that deal with diverse structures of representation. Aspects of globalization and the geographic displacement of context play a central role in her work, as well as the representation of women through new media, film, and architecture. In 2004 her work was shown in solo exhibitions at Museum Moderner Kunst Stiftung Ludwig (Vienna), Art Basel Miami Beach, Kunstforum Montafon, and in group exhibitions at Liverpool Biennial, Tate Liverpool, Secession (Vienna), and Galerie für zeitgenössische Kunst (Leipzig).

Raimundas Malasauskas
Freelance journalist and curator at the Contemporary Art Centre in Vilnius (LT). Currently based in Vilnius. Works with *The File Room* and *The So-Called Records*. Guest advisor at Jan Van Eyck Academy (Maastricht). Member of the curatorial board of Museo de Arte Sacramento. Researches issues of copyright, remixology, and media. Upcoming projects will be on show at CAC TV Program, The 9th Baltic Triennial of International Art at CAC Vilnius, and ICA London. www.thefileroom.org, www.socalledrecords.com, www.cac.lt/tv

Boris Ondreička
Born in 1969. Lives and works in Bratislava and Bernolakovo (SK). Participated in numerous exhibitions in Europe and USA, among others 51st Venice Biennial (Venice, 2005), Kunsthalle Loppem (2004), Magazin 4 (Bregenz, 2004), At & Kjubh (Cologne, 2003), Kiasma (Helsinki, 2003), bak (Utrecht, 2003), Österreichische Galerie Belvedere (Vienna, 2000), PS1 (New York, 1999), Manifesta 2 (Luxembourg, 1998).

Kirsten Pieroth
Born in 1970 in Offenbach am Main (D). Lives and works in Berlin. Her works have been shown among others at Contemporary Art Gallery (Vancouver), Portikus (Frankfurt a. M.), Galerie Klosterfelde (Berlin), Manifesta 5 (San Sebastian), Royal College of Art (London), Kunstverein Frankfurt, Palais de Tokyo (Paris).

Gerald Raunig
Philosopher and art theoretician. Lives in Vienna. Co-director of *eipcp* (European Institute for Progressive Cultural Policies) in Vienna. Coordinator of the transnational research project *republicart*. Numerous lectures, essays, and publications in the fields of contemporary philosophy, art theory, political aesthetics, and cultural politics. Latest publication: *Kunst und Revolution. Künstlerischer Aktivismus im langen 20. Jahrhundert* (Vienna, 2005).
www.eipcp.net, www.republicart.net

Oliver Ressler
Born in 1970. Lives and works in Vienna. Ressler is an artist who carries out theme-specific exhibitions, projects in public space and videos on issues such as racism, migration, genetic engineering, economics, forms of resistance, and

social alternatives. His ongoing project *Alternative Economics, Alternative Societies* was realized in solo-exhibitions in Galerija Škuc (Ljubljana, 2003), Kunstraum der Universität Lüneburg (2004), Centro Cultural Conde Duque, MediaLab-Madrid (2004), Platform Garanti Contemporary Art Center (Istanbul, 2005). Many of Ressler's works are being realized in collaborations, such as *European Corrections Corporation* (with Martin Krenn), *Boom!* (with David Thorne), and the film *Venezuela from Below* (with Dario Azzellini). In 2005, Ressler participates in group exhibitions at ZKM (Karlsruhe), Prague Biennial 2, and the 9th International Festival of Video/Arte/Electrónica (Lima). www.ressler.at

Hinrich Sachs
Born in 1962 in Osnabrück. Lives in Basel. Studied fine art and art theory in Hamburg and Paris. He has been exhibiting frequently since 1985, and has focused on project-based work since 1992. Since 1999 he has worked together with architects, exhibition designers, and publishers. He currently holds a position as advising researcher at the Jan van Eyck Academy (Maastricht).

Angela Sanders
Studied visual anthropology and film at the Universities of Zurich and Edinburgh. Her research and video practice focuses on the Spanish-Moroccan borderlands and on the living spaces of Moroccan domestic workers in Spain. In 2003 she co-produced *Europlex* with Ursula Biemann, and later produced the video *Domestic Scapes* (2004). Her videos have been exhibited internationally, e.g. at *Femme Totale video* festival (Dortmund), Center for Contemporary Culture (Barcelona), and in *Urban Diaries* at ARCO Madrid. Sanders publishes on subjects related to gender, identity and media. She is on the editorial team of *FRAZ*, a Swiss feminist magazine where she signed for the issue on the Mediterranean.

Sabine Schaschl-Cooper
Art historian and art critic. Director and curator of Kunsthaus Baselland (Muttenz/Basel, CH) since 2001. She has curated numerous solo and group exhibitions and has been curator of *Urban Diaries: Young Swiss Art* in Madrid. She is editor of numerous publications on contemporary art and co-author of *Skandal:Kunst* (Vienna and New York, 2000).

Georg Schöllhammer
Editor-in-chief of *springerin Hefte für Gegenwartskunst* and director of the publication project of documenta 12.

Jiří Skála
Born in 1976. Lives in Prague. Studied fine art at the Academy of Fine Arts in Prague and participated on the post-graduate program at the Palais de Tokyo (Paris). His work has been shown among others at Galerie A.M.180 (Prague), Fundação Cultural de Curitiba (Brazil), Art Klazma (Moscow), Palais de Tokyo (Paris); 1st Tirana Biennial (AL), Jeleni Gallery (Prague).

Claudia Spinelli
Born in 1964. Lives and works in Basel and Zurich (CH). Art historian and curator. 1996–98 curator at Kleines Helmhaus, Zurich. 1998–2000 director of Galerie Walcheturm, Zurich. In 2002 she was awarded the curatorial prize of the "Schweizerischen Bundesamtes für Kultur". She publishes regularly in art magazines and the weekly magazine *Die Weltwoche*. Curator of *Reprocessing Reality. New Perspectives on Art and the Documentary* within the framework of the film festival *Visions du Réel* (Nyon, 2005).

Bettina Steinbrügge
Curator and writer. Lives and works in Lüneburg. She studied art history, English philology and comparative literature, MA. Director of Halle für Kunst Lüneburg eV since 2001. Academic

lecturer at the Lüneburg University. Advisor of the artist-in-residence program at Künstlerstätte Schloss Bleckede.

Hito Steyerl
Filmmaker and author. Lives in Berlin and London. Academic lecturer at Goldsmiths College (London). Most recent publication: *Die Farbe der Wahrheit. Dokumentarismus im Kunstfeld* (Vienna, 2005).

Mark Ther
Born in 1977. Lives in Prague. He studied fine arts at the Art School of Václav Hollar (Prague) and at the Academy of Fine Arts (Prague). His work has been shown among others at The Cooper Union for the Advancement of Science and Art (New York), P.S.1 Contemporary Art Center (New York), Gallery Art Factory (Prague), Galerie & Projekte Mathias Kampl (Berlin), Gallery Jeleni (Prague), Foundation and Center for Contemporary Arts (Prague), Gallery Eskort (Brno), Stuttgarter Kunstverein.

Attila Tordai-S.
Founder of Protokoll Studio in Cluj (RO). Editor of *IDEA Arts + Society* since 2003. From 2001–2003, editor of the contemporary art magazine *Balkon*. From 1999–2003, lecturer of art theory and art history at Babes-Bolyai University (Cluj). He regularly publishes essays on contemporary art and has curated many exhibitions, including *UnoccupiedTerritories* (K&S Gallery Berlin, 2003) and *Unstable Narratives* (hARTware medien kunstverein, Dortmund, 2002). Recently he was appointed co-curator of the Periferic Biennial, Iasi (RO).

Jan Verwoert
Lives in Hamburg. He is contributing editor for *frieze* and works as freelance author among others for *Afterall, Metropolis M, Camera Austria,* and *springerin Hefte für Gegenwartskunst*. He is guest lecturer at the Academy of Fine Arts Umeå (S).

Olivier Zabat
Studied fine arts at Ecole des Beaux-Arts Grenoble. After a basic work on photography, he started his video praxis in Brazil where he held several scholarships in fine arts. There, he realized his first film, *Zona Oeste*. It was followed by *Miguel et les Mines* and *1/3 des yeux* that was awarded the prize of the French competition at the *Festival du Documentaire Marseille* 2004. His work has been featured at film festivals (Rotterdam, Belfort, Buenos Aires) and in shows in galleries and institutions such as Walker Art Center (Minneapolis), MACBA (Barcelona), Jeu de Paume (Paris), Musée d'Art Moderne (Paris), Centre Georges Pompidou (Paris). His recent film will be in the cinemas in October 2005.

Gerhard Zarbock
Student of philosophy and art sciences at the Academy of Fine Arts and the University of Kassel.

Ella Ziegler
Born in 1970 in Ilshofen. Lives and works in Berlin since 2000. While traveling in Europe, Asia, and the Americas, she gained fundamental experiences that form the basis of her interventions and performances. Her work has been shown in several solo and group exhibitions among others at Kunsthalle Fridericianum (Kassel), Kultursommer 2002 (Wiesbaden), Kunstraum Kreuzberg (Berlin), Nassauischer Kunstverein (Wiesbaden), Art Gallery of Hamilton (CAN), Art Cologne 2004, european media art festival (Osnabrück), O.K. centrum für Gegenwartskunst (Linz), Capri (Berlin).

Europlex

Ursula Biemann & Angela Sanders

Europlex tracks distinct cross-border activities through the Spanish-Moroccan borderland and seeks to make these obscure paths visible. On their repetitive circuit around the check-point to the Spanish enclave Ceuta, the video follows in three borderlogs the smuggling women who strap multiple layers of clothes to their bodies; the daily commute of "domesticas" who turn into time travellers as they move back and forth between the Moroccan and European time zones; and the Moroccan women working in the transnational zones in Northafrica for the European market. All these trajectories move around and in between the imperative of the territorial borders. They form, however, a vital layer of the cultural and economic space between Europe and Africa.

تسجيل الحدود ا / border log I

Border log I is first of all a meticulous observation of the extensive smuggling activities that circumscribe the border to Ceuta. Filming is strictly prohibited so that images can be made only under constant interruptions, with a hidden camera or from a distance. The liveliness begins at 6 am when the gates open to the crowd of impatiently waiting Moroccans and continues through the day. Smuggling takes place in the daylight in front of the eyes of the officials and is part of the everyday culture. The aim of the border crossing is not to get into the city of Ceuta but to pursue their semi-legal business in the expanded border complex. Wholesale warehouses and street markets are just around the corner from the checkpoint. Here they rummage around for good deals and buy as much as they can carry. These goods will be marketable in the Moroccan town Tétuan. On their way back, the smugglers pass, this time heavily loaded, in front of the same officials who get compensated for their forebearance. Circumscribing the architecture of the authorities up to eleven times a day, they inhabit the border in a non-linear, circular way, carving out an existence for themselves. Towards the best possible mobility for crossing, the female smugglers strap shirts and cloths to their body, layer by layer, until they have doubled their body volume. This seems to be a technique only women use. Every piece will increase the profit margin of her passage. The economic logic inscribes itself onto every layer of the transforming, mobile, female body.

border log II
تسجيل الحدود ٢

Border Log II follows the daily journey of the Moroccan maids who live in Tétuan and work in the enclave. Since Spanish women increasingly seek paid work outside her home, the need for cheap domestic personal in the enclave city has grown. Most of the service personal gets recruited from the neighboring Moroccan region, only very few will be given a work contract which would guarantee minimum salary and facilitate easier entrance into the enclave. Yet Europlex doesn't focus on the difficult conditions young Moroccan women are facing when they enter the European labor market. It rather takes a look at the casual but unusual detail that the workers commute between the Moroccan and the European time zones. Due to the fact that the two adjacent territories are located in distinct time zones with a two hour time lapse, the domestic workers turn into permanent time travelers within the border economy. Her life rhythm is off beat, it is performed through an alternating delay and acceleration with respect to her social context. Deferred time becomes the mode of their cultural positionality. In the video, the gesture and smile of the time travelling maid appear unnaturally repetitive, they are interrupted by drop-outs, i.e. missing images which stop and restart in a choppy fashion. The animated portrait of the Muslim woman takes on likeable robotic features that withdraw her from our time measurement.

border log III

تسجيل الحدود ٣

Border log III enters the transnational zone near Tangier where Moroccan women manufacture biological and technological products for European subcontractors: shrimp peelers, aroma makers, toy moulders. As in so many other global production sites, in Tangier too there is mainly a female work force being taken into consideration for jobs in the disfranchised zone. The border crossed by these women on a daily basis is a lot less visible than the fortified one around Ceuta passed by the smugglers and domestic workers. Still, upon entering the transnational zone the worker experiences a distinctive split from her cultural environment. In Europlex this fissure comes to expression in a series of female workers portraits captured at the exit of a factory in the harbor of Tangier.

These log journals describe three diverse practices which transform the border space into a translocal reality. What the border recordings aim at and attempt to impact on is not the consolidation of a national unity but on the contrary the permeability and constant subversion of it. Television reports on clandestine boat passengers do that too, to some extent, but it seems crucial to me that the shadowy and partially subversive circumstances of these border passages are not assimilated all too quickly into a disciplined national order, where intervening state officials play the leading part, but that they are allowed to cultivate an alternative imaginary based in translocal existences and transformative cultural practices.

List of Illustrations

Page 001–004
Zbyněk Baladrán, *Working process*, 2005, Storyboard, courtesy the artist

Page 007–010
Azorro, *Everything has been done*, 2003, parallel projection of two films: projection 1 / Wroclaw, color, 11:29 min., projection 2 / Bialystok, color, 25:06 min., Polish with English subtitles, courtesy the artists. The text is part of the book Azorro, *Wszystko juz bylo [Everything has been Done]*, Ed. Galeria Bunkier Sztuki, Krakow 2003

Page 013–016
Klub Zwei, *Schwarz auf Weiss. Die Rückseite der Bilder*, 2003, Beta SP, 4:3, b/w, stereo, 5 min., English, German, Polish, French, Bulgarian, Czech, Romanian, courtesy the artists

Page 020
Joachim Koester, *From the Travel of Jonathan Harker*, 2003, photographs, installation view *The Need to Document*, Kunsthaus Baselland, 2005, courtesy Galerie Jan Mot and Galleri Nicolai Wallner, Copenhagen, photo: Serge Hasenböhler

Page 021
Duncan Campbell, *Falls Burns Malone Fiddles*, 2003, video, 33 min., courtesy Galerie Luis Campaña, Cologne, photo: Belfast Exposed and Community Visual Images, Belfast

Page 022
Dorit Margreiter, *10104 Angelo View Drive*, 2004, 16 mm film on DVD, 6:56 min., installation view *The Need to Document*, Kunsthaus Baselland, 2005, courtesy the artist, photo: Serge Hasenböhler

Page 024
Oliver Ressler and Dario Azzellini, *Venezuela from Below*, 2004, film, 67 min., courtesy Dario Azzellini and Oliver Ressler, photo: Serge Hasenböhler

Page 027
Big Hope: Miklós Erhardt & Dominic Hislop & Elske Rosenfeld, *Commonopoly*, 2004, object, 200 x 200 x 20 cm, installation view *Open House*, O.K Centrum für Gegenwartskunst, Linz, 2004, courtesy the artists, photo: Otto Saxinger

Page 028
Loulou Cherinet, *White Women*, 2002, DVD auto-loop, 52 min., courtesy the artist

Page 031–034
Jiří Skála and Mark Ther, *Microfiltration*, 2001, performance, courtesy the artists, photo: Lindá Urbánková

Page 036
Image taken on the way from the Otepeni Bucarest Airport to the city center, 2004, photo: Vít Havránek

Page 039
Roman Ondák, *Antinomads*, 2000, set of 12 postcards, print on paper, 10,5 x 15 cm, courtesy the artist

Page 041
Little Warsaw, *Poster for Contra Monument Cathedral*, 2005, print on paper, dimensions variable, courtesy the artist

Page 042
Zbyněk Baladrán and Jan Mánčuška, *Vide*, 2003, video, 30 min., courtesy the artists

Page 049
Big Hope: Miklós Erhardt & Dominic Hislop, *Re:route*, 2002, composite map for the project, digital image, 29 x 21 cm, courtesy the artists

Page 050
Big Hope: Miklós Erhardt & Dominic Hislop, *Re:route*, 2002/2005, installation view *The Need to Document*, Kunsthaus Baselland, 2005, courtesy the artists, photo: Serge Hasenböhler

Page 051 (above)
Big Hope: Miklós Erhardt & Dominic Hislop, *Re:route*, 2002, mental map sketched for the project, Mahmoud, drawing on paper, 21 x 29 cm, courtesy the artists

Page 051 (below)
Big Hope: Miklós Erhardt & Dominic Hislop, *Re:route*, 2002, photograph taken for the project, Mahmoud, photograph, 10 x 15 cm, courtesy the artists

Page 052 (above)
Big Hope: Miklós Erhardt & Dominic Hislop, *Re:route*, 2002, photograph taken for the project, Evelyn, photograph, 10 x 15 cm, courtesy the artists

Page 052 (middle)
Big Hope: Miklós Erhardt & Dominic Hislop, *Re:route*, 2002, photograph taken for the project, Jefferson, photograph, 10 x 15 cm, courtesy the artists

Page 052 (below)
Big Hope: Miklós Erhardt & Dominic Hislop, *Re:route*, 2002, photograph taken for the project, Nali, photograph, 10 x 15 cm, courtesy the artists

Page 065
Kaucyila Brooke, *Untitled #76 from Vitrinen in Arbeit*, 2002–2005, color photograph, 76,2 x 76,2 cm, courtesy the artist and Michael Dawson Gallery, Los Angeles

Page 066
Kaucyila Brooke, *Untitled #99 from Vitrinen in Arbeit*, 2002–2005, color photograph, 76,2 x 76,2 cm, courtesy the artist and Michael Dawson Gallery, Los Angeles

Page 067
Kaucyila Brooke, *Untitled #118 from Vitrinen in Arbeit*, 2002–2005, color photograph, 76,2 x 76,2 cm, courtesy the artist and Michael Dawson Gallery, Los Angeles

Page 068
Kaucyila Brooke, *Untitled #127 from Vitrinen in Arbeit*, 2002–2005, color photograph, 76,2 x 76,2 cm, courtesy the artist and Michael Dawson Gallery, Los Angeles

Page 073–076
Taken from the artist's book, Edgar Arceneaux, *Lost Library*, Kunstverein Ulm (ed.), Ulm 2003, courtesy Galerie Joanna Kamm, Berlin and Galerie Adamski, Aachen

Page 085
Olivier Zabat, *Domingo 1*, 2001, color photograph, 80 x 80 cm, courtesy the artist

Page 086
Olivier Zabat, *Domingo 2*, 2001, color photograph, 80 x 80 cm, courtesy the artist

Page 087–088
Olivier Zabat, *La femme est sentimentale*, 2001, video, 10 min., courtesy the artist

Page 090
Bernadette Corporation, *Get Rid of Yourself*, 2003, digital video (color, sound), 61 min., available through EAI, NYC, courtesy the artists

Page 092
Oliver Ressler and Dario Azzellini, *Disobbedienti*, 2002, video, 54 min., courtesy Dario Azzellini and Oliver Ressler

Page 099
Ella Ziegler, *Hotelroom*, 2004, slides, courtesy the artist

Page 100
Ella Ziegler, *Lean on*, 2001, slides, courtesy the artist

Page 101
Ella Ziegler, *Exercise Book*, 1999, slides, courtesy the artist

Page 102
Ella Ziegler, *Fountain*, 2002, slide, courtesy the artist

Page 105 (above)
Johanna Kandl, *o.T.*, 2003, tempera on wood, 56,5 x 80 cm, courtesy Galerie Christine König, Vienna

Page 105 (below)
Johanna Kandl, *o.T.*, 2005, tempera on wood, 56,5 x 80 cm, courtesy Galerie Christine König, Vienna

Page 106–107
Johanna Kandl, *o.T.*, 2005, tempera on wood, 115 x 150 cm, courtesy Galerie Christine König, Vienna

Page 108
Johanna Kandl, *o.T.*, 2002, tempera on wood, 150 x 115 cm, courtesy Galerie für zeitgenössische Kunst, Leipzig

Page 110
Rainer Ganahl, *A Reading Seminar...*, in Stuttgart, 1995, video, courtesy the artist

Page 113
Marion von Osten and Sans Papiers Belgium, *nordreise-südreise*, 2000, video, 30 min., courtesy the artist

Page 114
Hilary Lloyd, *Colin #2*, 2000, video, installation view *Kino der Dekonstruktion*, Frankfurter Kunstverein, 2000, courtesy the artist, photo: Kathrin Schilling

Page 115
Isa Rosenberger, *Sarajevo Guided Tours*, 2001, video, courtesy the artist

Page 116
Nasrin Tabatabai, *Old House*, 1999, video, courtesy the artist
Page 118
Esra Ersen, *If you Could Speak Swedish*, 2001, video, courtesy the artist
Page 121
Annika Eriksson, *Arbeitswelt – Martin Hartmann*, 2003, video, courtesy the artist
Page 123
Ruth Kaaserer, *Balance*, 2000, video, courtesy the artist
Page 124
Ruth Kaaserer, *mädchen sind.*, 2004, video, courtesy the artist
Page 126
kpD, *Kamera läuft!*, 2004, video, courtesy the artists
Page 127
kpD, *Kamera läuft!*, 2004, video, courtesy the artists
Page 133–136
Duncan Campbell, *That time*, 2005, courtesy the artist, photo: Belfast Exposed and Community Visual Images, Belfast
Page 138 (left)
Big Hope: Miklós Erhardt & Dominic Hislop, *Inside Out*, László Hudák, 1997–1998, courtesy the artists
Page 138 (right)
Video still from *The Tequila Gang*, László Hudák, Imre Lénárt (dir.), produced by Miklós Erhardt, Balázs Béla Studio, 1999, 58 min., courtesy the artists and BBS
Page 139
Big Hope: Miklós Erhardt & Dominic Hislop, *Talking About Economy*, 2003, installation view *Permanent Produktiv*, Kunsthalle Exnergasse, Vienna, 2004, courtesy the artists, photo: Gabriele Mackert
Page 140
Film still from *Kentaur*, Tamás Szentjóby (dir.), Balázs Béla Studio, 1975, 38 min., courtesy the artist
Page 141
Film still from *Kentaur*, Tamás Szentjóby (dir.), Balázs Béla Studio, 1975, 38 min., courtesy the artist

Page 143–145
Dorit Margreiter, *10104 Angelo View Drive*, 2004, film still, courtesy Sammlung MUMOK, Vienna and Galerie Krobath Wimmer, Vienna
Page 146
Dorit Margreiter, *10104 Angelo View Drive*, 2004, production still, courtesy Sammlung MUMOK, Vienna and Galerie Krobath Wimmer, Vienna
Page 152–153
Kirsten Pieroth, *Edison's Workbench*, 2003, wooden table, vises, b/w photograph, 82,5 x 205 x 200 cm (table), 33 x 48,5 cm (photograph), courtesy Klosterfelde, Berlin, photo: Jens Ziehe
Page 156
Pierre Huyghe, *Block Party, Africa Bambaataa*, 2002, Polaroid photograph from the work *Block Party*, 2002, 16 mm film, 5:30 min., transferred onto hard disk, courtesy Marian Goodman Gallery, New York/Paris
Page 175–178
Boris Ondreička, *Dreambarter (in progress)*, 2004 –..., text, dimension variable, courtesy the artist
Page 184 (above)
Zbyněk Baladrán, *Archaeology: Google 1*, 2005, electronic illustration for the text, courtesy the author
Page 184 (below)
Zbyněk Baladrán, *Archaeology: Google 2*, 2005, electronic illustration for the text, courtesy the author
Page 187–189
Mircea Cantor, *Double Heads Matches*, 2002–2003, film (color, sound), 17 min., courtesy the artist and Yvon Lambert, Paris/New York, text copyright © Ami Barak, 2003
Page 190
Mircea Cantor, *Smen*, 2002, film (color, sound), 6:12 min., courtesy the artist and Yvon Lambert, Paris/New York
Page 218
Joachim Koester, *Hotel Castle Dracula #2*, 2003, Gelatin silver print, 47 x 60 cm, courtesy Galerie Jan Mot and Galleri Nicolai Wallner, Copenhagen
Page 219
Joachim Koester, *Hotel Castle Dracula #3*, 2003, c-print, 47 x 60 cm, courtesy Galerie Jan Mot and Galleri Nicolai Wallner, Copenhagen

Page 220
Joachim Koester, *The Borgo Pass #4*, 2003, c-print, 47 x 60 cm, courtesy Galerie Jan Mot and Galleri Nicolai Wallner, Copenhagen

Page 223
Jens Haaning, *Deniz*, 2000, light jet c-print on photographic paper, 68 x 47,4 cm, collection migros museum für gegenwartskunst, Zurich, courtesy Galleri Nicolai Wallner, Copenhagen

Page 224
Jens Haaning, *Shabeer*, 2000, light jet c-print on photographic paper, 68 x 47,4 cm, collection migros museum für gegenwartskunst, Zurich, courtesy Galleri Nicolai Wallner, Copenhagen

Page 225
Jens Haaning, *Dennis*, 2000, light jet c-print on photographic paper, 68 x 47,4 cm, collection migros museum für gegenwartskunst, Zurich, courtesy Galleri Nicolai Wallner, Copenhagen

Page 226
Jens Haaning, *Antonio*, 2000, light jet c-print on photographic paper, 68 x 47,4 cm, collection migros museum für gegenwartskunst, Zurich, courtesy Galleri Nicolai Wallner, Copenhagen

Page 233–236
Hinrich Sachs, *Dominique Noah (as speaker)*, 2004, in collaboration with Barnaby Drabble, Solveig Dufour, Albert Liebl, and Peter Stoffel, courtesy the artist

Page 241–244
Oliver Ressler and Dario Azzellini, *Venezuela from Below*, 2004, film, 67 min., courtesy Dario Azzellini and Oliver Ressler

Page 253–256
Laura Horelli, *712 Interviews?*, 2005, two-channel video, 16 min., with Ramin Baghir-Zada, Gunilla Holmlin / Sofia Karlsson / Linda Harju, and Araz Zeighami, courtesy Galerie Barbara Weiss, Berlin

Page 263–266
Ursula Biemann and Angela Sanders, *Europlex*, 2003, DVD, 20 min., courtesy the artists

Colophon

This book is published on the occasion of the exhibitions:

The Need to Document
Kunsthaus Baselland, Muttenz/Basel, Switzerland, March 19–May 1, 2005
Halle für Kunst eV, Lüneburg, Germany, April 3–May 29, 2005

and the round tables at:
Kunsthaus Baselland, Muttenz/Basel, Switzerland, April 6, 2005
Halle für Kunst eV, Lüneburg, Germany, April 23, 2005
tranzit, Prague, Czech Republic, May 27, 2005

Kunsthaus Baselland
Director and Curator: Sabine Schaschl-Cooper
Exhibition Assistants: Margrit Schmid, Eva Scharrer
Technical Assistant: Peter Wenger
www.kunsthausbaselland.ch

Halle für Kunst eV
Director and Curator: Bettina Steinbrügge
Exhibition Assistant: Bärbel Hartje
Trainees: Christin Müller, Jasmin Matthies
www.halle-fuer-kunst.de

tranzit
tranzit.cz Project Leader: Vít Havránek
Assistant: Markéta Strnadová
www.tranzit.org
tranzit is a contemporary art initiative supported by Česká spořitelna, a.s., Slovenská sporitel'ňa, a.s., Erste Bank Group

Editor: Vít Havránek, Sabine Schaschl-Cooper, Bettina Steinbrügge
Copy-editing: Bärbel Hartje
Proofreading: Linde Müller, Tim Schmalfeldt
Translation: Karl Hoffmann (German/English), Kathleen Hayes (Czech/English), Berit Francke (French/German), Anne Blonstein (Text Claudia Spinelli)
Graphic design: Simone Mutert Kommunikationsdesign, Cologne
Printed by: Vier-Türme GmbH, Benedict Press, Münsterschwarzach
Edition: 1500
Printed in Germany

© 2005 Vít Havránek, Sabine Schaschl-Cooper, Bettina Steinbrügge
© Texts: authors
© Photographs: Serge Hasenböhler, Gabriele Mackert, Otto Saxinger, Kathrin Schilling, Linda Urbánková, Jens Ziehe
© VG Bild-Kunst, Bonn, 2005: Serge Hasenböhler, Hinrich Sachs

Published by:

JRP|Ringier
Letzigraben 134
8047 Zürich
Switzerland
T +41 (0)43 311 27 50
F +41 (0)43 311 27 51
info@jrp-ringier.com
www.jrp-ringier.com

ISBN 3-905701-30-8

JRP|Ringier books are available internationally at selected bookstores and the following distribution partners:

Switzerland
Buch 2000, AVA Verlagsauslieferung AG, Centralweg 16, CH-8910 Affoltern a.A., buch2000@ava.ch, www.ava.ch

France
Les Presses du réel, 16 rue Quentin, F-21000 Dijon, info@lespressesdureel.com, www.lespressesdureel.com

UK
Art Data, 12 Bell Industrial Estate, 50 Cunnington Street, London W4 5 HB, info@artdata.co.uk, www.artdata.co.uk

USA
D.A.P./Distributed Art Publishers, 155 Sixth Avenue, 2nd Floor, New York, NY 10013, dap@dapinc.com, www.artbook.com

Other countries
IDEABooks, Nieuwe Herengracht 11, 1011 RK Amsterdam, idea@ideabooks.nl, www.ideabooks.nl

For a list of our partner bookshops or for any general questions, please contact JRP|Ringier directly at info@jrp-ringier.com, or visit our homepage www.jrp-ringier.com for further information about our program.

The project is supported by:

Ambassade de France en Suisse

Česká Spořitelna

ERSTE Bank

Gemeinde Muttenz

Goethe-Institut Prag

Danish Arts Council

Land Niedersachsen

Lüneburgischer Landschaftsverband

Migros-Kulturprozent

Novartis

österreichisches kulturforum brn

Schweizer Kulturstiftung

SLOVENSKÁ SPORITEĽŇA

Stadt Lüneburg

STIFTUNG KUNSTFONDS

The Ministry of Culture of the Czech Republic

Many thanks to:

All artists, galleries, all lenders, authors, and panelists, JRP|Ringier (Lionel Bovier, Salome Schnetz)

and Galerie Adamski, Jesper Alvaer, Christoph Behnke, Frederique Bergholtz and her construction team, Christine Boehler, Dusan Brozman, Bruder Sturmius, Candela2 (Oliver Schulte, Maik Timm), Karel Cisar, Display – space for contemporary art, Bianca Drebber, András Edit, Xavier Esnault of Capricci Films, Caroline Ferreira, Jörg Franzbecker, Christian Gatzert, Karin Gludovatz, Hedy Graber, Raphaël Grisey, Sophie Haaser, Julia Hahn, Mária Hlavajová, Christelle Havránek, Matthias Hayes, Galerie Joanna Kamm, Bettina Klein, Ingrid Klenner, Martin Klosterfelde, Ulrike Kremeier, Ula Kropiwiec, Nina Kuzmierz, Florence Lazar, Karin Lingl, Boris Marte, Matthias Michalka, Dirck Möllmann, Heike Munder, Nicolas Nahab, Stephan Nobbe, Rudolf Novak, Sanne Kofod Olsen, Anette Østerby, Jacques Pécheur, Tomáš Pospiszyl, Karin Rebbert, Kathrin Rhomberg, Tobias Ruderer, Ottheinz Rummert, Birte Schellmann, Georg Schöllhammer, Jiří Ševčík, Marco Sigmann, Claudia Spinelli, Kunstverein Springhornhof (Bettina von Dziembowski), Udo Steinbrügge, Monika Štěpánová, Diethelm Stoller, Transmission Gallery, Rudolf Velhagen, Aurélie Wacquant, Galerie Barbara Weiss, Ulf Wuggenig, Herbert Zöller (†) and the members of tranzit International Board.